The Muckrakers

THE ERA IN JOURNALISM

THAT MOVED AMERICA

TO REFORM—

THE MOST SIGNIFICANT

MAGAZINE ARTICLES OF

1902–1912

EDITED

AND WITH NOTES BY

ARTHUR AND LILA WEINBERG

Simon and Schuster • New York • 1961

The editors wish to express their gratitude for permission to reprint material from the following sources:

Brandt & Brandt, for "Peruna and the Bracers," from *The Great American Fraud* by Samuel Hopkins Adams. Copyright 1905 by P. F. Collier & Son.

Brandt & Brandt, for "The First Ward Ball" by Will Irwin. Copyright 1909 by P. F. Collier & Son.

Brandt & Brandt, for verses from "Joseph G. Cannon" by Wallace Irwin. Copyright 1907 by P. F. Collier & Son.

Cosmopolitan, for "The Hoe-Man in the Making" by Edwin Markham. Copyright 1906.

Cosmopolitan, for "The Treason of the Senate" by David Graham Phillips. Copyright 1906.

John J. Dacey, for "Mr. Ballinger and the National Grab Bag" by John L. Mathews, which appeared in *Hampton's*, December 1909. Copyright 1909, 1937.

William Hard, for " 'Uncle Joe' Cannon" by William Hard. Copyright 1908 by P. F. Collier & Son.

Mark Sullivan, Jr., for "Comment About Congress" by Mark Sullivan. Copyright 1909 by P. F. Collier & Son.

The Viking Press, Inc., for a section from *The Jungle* by Upton Sinclair. Copyright 1905, 1933 by Upton Sinclair.

For
Hedy, Anita, and Wendy Clare,
a new generation
of muckrakers

"Time was," Mr. Dooley pointed out to Mr. Hennessy over his Archey Road bar, "when the magazines was very ca'ming to th' mind. Angabel an' Alfonso dash' f'r a marredge license. Prom'nent lady authoressesses makin' pomes at th' moon.

"But now whin I pick me fav'rite magazine off th' flure, what do I find? Ivrything has gone wrong."

(*Collier's*, December 16, 1905)

"It looks to me," said Mr. Hennessy, "as though the counthry was goin' to th' divvle."

"Put down that magazine, Hinnissy!"

(*Collier's*, December 16, 1905)

"Yes sir, th' hand that rocks th' fountain pen is th' hand that rules th' wurruld."

(*American*, October 1906)

From F. P. Dunne in his
Mr. Dooley and Mr. Hennessy commentaries

CONTENTS

ᏗᏗ

ᏗᏗ

ℰℛ

INTRODUCTION

A NATION DOMINATED by laissez faire, dedicated to the status quo and paying homage to the dollar as a symbol of success, was shocked by a group of writers into awareness that this was not the best of all possible worlds.

That this rude awakening came upon the American scene at the opening of the twentieth century was the result of many events and conditions.

The nation was one of contrasts. Millions of immigrants who had come to the United States were ghettoed into tenements in growing cities, working in factories, doing the rough and menial work; millions of others moved westward to close the frontier. Americans of older stock, second- and third-generation Americans, made up the middle class, the white-collar workers, the owners of small businesses, and the professionals. At the top, the business tycoons—the speculators who directed the beef, iron, railroad and oil industries—lived in grandeur and luxury in palaces and on the Gold Coasts of cities.

It is estimated that in 1860 there were only three millionaires in the United States, but forty years later there were about 3,800: one-tenth of the population owned nine-tenths of the wealth of the nation. No wonder a visitor to New York City compared the city to "a lady in ball costume, with diamonds in her ears, and her toes out at her boots." Trusts and monopolies dominated business; factories and factory life became more important in the economy of the country; organized wealth flourished in its domination of politics, and political corruption was a daily love affair between big business and the big political boss.

Yet, at the opening of the new century, the magazines which were to play such an important role in the awakening of the social consciousness of the people—particularly the middle class—during the next decade and two years, were orderly, sober, respectable. The magazines of the nineties for the most part were literary: *Harper's*, *Scribner's*, *The Century* and *The Atlantic Monthly* set the tone. *Scribner's* sold for twenty-five cents and the other three for thirty-five cents. These magazines had no competition; they appealed to the snobbish taste of the so-called "cultivated classes."

The one major dissenter during this era was the *Arena*, founded in 1889. Its editor was Benjamin Orange Flower, the "editorial dean of democracy," a tireless agitator for social reform.

Just before the turn of the century there were a few magazines making overtures to the popular taste. Frank A. Munsey, publisher of *Munsey's*, felt that magazines were trying too hard to imitate the four successful periodicals, and that twenty-five or thirty-five cents a copy was too high a price for the average reader to pay for a magazine. Furthermore, the contents of the magazines were too heavy; the reader wanted a magazine "with pictures and art and good cheer and human interest throughout." [1]

John Brisben Walker at *Cosmopolitan* was also re-evaluating his magazine to find what changes were necessary to reach a new reading public.

While *Munsey's* and *Cosmopolitan* were making overtures to the popular taste, S. S. McClure came upon the scene in June 1893 with *McClure's Magazine*, and the era of the cheap mass-circulation periodical began.

The lower prices for magazines and the mass market were made possible by a number of circumstances. First, mechanical costs dropped because of the introduction of glazed paper made from wood pulp instead of from the more costly medium of rag paper; second, the newly developed, inexpensive technique of photoengraving; and third, the creation of a larger readership through the expansion of the high school system.

In 1870, public schools had an enrollment of about seven million pupils; by 1900, the attendance more than doubled to an estimated 15,500,000. In 1860, there were about 300 public high schools; by the opening of the new century, the number jumped to about 6,000. Illiteracy in 1880 was 17 per cent; in 1900, it dropped to 11 per cent.

McClure's with its first issue sold at fifteen cents. It was illustrated, well edited, and contained both fiction and nonfiction. The first issue included a dialogue between the noted literary figures William Dean Howells and Hjalmar Hjorth Boyesen, as well as a story by Joel Chandler Harris, author of *Uncle Remus*. It also promised among its future contributors Robert Louis Stevenson, Rudyard Kipling, A. Conan

Doyle, Thomas Hardy, John Burroughs, Edward Everett Hale, Hamlin Garland and others of similar caliber.

The price and content appealed to the public.

Cosmopolitan immediately dropped its price to 12½ cents, and *Munsey's* announced in October 1893 that at ten cents a copy and one dollar a year they were inaugurating "a new era in magazine publishing . . . healthy, reasonable, rational prices."

The sedate, respectable quality magazines looked askance on these innovators. *The Independent* editorialized: "The revolution in the art of engraving, not to say its destruction, is threatening a change in the conduct of monthly magazines. . . . With July *Cosmopolitan* and *McClure's* will reduce their prices to ten cents. . . . What will be the effect on the higher-priced illustrated magazines, like *Harper's, The Century* and *Scribner's*, it may not be easy to foresee; but it seems probable that they will not find it wise to reduce their price to a like figure. . . . The reason . . . is that they will wish to maintain that higher, purer literary standard which succeeds in securing the best but not the most numerous readers. . . . They cannot enlarge their constituency beyond the comparatively cultivated class that appreciates them." [2]

There was, nevertheless, a market for the new magazines, and circulation figures proved it. The ten-cent magazines recruited millions of new readers. For example, the total circulation for *McClure's* in August 1895 was 120,000; in November, 175,000; and by December it more than doubled the August figure. By 1900, circulation totaled 370,000; by 1907, it was close to half a million.*

The literature of exposure also played an important part in raising circulation for other magazines such as *Collier's, Everybody's, Hampton's, The Independent, Pearson's, Success* and *The American Magazine*. These, like *McClure's* and *Cosmopolitan*, used the muckraking type of journalism.

The American Magazine during its muckraking days was a unique experiment in periodical publishing. It was owned by a group of writers who had worked together for some time on *McClure's Magazine* and left when they found themselves in disagreement with S. S. McClure over business policies. They decided to pool their resources and purchase a magazine which they could edit according to their own ideas.

In 1905, *Frank Leslie's Popular Magazine* had been sold and renamed *The American Magazine*. Its new editor was Ellery Sedgwick. After two years on *The American*, Sedgwick attacked the muckrakers, charg-

---

* While these figures are low compared with today's mass-circulation magazines, at the turn of the century they represented a record number of readers.

ing that their writing was filled with all kinds of distortions, truths and half-truths, exaggerations and lies. *The American Magazine* under Sedgwick would not be part of the exposé movement.

But in 1907 the magazine was for sale again. It was then that Lincoln Steffens, Ray Stannard Baker, Ida Tarbell and John S. Phillips, *McClure's* editor, joined by Finley Peter Dunne, the social satirist, and William Allen White, who later became famous as the editor of the Kansas City *Emporia Gazette*, purchased *The American*.

It was in this magazine that Baker wrote his essays on "Adventures in Contentment" and "Adventures in Understanding," under the nom de plume of David Grayson, as well as his series of articles on the Negro; Steffens wrote on Hearst; Tarbell on the tariff situation; and Finley Peter Dunne lampooned the American scene with his fictitious character Mr. Dooley.

Muckraking as a movement began in 1902; it hit a militant stride in 1903-4, took on a sensational tinge in 1905-6. Circulation of the magazines engaged in muckraking began to drop in 1908; 1909 through 1910 saw a revitalization. By 1911, muckraking began its ebb tide; and it merged into the Progressive movement by 1912.

The heyday of the muckrakers ran almost parallel to Theodore Roosevelt's term as President of the United States. Roosevelt ascended to the presidency upon the death of William McKinley, in September 1901, a victim of an assassin's bullet. At his inauguration, Roosevelt proclaimed that he would continue McKinley's policies: "I wish to say that it shall be my aim to continue, absolutely unbroken, the policy of President McKinley for the peace, the prosperity, and the honor of our beloved country." [3]

The first indication that Roosevelt's term would not follow the complacency of Republicanism as personified in Mark Hanna and William McKinley came when newspapers reported that Roosevelt's attorney general, at the request of the President, had initiated action against J. P. Morgan's Northern Securities Corporation as being in violation of the Sherman Antitrust Act. The trust theme was a favorite of Roosevelt's. He worked at it not only in his messages to Congress, but in whistle-stop stumping as he traveled the country.

But it was the muckrakers, so named by Roosevelt, who detailed to the country the story of the trusts and how they made their money.

Roosevelt respected the popular magazines which were the vehicles of the muckrakers. He recognized their inherent power. He made it his business to be acquainted with their editors and their writers, and it was

not unusual for an author who had written something which was helping the President in one of his crusades, to be a luncheon guest at the
White House.

But even these writers who brought to light so many of the evils
upon which the President acted, were to learn, much to their surprise,
that he was not fully in agreement with their methods of exposure.
Soon after William Randolph Hearst's *Cosmopolitan* started its series
of articles in 1906 on "The Treason of the Senate," Roosevelt spoke
before the Gridiron Club of newspapermen in Washington, D.C. He
charged that the writers who were engaging in the exposure of corruption were "muckrakers," and likened them to the man with the muckrake in Bunyan's *Pilgrim's Progress* who could "look no way but downward, with a muckrake in his hands; who was offered a celestial crown
for his muckrake, but who would neither look up nor regard the crown
he was offered, but continued to rake to himself the filth of the floor."

The speech, like all Gridiron talks, was off the record. News of the
attack, however, became common gossip. The President was delighted.
He had a flare for the dramatic, and he announced he would make the
same talk when he dedicated the cornerstone of the House of Representatives office building on April 14, 1906. It was this speech which
labeled these writers as muckrakers.

While it is generally agreed that *The Arena* was the forerunner of
the muckraking magazines, and *McClure's* the first, the decision as to
who is the first muckraker remains moot.

Both Baker and Mark Sullivan claimed the title for themselves, as
did Steffens.

Baker, in a letter to Louis Filler,* suggested: "I note that you quote
Steffens to the effect that the first muckraking article was on October 2,
1902. But look up two articles of mine, one in *Collier's Weekly*, No-
vember 30, 1901, on 'The Northern Pacific Deal,' the other in *McClure's*
Magazine, November 1901, the leading article, entitled 'What the
United States Steel Corporation Really Is and How It Works.'"

In his *The Education of an American*, Sullivan asserted: "Actually
the first article of political muckraking was the one I wrote, 'The Ills
of Pennsylvania,' for the *Atlantic Monthly* just a year before, in October
1901."

Then again, Ida Tarbell started working on the "History of the
Standard Oil" five years before publication of the series started in
November 1902. She herself, however, never decided whether she was an
"historian" or a "muckraker."

* Professor of History of American Civilization at Antioch College.

Steffens made no bones about his contentions. In his autobiography, he captioned a photo of his article "Tweed Days in St. Louis" as "The first muckraking article."

Most historians are agreed that the title goes to Lincoln Steffens by default.

Actually, the "literature of exposure" as such was not anything new. The writings of the abolitionists border on muckraking, as does that of the great pamphleteer of the American revolution, Thomas Paine. Jesus, suggested Ray Stannard Baker, was one of the greatest muckrakers.

History is filled with the exploits of muckrakers—men who participated in the "literature of exposure" of their day. Prophets, honored or decried by their own generation, they pointed a finger at the wrongs and injustices in their society. Elijah and Socrates are examples. In modern history, before the era of the muckrake, there were Harriet Beecher Stowe of *Uncle Tom's Cabin* fame; Henry George, father of the single tax; Edward Bellamy, who foretold a new social order in his novel *Looking Backward*; and Henry Demarest Lloyd, who wrote a bitter attack on Standard Oil in *Wealth Against Commonwealth*.

What was new and makes the muckraking era unique, however, is that for the first time there was a group of writers and a concentration of magazines hammering away at the ills they found in society. Neither before nor since has there been in periodical literature anything which can compare to the relentless drive for exposure.

Because of the mass-circulation magazines, muckraking now had the ability to attract a national audience. The average muckraking article did not offer curative proposals. It was factual, though critical. It was primarily directed at the social conscience of the nation. Its aim was to expose, not to solve.

The muckrakers were "the publicity men for reform"; [4] they were the press agents for the Progressive movement. To these writers and to the fast-growing muckraking magazines goes the credit for arousing a lethargic public to righteous indignation. They spotlighted Progressivism, and gave this political movement the impetus that aided it in the passage of social and economic legislation.

There was a need for aggressive and sensational measures. This is where the muckrakers were important. There can be no intelligent discussion or action unless there are facts; the muckrakers furnished the facts and made them alive for a reading public. As Professor Louis Filler observed, "From it [these writings] stemmed the reforming zeal that was to leaven future American politics." [5]

The muckrake touched practically every phase of American life; nothing was immune from it. The flaws were photographed, analyzed, pinpointed. The men engaged in muckraking were bold. Their accusations were specific, direct. Names were named. They pointed to sore spots in business, in politics. They found food adulteration, unscrupulous practices in finance and insurance companies, fraudulent claims for and injurious ingredients in patent medicines, rape of natural resources, bureaucracy, prostitution, a link between government and vice. Prison conditions were exposed, as were newspapers and their domination by advertisers. The church was not spared from the muckrakers' probing, particularly the famous, highly revered Trinity Church of New York and its tenement houses. The evils of child labor were exposed.

Vernon Louis Parrington, social historian, summed up the muckraking era as "a time of brisk housecleaning that searched out old cobwebs and disturbed the dust that lay thick on the antiquated furniture." [6]

Walter Lippmann in his *Drift and Mastery* * emphasized that "the mere fact that muckraking was what people wanted to hear is in many ways the most important revelation of the whole campaign.

"There is no other way of explaining the quick approval which the muckrakers won. They weren't voices crying in a wilderness, or lonely prophets who were stoned. They demanded a hearing; it was granted. They asked for belief; they were believed. . . . There must have been real causes for dissatisfaction, or the land notorious for its worship of success would not have turned so savagely upon those who had achieved it." [7]

Some of the muckraking was conscientious and scholarly, based on detailed research for which expense was not spared. *McClure's* emphasized this type. Series like Thomas Lawson's "Frenzied Finance" and David Graham Phillips' "The Treason of the Senate" exemplify the more sensational kind of articles. John Chamberlain, editor and critic, refers to Tarbell and Steffens as "the scholars of the movement," and to Phillips and Lawson as "dealers in pyrotechnics." [8]

At the midpoint of the movement, the muckrakers themselves admitted that exposé was catching on as a fad. *Collier's* lamented on May 25, 1905, that the true investigator of the Steffens and Tarbell type were finding their "authority diminish[ed]. Why listen to facts when diatribes are at hand?"

Ellery Sedgwick, who prior to assuming the editorship of *The Atlantic Monthly* was a McClure editor for a year, commented that theories

* 1914.

instead of facts began to dominate muckraking, and he charged that "men are tried and found guilty in magazine counting-rooms before the investigation is begun." [9]

The muckrakers were also bitterly charged by the most conservative *Critic* magazine with being "a colossal scheme to make money by doing the greatest harm to men who do not deserve it. The people are laboring under the misapprehension of believing that these men in high places are all wrong-doers and that the newspapers and magazines are defenders of the public good in exposing them, but they are not. They are on the scent for scandal and blackmail because that sort of stuff is salable, and in most cases for that reason alone." [10]

Whether the motives of the muckrakers were financial, personal, or grew from a desire to see reform is not the main issue. Probably it was a little of all three. Historians generally, however, are agreed that muckraking during the first twelve years of the twentieth century was directly responsible for such legislation as the Pure Food and Drug Act, the reform in life insurance, the improvement in advertising.

The writings of the muckrakers gave new power to the demand for prison reform, direct election of senators, vice investigation, city and state reform, railroad legislation.

Everybody's—surely overly optimistic—listed in January 1908 the muckrakers' accomplishments: "Wall Street cannot gull the public as it once did. Insurance is on a sounder basis; banking is adding new safeguards; advertising is nearly honest. Food and drug adulterations are dangerous. Human life is more respected by common carriers. The hour of the old-time political boss has struck. States and municipalities are insisting upon clean administrations. The people are naming their own candidates. . . . Children are having their day in court. Protection is offered to the weak against the gambling shark and saloon. Our public resources are being conserved."

Business particularly felt the heavy hand of the muckrakers. Though it is impossible to substantiate that its workings were specifically improved as a result of the muckrake, it is argued by some that "the whole tone of business in the United States was raised because of the persistent exposures of corruption and injustice." [11] Business, at any rate, began to defend itself against the attacks.

Professor Eric Goldman of Princeton University proposes the thesis: "Perhaps the most helpful point I could make about the muckrakers is their critically important role in discovering 'publicity.' . . . Up to the early 1900's, most Americans, including much of American industry, considered publicity a bad thing. The idea was to operate in secrecy.

Then T.R. led in discovering publicity as a political weapon. The muckrakers used publicity as an anti-business weapon and industry, in direct reply to the muckrakers, began to feel that if publicity could be used against them, it could also be used for them. Hence the birth of the whole public relations industry." [12]

Harold Laski, a modern English critic, wrote: "In that remarkable epoch of the 'muckrakers,' which led, if in a circuitous way, through 'progressivism' to the reign of Woodrow Wilson in the White House, and thence, after the flamboyant nihilism of the nineteen-twenties, to the New Deal of Franklin Roosevelt, the relentless exposures of Lincoln Steffens and of Upton Sinclair put both the boss system in the cities and the great trusts on the defensive; and though each of them emerged from the attack successfully, they were not wholly unscathed by the ordeal.

"Indeed I do not think it is an exaggeration to say that it was the exposure of the methods of the Rockefeller empire by Miss Ida Tarbell in her 'History of the Standard Oil Company' which led Mr. Rockefeller to accept the advice of his public relations officer, the notorious Ivy Lee, to seek to regain by public benefactions the moral loss his reputation suffered as the ugly story of the corruption, brutality, and dishonesty upon which his fortune was founded came to be a matter of public knowledge." [13]

"Muckraking, indeed," wrote Chamberlain, "provided the basis for the entire movement toward Social Democracy that came to its head in the first Wilson Administration." [14]

This view is also reinforced by Jacob Scher, professor of journalism at Northwestern University and chief counsel for the United States House of Representatives Subcommittee on Government Information. Professor Scher points out that when the muckrakers focused on a problem, they laid the groundwork for the future climate of opinion which may have found expression years later, either under the Wilson administration or that of F.D.R.* [15]

Muckraking also had its fiction writers who exposed, appealed, exhorted and dramatized the various problems which the muckrakers posed.

Among the more famous of these was Frank Norris. His novel *The Octopus* told of the dominant hand the South Pacific railroad had in California politics; and in *The Pit* he showed how grain speculators controlled the grain wheat market.

* President Franklin D. Roosevelt and the New Deal.

Booth Tarkington and Brand Whitlock took a critical view of American political life, as did the American novelist Winston Churchill. David Graham Phillips unmasked political conditions in *The Plum Tree,* and in his *Great God Success* and *The Second Generation* he showed the corrupting power of money. In his *Susan Lenox* he played up the social forces which led a country girl into prostitution.

In addition to *The Jungle,* Upton Sinclair wrote such books as *The Money Changers,* which dealt with Wall Street, and *The Metropolis,* which was based on the antics of the gilded rich of New York. Theodore Dreiser exploited the life of a Chicago tractor magnate as a theme for one of his novels. Robert Herrick touched on the ethics of the Chicago meat packing industry in his *The Memoirs of an American Citizen.* William Allen White's *A Certain Rich Man* was an attack on predatory wealth. Jack London was intellectually a muckraker, as exemplified in his essays.

These novelists, with such near-muckrakers as Judge Ben B. Lindsey, Alfred Henry Lewis, John Spargo, Rheta Childe Dorr, George Kennan and Josiah Flynt, together with the muckrakers who are included in this anthology, influenced the country toward a self-examination unique in its history.

Many reasons are given for the decline of the muckraking movement, which pretty well came to a halt soon after the first decade of the twentieth century:

Professor Scher sees World War I as a turning point. The war directed people's attention away from the national onto the international scene; Wilson's new freedom absorbed much of the reform which was preached in the "literature of exposure"; advertisers began to withdraw from these magazines; and, finally, the era of the press agent which had its emergence with Rockefeller's employment of Ivy Lee, made it possible for big business to "unsell the public on practically anything." [16]

Charles Edward Russell, a muckraker in his own right, in an article in *Pearson's,* "The Magazines Soft Pedal," put the blame on the advertising departments of magazines who put the damper on the muckrakers. He also pointed to advertisers, and cited the fact that *Everybody's,* as an example, lost seven pages of advertising when his own series on the beef trust was running. The ads which were withdrawn were those for ham, preserved meats, soaps, patent cleaners and fertilizers, and a railroad. [17]

"More potent than the advertiser's garrotte," wrote Chamberlain, "and the garrotte played its part, we may be sure, whether openly or through the growth of a new 'community of interest' in the magazine field—was the indifference of a public that still allowed itself to be destroyed through lack of knowledge." [18]

Will Irwin—who had written a definitive study on "The American Newspaper" for *Collier's* *—pointed out that the average subscriber to a magazine grew tired of reading about civic corruption, predatory trusts, injustice to labor, and the stripping of natural resources. The public felt that the politicians had taken notice in such proceedings as the Industrial Commission, and that through these the government was doing its own muckraking.

He further asserted that magazines as a whole "were watering the milk, as the professional mediums used to say." [19]

According to Upton Sinclair, the decline came for a number of reasons, including the fact that "Phillips in his 'Treason of the Senate' went too far. Some of the magazines, such as *Everybody's* and the *American*, were forced into bankruptcy when the banks stopped extending credit. *Collier's* quit muckraking and was able to survive, until recently. Today, there is no magazine worthy of the name of muckraker." [20]

Is muckraking being done today?

Yes, in isolated instances. Now and then a magazine, a newspaper, a television documentary falls into the best tradition of muckraking. But the concentrated drive for exposure—which marked the opening years of this century—is lacking.

Is there a need for muckraking today? Are some of the sore spots, which were alleviated as a result of the work of the man with the muckrake, still festering in our society?

We leave these questions open to debate. It was not the intention of the editors to pass judgment, but rather to present a period in this country's history through magazine writers and their writings.

There were hundreds of articles written during the era of the muckrakers by magazine writers who almost seemed to be Don Quixotes fighting windmills. But from a historical perspective, their writings did have a part in changing the course of American political, economic and social history and thought. They affected individual lives, as well as the community. Their writings are historical documents.

This book attempts to re-create an era in American history through the efforts of these men and women who were writing about their generation. They were the "angry young men" of the early twentieth century. They talked and a country listened.

* January 21–July 29, 1911.

The articles included in this volume are not necessarily the most literary of the muckraking pieces. The editors have endeavored to select what they consider the most important and most significant magazine articles of the literature of exposure, written during the first twelve years of the twentieth century. In instances where an article is long, overly detailed and overwritten to present its case, it has been edited. Otherwise, the writings are those of the muckrakers as they wrote.

The idea for this book was first suggested to us by our friend Harry Sholl. For his idea and his encouragement during the years of our research and writing, we are most grateful.

The editors again express thanks to Richard L. Grossman, vice-president, Simon and Schuster, who has always been available for advice and has been most cooperative.

In our research we have spoken to scores of historians, writers, newspapermen. Upton Sinclair, veteran muckraker, and his wife Mary Craig Sinclair, spent time with the editors reminiscing about "those days" and thus helped re-create the era of exposure. William Hard, another survivor of the muckraking era, was very helpful in his comments.

Our friends Jacob Scher, professor of journalism, Northwestern University, and Louis Filler, professor of History of American Civilization at Antioch College, have spent time with the editors and their enthusiasm for this work has been most encouraging. Professor Filler read parts of the manuscript and we are indebted to him for suggestions, as we are to Professor Scher.

Jack Ryan, Director of Publications and News Service, Montana State University, who spoke with members of the university staff, helped prepare the chapter on Montana.

Others who have spent time with the editors are Professors John T. Frederick and Aaron I. Abell of the University of Notre Dame; Professor Walter Johnson, University of Chicago; United States Senator Paul Douglas (Illinois); Professor Arthur Schlesinger, Jr., Harvard University; Professor Allan Nevins, Columbia University; and Dr. Morton Frisch, College of William and Mary. Among others who cooperated are Professor Eric F. Goldman, Princeton University; Frank Luther Mott, University of Missouri; Roland E. Wolseley, Syracuse University; United States Congressman Barratt O'Hara (Illinois); Dr. Morris Fishbein; Stewart H. Holbrook; Herman Kogan; Gwynne Winsberg; Dr. Stanley Chyet; and J. A. Genier, El Camino College.

A special word of appreciation must be extended to Ben C. Bowman, of Newberry Library, Chicago, for extra help he gave the editors during

their research at the library. The editors also want to express apprecia-
tion to the University of Chicago's Harper Library, the Chicago Public
Library, and the Library of Indiana State Teachers College at Terre
Haute, Indiana.

The usual warning, however, must be sounded at this time: the
editors alone are responsible for the selections in this book, the facts
reported, and the interpretation given to the era of the muckrakers.

ARTHUR AND LILA WEINBERG

Chicago, Illinois, March 1961

PART ONE

In the Beginning

SAMUEL S. McCLURE was a magazine-maker; a businessman with the temperament of an artist.

He was an idea man. But not all of his ideas were good; the chaff had to be separated from the wheat, and this was the responsibility of the staff members of his *McClure's Magazine*.

He was always surging with enthusiasm. So insistent did he become at times for a particular article that the staff, in self-defense to complete a story they were working on, would rent a hotel room. His letters to his office while he was traveling around the world always carried ideas for articles and assignments. He sent newspaper clippings from wherever he was at the time, with sentences underscored for what he considered an idea for the magazine. "A week in the McClure office," wrote Ellery Sedgwick, who for a year before assuming the editorship of *The Atlantic Monthly* was a McClure editor, "was the precise reversal of the six busy days described in the first chapter of Genesis. It seemed to end in a world without form and void. From Order came forth Chaos. . . . Yet with all his pokings and proddings the fires he kindled were brighter than any flames his staff could produce without him." [21]

McClure's theme and insistence to his writers was accuracy. He demanded facts, and they had to be presented in a high standard of writing. Though *McClure's Magazine* became a reform vehicle, it was not because of any reforming zeal on the part of its owner, but rather because McClure felt that was what his readers wanted. The circulation figures of *McClure's* testified to how right he was. And the articles that made *McClure's* circulation soar belonged in the school that later came to be called muckraking. Ray Stannard Baker reported that "the public response to these articles, by any test, was astonishing." [22]

The unplanned but simultaneous publication of three articles in *McClure's* set muckraking on its "historic way" and more or less defined its future course. Lincoln Steffens' article, "Tweed Days in St. Louis" (which also carried the by-line of Claude H. Wetmore), appeared in the October 1902 issue of the magazine. Ida Tarbell started her series, "The History of the Standard Oil Company," a month later.

It was while the January 1903 issue was being dummied that the editors discovered that Steffens' article on Minneapolis, "The Shame of Minne-apolis," Tarbell's chapter on Standard Oil and an article by Baker on "The Right to Work" * underlined the same theme.

It was then the editors inserted an editorial entitled "Concerning Three Articles in This Number of *McClure's,* and a Coincidence that May Set Us Thinking." Henceforth, the trumpeting of exposures became the theme for *McClure's,* as well as for other magazines who readily joined the band-wagon. At one time, it is estimated, there were more than a dozen maga-zines muckraking one or more phases of American life.

These magazines became important to the Progressive movement, a fact exemplified by a story which was popular among the muckrakers: A wealthy Alaska miner urged a newspaper editor to start a crusade. He had the evidence.

"You certainly are a Progressive," said the editor to the miner.

"Progressive," retorted the miner. "Progressive! I tell you I'm a full-fledged Insurgent. Why, man, I subscribe to thirteen magazines!" [23]

A McClure article was detailed, accurate and thorough. He gave his writers adequate time for research and writing, and he paid them for "their study rather than for the amount of copy they turned out." He "put the writer on such a salary as would relieve him of all financial worry and let him master a subject to such a degree that he could write upon it, if not with the authority of the specialist, at least with such accuracy as could inform the public and meet with the corroboration of experts." [24]

Ida Tarbell, for example, took five years to write her series on Standard Oil, at a cost to McClure of about $4,000 an article. Lincoln Steffens averaged about four articles a year, at about $2,000 each.[25]

---

* Baker, in his autobiography published in 1945, recalls his insistence after his article, "The Right to Work," was written, that the magazine "clearly state[d] that I had treated only one aspect of a highly complex problem. It was true only as far as it went; I did not wish to be making ammunition for mere stupid opposi-tion to all labor organization, or even all strikes." (*An American Chronicle,* p. 168.)

The editor in his introduction to the article in *McClure's* wrote: "Public opinion seems to be coming around to the view that the trades' union is here to stay. From many unexpected quarters we hear every now and then a more generous acknowl-edgment that the organization of labor is not only as inevitable as the combination of capital, but a good thing in itself. At the same time, and from the same fair minds, you hear expressions of passionate indignation at the abuse of power by unions. This means that public opinion is beginning to distinguish between unionism and the sins of unionists, as it is between organized capital and the sins of capitalists.

"Clear-headed labor leaders say that violence hurts the union cause, and they denounce it in general. In general, too, violence of the old brick-throwing sort has decreased. It has not disappeared, however, but has taken on a subtler, more delib-erate, more terrible form, in many cases, nowadays. Consequently, conditions arise which make liberty and the pursuit of happiness, not to speak of life itself, well nigh impossible to certain of the strikers' fellow men and citizens. The public at large, and often the leaders of unions, do not realize these conditions. But it is manifestly the duty of both to understand them clearly.

"We believe that the presentation of the facts—the conditions under which the seventeen thousand nonstriking miners worked—will be helpful to the public, which is the final arbiter, and beneficial to those also who have in charge the ad-ministration of labor unions. Mr. Baker was, therefore, asked to make an impartial investigation and report, and the following article is the result."

McClure Editorial

CONCERNING THREE ARTICLES IN
THIS NUMBER OF MC CLURE'S, AND
A COINCIDENCE THAT MAY SET US
THINKING

How MANY of those who have read through this number of the magazine noticed that it contains three articles on one subject? We did not plan it so; it is a coincidence that the January *McClure's* is such an arraignment of American character as should make every one of us stop and think. How many noticed that?

The leading article, "The Shame of Minneapolis," might have been called "The American Contempt of Law." That title could well have served for the current chapter of Miss Tarbell's History of Standard Oil. And it would have fitted perfectly Mr. Baker's "The Right to Work." All together, these articles come pretty near showing how universal is this dangerous trait of ours.

Miss Tarbell has our capitalists conspiring among themselves, deliberately, shrewdly, upon legal advice, to break the law so far as it restrained them, and to misuse it to restrain others who were in their way. Mr. Baker shows labor, the ancient enemy of capital, and the chief complainant of the trusts' unlawful acts, itself committing and excusing crimes. And in "The Shame of Minneapolis" we see the administration of a city employing criminals to commit crimes for the profit of the elected officials, while the citizens—Americans of good stock and more than average culture, and honest, healthy Scandinavians—stood by complacent and not alarmed.

Capitalists, workingmen, politicians, citizens—all breaking the law, or letting it be broken. Who is left to uphold it? The lawyers? Some of the best lawyers in this country are hired, not to go into court to defend cases, but to advise corporations and business firms how they can get around the law without too great a risk of punishment. The judges? Too many of them so respect the laws that for some "error" or quibble they restore to office and liberty men convicted on evidence overwhelmingly convincing to common sense. The churches? We know of one, an ancient and wealthy establishment, which had to be compelled by a Tammany hold-over health officer to put its tenements in sanitary condition. The colleges? They do not understand.

There is no one left; none but all of us. Capital is learning (with indignation at labor's unlawful acts) that its rival's contempt of law is a menace to property. Labor has shrieked the belief that the illegal power of capital is a menace to the worker. These two are drawing together. Last November when a strike was threatened by the yard-men on all the railroads centering in Chicago, the men got together and settled by raising wages, and raising freight rates too. They made the public pay. We all are doing our worst and making the public pay. The public is the people. We forget that we all are the people; that while each of us in his group can shove off on the rest the bill of today, the debt is only postponed; the rest are passing it on back to us. We have to pay in the end, every one of us. And in the end the sum total of the debt will be our liberty.

McClure's Magazine
January 1903

LINCOLN STEFFENS

The Shame of Minneapolis

WHENEVER ANYTHING extraordinary is done in American municipal politics, whether for good or for evil, you can trace it almost invariably to one man. The people do not do it. Neither do the "gangs," "combines" or political parties. These are but instruments by which bosses (not leaders; we Americans are not led, but driven) rule the people, and commonly sell them out. But there are at least two forms of autocracy which has supplanted the democracy here as it has everywhere it has been tried. One is that of the organized majority by which, as in Tammany Hall in New York and the Republican machine in Philadelphia, the boss has normal control of more than half the voters. The other is that of the adroitly managed minority. The "good people" are herded into parties and stupefied with convictions and a name, Republican or Democrat; while the "bad people" are so organized or interested by the boss that he can wield their votes to enforce terms with party managers and decide elections. St. Louis is a conspicuous example of this form. Minneapolis is another. Colonel Ed Butler is the unscrupulous opportunist who handled the nonpartisan minority which turned St. Louis into a "boodle town." In Minneapolis "Doc" Ames was the man.

Minneapolis is a New England town on the upper Mississippi. The metropolis of the Northwest, it is the metropolis also of Norway and Sweden in America. Indeed, it is the second largest Scandinavian city in the world. But Yankees, straight from Down East, settled the town, and their New England spirit predominates. They had Bayard Taylor lecture there in the early days of the settlement; they made it the seat of the University of Minnesota. Yet even now, when the town has grown to a population of more than 200,000, you feel that there is

6

something western about it too—a Yankee with a small Puritan head, an open prairie heart, and a great, big Scandinavian body. The Round-head takes the Swede and Norwegian bone out into the woods, and they cut lumber by forests, or they go out on the prairies and raise wheat and mill it into fleet-cargoes of flour. They work hard, they make money, they are sober, satisfied, busy with their own affairs. There isn't much time for public business. Taken together, Miles, Hans and Ole are very American. Miles insists upon strict laws, Ole and Hans want one or two Scandinavians on their ticket. These things granted, they go off on raft or reaper, leaving whoso will to enforce the laws and run the city.

The people who were left to govern the city hated above all things strict laws. They were the loafers, saloonkeepers, gamblers, criminals, and the thriftless poor of all nationalities. Resenting the sobriety of a staid, industrious community, and having no Irish to boss them, they delighted to follow the jovial pioneer doctor, Albert Alonzo Ames. He was the "good fellow"—a genial, generous reprobate. Devery, Tweed, and many more have exposed in vain this amiable type. "Doc" Ames, tall, straight and cheerful, attracted men, and they gave him votes for his smiles. He stood for license. There was nothing of the Puritan about him. His father, the sturdy old pioneer, Dr. Alfred Elisha Ames, had a strong strain of it in him, but he moved on with his family of six sons from Garden Prairie, Illinois, to Fort Snelling reservation, in 1851, before Minneapolis was founded, and young Albert Alonzo, who then was ten years old, grew up free, easy and tolerant. He was sent to school, then to college in Chicago, and he returned home a doctor of medicine before he was twenty-one. As the town waxed soberer and richer, "Doc" grew gayer and more and more generous. Skillful as a surgeon, devoted as a physician, and as a man kindly, he increased his practice till he was the best-loved man in the community. He was especially good to the poor. Anybody could summon "Doc" Ames at any hour to any distance. He went, and he gave not only his professional service, but sympathy, and often charity. "Richer men than you will pay your bill," he told the destitute. So there was a basis for his "good-fellow-ship." There always is; these good fellows are not frauds—not in the beginning.

But there is another side to them sometimes. Ames was sunshine not to the sick and destitute only. To the vicious and the depraved also he was a comfort. If a man was a hard drinker, the good Doctor cheered him with another drink; if he had stolen something, the Doctor helped to get him off. He was naturally vain; popularity developed his love of approbation. His loose life brought disapproval only from the good people, so gradually the Doctor came to enjoy best the society of the barroom and the streets. This society, flattered in turn, worshiped the good Doctor, and, active in politics always, put its physician into the arena.

Had he been wise, or even shrewd, he might have made himself a real power. But he wasn't calculating, only light and frivolous, so he did not organize his forces and run men for office. He sought office himself from the start, and he got most of the small places he wanted by changing his party to seize the opportunity. His floating minority, added to the regular partisan vote, was sufficient ordinarily for his useless victories. As time went on he rose from smaller offices to be a Republican mayor, then twice at intervals to be a Democratic mayor. He was a candidate once for Congress; he stood for governor once on a sort of Populist-Democrat ticket. Ames could not get anything outside of his own town, and after his third term as mayor it was thought he was out of politics altogether. He was getting old, and he was getting worse.

Like many a "good fellow" with hosts of miscellaneous friends downtown to whom he was devoted, the good Doctor neglected his own family. From neglect he went on openly to separation from his wife and a second establishment. The climax came not long before the election of 1900. His wife was dying, and his daughter wrote to her father a note saying that her mother wished to see and forgive him. The messenger found him in a saloon. The Doctor read the note, laid it on the bar, and scribbled across it a sentence incredibly obscene. His wife died. The outraged family would not have the father at the funeral, but he appeared, not at the house, but in a carriage on the street. He sat across the way, with his feet up and a cigar in his mouth, till the funeral moved; then he circled around, crossing it and meeting it, and making altogether a scene which might well close any man's career.

It didn't end his. The people had just secured the passage of a new primary law to establish direct popular government. There were to be no more nominations by convention. The voters were to ballot for their party candidates. By a slip of some sort, the laws did not specify that Republicans only should vote for Republican candidates, and only Democrats for Democratic candidates. Any voter could vote at either primary. Ames, in disrepute with his own party, the Democratic, bade his followers vote for his nomination for mayor on the Republican ticket. They all voted; not all the Republicans did. He was nominated.

Nomination is far from election, and you would say that the trick would not help him. But that was a presidential year, so the people of Minneapolis had to vote for Ames, the Republican candidate for Mayor. Besides, Ames said he was going to reform; that he was getting old, and wanted to close his career with a good administration. The effective argument, however, was that, since McKinley had to be elected to save the country, Ames must be supported for Mayor of Minneapolis. Why? The great American people cannot be trusted to scratch a ticket.

Well, Minneapolis got its old mayor back, and he was reformed. Up to this time Ames had not been very venal personally. He was a "spender," not a "grafter," and he was guilty of corruption chiefly by proxy; he took the honors and left the spoils to his followers. His administrations were no worse than the worst. Now, however, he set out upon a career of corruption which for deliberateness, invention and avarice has never been equaled. It was as if he had made up his mind that he had been careless long enough, and meant to enrich his last years. He began early.

Immediately upon his election, before he took office (on January 7), he organized a cabinet and laid plans to turn the city over to outlaws who were to work under police direction for the profit of his administration. He chose for chief his brother, Colonel Fred W. Ames, who had recently returned under a cloud from service in the Philippines. The Colonel had commanded a Minnesota regiment out there till he proved a coward under fire; he escaped court-martial only on the understanding that he should resign on reaching San Francisco, whither he was immediately shipped. This he did not do, and his brother's influence at Washington saved him to be mustered out with the regiment. But he was a weak vessel for chief of police, and the mayor picked for chief of detectives an abler man, who was to direct the more difficult operations. This was Norman W. King, a former gambler, who knew the criminals needed in the business ahead. King was to invite the Minneapolis thieves, confidence men, pickpockets, and gamblers, and release some that were in the local jail. They were to be organized into groups, according to their profession, and detectives were assigned to assist and direct them. The head of the gambling syndicate was to have charge of the gambling, making the terms and collecting the "graft," just as King and a Captain Hill were to collect from the thieves. The collector for women of the town was to be Irwin A. Gardner, a medical student in the Doctor's office, who was made a special policeman for the purpose. These men looked over the force, selected those men who could be trusted, charged them a price for their retention, and marked for dismissal 107 men out of 225, the 107 being the best policemen in the department from the point of view of the citizens who afterward reorganized the force. John Fitchette, better known as "Coffee John," a Virginian (who served on the Jeff Davis jury), the keeper of a notorious coffeehouse, was to be a captain of police, with no duties except to sell places on the police force.

And they did these things that they planned—all and more. The administration opened with the revolution on the police force. They liberated the thieves in the local jail, and made known to the underworld generally that "things were doing" in Minneapolis. The incoming swindlers reported to King or his staff for instructions, and went to work, turning the "swag" over to the detectives in charge. Gambling went on openly, and disorderly houses multiplied under the fostering care of Gardner, the medical student. But all this was not enough. Ames dared to break openly into the municipal system of vice protection.

There was such a thing. Minneapolis, strict in its laws, forbade vices which are inevitable, then regularly permitted them under certain conditions. Legal limits, called "patrol lines," were prescribed, within which saloons might be opened. These ran along the river front, out through part of the business section, with long arms reaching into the Scandinavian quarters, north and south. Gambling also was confined, but more narrowly. And there were limits, also arbitrary, but not always identical with those for gambling, within which the social evil was allowed. But the novel feature of this scheme was that disorderly houses were practically licensed by the city, the women appearing before the clerk of the Municipal Court each month to pay a "fine" of $100. Unable at first to get this "graft," Ames's man Gardner persuaded women to start houses, apartments, and, of all things, candy stores, which sold sweets to children and tobacco to the "lumberjacks" in front, while a nefarious traffic was carried on in the rear. But they paid Ames, not the city, and that was all the reform administration cared about.

The revenue from all these sources must have been enormous. It only whetted the avarice of the mayor and his cabinet. They let gambling privileges without restriction to location or "squareness"; the syndicate could cheat and rob as it would. Peddlers and pawnbrokers, formerly licensed by the city, bought permits now instead from "Gardner's father," A. L. Gardner, who was the mayor's agent in this field. Some two hundred slot machines were installed in various parts of the town, with owner's agent and mayor's agent watching and collecting from them enough to pay the mayor $15,000 a year as his share. Auction frauds were instituted. Opium joints and unlicensed saloons, called "blind pigs," were protected. Gardner even had a police baseball team, for whose games tickets were sold to people who had to buy them. But the women were the easiest "graft." They were compelled to buy illustrated biographies of the city officials; they had to give presents of money, jewelry and gold stars to police officers. But the money they still paid direct to the city in fines, some $35,000 a year, fretted the mayor, and at last he reached for it. He came out with a declaration, in his old character as friend of the oppressed, that $100 a month was too much for these women to pay. They should be required to pay the city fine only once in two months. This puzzled the town till it became generally known that Gardner collected the other month for the mayor. The final outrage in this department, however, was an order of the mayor for the periodic visits to disorderly houses, by the city's physicians, at from $5 to $20 per visit. The two physicians he appointed called when they willed, and more and more frequently, till toward the end the calls became a pure formality, with the collections as the one and only object.

In a general way all this business was known. It did not arouse the citizens, but it did attract criminals, and more and more thieves and swindlers came hurrying to Minneapolis. Some of them saw the police, and made terms. Some were seen by the police and invited to go to work. There was room for all. This astonishing fact that the government of a city asked criminals to rob the people is fully established. The police and the criminals have confessed it separately. Their statements agree in detail. Detective Norbeck made the arrangement, and introduced the swindlers to Gardner, who, over King's head, took the money from them. Here is the story "Billy" Edwards, a "big mitt" man, told under oath of his reception in Minneapolis:

"I had been out to the coast, and hadn't seen Norbeck for some time. After I returned I boarded a Minneapolis car one evening to go down to South Minneapolis to visit a friend. Norbeck and Detective DeLaittre were on the car. When Norbeck saw me he came up and shook hands, and said, 'Hullo, Billy, how goes it?' I said, 'Not very well.' Then he says, 'Things have changed since you went away. Me and Gardner are the whole thing now. Before you left they thought I didn't know anything, but I turned a few tricks, and now I'm It.' 'I'm glad of that, Chris,' I said. He says, 'I've got great things for you. I'm going to fix up a joint for you.' 'That's good,' I said, 'but I don't be-

lieve you can do it.' 'Oh, yes, I can,' he replied. 'I'm It now—Gardner
and me.' 'Well, if you can do it,' says I, 'there's money in it.' 'How
much can you pay?' he asked. 'Oh, $150 or $200 a week,' says I. 'That
settles it,' he said; 'I'll take you down to see Gardner, and we'll fix it
up.' Then he made an appointment to meet me the next night, and
we went down to Gardner's house together."

There Gardner talked business in general, showed his drawer full of
bills, and jokingly asked how Edwards would like to have them. Edwards says:

"I said, 'That looks pretty good to me,' and Gardner told us that he
had 'collected' the money from the women he had on his staff, and
that he was going to pay it over to the 'old man' when he got back
from his hunting trip next morning. Afterward he told me that the
mayor had been much pleased with our $500, and that he said every-
thing was all right, and for us to go ahead."

"Link" Crossman, another confidence man who was with Edwards,
said that Gardner demanded $1,000 at first, but compromised on $500
for the mayor, $50 for Gardner, and $50 for Norbeck. To the chief,
Fred Ames, they gave tips now and then of $25 or $50. "The first week
we ran," said Crossman, "I gave Fred $15. Norbeck took me down
there. We shook hands, and I handed him an envelope with $15. He
pulled out a list of steerers we had sent him, and said he wanted to go
over them with me. He asked where the joint was located. At another
time I slipped $25 into his hand as he was standing in the hallway of
City Hall." But these smaller payments, after the first "opening, $500,"
are all down on the pages of the "big mitt" ledger. This notorious book,
which was kept by Charlie Howard, one of the "big mitt" men, was
much talked of at the subsequent trials, but was kept hidden to await
the trial of the mayor himself.

The "big mitt" game was swindling by means of a stacked hand at
stud poker. "Steerers" and "boosters" met "suckers" on the street, at
hotels, and railway stations, won their confidence, and led them to the
"joint." Usually the "sucker" was called, by the amount of his loss,
"the $102 man" or "the $35 man." Roman Meix alone had the distinction among all the Minneapolis victims of going by his own name.
Having lost $775, he became known for his persistent complainings.
But they all "kicked" some. To Norbeck at the street door was assigned
the duty of hearing their complaints, and "throwing a scare into them."
"Oh, so you've been gambling," he would say. "Have you got a license?
Well, then, you better get right out of this town." Sometimes he ac-

companied them to the station and saw them off. If they were not to be put off thus, he directed them to the chief of police. Fred Ames tried to wear them out by keeping them waiting in the anteroom. If they outlasted him, he saw them and frightened them with threats of all sorts of trouble for gambling without a license. Meix wanted to have payment on his check stopped. Ames, who had been a bank clerk, told him so, and then had the effrontery to say that payment on such a check could not be stopped.

Burglaries were common. How many the police planned may never be known. Charles F. Brackett and Fred Malone, police captains and detectives, were active, and one well-established crime of theirs is the robbery of the Pabst Brewing Company office. They persuaded two men, one an employee, to learn the combination of the safe, open and clean it out one night, while the two officers stood guard outside.

The excesses of the municipal administration became so notorious that some of the members of it remonstrated with the others, and certain county officers were genuinely alarmed. No restraint followed their warnings. Sheriff Megaarden, no Puritan himself, felt constrained to interfere, and he made some arrests of gamblers. The Ames people turned upon him in a fury; they accused him of making overcharges in his accounts with the county for fees, and laying the evidence before Governor Van Sant, they had Megaarden removed from office. Ames offered bribes to two county commissioners to appoint Gardner sheriff, so as to be sure of no more trouble in that quarter. This move failed, but the lesson taught Megaarden served to clear the atmosphere, and the spoliation went on as recklessly as ever. It became impossible.

Even lawlessness must be regulated. Dr. Ames, never an organizer, attempted no control, and his followers began to quarrel among themselves. They deceived one another; they robbed the thieves; they robbed Ames himself. His brother became dissatisfied with his share of the spoils, and formed cabals with captains who plotted against the administration and set up disorderly houses, "panel games," and all sorts of "grafts" of their own. The one man loyal to the mayor was Gardner, and Fred Ames, Captain King and their pals plotted the fall of the favorite. Now, anybody could get anything from the Doctor, if he could have him alone. The Fred Ames clique chose a time when the mayor was at West Baden; they filled him with suspicion of Gardner and the fear of exposure, and induced him to let a creature named "Reddy" Cohen, instead of Gardner, do the collecting, and pay over all the moneys, not directly, but through Fred. Gardner made a touching appeal. "I have been honest. I have paid you all," he said to the mayor. "Fred and the rest will rob you." This was true, but it was of no avail.

Fred Ames was in charge at last, and he himself went about giving notice of the change. Three detectives were with him when he visited the women, and here is the women's story, in the words of one, as it was told again and again in court: "Colonel Ames came in with the detectives. He stepped into a side room and asked me if I had been paying Gardner. I told him I had, and he told me not to pay no more, but to come to his office later, and he would let me know what to do. I went to the City Hall in about three weeks, after Cohen had called and said he was 'the party.' I asked the chief if it was all right to pay Cohen, and he said it was."

The new arrangement did not work so smoothly as the old. Cohen was an oppressive collector, and Fred Ames, appealed to, was weak and lenient. He had no sure hold on the force. His captains, free of Gardner, were undermining the chief. They increased their private operations. Some of the detectives began to drink hard and neglect their work. Norbeck so worried the "big mitt" men by staying away from the joint that they complained to Fred about him. The chief rebuked Norbeck, and he promised to "do better," but thereafter he was paid, not by the week, but by piecework—so much for each "trimmed sucker" that he ran out of town. Protected swindlers were arrested for operating in the street by "Coffee John's" new policemen who took the places of the negligent detectives. Fred let the indignant prisoners go when they were brought before him, but the arrests were annoying, inconvenient, and disturbed business. The whole system became so demoralized that every man was for himself. There was not left even the traditional honor among thieves.

It was at this juncture, in April 1902, that the grand jury for the summer term was drawn. An ordinary body of unselected citizens, it received no special instructions from the bench; the county prosecutor offered it only routine work to do. But there was a man among them who was a fighter—the foreman, Hovey C. Clarke. He was of an old New England family. Coming to Minneapolis when a young man, seventeen years before, he had fought for employment, fought with his employers for position, fought with his employees, the lumberjacks, for command, fought for his company against competitors; and he had won always, till now he had the habit of command, the impatient, imperious manner of the master, and the assurance of success which begets it. He did not want to be a grand juryman, he did not want to be a foreman; but since he was both, he wanted to accomplish.

Why not rip up the Ames gang? Heads shook, hands went up; it was useless to try. The discouragement fired Clarke. That was just what he would do, he said, and he took stock of his jury. Two or three were men with backbone; that he knew, and he quickly had them with him. The rest were all sorts of men. Mr. Clarke won over each man to himself, and interested them all. Then he called for the county prosecutor. The prosecutor was a politician; he knew the Ames crowd; they were too powerful to attack.

"You are excused," said the foreman.

There was a scene; the prosecutor knew his rights.

"Do you think, Mr. Clarke," he cried, "that you can run the grand jury and my office too?"

"Yes," said Clarke, "I will run your office if I want to; and I want to. You're excused."

Mr. Clarke does not talk much about his doings last summer; he isn't the talking sort. But he does say that all he did was to apply simple business methods to his problem. In action, however, these turned out to be the most approved police methods. He hired a lot of local detectives who, he knew, would talk about what they were doing, and thus would be watched by the police. Having thus thrown a false scent, he hired some other detectives whom nobody knew about. This was expensive; so were many of the other things he did; but he was bound to win, so he paid the price, drawing freely on his own and his colleagues' pockets. (The total cost to the county for a long summer's work by this grand jury was $259.) With his detectives out, he himself went to the jail to get tips from the inside, from criminals who, being there, must have grievances. He made the acquaintance of the jailor, Captain Alexander, and Alexander was a friend of Sheriff Megaarden. Yes, he had some men there who were "sore" and might want to get even.

Now two of these were "big mitt" men who had worked for Gardner. One was "Billy" Edwards, the other "Cheerful Charlie" Howard. I heard too many explanations of their plight to choose any one; this general account will cover the ground: In the Ames melee, either by mistake, neglect, or for spite growing out of the network of conflicting interests and gangs, they were arrested, arraigned, not before Fred Ames, but a judge, and held in bail too high for them to furnish. They had paid for an unexpired period of protection, yet could get neither protection nor bail. They were forgotten. "We got the double cross all right," they said, and they bled with their grievance; but squeal, no, sir!—that was "another deal."

But Mr. Clarke had their story, and he was bound to force them to tell it under oath on the stand. If they did, Gardner and Norbeck would be indicted, tried, and probably convicted. In themselves, these men were of no great importance; but they were the key to the situation, and a way up to the mayor. It was worth trying. Mr. Clarke went into the jail with Messrs. Lester Elwood and Willard J. Hield, grand jurors on whom he relied most for delicate work. They stood by while the foreman talked. And the foreman's way of talking was to smile, swear, threaten, and cajole. "Billy" Edwards told me afterward that he and Howard were finally persuaded to turn state's evidence, because they believed that Mr. Clarke was the kind of a man to keep his promises and fulfill his threats. "We," he said, meaning criminals generally, "are always stacking up against juries and lawyers who want us to holler. We don't because we see they ain't wise, and won't get there. They're quitters; they can be pulled off. Clarke has a hard eye. I know men. It's my business to size 'em up, and I took him for a winner, and I played in with him against that whole big bunch of easy things that was running things on the bum." The grand jury was ready at the end of three weeks of hard work to find bills. A prosecutor was needed. The public prosecutor was being ignored, but his first assistant and friend, Al J. Smith, was taken in hand by Mr. Clarke. Smith hesitated; he knew better even than the foreman the power and resources of the Ames gang. But he came to believe in Mr. Clarke, just as Edwards had; he was sure the foreman would win; so he went over to his side, and, having once decided, he led the open fighting, and, alone in court, won cases against men who had the best lawyers in the state to defend them. His court record is extraordinary. Moreover, he took over the negotiations with criminals for evidence, Messrs. Clarke, Hield, Elwood, and the other jurors providing means and moral support. These were needed. Bribes were offered to Smith; he was threatened; he was called a fool. But so was Clarke, to whom $28,000 was offered to quit, and for whose slaughter a slugger was hired to come from Chicago. What startled the jury most, however, was the character of the citizens who were sent to them to dissuade them from their course. No reform I ever studied has failed to bring out this phenomenon of virtuous cowardice, the baseness of the decent citizen.

Nothing stopped this jury, however. They had courage. They indicted Gardner, Norbeck, Fred Ames, and many lesser persons. But the gang had courage, too, and raised a defense fund to fight Clarke. Mayor Ames was defiant. Once, when Mr. Clarke called at the City Hall, the mayor met and challenged him. The mayor's heelers were all about him, but Clarke faced him.

"Yes, Doc Ames, I'm after you," he said. "I've been in this town for seventeen years, and all that time you've been a moral leper. I hear you were rotten during the ten years before that. Now I'm going to put you where all contagious things are put—where you cannot contaminate anybody else."

The trial of Gardner came on. Efforts had been made to persuade him to surrender the mayor, but the young man was paid $15,000 "to stand pat," and he went to trial and conviction silent. Other trials followed fast—Norbeck's, Fred Ames's, Chief of Detectives King's. Witnesses who were out of the state were needed, and true testimony from women. There was no county money for extradition, so the grand jurors paid these costs also. They had Meix followed from Michigan down to Mexico and back to Idaho, where they got him, and he was presented in court one day at the trial of Norbeck, who had "steered" him out of town. Norbeck thought Meix was a thousand miles away, and had been bold before. At the sight of him in court he started to his feet, and that night ran away. The jury spent more money in his pursuit, and they caught him. He confessed, but his evidence was not accepted. He was sentenced to three years in state's prison. Men caved all around, but the women were firm, and the first trial of Fred Ames failed. To break the women's faith in the ring, Mayor Ames was indicted for offering the bribe to have Gardner made sheriff—a genuine, but not the best case against him. It brought the women down to the truth, and Fred Ames, retried, was convicted and sentenced to six and a half years in state's prison. King was tried for accessory to felony (helping in the theft of a diamond, which he afterward stole from the thieves), and sentenced to three and a half years in prison. And still the indictments came, with trials following fast. Al Smith resigned with the consent and thanks of the grand jury; his chief, who was to run for the same office again, wanted to try the rest of the cases, and he did very well.

All men were now on the side of law and order. The panic among the "grafters" was laughable, in spite of its hideous significance. Two heads of departments against whom nothing had been shown suddenly ran away, and thus suggested to the grand jury an inquiry which revealed another source of "graft," in the sale of supplies to public institutions and the diversion of great quantities of provisions to the private residences of the mayor and other officials. Mayor Ames, under indictment and heavy bonds for extortion, conspiracy, and bribe-offering, left the state on a night train; a gentleman who knew him by sight saw him sitting up at eleven o'clock in the smoking room of the sleeping car, an unlighted cigar in his mouth, his face ashen and drawn, and at six o'clock the next morning he still was sitting there, his cigar still unlighted. He went to West Baden, a health resort in Indiana, a sick and broken man, aging years in a month. The city was without a mayor, the ring was without a leader; cliques ruled, and they pictured one another hanging about the grand-jury room begging leave to turn state's evidence. Tom Brown, the mayor's secretary, was in the mayor's chair; across the hall sat Fred Ames, the chief of police, balancing Brown's light weight. Both were busy forming cliques within the ring. Brown had on his side Coffee John and Police Captain Hill. Ames had Captain "Norm" King (though he had been convicted and had resigned), Captain Krumweide, and Ernest Wheelock, the chief's secretary. Alderman D. Percy Jones, the president of the council, an honorable man, should have taken the chair, but he was in the East; so this unstable equilibrium was all the city had by way of a government.

Then Fred Ames disappeared. The Tom Brown clique had full sway, and took over the police department. This was a shock to everybody, to none more than to the King clique, which joined in the search for Ames. An alderman, Fred M. Powers, who was to run for mayor on the Republican ticket, took charge of the mayor's office, but he was not sure of his authority or clear as to his policy. The grand jury was the real power behind him, and the foreman was telegraphing for Alderman Jones. Meanwhile the cliques were making appeals to Mayor Ames, in West Baden, and each side that saw him received authority to do its will. The Coffee John clique, denied admission to the grand-jury room, turned to Alderman Powers, and were beginning to feel secure, when they heard that Fred Ames was coming back. They rushed around, and obtained an assurance from the exiled mayor that Fred was returning only to resign. Fred—now under conviction—returned, but he did not resign; supported by his friends, he took charge again of the police force. Coffee John besought Alderman Powers to remove the chief, and when the acting mayor proved himself too timid, Coffee John, Tom Brown and Captain Hill laid a deep plot. They would ask Mayor Ames to remove his brother. This they felt sure they could persuade the "old man" to do. The difficulty was to keep him from changing his mind when the other side should reach his ear. They hit upon a bold expedient. They would urge the "old man" to remove

Fred, and then resign himself, so that he could not undo the deed that they wanted done. Coffee John and Captain Hill slipped out of town one night; they reached West Baden on one train and they left for home on the next, with a demand for Fred's resignation in one hand and the mayor's own in the other. Fred Ames did resign, and though the mayor's resignation was laid aside for a while, to avoid the expense of a special election, all looked well for Coffee John and his clique. They had Fred out, and Alderman Powers was to make them great. But Mr. Powers wobbled. No doubt the grand jury spoke to him. At any rate he turned most unexpectedly on both cliques together. He turned out Tom Brown, but he turned out also Coffee John, and he did not make their man chief of police, but another of someone else's selection. A number of resignations was the result, and these the acting mayor accepted, making a clearing of astonished rascals which was very gratifying to the grand jury and to the nervous citizens of Minneapolis.

But the town was not yet easy. The grand jury, which was the actual head of the government, was about to be discharged, and, besides, their work was destructive. A constructive force was now needed, and Alderman Jones was pelted with telegrams from home bidding him hurry back. He did hurry, and when he arrived, the situation was instantly in control. The grand jury prepared to report, for the city had a mind and a will of its own once more. The criminals found it out last.

Percy Jones, as his friends call him, is of the second generation of his family in Minneapolis. His father started him well-to-do, and he went on from where he was started. College graduate and businessman, he has a conscience which, however, he has brains enough to question. He is not the fighter, but the slow, sure executive. As an alderman he is the result of a movement begun several years ago by some young men who were convinced by an exposure of a corrupt municipal council that they should go into politics. A few did go in; Jones was one of these few.

The acting mayor was confronted at once with all the hardest problems of municipal government. Vice rose right up to tempt or to fight him. He studied the situation deliberately, and by and by began to settle it point by point, slowly but finally, against all sorts of opposition. One of his first acts was to remove all the proved rascals on the force, putting in their places men who had been removed by Mayor Ames. Another important step was the appointment of a church deacon and personal friend to be chief of police, this on the theory that he wanted at the head of his police a man who could have no sympathy with crime, a man whom he could implicitly trust. Disorderly houses, forbidden by law, were permitted, but only within certain patrol lines, and they were to pay nothing, in either blackmail or "fines." The number and the standing and the point of view of the "good people" who opposed this order was a lesson to Mr. Jones in practical government. One very prominent citizen and church member threatened him for driving women out of two flats owned by him; the rent was the surest means of "support for his wife and children." Mr. Jones enforced his order.

Other interests—saloonkeepers, brewers, etc.—gave him trouble enough, but all these were trifles in comparison with his experience with the gamblers. They represented organized crime, and they asked for a hearing. Mr. Jones gave them some six weeks for negotiations. They proposed a solution. They said that if he would let them (a syndicate) open four gambling places downtown, they would see that no others ran in any part of the city. Mr. Jones pondered and shook his head, drawing them on. They went away, and came back with a better promise. Though they were not the associates of criminals, they knew that class and their plans. No honest police force, unaided, could deal with crime. Thieves would soon be at work again, and what could Mr. Jones do against them with a police force headed by a church deacon? The gamblers offered to control the criminals for the city.

Mr. Jones, deeply interested, declared he did not believe there was any danger of fresh crimes. The gamblers smiled and went away. By an odd coincidence there happened just after that what the papers called "an epidemic of crime." They were petty thefts, but they occupied the mind of the acting mayor. He wondered at their opportuneness. He wondered how the news of them got out.

The gamblers soon reappeared. Hadn't they told Mr. Jones crime would soon be prevalent in town again? They had, indeed, but the mayor was unmoved; "porch climbers" could not frighten him. But this was only the beginning, the gamblers said: the larger crimes would come next. And they went away again. Sure enough, the large crimes came. One, two, three burglaries of jewelry in the houses of well-known people occurred; then there was a fourth, and the fourth was in the house of a relative of the acting mayor. He was seriously amused. The papers had the news promptly, and not from the police.

The gamblers called again. If they could have the exclusive control of gambling in Minneapolis, they would do all that they had promised before, and, if any large burglaries occurred, they would undertake to recover the "swag," and sometimes catch the thief. Mr. Jones was skeptical of their ability to do all this. The gamblers offered to prove it. How? They would get back for Mr. Jones the jewelry recently reported stolen from four houses in town. Mr. Jones expressed a curiosity to see this done, and the gamblers went away. After a few days the stolen jewelry, parcel by parcel, began to return; with all due police-criminal mystery it was delivered to the chief of police.

When the gamblers called again, they found the acting mayor ready to give his decision on their propositions. It was this: There should be no gambling, with police connivance, in the city of Minneapolis during his term of office.

Mr. Jones told me that if he had before him a long term, he certainly would reconsider this answer. He believed he would decide again as he had already, but he would at least give studious reflection to the question—Can a city be governed without any alliance with crime? It was an open question. He had closed it only for the four months of his emergency administration. Minneapolis should be clean and sweet for a little while at least, and the new administration should begin with a clear deck.

McClure's Magazine
January 1903

IDA M. TARBELL

C&X

The History of the Standard Oil Company:

THE OIL WAR OF 1872

FOR SEVERAL DAYS an uneasy rumor had been running up and down the Oil Regions. Freight rates were going up. Now, an advance in a man's freight bill may ruin his business; more, it may mean the ruin of a region. Rumor said that the new rate meant just this; that is, that it more than covered the margin of profit in any branch of the oil business. There was another feature to the report; the railroads were not going to apply the proposed tariffs to everybody. They had agreed to give to a company unheard of until now—the South Improvement Company—a special rate considerably lower than the new open rate. It was only a rumor and many people discredited it. *Why* should the railroads ruin the Oil Regions to build up a company of outsiders?

On the morning of February 26, 1872, the oil men read in their morning papers that the rise which had been threatened had come; moreover, that all members of the South Improvement Company were exempt from the advance. At the news all Oildom rushed into the streets. Nobody waited to find out his neighbor's opinion. On every lip there was but one word, and that was "conspiracy." In the vernacular of the region, it was evident that "a torpedo was filling for that scheme."

In twenty-four hours after the announcement of the increase in freight rates a mass meeting of three thousand excited, gesticulating oil men was gathered in the Opera House at Titusville. Producers, brokers, refiners, drillers, pumpers were in the crowd. Their temper was shown by the mottoes on the banners which they carried: "Down with the conspirators"—"No compromise"—"Don't give up the ship!" Three days later, as large a meeting was held at Oil City, its temper more warlike if possible; and so it went. They organized a Petroleum Producers' Union, pledged themselves to reduce their production by starting no new wells for sixty days and by shutting down on Sundays, to sell no oil to any person known to be in the South Improvement Company, but to support the Creek refiners and those elsewhere who had refused to go into the combination, to boycott the offending railroads, and to build lines which they would own and control themselves. They sent a committee to the Legislature asking that the charter of the South Improvement Company be repealed, and another to Congress demanding an investigation of the whole business on the ground that it was an interference with trade. They ordered that a history of the conspiracy, giving the names of the conspirators and the designs of the company, should be prepared, and 30,000 copies sent to "judges of all courts, Senators of the United States, members of Congress and of State Legislatures, and to all railroad men and prominent businessmen of the country, *to the end that enemies of the freedom of trade may be known and shunned by all honest men.*"

They prepared a petition ninety-three feet long, praying for a free pipe-line bill, something which they had long wanted, but which, so far, the Pennsylvania Railroad had prevented their getting, and sent it by a committee to the Legislature; and for days they kept a thousand men ready to march on Harrisburg at a moment's notice if the Legislature showed signs of refusing their demands. In short, for weeks the whole body of oil men abandoned regular business and surged from town to town intent on destroying the "Monster," the "Forty Thieves," the "Great Anaconda," as they called the mysterious South Improvement Company. Curiously enough, it was chiefly against the combination from the railroads—not the railroads which had granted it—that their fury was directed. They expected nothing but robbery from the railroads, they said. They were used to that; but they would not endure it from men in their own business.

When they began the fight, the mass of the oil men knew nothing more of the South Improvement Company than its name and the fact that it had secured from the railroads advantages in rates which were bound to ruin all independent refiners of oil and to put all producers at its mercy. Their tempers were not improved by the discovery that it was a secret organization, and had been at work under their very eyes for some weeks without their knowing it. At the first public meeting this fact came out, leading refiners of the region relating their experience with the "Anaconda." According to one of these gentlemen, Mr. J. D. Archbold—the same who afterward became vice-president of the Standard Oil Company, which office he now holds—he and his partners had heard of the scheme some months before. Alarmed by the rumor, a committee of independent refiners had attempted to investigate, but could learn nothing until they had given a promise not to reveal what was told them. When convinced that a company had been formed actually strong enough to force or persuade the railroads to give to it special rates and refuse them to all persons outside, Mr. Archbold said that he and his colleagues had gone to the railway kings to remonstrate, but all to no effect. The South Improvement Company by some means had convinced the railroads that they owned the Oil Regions, producers and refiners both, and that hereafter no oil of any account would be shipped except as they shipped it. Mr. Archbold and his partners had been asked to join the company, but had refused, declaring that the whole business was iniquitous, that they would fight it to the end, and that in their fight they would have the backing of the oil men, as a whole. They excused their silence up to this time by citing the pledge * exacted from them before they were informed of the extent and nature of the South Improvement Company.

Naturally the burning question throughout the Oil Region, convinced as it was of the iniquity of the scheme, was: who are the conspirators? Whether the gentlemen concerned regarded themselves in the light of "conspirators" or not, they seem from the first to have realized that it would be discreet not to be identified publicly with the scheme, and to have allowed one name alone to appear in all signed negotiations. This was the name of the president, Peter H. Watson. However anxious the members of the South Improvement Company were that Mr. Watson should combine the honors of president with the trials of scapegoat, it was impossible to keep their names concealed. The *Oil City Derrick*, at that time one of the most vigorous, witty, and daring newspapers in the country, began a blacklist at the head of its editorial columns the day after the raise in freights was announced, and it kept it there until it was believed complete. It stood finally as follows:

THE BLACKLIST

P. H. Watson, Pres. S.I. Co.
Charles Lockhart
W. P. Logan

* See "Mother of Trusts," p. 242.

R. S. Waring
A. W. Bostwick
W. G. Warden
John Rockefeller
Amasa Stone

These seven are given as the Directors of the Southern Improvement Company. They are refiners for merchants of petroleum.

Atlantic & Gt. Western Railway,
L. S. & M. S. Railway,
Philadelphia & Erie Railway,
Pennsylvania Central Railway,
New York Central Railway,
Erie Railway.

Behold "The Anaconda" in all his hideous deformity!

This list was not exact,* but it was enough to go on, and the oil blockade, to which the Petroleum Producers' Union had pledged itself, was now enforced against the firms listed, and as far as possible against the railroads. All of these refineries had their buyers on the Creek, and although several of the buyers were young men generally liked for their personal and business qualities, no mercy was shown them. They were refused oil by everybody, though they offered from seventy-five cents to a dollar more than the market price. They were ordered at one meeting "to desist from their nefarious business or leave the Oil Region," and when they declined they were invited to resign from the Oil Exchanges of which they were members. So strictly, indeed, was the blockade enforced that in Cleveland the refineries were closed and meetings for the relief of the workmen were held. In spite of the excitement there was little vandalism, the only violence at the opening of the war being at Franklin, where a quantity of the oil belonging to Mr. Watson was run on the ground.

The sudden uprising of the Oil Regions against the South Improvement Company did not alarm its members at first. The excitement would die out, they told one another. All that they needed to do was to keep quiet, and stay out of the oil country. But the excitement did not die out. Indeed, with every day it became more intense and more widespread. When Mr. Watson's tanks were tapped he began to protest in letters to a friend, F. W. Mitchell, a prominent banker and oil man of Franklin. The company was misunderstood, he complained. "Have a committee of leading producers appointed," he wrote, and "we will show that the contracts with the railroad are as favorable to

* See "Mother of Trusts," p. 242.

the producing as to other interests; that the much-denounced rebate will enhance the price of oil at the wells, and that our entire plan in operation and effect will promote every legitimate American interest in the oil trade." Mr. Mitchell urged Mr. Watson to come openly to the Oil Regions and meet the producers as a body. A mass meeting was never a "deliberative body," Mr. Watson replied, but if a few of the leading oil men would go to Albany or New York, or any place favorable to calm investigation and deliberation, and therefore outside of the atmosphere of excitement which enveloped the Oil Country, he would see them. These letters were read to the producers, and a motion to appoint a committee was made. It was received with protests and jeers. Mr. Watson was afraid to come to the Oil Regions, they said. The letters were not addressed to the association, they were private— an insult to the body. "We are lowering our dignity to treat with this man Watson," declared one man. "He is free to come to these meetings if he wants to." "What is there to negotiate about?" asked another. "To open a negotiation is to concede that we are wrong. Can we go halves with these middlemen in their swindle?" "He has set a trap for us," declared another. "We cannot treat with him without guilt," and the motion was voted down.

The stopping of the oil supply finally forced the South Improvement Company to recognize the Producers' Union officially, by asking that a committee of the body be appointed to confer with them, on a compromise. The producers sent back a pertinent answer. They believed the South Improvement Company meant to monopolize the oil business. If that was so they could not consider a compromise with it. If they were wrong, they would be glad to be enlightened, and they asked for information. First: the charter under which the South Improvement Company was organized. Second: the articles of association. Third: the officers' names. Fourth: the contracts with the railroads and who signed them. Fifth: the general plan of management.

Until we know these things, the oil men declared, we can no more negotiate with you than we could sit down to negotiate with a burglar as to his privileges in our house.

The Producers' Union did not get the information they asked from the company at that time, but it was not long before they did, and much more, too. The committee which they had appointed to write a history of the South Improvement Company reported on March 20, and in April the Congressional Committee appointed at the insistence of the oil men made its investigation. The former report was published broadcast, and is readily accessible today. The Congressional investigation was not published officially, and no trace of its work can now be found in Washington, but while it was going on, reports were made in the newspapers of the Oil Regions, and at its close the Producers' Union published in Lancaster, Pennsylvania, a pamphlet called the "Rise and Fall of the South Improvement Company," which contains the full testimony taken by the committee. This pamphlet is rare, the writer never having been able to find a copy save in three or four private collections. The most important part of it is the testimony of Peter H. Watson, the president, and W. G. Warden, the secretary of the South Improvement Company. It was in these documents that the oil men found full justification for the war they were carrying on and for the losses they had caused themselves and others. Nothing, indeed, could have been more damaging to a corporation than the publication of the charter of the South Improvement Company. As its president told the Congressional Investigating Committee, when he was under examination, "this charter was a sort of clothes-horse to hang a scheme upon." As a matter of fact, it was a clothes-horse big enough to hang the earth upon. It granted powers practically unlimited. There really was no exaggeration in the summary of its powers made and scattered broadcast by the irate oil men in their "History of the South Improvement Company":

The South Improvement Company can own, contract or operate any work, business or traffic (save only banking); may hold and transfer any kind of property, real or personal; hold and operate on any leased property (oil territory, for instance); make any kind of contract; deal in stocks, securities and funds; loan its credit; guarantee anyone's paper; manipulate any industry; may seize upon the lands of other parties for railroading or any other purpose; may absorb the improvements, property or franchises of any other company, ad infinitum; may fix the fares, tolls or freights to be charged on lines of transit operated by it, or on any business it gives to any other company or line, without limit.

Its capital stock can be expanded or "watered" at liberty; it can change its name and location at pleasure; can go anywhere and do almost anything. It is not a Pennsylvania corporation, only; it can, so far as these enactments are valid, or are confirmed by other legislatures, operate in any state or territory; its directors must be only citizens of the United States—not necessarily of Pennsylvania. It is responsible to no one; its stockholders are only liable to the amount of their stock in it; its directors, when wielding all the princely powers of the corporation, are also responsible only to the amount of their stock in it;

it may control the business of the continent and hold and transfer millions of property and yet be rotted to the core. It is responsible to no one; makes no reports of its acts or financial condition; its records and deliberations are secret; its capital illimitable; its object unknown. It can be here today, tomorrow away. Its domain is the whole country; its business everything. Now it is petroleum it grasps and monopolizes; next year it may be iron, coal, cotton or breadstuffs. They are landsmen granted perpetual letters of marque to prey upon all commerce everywhere.

When the course of this charter through the Pennsylvania Legislature came to be traced, it was found to be devious and uncertain. The company had been incorporated in 1870, and vested with all the "powers, privileges, duties, and obligations" of two earlier companies—the Continental Improvement Company and the Pennsylvania Company, both of which were children of that interesting body known as the "Tom Scott Legislature." The act incorporating the company was never published, the name of the member introducing it was never known, and no votes on it are recorded. The origin of the South Improvement Company has always remained in darkness. It was one of thirteen "improvement" companies chartered in Pennsylvania at about the same time, and enjoying the same commercial carte blanche.

Bad as the charter was in appearance, the oil men found that the contracts which the new company had made with the railroads were worse. These contracts advanced the rates of freight from the Oil Regions over 100 per cent, but it was not the railroad that got the greater part of this advance; it was the South Improvement Company. Not only did it ship its own oil at fully a dollar a barrel cheaper on an average than anybody else could, but it received fully a dollar a barrel "rake-off" on every barrel its competitors shipped. It was computed and admitted by the members of the company who appeared before the investigating committee of Congress that this discrimination would have turned over to them fully $6,000,000 annually on the carrying trade. It is hardly to be wondered at that when the oil men had before them the full text of these contracts they refused absolutely to accept the repeated assertions of the members of the South Improvement Company that their scheme was intended only for "the good of the oil business." The committee of Congress could not be persuaded to believe it either. "Your success meant the destruction of every refiner who refused for any reason to join your company, or whom you did not care to have in, and it put the producers entirely in your power. It would make a monopoly such as no set of men are fit to handle," the chairman of the committee declared. Mr. Warden, the secretary of the company, protested again and again that they meant to take in all the refiners, though he had to admit that the contracts with the railroads were not made on this condition. Mr. Watson affirmed and reaffirmed before the committee that it was the intention of the company to take care of the producers. "It was an essential part of this contract that the producers should join it," he declared. But no such condition was embodied in the contract. It was verbal only, and, besides, it had never been submitted to the producers themselves in any form until after the trouble in the Oil Region began. The committee, like the oil men, insisted that under the circumstances no such verbal understanding was to be trusted.

No part of the testimony before the committee made a worse impression than that showing that one of the chief objects of the combination was to put up the price of refined oil. "Under your arrangement," said the chairman, "the public would have been put to an additional expense of $7,500,000 a year." "What public?" said Mr. Warden. "They would have had to pay it in Europe." "But to keep up the price abroad you would have to keep up the price at home," said the chairman. Mr. Warden conceded the point: "You could not get a better price for that exported without having a better price here." Thirty-two cents a gallon was the ideal price they had in view, though refined had not sold for that since 1869, the average price in 1870 being 26⅜ and in 1871 24¼. The average price of crude in 1870 was $3.90 a barrel; in 1871, $4.40. The Congressional Committee claimed that any combination formed for the purpose of putting up the price of an article of general consumption was an injury to the public, but the members of the company would not admit it as such. Everybody in the business should make more money, they argued; the profits were too small—the consumer ought to be willing to pay more.

It did not take the full exposition of the objects of the South Improvement Company, brought out by the Congressional Investigating Committee, with the publication of charters and contracts, to convince the country at large that the Oil Regions were right in their opposition. From the first the sympathy of the press and the people was with the oil men. It was evident to everybody that if the railroads had made the contracts as charged (and it daily became more evident they had done so), nothing but an absolute monopoly of the whole oil business by this combination could result. It was robbery, cried the newspapers all over the land. "Under the thin guise of assisting in the development of oil refining in Pittsburg and Cleveland," said the New York *Tribune*, "this corporation has simply laid its hand upon the throat of the oil traffic with a demand to 'stand and deliver.'" And if this could be done in the oil business, what was to prevent its being done in any other industry? Why should not a company be formed to control wheat or beef or iron or steel, as well as oil? If the railroads would do this for one company, why not for another? The South Improvement Company, men agreed, was a menace to the free trade of the country. If the oil men yielded now, all industries must suffer from their weakness. The railroads must be taught a lesson as well as would-be monopolists.

The oil men had no thought of yielding. With every day of the war their backbones grew stiffer. The men were calmer, too, for their resistance had found a moral ground which seemed impregnable to them, and arguments against the South Improvement Company now took the place of denunciations. The country so buzzed with discussion on the duties of the railroads that reporters sent from the eastern newspapers commented on it. Nothing was commoner, indeed, on the trains which ran the length of the region, and were its real forums, than to hear a man explaining that the railways derived their existence and power from the people, that their charters were contracts with the people, that a fundamental provision of these contracts was that there should be no discriminating in favor of one person or one town, that such a discrimination was a violation of charter, that therefore the South Improvement Company was founded on fraud, and the courts must dissolve it if the railways did not abandon it.

They now met the very plausible reasons given by the members of the company for their combination more intelligently than at first. There were grave abuses in the business, they admitted; there was too great refining capacity; but this they argued was a natural development in a new business whose growth had been extraordinary and whose limits were by no means defined. Time and experience would regulate it. Give the refiners open and regular freights, with no favors to any one, and the stronger and better equipped would live, the others die— but give all a chance. In fact, time and energy would regulate all the evils of which they complained if there was fair play.

The oil men were not only encouraged by public opinion and by getting their minds clear on the merits of their case; they were upheld by repeated proofs of aid from all sides; even the women of the region were asking what they could do, and offering to wear their "black velvet bonnets" all summer if necessary. Solid support came from the independent refiners and shippers in other parts of the country, who were offering to stand in with them in their contest. New York was already one of the chief refining centers of the country, and the South Improvement Company had left it entirely out of its combination. As incensed as the Creek itself, the New York interests formed an association, and about the middle of March sent a committee of three, with H. H. Rogers of Charles Pratt & Company at its head, to Oil City, to consult with the Producers' Union. Their arrival in the Oil Regions was a matter of great satisfaction. What made the oil men most exultant, however, was their growing belief that the railroads—the crux of the whole scheme—were weakening.

However fair the great scheme may have appeared to the railroad kings in the privacy of the council chamber, it began to look dark as soon as it was dragged into the open, and signs of a scuttle soon appeared. General G. B. McClellan, president of the Atlantic and Great Western, sent to the very first mass meeting this telegram:

New York, February 27, 1872

Neither the Atlantic and Great Western, or any of its officers, are interested in the South Improvement Company. Of course, the policy of the road is to accommodate the petroleum interest.

G. B. McClellan

A great applause was started, only to be stopped by the hisses of a group whose spokesman read the following:

Contract with South Improvement Company signed by Geo. B. McClellan, president, for the Atlantic and Great Western Railroad. I only signed it after it was signed by all the other parties.

Jay Gould

The railroads tried in various ways to appease the oil men. They did not enforce the new rates. They had signed the contracts, they declared, only after the South Improvement Company had assured them that all the refineries and producers were to be taken in. Indeed, they seem to have realized within a fortnight that the scheme was doomed, and to have been quite ready to meet cordially a committee of oil men which went east to demand that the railroads revoke their contracts with the South Improvement Company. This committee, which was composed of twelve persons, three of them being the New York representatives already mentioned, began its work by an interview with Colonel Scott at the Colonial Hotel in Philadelphia. With evident pride the committee wrote back to the Producers' Union that: "Mr. Scott differing in this respect from the railroad representatives whom we afterwards met, notified us that he would call upon us at our hotel."

An interesting account of their interview was given to the Hepburn
Committee in 1879 by Mr. W. T. Scheide, one of the number:

> We saw Mr. Scott on the 18th of March, 1872, in Philadelphia,
> and he said to us that he was very much surprised to hear of this
> agitation in the Oil Regions; that the object of the railroads in mak-
> ing this contract with the South Improvement Company was to
> obtain an evener to pool the freight—pool the oil freights among
> the different roads; that they had been cutting each other on oil
> freights for a number of years, and had not made any money out of
> it, although it was a freight they should have made money from; that
> they had endeavored to make an arrangement among themselves, but
> had always failed; he said that they supposed that the gentlemen
> representing the South Improvement Company represented the pe-
> troleum trade, but as he was now convinced they did not, he would
> be very glad to make an arrangement with this committee, who un-
> doubtedly did represent the petroleum trade; the committee told him
> that they could not make any such contract; that they had no legal
> authority to do so; he said that could be easily fixed, because the
> Legislature was then in session, and by going to Harrisburg a charter
> could be obtained in a very few days; the committee still said that
> they would not agree to any such arrangement, that they did not
> think the South Improvement Company's contract was a good one,
> and they were instructed to have it broken, and so they did not feel
> that they could accept a similar one, even if they had the power.

Leaving Colonel Scott, the committee went on to New York, where
they stayed for about a week, closely watched by the newspapers, all
of which treated the "Oil War" as a national affair. Various conferences were held, leading up to a final all-important one on March 25,
at the Erie offices. Horace Clark, president of the Lake Shore and
Michigan Southern Railroad, was chairman of this meeting, and, according to H. H. Rogers's testimony before the Hepburn Committee,
in 1879, there were present, besides the oil men, Colonel Scott, General
McClellan, Director Diven, William H. Vanderbilt, Mr. Stebbins, and
George Hall.

The meeting had not been long in session before Mr. Watson, president of the South Improvement Company, and Mr. John D. Rockefeller, presented themselves for admission. Up to this time Mr. Rockefeller had kept well out of sight in the affair. He had given no
interviews, offered no explanations. He had allowed the president of
the company to wrestle with the excitement in his own way, but things
were now in such critical shape that he came forward in a last attempt
to save the organization by which he had been able to concentrate
in his own hands the refining interests of Cleveland. With Mr. Watson,
he knocked for admission to the council going on in the Erie offices.

The oil men flatly refused to let them in. A dramatic scene followed, Mr. Clark, the chairman, protesting in agitated tones against shutting out his "life-long friend, Watson." The oil men were obdurate. They would have nothing to do with anybody concerned with the South Improvement Company. So determined were they that although Mr. Watson came in, he was obliged at once to withdraw. A *Times* reporter who witnessed the little scene between the two supporters of the tottering company after its president was turned out of the meeting remarks sympathetically that Mr. Rockefeller soon went away, "looking pretty blue."

The acquiescence of the "railroad kings" in the refusal of the oil men to recognize representatives of the South Improvement Company was followed by an unwilling promise to break the contracts with the company. A strong effort was made to persuade the independents to make the same contracts on condition that they shipped as much oil, but they would not hear of it. They demanded open rates, with no rebates to anyone. The Vanderbilts particularly stuck for this arrangement, but were finally obliged to consent to revoke the contracts and to make a new one embodying the views of the Oil Regions. The contract finally signed at this meeting by H. F. Clark for the Lake Shore Road, O. H. P. Archer for the Erie, W. H. Vanderbilt for the Central, George B. McClellan for the Atlantic and Great Western, and Thomas A. Scott for the Pennsylvania, agreed that all shipping of oil should be made on "a basis of perfect equality to all shippers, producers, and refiners, and that no rebates, drawbacks, or other arrangements of any character shall be made or allowed that will give any party the slightest difference in rates or discriminations of any character whatever."

The same rate was put on refined oil from Cleveland, Pittsburg, and the Creek, to eastern shipping points; that is, Mr. Rockefeller could send his oil from Cleveland to New York at $1.50 per barrel; so could his associates in Pittsburg, and this was what it cost the refiner on the Creek; but the latter had this advantage: he was at the wells. Mr. Rockefeller and his Pittsburg allies were miles away, and it cost them, by the new contract, fifty cents to get a barrel of crude to their works. The Oil Regions meant that geographical position should count. Unless there was some way to get around this contract, it looked at that moment very much as if Mr. Rockefeller had bought a white elephant when he swept up the refineries of Cleveland.

This contract was the first effective thrust into the great bubble. Others followed in quick succession. On the 28th, the railroads officially annulled their contracts with the company. About the same time the

Pennsylvania Legislature repealed the charter. On March 30, the committee of oil men sent to Washington to be present during the Congressional investigation, now about to begin, spent an hour with President Grant. They wired home that on their departure he said: "Gentlemen, I have noticed the progress of monopolies, and have long been convinced that the National Government would have to interfere and protect the people against them." The President and the members of Congress of both parties continued to show the greatest interest in the investigation, and there was little or no dissent from the final judgment of the committee, given early in May, that the South Improvement Company was the "most gigantic and daring conspiracy" a free country had ever seen. This decision finished the work. The "monster" was slain, the Oil Regions proclaimed exultantly.

And now came the question: what should they do about the blockade established against the members of the South Improvement Company? The railroads they had forgiven; should they forgive the members of the South Improvement Company? This question came up immediately on the repeal of the charter. The first severe test to which their temper was put was early in April, when a firm of Oil City brokers sold some 20,000 barrels of oil to the Standard Oil Company. The moment the sale was noised a perfect uproar burst forth. Indignant telegrams came from every direction condemning the brokers. "Betrayal," "infamy," "mercenary achievement," "the most unkindest cut of all," was the gist of them. From New York, Porter and Archbold telegraphed annulling all their contracts with the guilty brokers. The Oil Exchange passed votes of censure, and the Producers' Union turned them out. A few days later it was learned that a dealer on the Creek was preparing to ship 5,000 barrels to the same firm. A mob gathered about the cars and refused to let them leave. It was only by stationing a strong guard that the destruction of the oil was prevented.

But something had to be done. The cooler heads argued that the blockade, which had lasted now forty days, and from which the region had, of course, suffered enormous loss, should be entirely lifted. The objects for which it had been established had been accomplished— that is, the South Improvement Company had been destroyed; now let free trade be established. If anybody wanted to sell to "conspirators," it was his lookout. A long and excited meeting of men from the entire oil country was held at Oil City to discuss the question. At this meeting telegrams to the president of the Petroleum Producers' Union, Captain William Hasson, from officials of the railroads were read, declaring that the contracts with the South Improvement Company were canceled. Also the following from the Standard Oil Company was read:

CLEVELAND, OHIO, April 8, 1872

To Captain William Hasson: In answer to your telegram, this company holds no contract with the railroad companies or any of them, or with the South Improvement Company. The contracts between the South Improvement Company and the railroads have been canceled, and I am informed you have been so advised by telegram. I state unqualifiedly that reports circulated in the Oil Region and elsewhere, that this company, or any member of it, threatened to depress oil, are false.

JOHN D. ROCKEFELLER, *President*

It was finally decided that "inasmuch as the South Improvement Company contracts were annulled, and the Pennsylvania Legislature had taken pains to safeguard the interests of the trade, and Congress was moving on the same line, after the 15th trade should be free to all." This resolution put an official end to the "oil war."

But no number of resolutions could wipe out the memory of the forty days of terrible excitement and loss which the region had suffered. No triumph could stifle the suspicion and the bitterness which had been sown broadcast through the region. Every particle of independent action had been outraged. Their sense of fair play, the saving force of the region in the days before law and order had been established, had been violated. These were things which could not be forgotten. There henceforth could be no trust in those who had devised a scheme which, the producers believed, was intended to rob them of their business.

It was inevitable that under the pressure of their indignation and resentment some person or persons should be fixed upon as responsible, and should be hated accordingly. Before the lifting of the embargo this responsibility had been fixed. It was the Standard Oil Company of Cleveland, so the Oil Regions decided, which was at the bottom of the business, and the "Mephistopheles of the Cleveland Company," as they put it, was John D. Rockefeller. Even the Cleveland *Herald* acknowledged this popular judgment. "Whether justly or unjustly," the editor wrote, "Cleveland has the odium of having originated the scheme." This opinion gained ground as the days passed. The activity of the president of the Standard in New York, in trying to save the contracts with the railroads, and his constant appearance with Mr. Watson, and the fact brought out by the Congressional investigation that a larger block of the South Improvement Company's stock was owned in the Standard than in any other firm, strengthened the belief.

But what did more than anything else to fix the conviction was what they had learned of the career of the Standard Oil Company in Cleveland. Before the oil war the company had been known simply as one of several successful firms in that city. It drove close bargains, but it paid promptly, and was considered a desirable customer. Now the Oil Regions learned for the first time of the sudden and phenomenal expansion of the company. Where there had been at the beginning of 1872 twenty-six refining firms in Cleveland, there were but six left. In three months before and during the oil war the Standard had absorbed twenty plants. It was generally charged by the Cleveland refiners that Mr. Rockefeller had used the South Improvement scheme to persuade or compel his rivals to sell to him. "Why," cried the oil men, "the Standard Oil Company has done already in Cleveland what the South Improvement Company set out to do for the whole country, and it has done it by the same means."

By the time the blockade was raised, another unhappy conviction was fixed on the Oil Regions—the Standard Oil Company meant to carry out the plans of the exploded South Improvement Company. The promoters of the scheme were partly responsible for the report. Under the smart of their defeat they talked rather more freely than their policy of silence justified, and their remarks were quoted widely. Mr. Rockefeller was reported in the *Derrick* to have said to a prominent oil man of Oil City that the South Improvement Company could work under the charter of the Standard Oil Company, and to have predicted that in less than two months the gentleman would be glad to join him. The newspapers made much of the following similar story reported by a New York correspondent:

> A prominent Cleveland member of what was the South Improvement Company had said within two days: "The business *now* will be done by the Standard Oil Company. We have a rate of freight by water from Cleveland to New York at seventy cents. No man in the trade shall make a dollar this year. We purpose so manipulating the market as to run the price of crude on the Creek as low as two and a half. We mean to show the world that the South Improvement Company was organized for business and means business in spite of opposition." The same thing has been said in substance by the leading Philadelphia member.

"The trade here regards the Standard Oil Company as simply taking the place of the South Improvement Company as being ready at any moment to make the same attempt to control the trade as its progenitors did," said the New York *Bulletin* about the middle of April. And the Cleveland *Herald* discussed the situation under the heading,

"South Improvement Company *alias* Standard Oil Company." The effect of these reports in the Oil Regions was most disastrous. Their open war became a kind of guerrilla opposition. Those who sold oil to the Standard were ostracized, and its president was openly scorned.

If Mr. Rockefeller had been an ordinary man, the outburst of popular contempt and suspicion which suddenly poured on his head would have thwarted and crushed him. But he was no ordinary man. He had the powerful imagination to see what might be done with the oil business if it could be centered in his hands—the intelligence to analyze the problem into its elements and to find the key to control. He had the essential element to all great achievement, a steadfastness to a purpose which once conceived nothing can crush. The Oil Regions might rage, call him a conspirator and those who sold him oil traitors; the railroads might withdraw their contracts and the legislature annul his charter; undisturbed and unresting he kept at his great purpose. Even if his nature had not been such as to forbid him to abandon an enterprise in which he saw promise of vast profits, even if he had not had a mind which, stopped by a wall, burrows under or creeps around, he would nevertheless have been forced to desperate efforts to save his business. He had increased his refining capacity in Cleveland to 10,000 barrels on the strength of the South Improvement Company contracts. These contracts were annulled, and in their place was one signed by officials of all the oil-shipping roads refusing rebates to everybody. His geographical position was such that it cost him under these new contracts fifty cents more to get oil from the wells to New York than it did his rivals on the Creek. What could he do?

He got a rebate. In spite of the binding nature of the contracts signed in New York on March 25 by representatives of all the railroads, before the middle of April the Standard Oil Company was shipping oil eastward from Cleveland for $1.25—this by the sworn testimony of Mr. H. M. Flagler before a commission of the Ohio State Legislature, in March 1879. How much less a rate than $1.25 Mr. Rockefeller had before the end of April the writer does not know. Of course the rate was secret, and he probably understood now, as he had not two months before, how essential it was that he keep it secret. His task was more difficult now, for he had an enemy active, clamorous, contemptuous, whose suspicions had reached that acute point where they could believe nothing but evil of him—the producers and independents of the Oil Regions. It was utterly impossible that he should ever silence this enemy, for their points of view were diametrically opposed.

They believed in independent effort—every man for himself and fair play for all. They wanted competition, loved open fight. They considered that all business should be done openly—that the railways were bound as public carriers to give equal rates—that any combination which favored one firm or one locality at the expense of another was unjust and illegal.

Mr. Rockefeller's point of view was different. He believed that the "good of all" was in a combination which would control the business as the South Improvement Company proposed to control it. Such a combination would end at once all the abuses the business suffered. As rebates and special rates were essential to this control, he favored them. Of course Mr. Rockefeller knew that the railroad was a public carrier, and that its charter forbade discrimination. But he knew that the railroads did not pretend to obey the laws governing them, that they regularly granted special rates and rebates to those who had large amounts of freight. That is, you could bargain with the railroads as you could with a man carrying on a strictly private business depending in no way on a public franchise. Moreover, Mr. Rockefeller knew that if he did not get rebates, somebody else would; that they were for the wariest, the shrewdest, the most persistent. If somebody was to get rebates, why not he? This point of view was no uncommon one. Many men held it and felt a sort of scorn, as practical men always do for theorists, when it was contended that the shipper was as wrong in taking rates as the railroads in granting them.   •

Thus, on one hand there was an exaggerated sense of personal independence, on the other a firm belief in combination; on one hand a determination to root out the vicious system of rebates practiced by the railway, on the other a determination to keep it alive and profit by it. Those theories which the body of oil men held as vital and fundamental Mr. Rockefeller and his associates either did not comprehend or were deaf to. This lack of comprehension by many men of what seems to other men to be the most obvious principles of justice is not rare. Many men who are widely known as good, share it. Mr. Rockefeller was "good." There was no more faithful Baptist in Cleveland than he. Every enterprise of that church he had supported liberally from his youth. He gave to its poor. He visited its sick. He wept with its suffering. Moreover, he gave unostentatiously to many outside charities of whose worthiness he was satisfied. He was simple and frugal in his habits. He never went to the theater, never drank wine. He was a devoted husband, and he gave much time to the training of his children, seeking to develop in them his own habits of economy and of charity. Yet he was willing to strain every nerve to obtain for himself special and illegal privileges from the railroads which were bound to ruin every man in the oil business not sharing them with him. Religious emotion and sentiments of charity, propriety and self-denial seem to have taken the place in him of notions of justice and regard for the rights of others.

Unhampered, then, by any ethical consideration, undismayed by the clamor of the Oil Regions, believing firmly as ever that relief for the disorders in the oil business lay in combining and controlling the entire refining interest, this man of vast patience and foresight took up his work. The day after the newspapers of the Oil Regions printed the report of the Congressional Committee on Commerce denouncing the South Improvement Company as "one of the most gigantic and dangerous conspiracies ever attempted," and declaring that if it had not been checked in time it "would have resulted in the absorption and arbitrary control of trade in all the great interests of the country," Mr. Rockefeller and several other members of the South Improvement Company appeared in the Oil Regions. They had come, they explained, to present a new plan of cooperation, and to show the oil men that it was to their interest to go into it. Whether they would be able to obtain by persuasion what they had failed to obtain by assault was now an interesting uncertainty.

McClure's Magazine
January 1903

RAY STANNARD BAKER

The Right to Work

During the closing weeks of the great coal strike, seventeen thousand men were at work in and around the anthracite coal mines. More than seven thousand of these were old employees of the companies, long resident in the communities where they worked, with knowledge of the conditions of life there existing. Of the remaining ten thousand, part was made up of workers recruited from one section of the coal fields into another, men who dared not work in their home villages, but ventured employment at collieries where they were not personally known; and part consisted of men having no special knowledge of mining, recruited from neighboring farms or more distant cities.

It seems profoundly important that the public should know exactly who these seventeen thousand American workers really were, how they fared, and why they continued to work in spite of so much abuse and even real danger. This inquiry may be made without bias without contravening the rights of labor to organize, or impugning the sincerity of the labor leader, or defending the operator.

In order, therefore, to learn more of these nonstriking workers I visited a large number of them, their families, and their neighbors, union and nonunion, in various parts of the anthracite regions, reaching them both in their homes and at their work in and around the mines. I saw the men themselves in each case, examining at firsthand the evidence of their difficulties and dangers, recording exactly the reasons they gave for continuing to work, securing corroboration and further light from all sources, both union and nonunion. The account of all the cases investigated would fill an entire number of this magazine; those here given are typical of the conditions generally prevailing, and show what the strike signified to the so-called scab, the nonstriking worker.

The first man visited was David Dick, of Old Forge, a small town south of Scranton. I was led to visit Mr. Dick by a letter bearing his signature published in the Scranton *Tribune*. Here is the letter:

MR. DICK'S VERSION OF THE ATTEMPT TO KILL HIM.

EDITOR, *Scranton Tribune*.

Sir: Your paper this morning [Monday] contained an account of the recent attempt on my life, which has several inaccuracies. I therefore send you a correct version, for I think the public ought to know how some persons are treated in this so-called "free country." On Tuesday evening, September 23, my next-door neighbor, Edward Miller, called at my house and spent some time with us. Shortly after 11 o'clock he left us to go home. I accompanied him to the gate in front of our house. Just as we said "good-night" I turned to re-enter the house. Two shots were fired behind me; the shots whistled past my head and lodged in the door in front of me. The night was dark and it was impossible to see any one. My wife is an invalid. Imagine the shock when my family realized that a deliberate attempt had been made on my life.

A short time ago, my son, James Dick, had his home attacked at night by an angry mob. The windows were smashed and the house so damaged that he had to move his family out and come to my place for shelter. Now, why these depredations? Because my son and I try to earn a living for our families. I have been in this country thirty years, and have worked all these years as an engineer. I have tried all my life to live peaceably with all men. I am not a member of the union or any other organization, except the Christian church. When the order was given for engineers to quit work, like many others, I did not obey the orders. Why should I? The company had given me a support in return for my work—I considered myself fairly treated; I had no grievance.

Further, I disagreed with the policy of destruction and revenge which the proposed flooding of the mines implied. I admired the attitude of Mr. Mitchell in the strike two years ago, when he said the property of the companies should be protected, and went so far as to say that men who served as deputies should not be discriminated against when the strike ended. Now, all this is reversed, and I claim my right as a free man to do what my conscience approves.

My forefathers died in Scotland for what they believed to be right, and now, once for all, let me say that I propose to work for my home and loved ones. If I am murdered for this, then I ask my enemies to face me in the daylight and not come skulking around a man's house in the dead of the night and fire when my back is turned.

No attempt has been made by the civil authorities to find a clue to the perpetrators of these outrages. I cannot but think if I occupied a position on the other side of the labor question what has happened would be heralded far and wide as an illustration of the tyranny of the operators or their friends. I write in the interest of freedom and justice and the rights of working men under the Stars and Stripes in this "land of the free and the home of the brave." We have our suspicions of the guilty parties, and if we are correct, they are not far away from us.

DAVID DICK

OLD FORGE, September 29, 1902

I found Mr. Dick in his engine house at No. 2 Colliery, Old Forge, a prosperous-appearing Scotchman who had a singularly clear way of expressing his decided views. He told me he had written the letter, and would reassert all it said. He had come to this country without money, and had been able to save enough to purchase himself a good home of his own. He was a member of the Scotch Presbyterian Church. The company, he said, had always treated him well, and he had no reason for striking. He had been repeatedly threatened, once surrounded by a mob of Italians, once shot at, narrowly escaping death, as his letter shows, and he and his family were ostracized by the strikers of the community. But he said he proposed to work or not to work as he saw fit, and that no threat would deter him. Every day he walked over a mile to his work, going unarmed, though he showed me the riot gun which he had in the engine house to protect him in case the colliery was attacked, as it had been at one time.

I talked with Charles Monie, another Scotch engineer of Moosic, Pennsylvania, who had worked for twenty-three years in the place he then occupied. He was a man of high intelligence, an elder in the Presbyterian Church of Avoca. He owned a good home, which I visited, and his children were finding good places in the greater world. I asked him why he had remained with the company. I quote his exact words:

"Unionism is all right when it is kept within bounds. But when it says to any man, 'You can't work until we give you permission,' and when it plans to destroy property, I claim that the individual has a right to quit.

"I have got a home over there without a cent of debt on it. I must have my regular wages to support it.

"I have a right to work when I like, for what I like, and for whom I like.

"I thought about this matter, and as long as my conscience approves my course I don't care who is against me. I don't know your beliefs, but I have faith that the great God will protect me, so I am not afraid."

Another nonunion engineer whom I called on in his engine house was J. R. Gorman, of Exeter Shaft, West Pittston, who had worked for the company twenty-five years. As he said, he was a "free-born American citizen, not a made citizen." This is his story:

At the beginning of the strike Paddy Brann, the president of the local union, came to me and said he was requested to inform me that my presence would be required at St. Alban's Hall that evening to discuss the strike.

"I can't go," I said, "I'm working."

"You understand," he said, "that when the strike is over you won't have no work."

"Won't I?" I said.

"No sir; we'll see to that, and you won't be able to buy any goods at the store. We'll boycott you."

"Partner," I said to him, "look here. Don't you bother your head about me; you've got troubles enough of your own."

They hung me in effigy and hooted me in the street. I had to go armed, but they didn't dare lay hands on me. I stand on my rights. I won't have anyone coming to me and telling me when I am to work and when I am to quit working. I don't join a union because I object to having some Dago I never saw before coming and ordering me to stop work or to go to work again. I can think for myself. I don't need any guardians. What is the object of their union anyway? Why strike, pure and simple, causing all this rioting and trouble. Some labor organizations give their members benefits and insurance, help take care of the sick and bury the dead. Do the mine workers? Not a bit of it. They pay in their money month after month, the officers draw fat salaries, and by and by they all strike, and begin persecuting and assaulting honest men who want to work.

One particularly determined worker was a teamster named Bellas, of the Lehigh Company. They heaped a mock grave in front of his house and set up the inscription:

> HERE LIES THE BODY
> OF BELLAS THE SCAB.

That did not bother Bellas, nor did any of the threats. Once when they stopped him he said, "My father fought for this country up in the Wyoming Valley during the Revolutionary War, and I think I've got a right to work where I please."

At another time they surrounded him and asked him for his union card. He pulled a revolver out of his boot with the remark:

"Here's my card."

They stoned his house, hung him in effigy, and fired at him at night. Part of the time, to prevent his house from being blown up, he watched half the night and his son the other half.

At Wilkes-Barre I met John Snyder, a nonstriking worker, and his wife. Snyder is a strong-built young fellow, brought up in the coal regions, a fireman by trade, though he never had worked in the mines until this summer. His wife had been a shopgirl in New York City. Just before the strike began she inherited a legacy of $450.

"When we got that," she said, "we thought that now we could have a little home of our own—I mean we could start one."

But the legacy was small, and homes were costly, so Mrs. Snyder finally went out of the city to Stanton Hill, and bought a lot in a miners' neighborhood, paying $100 for it. Then her husband and his father built a house, mostly of second-hand lumber, leaving the plastering until Snyder should be able to save something from his wages. There was now just money enough left to furnish the house meagerly, and they moved into it, with what joy one may imagine. At last they had a place, a home, in the world. Mrs. Snyder bought a hive of bees, her husband fitted up a chicken house and made a little garden, hoping thus to add to their income and make the life of their children more comfortable. Every penny they possessed was expended on the home. But Snyder was an industrious fellow, did not "touch, taste, nor handle," as his wife told me, and they knew that he could easily earn enough to support them comfortably.

In the meantime, however, the great strike was on, and every sort of job not connected with the mines was seized upon by union men who were willing to work for almost nothing while the strike lasted, so that Snyder, in order that his family might not be reduced to starvation, was forced, as he told me, to go to work in the mines. He had been thus employed barely four days when one of his neighbors—an Irish striker— came to him. Snyder thus reported to me the conversation which ensued:

" 'You're working, are you?'

" 'No,' I said.

" 'We've got spies on you, and we find that you're firing at the Dorrance.'

" 'I am a citizen,' I said, 'and I have a right to work where I please.'

" 'Well, I tell you,' he said, 'you can't scab and live here. You ought to be killed, and you'll find your house blown up some morning if you don't quit.'

"Then a big crowd gathered, mostly Irish, and began to yell 'Scab! Kill him! Kill him!' and throw stones at me. I jumped on my bicycle and escaped."

Snyder now remained within the stockade at the Dorrance colliery day and night, fearing death if the strikers caught him, leaving his wife and two babies in the new home on the hill, not dreaming that any harm would come to defenseless women. But crowds, both grown men and boys, gathered daily under the trees near the house, and every time Mrs. Snyder appeared they hooted at her, often insultingly, sometimes threateningly. After a few days of this treatment she became so fearful of personal injury—for she had seen more than one account in the newspapers of what had happened to the wives of nonstriking workers— that she took her babies and, having not even money enough to pay carfare, fled to the city, where she found shelter for the night. For several days she returned to her home to feed the chickens and look after the bees, always subjected coming and going to the jeers and insults of her neighbors. One day she found that her bees had swarmed, and that the swarm was attached to a nearby tree. Here was the first of the increase. She tried her best to get them down and rehived, but, not strong and a woman, she could not do it. Venturing even insult, she ran out to the men on the hill asking help. Not a man of them would assist her. Instead, they hooted her back to her home, and presently she saw her bees rise and disappear to the hills. She could not tell this part of the story without a quivering lip and a tearful eye.

A few days later she returned to find that her home had been entered, her new lamp smashed, a prized clock stolen, her husband's trunk broken open, rifled and thrown out of the window. In terror she started back toward the city, but turned back to get her canary bird and two or three pet chickens, which, fortunately, she carried away with her. There was nothing now but to desert the new home. The terrified woman sought her husband but he dared not leave the colliery, though he finally succeeded in getting an advance of $5 on his wages. With this money in hand, Mrs. Snyder hurriedly employed a drayman to move her furniture. When the team reached the house, however, the drivers were stopped by the crowd. She told me they shouted at her: "We'll kill you and your husband if it takes twenty years. Your house will go up in smoke."

And they turned back the teams, not permitting the removal of any of the furniture. In desperation now at the prospect of seeing her little home destroyed, Mrs. Snyder went to Mr. Mitchell's * headquarters in the Hart Hotel. She told me she had read somewhere that Mr. Mitchell wanted to have no violence committed—that he had promised to prevent violence to nonunion men and the blowing up of houses. She met John Fallon, one of Mr. Mitchell's assistants and chairman of the district board of the union, and to him she told her story.

* President, United Mine Workers Union.

"Why, yes," he said, "I'll see to that; I'll go right out now"—looking at his watch.

Mrs. Snyder went away relieved. The next morning when she climbed Stanton Hill and looked up to see her home its place was vacant. She found only a cellar full of ashes. The chicken house was also gone, and of all the chickens not one was left. Even the bees had been burned up, and the little garden was trampled and ruined. An old family dog that had recently brought a family of pups to the house was the only creature left, wandering about whining, looking for her pups. In the telling of this part of their story neither Mr. nor Mrs. Snyder could keep back the tears.

They searched in the ashes, hoping to find something left, but there was not even any remains of their cook stove, or sewing machine, or bedsprings, and they learned subsequently—so they told me—that their house had been looted before burning, and that the furniture had been distributed among their neighbors on the hill. Everything was gone. Mrs. Snyder did not even have left a change of clothing for her children. While she and her mother were looking into the ruins the crowd gathered and hooted "Scab, scab! Dynamite them!" so the two helpless women turned back toward the city.

Fresh from her loss, Mrs. Snyder went to see John Fallon, who said: "I didn't see about it in the newspapers."

Snyder continued to work until the strike was over and the union men came back to the colliery. At once every means was exerted by the strikers to displace nonunion workers, Snyder among them, and such influence was brought to bear that the foreman finally discharged Snyder, and when I saw him two weeks after the strike closed he was still out of work, though the company had offered him another position. And Mrs. Snyder has been haunting the second-hand stores of Wilkes-Barre, hoping against hope that some of her household goods may be pawned by the thieves, and that she may thus recover them.

I asked Snyder why he did not try to have the criminals arrested.

"In the first place," he said, "if they were arrested they'd never be punished, because everybody is in favor of the strikers, and they could get all their friends to swear they were not present when the house was burned. Besides, I am afraid they'd take it out of me if I did anything."

So nothing has been done, and it seems likely, from what I can learn, that nothing ever will be done to bring the perpetrators of these outrages to justice.

The case of the Snyders is by no means exceptional. There were many instances which I investigated of similar persecution.

"All we want is investigation," a strike leader said to me. "Now, these murders they talk about. Look into them and you will find that they were the result of the presence of the armed coal and iron police, who were mostly city thugs with orders to shoot and kill. It's a trick of the operators to try to lay all the blame for disturbances on us; they want to work up public sentiment against us." So I went from Scranton to look into the case of James Winstone, of Olyphant.

Olyphant is a more than usually prosperous mining town of some 6,100 inhabitants, nearly all mine workers, over 70 per cent of whom own their own homes. The population is very diverse, being made up of some dozen different nationalities, but with an unusually large proportion of the English, Welsh, and Irish, the better elements among the miners. * James Winstone lived in a neighborhood known as Grassy Island, of which he was the foremost citizen, having by far the best home and the most means.

His home was really a pretty place, a two-story house with trees in front, which Winstone himself set out, an arbor where there was shade in summer, a fine garden in which Winstone grew vegetables, and was experimenting with grapes. I came in by the back door to a shining kitchen, spotlessly clean. Indeed, the home was more than comfortably furnished, with an organ, books, pictures, and other evidences of enlightenment and comfort. Mrs. Winstone came in and told us quietly and sadly some of her story. Then we went out again through the spotless kitchen, and crossed to the next house, also the property of James Winstone, and the home of his son-in-law, S. J. Lewis, a worker in the mines. Here, too, was every evidence of comfort and spotless cleanness. The daughter, James Winstone's oldest, had been married only a year. Little by little the story came out, mostly through Mr. D. E. Lewis, a highly intelligent Welshman, the foreman of the mine where Winstone and his son-in-law were employed.

Winstone had been in America only fourteen years, having come from Yorkshire, England. Reaching Pennsylvania without money, he was able, working as a common miner and supporting a family, to save enough in fourteen years to make him the possessor of two fine homes and everything paid for. Mr. D. E. Lewis told me that Winstone averaged a net earning of $3.50 a day, for which he found it necessary to work only five or six hours. His son-in-law, young Lewis, earned $2.26 a day. Winstone was in the prime of life, forty-eight years old, with a

---

* As an indication of the diversity of nationality, Grassy Slope mine, in which James Winstone worked, had 401 adult employes. Of this number 24 were Americans, 48 English, 60 Welsh, 59 Irish, 5 Scotch, 2 Swedish, 152 Polish, 5 German, 41 Hungarian, 5 Italian.

wife and three children. His wife told me with sad pride how he had
been respected in his community. He was treasurer, she said, for eight
years of the Lackawanna Accident Fund, a member of the Sons of
St. George and of the Red Men, and even, at one time, an officer in
the United Mine Workers. She said he had not an enemy in the world,
that all he wanted was to live peaceably and see his sons properly educated. He meant to keep them in school until they could work into
good positions. They had done well in the mines, but they hoped the
boys would do something better.

Winstone, a natural leader, opposed the strike from the beginning,
as did others of the conservative element. He asserted publicly that he
saw no cause for striking, that any man who was willing to work and
was temperate could get ahead, that there was too much agitation. But
he and the conservatives were overwhelmed and the strike declared.
Winstone went out with the others, found employment for several
weeks outside the mines at a fraction of his former wages, and then came
back home. He now saw that he must mortgage his property to live.
He went to the union, and was told that he would be given no assist-
ance. He had property and he could raise money on that. This, however, he refused to do.

So Winstone went back to the mine to work. His son-in-law, S. J.
Lewis, had already gone back, in company with some of the other mine
workers of the community. Immediately the strikers began their tactics
of intimidation and threats. Every morning and evening they gathered
in the road and hooted Winstone, Lewis, Doyle and others on their
way to work. Sometimes they gathered in front of his home, threateningly, but Winstone would not be cowed. One night a larger crowd
than usual appeared, and Patrick Fitzsimmons, secretary of the local
and auditor of the general assembly, stood up and shouted a violent
tirade against scabs. One of the things he said, reported to me by Mr.
Lewis, was: "If there were half a dozen of loyal union men like me
there wouldn't be one of the scabs that would dare to go to work."

These crowds were composed of Irish and English, with a large rally-
ing force of Poles and others. Most of them were Winstone's neighbors
and fellow workmen, and many of them had been his good friends.

A week before the final tragedy, a committee waited on Winstone
and requested him to stop work, threatening him if he did not. Winstone
told them that he would not desert his place.

The persecutions now became so severe that Winstone and Lewis,
instead of going to the mine by the road, were accustomed to go back
through the garden, climb a fence, cross the rear of a lot occupied by a

Polish miner named Harry Shubah, a neighbor well known to Winstone, and join William Doyle, another nonunion man, the three men going together. They carried no arms.

The morning of September 25 was rainy. Winstone and Lewis had gone down through the garden. When they had climbed the fence into Shubah's yard, Lewis took his father-in-law's arm, and was holding an umbrella over his head. Suddenly, hearing a noise, he glanced behind and saw Harry Simuralt, another Polish neighbor with whom both were well acquainted. Simuralt had a club lifted. Lewis cried:

"Don't strike us with that."

The words were hardly out of his mouth when he was felled to the earth. Jumping up again, half dazed, he ran toward Doyle's house. Hearing Winstone shout, "Don't kill me," he glanced behind and saw several men pounding him with clubs. Lewis himself was now pursued and struck in the back with a heavy stick, but he succeeded in escaping. The assaulters having pounded Winstone to their satisfaction, left him lying in his blood. He was carried into Doyle's house, where he died a few hours later without regaining consciousness. Lewis was in bed three weeks.

Everything evidently had been plotted beforehand. The murderers were perfectly sober, making an evidently planned escape by train. Fortunately they were arrested at Hoboken, New Jersey, and brought back to Scranton, where they are now in jail. According to Lewis, the three men most concerned were Harry Simuralt, Harry Shubah, and Tom Priston, all Polish miners, union men, and strikers—all near neighbors of Winstone, long known to him. The astonishing thing is that they had been in the country for years and spoke English well; one of them, Simuralt, owned his own home, a very comfortable place. Foreman Lewis told me that they all bore good reputations as industrious and temperate workers.

It is interesting, as showing the difficulty of protecting life, that seven hundred soldiers were camped within less than half a mile of the scene of this murder.

Through some peculiarity of location, the valley of the Susquehanna is singularly subject to fogs—not unlike those of southern England, appearing before dawn and often continuing until long after sunrise. Such a fog filled the valley on the early morning of September 8, 1902. It was so thick that a man could see only a few paces before him— familiar houses, fences, road-marks, seemed mysterious. It was on this foggy morning that a number of important things were happening in the vicinity of the Maltby Colliery. Though no one could see any evidence of life, nor hear any sound, yet men were gathering from several directions—men who hated one another. There were three parties of them, all armed. On the previous Saturday night there had been a joint meeting of three locals of the United Mine Workers of America—the Luzerne, the Broderick, and the Maltby. It was a special occasion. Reports were made by an officer that the company intended to add a large number of nonunion men to its force at the Maltby Colliery on the following Monday morning. This news was received with jeers, and after much discussion a motion was made and passed calling upon all the members of the three locals to be present at the entrance to the colliery on Monday morning. Great secrecy was enjoined, but there was a man present whose business it was to listen to just such news; he carried the word immediately to the officials of the Lehigh Valley Coal Company. Sheriff Jacobs being notified, armed deputies were provided to escort the nonunion men on Monday morning. This accounted for two of the parties gathered in the fog. The mob appeared in great force, many armed with clubs, some having large iron nuts at the end; some with stones; others with cheap revolvers. Lining themselves up along the roadways, they awaited the coming of the car with the nonunion men.

In the meantime another party of two men was out in the fog. Sistieno Castelli and his friend and brother-in-law, Kiblotti, were going hunting. Castelli was a peaceable citizen, whose family was hungry. He had his gun on his shoulder and was tramping by the Lackawanna Railroad tracks on his way to the hills, hoping to find some rabbits or squirrels. Just as he and his friend reached a point behind the house of John Keeler, outside foreman of the mine, the car with the nonunion men had come to a stop. The mob, fully expecting to surprise the nonunion men and have them instantly at their mercy, came up out of the fog to find themselves facing armed deputies. Under cover of this surprise the nonunion men were hurried into Keeler's house, guarded by the deputies. The mob, gathering quickly, foresaw that an attempt would be made to rush the workmen from Keeler's house by the back way to the mine, so they turned and streamed up the tracks of the Lackawanna Railroad, between the colliery and the foreman's home. And here they came suddenly upon Castelli and Kiblotti there in the fog. Castelli cried out. Someone, said to be a Hungarian, struck him a frightful blow on the head, felling him to the earth. And then they seized his shotgun, placed the muzzle against Castelli's body, and pulled the trigger. In the meantime several others pitched upon his companion, but in the confusion Kiblotti succeeded in escaping. The mob then turned their attention to Castelli, in their fury horribly beating his lifeless body. Having glutted their passion, they turned the body over and went through the pockets, and this is what they found—a union card and receipt for dues paid, showing that Castelli was a good union man, a member of the Broderick Local No. 452. They had killed him and left another widow and children, visiting upon him the fate they had planned for the nonunion men. In the meantime the deputies and their charges were safe in the colliery.

In the list read before the Arbitration Commission of the men murdered during the strike was the name of John Colson, and the memorandum, "Nonunion man beaten to death at Shenandoah." I went to Shenandoah to learn more of the story of John Colson.

At first I could find no record of any workman named Colson. Shenandoah had her share of riot and bloodshed, but Colson was not remembered among those injured. But I finally heard of a man of that name who had been working at Shamokin, and I went down to find John Colson, not dead, but living and working tenaciously after an experience that would have daunted most men. He is an English-born engineer. Previous to the strike he had lived at Gilberton, working as an engineer, the best position at the colliery. He did not believe in the strike, nor in the order withdrawing the engineers, and he had not been slow in saying so. But he went out with the other strikers and remained a month; then he went to work at the Henry Clay Colliery, at Shamokin. Spies at once found him out, but, living in a car close to the colliery, they could not reach him personally, so they brought to bear the usual pressure on his wife and family at Gilberton. She was boycotted at some of the stores, so that she could not buy the necessaries of life. She was jeered and insulted in the streets, and her home was stoned.

"Every night," she told me, "I was afraid to go to bed for fear they would blow up my home with dynamite. They did dynamite three houses in the same neighborhood."

So she finally wrote to her husband that she could bear it no longer, and he rented a house in Shamokin, and told her to move the furniture. This she tried to do, but the teamsters refused to assist her, and she feared that if she attempted to get away the strikers would attack her. Accordingly, Colson bought furniture at Shamokin to fit up a new home. On the evening of October 7 he came up from his work with several coal and iron police to look after the arrangement of his purchases, and when he had finished he started back alone along the railroad tracks. The police had warned him of his danger, and he had, indeed, already been stoned, and yet, naturally fearless, he was going back alone. Having a revolver, he thought he could defend himself. A trainload of soft coal was passing; a mob of men appeared, shouting at him threateningly. He reached to draw his revolver, and a man on one of the cars dropped a huge block of coal on his head. Colson fell in his tracks, and after further beating him, the mob robbed him of his revolver and a new pair of boots, and left him for dead. For three days he lay unconscious in the hospital, and there, slowly, with careful nursing, he recovered, and as soon as he could walk went back to work again. His wife now succeeded in getting an undertaker from an adjoining town to move her goods, under guard of a deputy, and they settled at Shamokin. I found them in a comfortable, pleasant home—two boys at work in the mines and a comely daughter.

In this case of John Colson I had an opportunity of seeing what it means, socially, for a man to work during a strike. At Mahoney City, in the last house in the town, one of the dingy red company houses, almost in the shadow of an enormous pile of culm, I found John Colson's father and mother. The old miner had just come in from his work, his face and clothing black with coal dust. His wife had hot water ready for him, and a tub stood waiting on her kitchen floor, so that he might wash off the marks of the mine. Yet some of the marks he could not wash off—the blue tattooing of powder which covered his face with ugly scars. Five years before he had been in a mine explosion. A careless Hungarian, cross-cutting through the coal, had set off his blast without giving warning, and Colson had been taken from the mine for dead, but he finally lived, blue-scarred, wholly blind in one eye and almost blind in the other. He was an old man even then; he had been mining, here and in England, for nearly fifty years, and his seven sons, miners all, told him that he might rest the remainder of his days. So for four years previous to the great strike he had lived quietly a comfortable old age, he and his wife alone in the red house at the end of the village, their sons and daughters around them.

But with the strike came hard times, and the sons, though willing to help their parents, had many mouths of their own to feed, and by the time the miners were ordered back to work in October they were all in straitened circumstances, so that old John Colson was compelled to go back into the mines. He told me he was doing a boy's job now— turning a fan in a deep working, and that he earned only seventy-five cents a day, but he was glad to be employed again. The mother told me with pride of her boys—Anthony with his family of eight children, her other boys, and the married daughters. And so we came to speak of John, her oldest son, the one reported beaten to death. She flushed at the mention of his name, said at first that she would have nothing to say about him, and then, bitterly:

"He might better be dead, for he's brought disgrace on the name."

All the brothers, the old miner said, had been members of the union, and had come out when the strike was called, but John had gone back to work.

"He deserved all he got," said his mother. "He wasn't raised a scab."

Then she told how, when he lay hovering between life and death in the hospital, she had not gone to him once, and yet she wanted so much to know whether he would live or die that she called up the hospital on the telephone.

"But I didn't give my name," she said, "so he didn't know about it."

Since he was well again none of the family had visited him or paid the least attention to him. The strike had wholly crushed all family feeling. John was not again to be recognized.

Such a story as this gives a faint idea of the meaning of a strike in the coal fields.

McClure's Magazine
January 1903

PART TWO

A Name Is Born

It was in a speech on April 14, 1906, that the reform journalists were publicly named "muckrakers." The man who named them was President Theodore Roosevelt, and the name stuck.

The occasion was the laying of the cornerstone of the United States House of Representatives office building in Washington. The President's speech was a repeat of his off-the-record remarks at the Gridiron Club.

On the day the President made his muckrake speech, members of the Senate and the House, cabinet members, Supreme Court Justices and representatives of foreign governments were present. The "scheme of seating was such that the Senate was literally at the President's feet and the executive could have reached over the rail of the speaker's stand and touched the heads" of some of the leaders of the Senate "who occupied the front pew." [26] The area of the ceremony was draped with flags and bunting.

The President had neither a military nor a naval aide when he came upon the platform. He was escorted by the building commissioner, Senator Hepburn of Iowa, and Speaker Joseph Cannon of Illinois, who was to introduce him.

At the end of the Masonic rites and a prayer for the American people and its present Chief Executive, by the Grand Chaplain of the Grand Lodge of Masons, the trumpets of the Marine Band announced the cornerstone-laying dedication.

A hermetically sealed copper box, containing a copy of the Declaration of Independence, the Constitution of the United States, and a collection of American coins and stamps, was placed in position to become part of the new building.

Then the President spoke.

Headlines the next day proclaimed:

Roosevelt Brands
Muckrake Misuse
as Foe of Reform

President Standing Firm in
War on Real Public Evils,
Warns of Danger in
Rash Agitation

Would Curb Big Fortunes

Need of Law to Prevent by National Tax the Bequesting
of Vast Wealth Is
Suggested

(Chicago *Sunday Record-Herald,*
April 15, 1906)

Roosevelt for
Tax on Wealth

Would Prevent Inheritance
of Great Fortunes

Favors a Federal Law

Congress Leaders Talk of
a New Political Issue

President on Muckrake

Considers Indiscriminate As-
saults on Public Men—
Cornerstone of House
Office Building Laid

(*New York Times,* April 15, 1906)

Before he made the talk, Roosevelt assured Ray Stannard Baker, one of the writers who accepted the muckraker label for himself, that he was not referring to him but had "in mind at the moment" the Hearst magazines and newspapers.

He wrote to Baker: "One reason I want to make that address is because people so persistently misunderstand what I said, that I want to have it reported in full. For instance, you misunderstand it. I want to 'let in light and air,' but I do not want to let in sewer gas. If a room is fetid and the windows are bolted I am perfectly contented to knock out the windows; but I would not knock a hole into the drain pipe. In other words, I feel that the man who in a yellow newspaper or in a yellow magazine . . . makes a ferocious attack on good men or even attacks bad men with exaggeration or for things they have not done, is a potent enemy of those of us who are really striving in good faith to expose bad men and drive them from power. I disapprove of the whitewash brush quite as much as of mud slinging, and it seems to me that the disapproval of one in no shape or way implies approval of the other. This I shall try to make clear." [27]

Lincoln Steffens, one of the most historically famous of the muckrakers, calling on the President the day after the talk, said to him: "Well, Mr. President, you have put an end to all these journalistic investigations that have made you."

Roosevelt answered "that he had no such intention," that he didn't mean Steffens. "He had been aroused to wrath by an article on 'poor old Chauncey Depew' * by David Graham Phillips. . . . T.R. said that he spoke 'to comfort Depew.' " [28]

However, in 1915 Roosevelt wrote to the American novelist Winston Churchill—who was so popular during that era that the future Prime Minister of England added the middle initial "S" to his own name: "Even of the more honest muckrakers I found by lamentable experience that there were hardly any whose statements of fact I could trust." [29]

* United States Senator from New York.

THEODORE ROOSEVELT

The Man with the Muckrake

Over a century ago Washington laid the cornerstone of the Capitol in what was then little more than a tract of wooded wilderness here beside the Potomac. We now find it necessary to provide by great additional buildings for the business of the government. This growth in the need for the housing of the government is but a proof and example of the way in which the nation has grown and the sphere of action of the national government has grown. We now administer the affairs of a nation in which the extraordinary growth of population has been outstripped by the growth of wealth and the growth in complex interests. The material problems that face us today are not such as they were in Washington's time, but the underlying facts of human nature are the same now as they were then. Under altered external form we war with the same tendencies toward evil that were evident in Washington's time, and are helped by the same tendencies for good. It is about some of these that I wish to say a word today.

In Bunyan's *Pilgrim's Progress* you may recall the description of the Man with the Muckrake, the man who could look no way but downward, with a muckrake in his hands; who was offered a celestial crown for his muckrake, but who would neither look up nor regard the crown he was offered, but continued to rake to himself the filth of the floor.

In *Pilgrim's Progress* the Man with the Muckrake is set forth as the example of him whose vision is fixed on carnal instead of on spiritual things. Yet he also typifies the man who in this life consistently refuses to see aught that is lofty, and fixes his eyes with solemn intentness only on that which is vile and debasing. Now, it is very necessary that we should not flinch from seeing what is vile and debasing. There is filth on the floor, and it must be scraped up with the muckrake; and there are times and places where this service is the most needed of all the services that can be performed. But the man who never does anything else, who never thinks or speaks or writes save of his feats with the muckrake, speedily becomes, not a help to society, not an incitement to good, but one of the most potent forces of evil.

There are in the body politic, economic and social, many and grave evils, and there is urgent necessity for the sternest war upon them. There should be relentless exposure of and attack upon every evil man, whether politician or businessman, every evil practice, whether in politics, in business or in social life. I hail as a benefactor every writer or speaker, every man who, on the platform or in book, magazine or newspaper, with merciless severity makes such attack, provided always that he in his turn remembers that the attack is of use only if it is absolutely truthful. The liar is no whit better than the thief, and if his mendacity takes the form of slander he may be worse than most thieves. It puts a premium upon knavery untruthfully to attack an honest man, or even with hysterical exaggeration to assail a bad man with untruth. An epidemic of indiscriminate assault upon character does not good but very great harm. The soul of every scoundrel is gladdened whenever an honest man is assailed, or even when a scoundrel is untruthfully assailed.

Now, it is easy to twist out of shape what I have just said, easy to affect to misunderstand it, and, if it is slurred over in repetition, not difficult really to misunderstand it. Some persons are sincerely incapable of understanding that to denounce mudslinging does not mean the indorsement of whitewashing; and both the interested individuals who need whitewashing and those others who practice mudslinging like to encourage such confusion of ideas. One of the chief counts against those who make indiscriminate assault upon men in business or men in public life is that they invite a reaction which is sure to tell powerfully in favor of the unscrupulous scoundrel who really ought to be attacked, who ought to be exposed, who ought, if possible, to be put in the penitentiary. If Aristides is praised overmuch as just, people get tired of hearing it; and overcensure of the unjust finally and from similar reasons results in their favor.

Any excess is almost sure to invite a reaction; and, unfortunately, the reaction, instead of taking the form of punishment of those guilty of the excess, is very apt to take the form either of punishment of the unoffending or of giving immunity, and even strength, to offenders. The effort to make financial or political profit out of the destruction of character can only result in public calamity. Gross and reckless assaults

on character—whether on the stump or in newspaper, magazine or book
—create a morbid and vicious public sentiment, and at the same time act
as a profound deterrent to able men of normal sensitiveness and tend
to prevent them from entering the public service at any price. As an
instance in point, I may mention that one serious difficulty encountered
in getting the right type of men to dig the Panama Canal is the certainty that they will be exposed, both without, and, I am sorry to say,
sometimes within, Congress, to utterly reckless assaults on their character and capacity.

At the risk of repetition let me say again that my plea is, not for
immunity to, but for the most unsparing exposure of, the politician
who betrays his trust, of the big businessman who makes or spends his
fortune in illegitimate or corrupt ways. There should be a resolute
effort to hunt every such man out of the position he has disgraced.
Expose the crime and hunt down the criminal; but remember that
even in the case of crime, if it is attacked in sensational, lurid and un-
truthful fashion, the attack may do more damage to the public mind
than the crime itself. It is because I feel that there should be no rest in
the endless war against the forces of evil that I ask that the war be
conducted with sanity as well as with resolution. The men with the
muckrakes are often indispensable to the well-being of society, but only
if they know when to stop raking the muck, and to look upward to the
celestial crown above them, to the crown of worthy endeavor. There
are beautiful things above and round about them; and if they gradually
grow to feel that the whole world is nothing but muck their power of
usefulness is gone. If the whole picture is painted black there remains
no hue whereby to single out the rascals for distinction from their
fellows. Such painting finally induces a kind of moral color blindness;
and people affected by it come to the conclusion that no man is
really black and no man really white, but they are all gray. In other
words, they neither believe in the truth of the attack nor in the honesty
of the man who is attacked; they grow as suspicious of the accusation
as of the offense; it becomes well-nigh hopeless to stir them either to
wrath against wrongdoing or to enthusiasm for what is right; and such
a mental attitude in the public gives hope to every knave, and is the
despair of honest men.

To assail the great and admitted evils of our political and industrial
life with such crude and sweeping generalizations as to include decent
men in the general condemnation means the searing of the public conscience. There results a general attitude either of cynical belief in and
indifference to public corruption or else of a distrustful inability to

discriminate between the good and the bad. Either attitude is fraught with untold damage to the country as a whole. The fool who has not sense to discriminate between what is good and what is bad is well-nigh as dangerous as the man who does discriminate and yet chooses the bad. There is nothing more distressing to every good patriot, to every good American, than the hard, scoffing spirit which treats the allegation of dishonesty in a public man as a cause for laughter. Such laughter is worse than the crackling of thorns under a pot, for it denotes not merely the vacant mind, but the heart in which high emotions have been choked before they could grow to fruition.

There is any amount of good in the world, and there never was a time when loftier and more disinterested work for the betterment of mankind was being done than now. The forces that tend for evil are great and terrible, but the forces of truth and love and courage and honesty and generosity and sympathy are also stronger than ever before. It is a foolish and timid no less than a wicked thing to blink the fact that the forces of evil are strong, but it is even worse to fail to take into account the strength of the forces that tell for good. Hysterical sensationalism is the very poorest weapon wherewith to fight for lasting righteousness. The men who with stern sobriety and truth assail the many evils of our time, whether in the public press, or in magazines, or in books, are the leaders and allies of all engaged in the work for social and political betterment. But if they give good reason for distrust of what they say, if they chill the ardor of those who demand truth as a primary virtue, they thereby betray the good cause and play into the hands of the very men against whom they are nominally at war.

In his *Ecclesiastical Polity* that fine old Elizabethan divine, Bishop Hooker, wrote:

"He that goeth about to persuade a multitude that they are not so well governed as they ought to be, shall never want attentive and favorable hearers; because they know the manifold defects whereunto every kind of regimen is subject, but the secret lets and difficulties, which in public proceedings are innumerable and inevitable, they have not ordinarily the judgment to consider."

This truth should be kept constantly in mind by every free people desiring to preserve the sanity and poise indispensable to the permanent success of self-government. Yet, on the other hand, it is vital not to permit this spirit of sanity and self-command to degenerate into mere mental stagnation. Bad though a state of hysterical excitement is, and evil though the results are which come from the violent oscillations such excitement invariably produces, yet a sodden acquiescence in evil is even worse. At this moment we are passing through a period of great unrest—social, political and industrial unrest. It is of the utmost importance for our future that this should prove to be not the unrest of mere rebelliousness against life, of mere dissatisfaction with the inevitable inequality of conditions, but the unrest of a resolute and eager ambition to secure the betterment of the individual and the nation. So far as this movement of agitation throughout the country takes the form of a fierce discontent with evil, of a determination to punish the authors of evil, whether in industry or politics, the feeling is to be heartily welcomed as a sign of healthy life.

If, on the other hand, it turns into a mere crusade of appetite against appetite, of a contest between the brutal greed of the "have-nots" and the brutal greed of the "haves," then it has no significance for good, but only for evil. If it seeks to establish a line of cleavage, not along the line which divides good men from bad, but along that other line, running at right angles thereto, which divides those who are well off from those who are less well off, then it will be fraught with immeasurable harm to the body politic.

We can no more and no less afford to condone evil in the man of capital than evil in the man of no capital. The wealthy man who exults because there is a failure of justice in the effort to bring some trust magnate to an account for his misdeeds is as bad as, and no worse than, the so-called labor leader who clamorously strives to excite a foul class feeling on behalf of some other labor leader who is implicated in murder. One attitude is as bad as the other, and no worse; in each case the accused is entitled to exact justice; and in neither case is there need of action by others which can be construed into an expression of sympathy for crime.

It is a prime necessity that if the present unrest is to result in permanent good the emotion shall be translated into action, and that the action shall be marked by honesty, sanity and self-restraint. There is mighty little good in a mere spasm of reform. The reform that counts is that which comes through steady, continuous growth; violent emotionalism leads to exhaustion.

It is important to this people to grapple with the problems connected with the amassing of enormous fortunes, and the use of those fortunes, both corporate and individual, in business. We should discriminate in the sharpest way between fortunes well won and fortunes ill won; between those gained as an incident to performing great services to the community as a whole, and those gained in evil fashion by keeping just within the limits of mere law-honesty. Of course no amount of charity in spending such fortunes in any way compensates for misconduct in making them. As a matter of personal conviction, and without pretending to discuss the details or formulate the system, I feel that we shall ultimately have to consider the adoption of some such scheme as that of a progressive tax on all fortunes, beyond a certain amount, either given in life or devised or bequeathed upon death to any individual—a tax so framed as to put it out of the power of the owner of one of these enormous fortunes to hand on more than a certain amount to any one individual; the tax, of course, to be imposed by the national and not the state government. Such taxation should, of course, be aimed merely at the inheritance or transmission in their entirety of those fortunes swollen beyond all healthy limits.

Again, the national government must in some form exercise supervision over corporations engaged in interstate business—and all large corporations are engaged in interstate business—whether by license or otherwise, so as to permit us to deal with the far-reaching evils of over-capitalization. This year we are making a beginning in the direction of serious effort to settle some of these economic problems by the railway rate legislation. Such legislation, if so framed, as I am sure it will be, as to secure definite and tangible results, will amount to something of itself; and it will amount to a great deal more in so far as it is taken as a first step in the direction of a policy of superintendence and control over corporate wealth engaged in interstate commerce, this superintendence and control not to be exercised in a spirit of malevolence toward the men who have created the wealth, but with the firm purpose both to do justice to them and to see that they in their turn do justice to the public at large.

The first requisite in the public servants who are to deal in this shape with corporations, whether as legislators or as executives, is honesty. This honesty can be no respecter of persons. There can be no such thing as unilateral honesty. The danger is not really from corrupt corporations; it springs from the corruption itself, whether exercised for or against corporations.

The eighth commandment reads, "Thou shalt not steal." It does not read, "Thou shalt not steal from the rich man." It does not read, "Thou shalt not steal from the poor man." It reads simply and plainly, "Thou shalt not steal." No good whatever will come from that warped and mock morality which denounces the misdeeds of men of wealth and forgets the misdeeds practiced at their expense; which denounces bribery, but blinds itself to blackmail; which foams with rage if a corporation secures favors by improper methods, but merely leers with hideous mirth if the corporation is itself wronged. The only public servant who can be trusted honestly to protect the rights of the public against the misdeed of a corporation is that public man who will just as surely protect the corporation itself from wrongful aggression. If a public man is willing to yield to popular clamor and do wrong to the men of wealth or to rich corporations, it may be set down as certain that if the opportunity comes he will secretly and furtively do wrong to the public in the interest of a corporation.

But, in addition to honesty, we need sanity. No honesty will make a public man useful if that man is timid or foolish, if he is a hot-headed zealot or an impracticable visionary. As we strive for reform we find that it is not at all merely the case of a long uphill pull. On the contrary, there is almost as much of breeching work as of collar work; to depend only on traces means that there will soon be a runaway and an upset. The men of wealth who today are trying to prevent the regulation and control of their business in the interest of the public by the proper government authorities will not succeed, in my judgment, in checking the progress of the movement. But if they did succeed they would find that they had sown the wind and would surely reap the whirlwind, for they ultimately provoke the violent excesses which accompany a reform coming by convulsion instead of by steady and natural growth.

On the other hand, the wild preachers of unrest and discontent, the wild agitators against the entire existing order, the men who act crookedly, whether because of sinister design or mere puzzleheadedness, the men who preach destruction without proposing any substitute for what they intend to destroy, or who propose a substitute which would be far worse than the existing evils—all these men are the most dangerous opponents of real reform. If they get their way they will lead the people into a deeper pit than any into which they could fall under the present system. If they fail to get their way they will still do incalculable harm by provoking the kind of reaction which in its revolt against the senseless evil of their teaching would enthrone more securely than ever the very evils which their misguided followers believe they are attacking.

More important than aught else is the development of the broadest sympathy of man for man. The welfare of the wage worker, the welfare of the tiller of the soil, upon these depend the welfare of the entire country; their good is not to be sought in pulling down others; but their good must be the prime object of all our statesmanship.

Materially, we must strive to secure a broader economic opportunity for all men, so that each shall have a better chance to show the stuff of which he is made. Spiritually and ethically we must strive to bring about clean living and right thinking. We appreciate that the things of the body are important; but we appreciate also that the things of the soul are immeasurably more important. The foundation stone of national life is, and ever must be, the high individual character of the average citizen.

New York *Tribune*
April 15, 1906

PART THREE

❦

Behind Political Doors

THE

UNITED STATES SENATE

AN EARTHQUAKE IN 1906 practically wiped out half the city of San Francisco.

The journalistic earthquake of the year was the series of articles by David Graham Phillips in *Cosmopolitan* Magazine, "The Treason of the Senate." It was this series which prompted President Roosevelt to give to Phillips and other writers the name which has tagged them ever since: muckrakers.

Inspiration for the articles had come from Charles Edward Russell, also a journalist. While sitting in the press gallery of the U.S. Senate one day, he became aware of "well-fed and portly gentlemen," and was struck with the idea that "almost nobody in that chamber had any other reason to be there than his skill in valeting for some powerful Interest." Russell then conceived the idea that a series of articles "might well be written on the fact that strictly speaking we had no Senate; we had only a chamber of butlers for industrialists and financiers." [30]

He suggested the idea to William Randolph Hearst, who had just purchased *Cosmopolitan*. Hearst liked it, and Russell started to gather facts. But he dropped the project when he was given an assignment by *Everybody's* Magazine, and *Cosmopolitan* looked for someone else to do the series.

Hearst picked the handsome, meticulously dressed Phillips, who at the age of thirty-nine was already a novelist of some repute. He was also a political journalist whose writing had appeared in the Cincinnati *Star* and the New York *Sun* and *World*.

In spite of his attention to fiction, Phillips was first and foremost a reporter.[31] His name was familiar to readers of *Everybody's*, *McClure's*, *Collier's* and *Harper's*. A series of articles in *Everybody's* touched such subjects as "How Roosevelt Became President," "The Man Who Made the Money Trust," and "The Madness of Much Power."

Though Phillips wrote the series, the research for "The Treason of the Senate" was done by Gustavus Myers, who had already written *The History of the Great American Fortunes*. Myers specialized in historical research.

In announcing the series, *Cosmopolitan* proclaimed: "This convincing story of revelation, to be told in several chapters, and to run well through the magazine year, has been called 'The Treason of the Senate' for the reason that that is a fit and logical title for this terrible arraignment of those who, sitting in the seats of the mighty at Washington, have betrayed the public to that cruel and vicious Spirit of Mammon which has come to dominate the nation." [32]

The series began in March 1906. Its theme, taken from the Constitution of the United States, Article III, Section 3: "Treason against the United States shall consist only in levying war against them, or in adhering to their enemies, giving them aid and comfort."

Its opening article charged: "The treason of the Senate! Treason is a strong word, but not too strong, rather too weak, to characterize the situation in which the Senate is eager, resourceful, indefatigable agent of interests as hostile to the American people as any invading army could be, and vastly more dangerous: interests that manipulate the prosperity produced by all, so that it heaps up riches for the few; interests whose growth and power can only mean the degradation of the people, of the educated into sycophants, of the masses toward serfdom. . . . The Senators are not elected by the people; they are elected by the 'interests.' "

Senators Chauncey M. Depew and Thomas Collier Platt * were the first to be put on the carpet. Phillips pointed out that Senator Depew was a member of the boards of directors of seventy corporations. He received more than $50,000 as fees for his services from these firms, which Phillips claimed was part payment from "the interests." He described Platt as having a "long . . . unbroken record of treachery to the people in legislation of privilege and plunder promoted and in decent legislation prevented."

After Depew and Platt, Phillips singled out Nelson W. Aldrich, the senator from Rhode Island, a Republican, and called him the right arm of "the interests." Senator Arthur Pue Gorman of Maryland, a Democrat, was called the left arm.

The series also included articles on John C. Spooner of Wisconsin, Joseph Weldon Bailey of Texas, Stephen B. Elkins of West Virginia, Philander C. Knox of Pennsylvania.

Phillips referred to Henry Cabot Lodge as "the familiar coarse type of machine politician disguised by the robe of the 'Gentleman Scholar.' " He called William B. Allison of Iowa the Interests' "craftiest agent," and Joseph Benson Foraker of Ohio the "best stump speaker" for "the interests."

The records of William J. Stone of Missouri, Shelby M. Cullom of Illinois and Winthrop Murray Crane of Massachusetts were reviewed, as well as a number of other senators, both the leaders and those who were led.

The series concluded: "Such is the stealthy and treacherous Senate as at present constituted. And such it will continue to be until people think instead of shout about politics; until they judge public men by what they do and are, not by what they say and pretend. However, the fact that the people are themselves responsible for their own betrayal does not mitigate contempt for their hypocritical and cowardly betrayers. A corrupt system

---

* Senators from New York.

explains a corrupt man; it does not *excuse* a corrupt man; it does not *excuse* him. The stupidity or negligence of the householder in leaving the door unlocked does not lessen the crime of the thief."

Upon the conclusion of the series, *Collier's*, which had been doing its own share of muckraking, commented: " 'The Treason of the Senate' has come to a close. These articles made reform odious. They represented sensational and money-making preying on the vogue of the 'literature of exposure,' which had been built up by truthful and conscientious work of writers like Miss Tarbell, Lincoln Steffens and Ray Stannard Baker. . . . Mr. Phillips' articles were one shriek of accusations based on the distortion of such facts as were printed, and on the suppression of facts which were essential." [33]

President Roosevelt, writing to the editor-in-chief of the *Saturday Evening Post*, George Horace Lorimer, said: "I do not believe that the articles that Mr. Phillips has written, and notably these articles on the Senate, do anything but harm. They contain so much more falsehood than truth that they give no accurate guide for those who are really anxious to war against corruption, and they do excite a hysterical and ignorant feeling against everything existing, good or bad. . . ." [34]

Professor Louis Filler contends that the political consequences of the series of articles "had at least broken down those adamant walls of the Senate. Freer discussion of Senatorial personages and powers followed. A number of Senators were unseated in the next election, and others were dropped from the rolls in succeeding years until, by 1912, the composition of the Chamber had changed completely. . . . An amendment to the Constitution was drafted and triumphantly adopted, and the power of direct election of Senators was at last given to the people." [35]

Phillips himself was disturbed about the outburst which followed the publication of the articles. He considered the series the one failure in his life.

He did not live long enough to derive the satisfaction of knowing what he had accomplished. An assassin's bullet killed him at the age of forty-three. But his series on the treason of the Senate was a major influence in the passage of the Seventeenth Amendment, which gave to the people the direct election of senators.

DAVID GRAHAM PHILLIPS

&

The Treason of the Senate:

ALDRICH, THE HEAD OF IT ALL

Platt and Depew * are significant only as showing how New York,
foremost state of our forty-five, is represented in the Senate, in the
body that is the final arbiter of the distribution of the enormous prosperity annually created by the American people. Long before Platt and
Depew were sent to the Senate by and for "the interests," treason had
been organized and established there; they simply joined the senatorial
rank and file of diligent, faithful servants of the enemies of their country. For the organizer of this treason we must look at Nelson W.
Aldrich, senior senator from Rhode Island.

Rhode Island is the smallest of our states in area and thirty-fourth
in population—twelve hundred and fifty square miles, less than half a
million people, barely seventy thousand voters with the rolls padded by
the Aldrich machine. But size and numbers are nothing; it contains as
many sturdy Americans proportionately as any other state. Its bad distinction of supplying the enemy with a bold leader is due to its ancient
and aristocratic constitution, changed once, away back before the
middle of the last century, but still an archaic document for class rule.
The apportionment of legislators is such that one-eleventh of the population, and they the most ignorant and most venal, elect a majority of
the legislature—which means that they elect the two United States
senators. Each city and township counts as a political unit; thus, the
five cities that together have two-thirds of the population are in an
overwhelming minority before twenty almost vacant rural townships—
their total population is not thirty-seven thousand—where the igno-

* U.S. Senators from New York.

71

rance is even illiterate, where the superstition is medieval, where tradition and custom have made the vote an article of legitimate merchandising.

The combination of bribery and party prejudice is potent everywhere; but there come crises when these fail "the interests" for the moment. No storm of popular rage, however, could unseat the senators from Rhode Island. The people of Rhode Island might, as a people and voting almost unanimously, elect a governor; but not a legislature. Bribery is a weapon forbidden those who stand for right and justice—who "fights the devil with fire" gives him choice of weapons, and must lose to him, though seeming to win. A few thousand dollars put in the experienced hands of the heelers, and the senatorial general agent of "the interests" is secure for another six years.

The Aldrich machine controls the legislature, the election boards, the courts—the entire machinery of the "republican form of government." In 1904, when Aldrich needed a legislature to re-elect him for his fifth consecutive term, it is estimated that carrying the state cost about two hundred thousand dollars—a small sum, easily to be got back by a few minutes of industrious pocket-picking in Wall Street; but a very large sum for Rhode Island politics, and a happy augury of a future day, remote, perhaps, but inevitable, when the people shall rule in Rhode Island. Despite the bribery, despite the swindling on registration lists and all the chicane which the statute book of the state makes easy for "the interests," Aldrich elected his governor by a scant eight hundred on the face of the returns. His legislature was, of course, got without the least difficulty—the majority for "the interests" is on joint ballot seventy-five out of a total of one hundred and seventeen. The only reason Aldrich disturbed himself about the governorship was that, through the anger of the people and the carelessness of the machine, a people's governor had been elected in 1903 and was up for re-election; this people's governor, while without any power whatever under the Constitution, still could make disagreeable demands on the legislature, demands which did not sound well in the ears of the country and roused the people everywhere to just what was the source of the most respectable politician's security. So, Aldrich, contrary to his habit in recent years, took personal charge of the campaign and tried to show the people of Rhode Island that they were helpless and might as well quiet down, accept their destiny and spare his henchmen the expense and labor of wholesale bribery and fraud.

But, as a rule, Aldrich no longer concerns himself with Rhode Island's petty local affairs. "Not until about a year or so before it comes time for him to be elected again, does he get active," says his chief henchman, Gen. Charles R. Brayton, the state's boss. "He doesn't pay much attention to details." Why should he? Politically, the state is securely "the interests'" and his; financially, "the interests" and he have incorporated and assured to themselves in perpetuity about all the graft—the Rhode Island Securities Company, capitalized at and paying excellent dividends upon thirty-nine million dollars, representing an actual value of less than nine million dollars, owns, thanks to the munificence of the legislature, the state's street and trolley lines, gas and electric franchises, etc., etc. It began in a street railway company of Providence in which Aldrich, president of the Providence council and afterward member of the legislature, acquired an interest. The sugar trust's Searles put in a million and a half shortly after the sugar trust got its license to loot through Aldrich at Washington; the legislature passed the necessary laws and gave the necessary franchises; Senator Steve Elkins and his crowd were invited in; more legislation; more franchises, more stocks and bonds, the right to loot the people of the state in perpetuity. Yes, Aldrich is rich, enormously rich, and his mind is wholly free for the schemes he plots and executes at Washington. And, like all the other senators who own large blocks of stocks and bonds in the great drainage companies fastened upon America's prosperity, his service is not the less diligent or adroit because he himself draws huge dividends from the people.

He was born in 1841, is only sixty-four years old, good for another fifteen years, at least, in his present rugged health, before "the interests" will have to select another for his safe seat and treacherous task. He began as a grocery boy, got the beginning of one kind of education in the public schools and in an academy at East Greenwich, Rhode Island. He became clerk in a fish store in Providence, then clerk in a grocery, then bookkeeper, partner, and is still a wholesale grocer. He was elected to the legislature, applied himself so diligently to the work of getting his real education that he soon won the confidence of the boss, then Senator Anthony, and was sent to Congress, where he was Anthony's successor as boss, and chief agent of the Rhode Island interests. He entered the United States Senate in 1881.

In 1901 his daughter married the only son and destined successor of John D. Rockefeller. Thus, the chief exploiter of the American people is closely allied by marriage with the chief schemer in the service of their exploiters. This fact no American should ever lose sight of. It is a political fact; it is an economic fact. It places the final and strongest seal upon the bonds uniting Aldrich and "the interests."

When Aldrich entered the Senate, twenty-five years ago, at the splendid full age of forty, the world was just beginning to feel the effects of the principles of concentration and combination, which were inexorably and permanently established with the discoveries in steam and electricity that make the whole human race more and more like one community of interdependent neighbors. It was a moment of opportunity, an unprecedented chance for Congress, especially its deliberate and supposedly sagacious senators, to "promote the general welfare" by giving those principles free and just play in securing the benefits of expanding prosperity to all, by seeing that the profits from the cooperation of all the people went *to* the people. Aldrich and the traitor Senate saw the opportunity. But they saw in it only a chance to enable a class to despoil the masses.

Before he reached the Senate, Aldrich had had fifteen years of training in how to legislate the proceeds of the labor of the many into the pockets of the few. He entered it as the representative of local interests engaged in robbing by means of slyly worded tariff schedules that changed protection against the foreigner into plunder of the native. His demonstrated excellent talents for sly, slippery work in legislative chambers and committee rooms and his security in his seat against popular revulsions and outbursts together marked him for the position of chief agent of the predatory band which was rapidly forming to take care of the prosperity of the American people.

Various senators represent various divisions and subdivisions of this colossus. But Aldrich, rich through franchise grabbing, the intimate of Wall Street's great robber barons, the father-in-law of the only son of *the* Rockefeller—Aldrich represents the colossus. Your first impression of many and conflicting interests has disappeared. You now see a single interest, with a single agent-in-chief to execute its single purpose—getting rich at the expense of the labor and the independence of the American people. And the largest head among the many heads of this monster is that of Rockefeller, father of the only son-in-law of Aldrich and his intimate in all the relations of life!

There are many passages in the Constitution in which a Senate, true to its oath and mindful of the welfare of the people and of the nation, could find mandates to stop wholesale robbery, and similar practices.

And yet, what has the Senate done—the Senate, with its high-flown pretenses of reverence for the Constitution? It has so legislated and so refrained from legislating that more than half of all the wealth created by the American people belongs to less than 1 per cent of them; that the income of the average American family has sunk to less than six hundred dollars a year; that of our more than twenty-seven million children of school age, less than twelve millions go to school, and more than two millions work in mines, shops, and factories.

And the leader, the boss of the Senate for the past twenty years has been—Aldrich!

In vain would "the interests" have stolen franchises, in vain would they have corrupted the public officials of states and cities, if they had not got absolute and unshakable control of the Senate. But, with the Senate theirs, how secure, how easy and how rich the loot!

The sole source of Aldrich's power over the senators is "the interests" —the sole source, but quite sufficient to make him permanent and undisputed boss. Many of the senators . . . are, like Depew and Platt, the direct agents of the various state or sectional subdivisions of "the interests," and these senators constitute about two-thirds of the entire Senate. Of the remainder several know that if they should oppose "the interests" they would lose their seats; several others are silent because they feel that to speak out would be useless; a few do speak out, but are careful not to infringe upon the rigid rule of "senatorial courtesy," which thus effectually protects the unblushing corruptionists, the obsequious servants of corruption, and likewise the many traitors to party as well as the people, from having disagreeable truths dinged into their ears. Tillman will "pitchfork" a President, but not a senator, and not the Senate in any but the most useless, futile way—this, though none knows better than he how the rights and the property of the people are trafficked in by his colleagues of both parties, with a few exceptions. There are a few other honest men from the South and from the West, as many of the few honest Republicans as honest Democrats. Yet party allegiance and "senatorial courtesy" make them abettors of treason, allies of Aldrich and Gorman.

"Senatorial courtesy!" We shall have to return to it, as it is the hypocritical mask behind which the few senators who pose as real representatives of the people hide in silence and inaction.

The greatest single hold of "the interests" is the fact that they are the "campaign contributors"—the men who supply the money for "keeping the party together," and for "getting out the vote." Did you ever think where the millions for watchers, spellbinders, halls, processions, posters, pamphlets, that are spent in national, state and local campaigns come from? Who pays the big election expenses of your congressman, of the men you send to the legislature to elect senators? Do you imagine those who foot those huge bills are fools? Don't you know that they make sure of getting their money back, with interest,

compound upon compound? Your candidates get most of the money
for their campaigns from the party committees; and the central party
committee is the national committee with which congressional and
state and local committees are affiliated. The bulk of the money for
the "political trust" comes from "the interests." "The interests" will
give only to the "political trust." And that means Aldrich and his
Democratic (!) lieutenant, Gorman of Maryland, leader of the minority in the Senate. Aldrich, then, is the head of the "political trust" and
Gorman is his right-hand man. When you speak of the Republican
party, of the Democratic party, of the "good of the party," of the "best
interests of the party," of "wise party policy," you mean what Aldrich
and Gorman, acting for their clients, deem wise and proper and "Republican" or "Democratic."

To relate the treason in detail would mean taking up bill after bill
and going through it, line by line, word by word, and showing how
this interpolation there or that excision yonder meant millions on
millions more to this or that interest, millions on millions less for the
people as merchants, wage or salary earners, consumers; how the killing
of this measure meant immunity to looters all along the line; how the
alteration of the wording of that other "trifling" resolution gave a
quarter of a cent a pound on every one of hundreds of millions of
pounds of some necessary of life to a certain small group of men; how
this innocent-looking little measure safeguarded the railway barons in
looting the whole American people by excessive charges and rebates.
Few among the masses have the patience to listen to these dull matters
—and, so, "the interests" and their agents have prosperity and honor
instead of justice and jail.

No railway legislation that was not either helpful to or harmless
against "the interests"; no legislation on the subject of corporations
that would interfere with "the interests," which use the corporate form
to simplify and systematize their stealing; no legislation on the tariff
question unless it secured to "the interests" full and free license to
loot; no investigations of wholesale robbery or of any of the evils resulting from it—there you have in a few words the whole story of the
Senate's treason under Aldrich's leadership, and of why property is
concentrating in the hands of the few and the little children of the
masses are being sent to toil in the darkness of mines, in the dreariness
and unhealthfulness of factories instead of being sent to school; and
why the great middle class—the old-fashioned Americans, the people
with the incomes of from two thousand to fifteen thousand a year—is
being swiftly crushed into dependence and the repulsive miseries of

"genteel poverty." The heavy and ever heavier taxes of "the interests" are swelling rents, swelling the prices of food, clothing, fuel, all the necessities and all the necessary comforts. And the Senate both forbids the lifting of those taxes and levies fresh taxes for its master.

Let us concentrate on three signal acts of treachery which Aldrich had to perpetrate publicly and which are typical and all-embracing in effect.

There are, of course, two honestly tenable views of the tariff question. But both the honest advocates of high tariff and the honest advocates of low tariff are agreed in opposition to tariff for plunder only. And we are noting here only that last kind of tariff, which is as hateful to protectionist as to free trader because it is in truth a treason.

Two years after Aldrich came to the Senate there was a revision of the tariff law enacted during the Civil War. In that revision Aldrich took an active part, and laid the foundations of his power with "the interests," then in their early formative period. But it was not until 1890 that he had an opportunity to make his first large contribution toward the firm establishment of conditions of unequal division of prosperity which have now resulted in expropriating the American people from the ownership of their own country. In 1890 the House of Representatives passed the so-called McKinley bill. As it left the House it was, on the whole, a fairly honest protective-tariff measure, extreme, in the opinion of some Republicans and of many Democrats, but on the whole an attempt to raise revenue and to protect all American industries. "The interests" had their representatives in the House by the score; but the House is so directly responsible to the people that it dared not originate and utter a measure of frank treason. The bill went to the Senate, was there handed to Aldrich and his committee for examination in the secrecy of the committee room. When Aldrich reported the bill, there was a wild outcry from the House—largely for political effect upon the astonished people, who almost awakened to the enormity of the treason. The McKinley bill had been killed; for it Aldrich had substituted a bill to enrich "the interests" with the earnings and savings of the masses. The sugar trust's schedule, for example, was so scandalous that even the mild and devotedly partisan McKinley exclaimed publicly that it was far too high. It gave the trust a loot of sixty cents the hundred pounds, of three million dollars a year over and above the high protection it already had, when sugar can be refined more cheaply in this country than anywhere else in the world, the labor cost being insignificant.

But the traitor Senate stood firm for its masters; and the House, in terror of Aldrich and his "campaign contributors," accepted what it knew meant temporary political ruin—better offend the short-memoried people than "the interests" that forgive and forget nothing and never. The Aldrich bill was passed and was signed by the President. The party and the President, and Congressman McKinley and all who had had anything to do with the bill went down in defeat—but not Aldrich, secure in his Rhode Island seat, and not any of the senators who were needed by "the interests." And "the interests" got their loot —literally, hundreds of millions a year, every penny of it coming out of the pockets of the people.

The Democrats came in, and in 1894 the Wilson bill passed the House—a fairly honest and really moderate expression of the low-tariff view of the tariff question. The Senate had a small Democratic majority, nominally. So, Aldrich was pretending to take a back seat; and his right bower, Gorman, was posing as leader of the Senate, that is, of its traitorous band of servants of "the interests"—more than half of all the senators. The Wilson bill reappeared from the secrecy of the Aldrich-Gorman committee so absolutely transformed from a thing of decency to a thing of shame that the whole country was convulsed. Again "the interests" had been looked after; there had been injected into the bill provisions for loot for each and every one of Aldrich's powerful clients, the electors of senators, Democratic and Republican, the suppliers of campaign funds and tips on stocks and shares in "good things," and of funds to be lost at poker to congressmen too "honest" and too "proud" to accept a direct bribe. The scandal was enormous— so enormous that there had to be a farcical investigation at which Havemeyer, the sugar king, and Chapman, the agent of the brokers through whom the senators and representatives gambled in stocks, refused to tell what they knew of the utter rottenness of the leaders of Senate and House. Chapman got a few days in jail for contempt; Havemeyer, tried for the same offense, and whistling softly all through this farcical trial, was acquitted. But the scandal did not stagger Aldrich and Gorman and their band. They, more than a majority of the Senate, most of them traitors to the people wearing the Republican disguise, enough of them from among the Democrats—Gorman, Jim Smith of New Jersey, Brice of Ohio, Ed Murphy of New York—formed a solid, brazen phalanx and forced the House—again in terror of the "campaign contributors"—to accept the Aldrich bill or nothing. The President denounced it, refused to sign it—he almost took the advice of Tom Johnson to veto it. But the "Aldrich-Gorman political trust" had been shrewd enough to leave in the bill some features popularly attractive that happened not to injure any of "the interests," some features that made it *seem* less predatory than the Aldrich bill of 1890; and the President let it become a law without his signature. In action, it soon demonstrated that as a whole it was quite as effective as the Aldrich bill of 1890 in doing all that a tariff law could to accelerate the expropriation of the people from ownership of any property whatever.

Poor Wilson! Had he been a "practical" tariff expert like Aldrich, how he would have cried out against that law which bore his name as a cover for Aldrich's treachery!

Aldrich's next great positive tariff opportunity came in 1897. The Dingley tariff bill left the House more satisfactory to "the interests" than any that had preceded it. The House had been gradually passing into the control of "the interests" and the doctrine that to serve "the interests" which financed the party and acted as fatherly guardians of the poor, helpless and so mysteriously impoverishing American people was to serve God and country, had gained ground, had become almost as axiomatic as it now is. Still, the leaders of the House had not dared wholly to lose their point of view—or, rather, to pretend to lose it. The Dingley bill entered the Senate, almost perfect from the standpoint of the agents of the enemies of the people there enthroned. But not quite perfect. The defects were all speedily remedied, however, in the secrecy of Aldrich's committee room. And the third Aldrich tariff bill became a law. Like the Aldrich-emasculated antitrust legislation, like the Aldrich-manipulated laws for the regulation of railways, this law is, in its main schedules—those dealing with the fundamental necessaries of civilized life used by all the people—a stupendous robbery, taking cognizance of the huge developments of American resources to arrange that all but a scanty share of them shall become profit for the plunderers. And since 1897 the up-piling of huge fortunes, the reduction of the American people toward wage and salary slavery has gone forward with amazing rapidity. The thieves use each year's rich haul to make larger nets for larger hauls the next.

The abounding prosperity, the immense amount of work to do, has caused the paying of salaries and wages that, as the reports of the commercial agencies show, are *in money* almost as high as they were fifteen years ago and about where they were *in purchasing power* thirty years ago. But the cost of living is going up, up, faster than incomes; and the number of tenant farmers, of renters, of paupers, of unemployed has increased as never before, even in straitened times. In place of the old proportion in the lot of the American people, there is gross disproportion. How Aldrich must laugh as he watches the American people meekly submitting to this plundering through tariff and railway rates and hugely overcapitalized corporations! And what, think you, must be his opinion of the man who in all seriousness attributes the astounding contrasts between the mountainous fortunes of the few and the ant-hill hoardings of the many to the superior intelligence of the few? Yet, Aldrich's contempt for the mentality of the masses is not unjustified, is it?

How does Aldrich work? Obviously, not much steering is necessary, when the time comes to vote. "The interests" have a majority and to spare. The only questions are such as permitting a senator to vote and at times to speak against "the interests" when the particular measure is mortally offensive to the people of his particular state or section. Those daily sham battles in the Senate! Those paradings of sham virtue! Is it not strange that the other senators, instead of merely busying themselves at writing letters or combing their whiskers, do not break into shouts of laughter?

Aldrich's real work—getting the wishes of his principals, directly or through their lawyers, and putting these wishes into proper form if they are orders for legislation or into the proper channels if they are orders to kill or emasculate legislation—this work is all done, of course, behind the scenes. When Aldrich is getting orders, there is of course never any witness. The second part of his task—execution—is in part a matter of whispering with his chief lieutenants, in part a matter of consultation in the secure secrecy of the Senate committee rooms. Aldrich is in person chairman of the chief Senate committee—finance. There he labors, assisted by Gorman, his right bower, who takes his place as chairman when the Democrats are in power; by Spooner, his left bower and public mouthpiece; by Allison, that Nestor of craft; by the Pennsylvania Railroad's Penrose; by Tom Platt of New York, corruptionist and lifelong agent of corruptionists; by Joe Bailey of Texas, and several other sympathetic or silent spirits. Together they concoct and sugar-coat the bitter doses for the people—the loot measures and the suffocating of the measures in restraint of loot. In the unofficial but powerful steering committee—which receives from him the will of "the interests" and translates it into "party policy"—he works through Allison as chairman—but Allison's position is recognized as purely honorary.

And, also, Aldrich sits in the powerful interstate commerce committee; there, he has his "pal," the brazen Elkins of West Virginia, as chairman. He is not on the committee on appropriations; but Allison is, is its chairman, and Cullom of Illinois is there—and in due time we shall endeavor to get better acquainted with both of them. In the commerce committee, he has Frye of Maine, to look after such matters as the projected, often postponed, but never abandoned, loot through ship subsidy; in the Pacific Railroad committee he has the valiant soldier, the honest lumber and railway multimillionaire, the embalmed-beef hero, Alger, as chairman; in the post office and post roads committee, which looks after the railways' postal graft, a clean steal from the Treasury of upward of ten millions a year—some put it as high as thirty millions—he has Penrose as chairman. In that highly important committee, the one on rules, he himself sits; but mouthpiece Spooner is naturally chairman. Their associates are Elkins and Lodge —another pair that need to be better known to the American people. Bailey is the chief "Democratic" member. What a sardonic jest to speak of these men as Republicans and Democrats!

These committees carry on their colorless routine and also their real work—promoting thievish legislation, preventing decent legislation, devising ways and means of making rottenest dishonesty look like honesty and patriotism—these committees carry on their work in secrecy. *Public* business in profound privacy! Once Vest, angered by some misrepresentation made by Aldrich, had part of the minutes of a meeting of the finance committee read in open Senate—a gross breach of "senatorial courtesy"! Before the rudely lifted curtain was dropped, the country had a rare, illuminatory view of Aldrich. Here is this official minute:

"At a meeting of the Committee on Finance on March 17, 1894, on motion of Mr. Aldrich, the committee proceeded to a consideration of the provisions [of the Wilson bill] in regard to an income tax. Mr. Aldrich moved that the whole provision be stricken out of the bill."

He and Allison, that lifelong professional friend of the "plain people," had both voted aye. A pitiful sight he and Allison were, flustering and red, as this damning fact was read in open Senate, with the galleries full and all the reporters in their places! It is the only time the people have ever had a look at Aldrich in his shirt sleeves and hard at his repulsive but remunerative trade. But the people do not need to see the processes. They see, they feel, they suffer from the finished result—the bad law enacted, the good law killed.

When Bacon, in 1903, moved to call on the Department of Commerce and Labor for full facts about the selling of American goods at prices from one-fourth to a full hundred per cent cheaper abroad than at home, Aldrich at once moved to refer the resolution to his committee, and his motion was carried. A year later, Bacon reminded the Senate of his former resolution and of how it was sleeping in Aldrich's committee, and reintroduced it. He backed it up with masses of facts—how "our" sewing machines sell abroad for fifteen dollars and here for twenty-five dollars; how "our" borax, a Rockefeller product, costs seven and a half cents a pound here and only two and a half cents abroad; how "our" nails, a Rockefeller-Morgan product, sell here for four dollars and fifty cents a keg and abroad for three dollars and ten cents; how the foreigner gets for one dollar as much of "our" window glass as we get for two dollars; how Schwab, in a letter to Frick on May 15, 1899, had said that, while steel rails sold here at twenty-eight dollars a ton, he could deliver them in England for sixteen dollars a ton and make four dollars a ton profit; how the beef trust sold meat from twenty-five to fifty per cent dearer in Buffalo than just across the Canadian line; how the harvester trust sold its reapers cheaper on the continent of Europe than to an Illinois farmer coming to its main factory at Chicago; how on every article in common use among the American people of city, town and country, "the interests" were boldly robbing the people.

And Mr. Aldrich said, "Absurd!" And the Senate refused even to call upon the Department of Labor for the facts.

An illustration of another form of Aldrich's methods: When House and Senate disagree on a bill, each appoints a conference committee; and the two committees meet and try to find common ground. At one of these conferences—on the war-tax bill—Aldrich appeared, as usual in all matters which concern "the interests," at the head of the Senate conferees. He pressed more than a score of amendments to a single paragraph in the House measure. The House committee resisted him, and he slowly retreated, yielding point after point until finally he had yielded all but one. He said: "Well, gentlemen of the House, we of the Senate have yielded practically everything to your body. We dare not go back absolutely empty-handed." And the House conferees gave him the one remaining point—the "mere trifle." It afterwards appeared that this was probably the only one of his more than a score of amendments that he really wanted; the others were mere blinds. For, that "mere trifle" subtly gave the tobacco "interests" (Rockefeller-Ryan) a license to use the war-revenue tax on tobacco to extort an additional four or five cents a pound from the consumer! There are half a dozen clauses, at least, in the present so-called Dingley tariff that protect the many-sided Standard Oil trust alone. But it takes an expert to find them, and doubtless many have escaped detection.

Such is Aldrich, the senator. At the second session of the last Congress his main achievements, so far as the surface shows, were smothering all inquiry into the tariff and the freight-rate robberies, helping Elkins and the group of traitors in the service of the thieves who control the railway corporations to emasculate railway legislation, helping Allison and Bailey to smother the bill against the food poisoners for dividends. During the past winter he has been concentrating on the "defense of the railways"—which means not the railways nor yet the railway corporations, but simply the Rockefeller-Morgan looting of the people by means of their control of the corporations that own the railways.

Has Aldrich intellect? Perhaps. But he does not show it. He has never in his twenty-five years of service in the Senate introduced or advocated a measure that shows any conception of life above what might be expected in a Hungry Joe. No, intellect is not the characteristic of Aldrich—or of any of these traitors, or of the men they serve. A scurvy lot they are, are they not, with their smirking and cringing and voluble palaver about God and patriotism and their eager offerings of endowments for hospitals and colleges whenever the American people so much as looks hard in their direction!

Aldrich is rich and powerful. Treachery has brought him wealth and rank, if not honor, of a certain sort. He must laugh at us, grown-up fools, permitting a handful to bind the might of our eighty millions and to set us all to work for them.

Cosmopolitan
March 1906

THE
UNITED STATES HOUSE
OF REPRESENTATIVES

To THE MUCKRAKERS, the autocratic power of Speaker Joseph G. Cannon of Illinois was like a cloth of red before a charging bull. The fundamental objections to the gentleman from Danville, Illinois was his espousal of trusts, and his defense of the status quo.

Wallace Irwin, light versifier and satirist, wrote of Cannon:

> First reared on a farm, with an old-fashioned notion
> Of Duty to honor's last ditch,
> He stands like a rock in his simple devotion
> A staunch friend of the rich.
>
> Enthusiasts laud him from belfry to steeple,
> Forgetting the truth, as they must,
> That statesmen are seldom so close to the People
> As when they are hugging some trust.[36]

Cannon ruled the House of Representatives of the United States with an iron hand, and was thus dubbed "Czar."

His power lay in his ability through the rules of the House to appoint "every member of every committee; consequently every member who wanted to be on a desirable committee was careful to act on bills the way Cannon wished them acted upon—to report out for action those that Cannon wanted out, to keep in committee those that Cannon wanted repressed." [37]

There were other objections to Cannon: he was vulgar, uncouth and unenlightened; he was a poker-playing old man of the era.

His third of a century in Congress was interrupted by a one-term defeat because of a "coarse joke" against an opponent in the House.

The struggle against Cannonism was carried on by such muckraking magazines as *Collier's*, the *American, Cosmopolitan,* and *Success. Collier's* as a weekly was the recognized leader. At the helm was Mark Sullivan with his "Comment About Congress." One of the first to expose Cannon was William Hard, at the suggestion of Sullivan.

Sullivan in his writings undertook to show the public how the working rules of the House hampered any democratic action on the part of its members. He asked his readers to write their congressmen who were up for election, asking them:

(1) If elected to Congress, will you vote for or against Cannon for Speaker in the Republican caucus?

(2) If the Republican caucus should nominate Cannon for Speaker, will you then vote for or against Cannon in the regular session of Congress?

Readers sent the replies they received to Sullivan, and he printed them on his page in *Collier's.* He excoriated those who did not come out and say they would vote against Cannon.

On the other hand, he complimented the twelve congressmen who previously voted against Cannon as Speaker. He printed the photographs of these Progressives or "Insurgents" as he called them and labeled them "Twelve Men of Courage." Included were George W. Norris of Nebraska, and Charles A. Lindbergh, Sr., of Minnesota.

Success, in an article, called Cannon "The Barnacles on the Ship of State." In January 1910, *Success* printed an article by Judson C. Welliver called "The End of Cannonism" and prophesied the Speaker's early defeat.

It is reported that when Cannon saw the articles, he shouted, "Damn *Success!* Who in hell is E. E. Higgins?" * 38

Simultaneously with the exposé of Cannonism, *Collier's* and *Hampton's,* particularly the former, were engaged in the Ballinger-Glavis bureaucracy controversy (see Bureaucracy, page 146).

It was on March 16, 1910 that George W. Norris, a skilled parliamentarian, who had been carrying in his pocket a resolution for a change of rules, was able to introduce his resolution.

One of Cannon's men had opened the subject on the floor by proposing an extension of the rules. Here was Norris' opportunity and he took advantage of it.

The House was in a turmoil for two days and the debate lasted for twenty-nine hours.

The Insurgents joined with the Democrats and they won the necessary rule change by thirty-five votes.

The last speech before Cannon's defeat was given in the House by Samuel W. McCall.† He said:

"Mr. Speaker . . . This proceeding, in my opinion, is aimed at the Speaker of the House of Representatives. I do not propose to vote for it. . . . I do not propose to vote to deliver the Speaker, bound hand and foot, over to the minority. . . . This movement does not originate in the House of Representatives. I am not undiscriminating. I do not condemn a whole class, but

* Publisher of *Success.*
† U.S. Congressman from Massachusetts.

you are about to do the behest of a gang of literary highwaymen who are entirely willing to assassinate a reputation in order to sell a magazine." [39]

The removal of the committee appointments from Cannon's hands was the first successful blow at Cannonism.

In the fall 1910 election, due to the attacks on Cannon and, even more important, the Ballinger-Glavis controversy, President Taft lost control of the House and his lead in the Senate was narrowed to ten.

George French, a journalist of the period, asserted that as a result of the *Success* article, "There can be no doubt that Cannon was booted out of the Speaker's chair of the national House of Representatives." [40]

Sullivan himself takes the credit for "unhorsing" Cannon as well as Senator Aldrich.[41]

WILLIAM HARD

"Uncle Joe" Cannon

M R. CANNON survived his "foul-mouth" speech and his subsequent
defeat in his congressional district in the fall of 1890 because
it was impossible to find anybody else with the same enormous grasp
of the details of the national government. "Uncle Joe" might be
narrow-minded and obscene, but there was no other congressman who
knew definitely that "if present plans are carried out there will be, on
July 15 next, at 3:27 in the afternoon, a gap of $37,483,093.78 (not
forgetting the seventy-eight cents) between the Government's pants
and its vest."

Mr. Cannon's industrious attention to public business was immor-
talized twenty-five years ago by being inserted into James G. Blaine's
political classic, *Twenty Years of Congress.*

"Mr. Joseph G. Cannon of Illinois," said Mr. Blaine, "soon acquired
a prominent position as an earnest worker in the House, and, indeed,
became an authority on all matters connected with the Post Office of
the United States."

Six years of indefatigable attention to detail raised Mr. Cannon from
the Committee on Post Office and Post Roads, in 1879, to the Committee on Appropriations.

Here he was finally at home. One story will suffice:

The Committee had granted $5,000 to the Patent Office for an
"abridgment of patents." Having spent it, the Patent Office wanted
$25,000 more. Mr. Cannon, though a new member, summoned the
Patent Office officials before the Committee. His careful cross-examination revealed the fact, previously unsuspected even by the Patent Office
officials themselves, that the "abridgment of patents" would, in the
end, cost $20,000,000. It was enthusiastically abandoned.

Next to industry, in Mr. Cannon's qualifications, came likableness. He talked then, as now, largely with his left fist. In the Forty-fourth Congress he had the following famous colloquy with Samuel Sullivan Cox of New York:

Mr. Cox—"Don't you shake your fist at me that way."

Mr. Cannon—"With the permission of the gentleman——"

Mr. Cox—"If the gentleman will keep his hands in his pockets, he may go on."

Mr. Cannon thereupon rose to speak.

Mr. Cox—"My friend must keep his hands in his pockets."

Mr. Cannon—"I have both my hands in my pockets. I wish to say this: I did not seek to interrupt the gentleman. I do not often interrupt gentlemen. But when gentlemen make remarks by innuendo——"

This was the end. Thirty-four words was Mr. Cannon's utmost possibility when deprived of his powers of gesticulation.

"The time of the gentleman is up," shouted Mr. Cox. "He has his hands out of his pockets and he is shaking his left fist at me again."

Mr. Cannon has endeared himself, wittingly and unwittingly, to the humor of the House of Representatives. He has also endeared himself, strange as it may seem, to the human weakness of even the artists and architects whose professional activities he so fanatically opposes. They hate him as a legislative force, but like him as an individual.

The architects of the United States once invited him to a big dinner in Washington. They issued his invitation as a pure formality, not supposing for a moment that he would turn up. But he did turn up, friendly and feeling quite homelike, at about 11:45 P.M., and he arose, totally unembarrassed, to make a little speech. He had been at a loss, he said, to understand why they had sent him a card, but he had recollected that when temperance lecturers came across the prairies of Illinois they always carried with them some hopeless drunken sot as a "horrible example." He supposed he was the most horrible example available for any gathering of esthetic persons, and he was glad to be able to do some good by being present.

"We were positively hypnotized," said a Washington architect in talking about it afterward. "His nerve was as funny as his humor."

His nerve and his humor would not have carried him very far without that persistent industry and that patient pursuit of financial facts which gave him his unrivaled knowledge of the money side of the national government.

Perhaps he was helped in this respect by his five years' experience, after his father's death, in the country store kept by Sam T. Ensly at

Annapolis, Indiana. There, as a young man, Mr. Cannon sold everything, from a quart of tar to a skein of silk, and learned to think in nickels. He has thought in nickels ever since, and in spite of having become, personally, a millionaire and, professionally, a financial leader of billion-dollar Congresses.

Mr. Cannon's personal fortune, like his political fortune, was not acquired by the exercise of imagination. His million dollars is due to nickels, thrift, a few more nickels, a little more thrift, and then the happy accident of a younger brother who turned out to be a real financial genius on a small-town scale.

The story of that younger brother, "Bill," is worth sketching, in short, because, in biographies of "Joe," a great deal has been said about the inappropriateness of a man's having a million dollars after thirty-six years at Washington, during which no signs have been evident of his having any occupation outside of politics.

Mr. Cannon's money is a matter of Tuscola and Danville, not of Washington. It was all accumulated west of the boundary line between Indiana and Illinois.

Not much of it was gathered, however, in Shelbyville, Mr. Cannon's first Illinois stopping-place. He arrived there in 1859, after having supplemented his training in his country store by a course of reading in a law office in Terre Haute and a law school in Cincinnati.

Shelbyville was sterile. At the end of six months "Uncle Joe" approached his landlord and presented him with a dazzling financial proposition.

"I want to go to Tuscola," he said, "and make another start. I owe you for my board; but I'm young and strong, and, if you'll back me financially in my present plans, you'll never be sorry."

"Well," said the landlord, "I'm willing. I'll take out some of my savings and back you. How much do you want?"

"Two dollars and forty-eight cents," said Mr. Cannon, "the fare to Tuscola."

He got it, and, after a year in Tuscola, he was elected prosecuting attorney for the judicial district in which Tuscola was situated.

Here he sent for "Bill" (who was still back in Indiana), and his kindness in remembering "Bill" was the happiest act of his life.

"Bill" was an albino, with white hair and pinky eyes. "You must always look after 'Bill'," old Mrs. Cannon had told "Joe." "He is so unfortunate."

Poor, unfortunate "Bill" had been in Tuscola just about three years when he organized a bank and gave "Joe" a minority interest. "Joe"

had saved a little stack of nickels from his income as prosecuting attorney, but he hadn't thought of organizing banks. That was one of
"Bill's" unfortunate frailties.

Having got a bank in Tuscola, "Bill" went to Danville and organized
another bank there, again admitting his elder brother as a minority
partner.

The two brothers were inseparable, or, rather, identical. Their two
lives were really one life. Country banks are all in politics. Country
politics all leads to banks. "Bill" did the banks. "Joe" did the politics.

"Bill" got bigger than "Joe." In Danville he continued to be so
unfortunate that he soon owned a street-car company, then a gas company, and then an electric-light company. He was the local magnate,
and, for all practical purposes, he was a much greater man than his
brother. He was Business. His brother was only Statesmanship.

But whenever "Bill" started a new enterprise he left an opening into
which "Joe" could throw his accumulating unproductive dividends
and change them into fresh, profitable investments. And that is all
there is to "Joe" Cannon's million. Thrift and "Bill"!

What "Joe" would have done without "Bill" is shown clearly enough
by what he has done since "Bill's" death. He now puts his money into
good, solid farm land, which he can see and touch, and into amply
secured farm mortgages. No new enterprises, no creative, imaginative
developments for "Joe" in business any more than in legislation! The
imaginative element in his business life was furnished by "Bill." The
imaginative element in his political life has been furnished by a long
series of fellow Republicans, beginning with Horace Greeley and ending with Theodore Roosevelt. He himself has done nothing but invest,
usually reluctantly, in the ideas of others.

"Uncle Joe's" first instinctive impulse, when he observes a new idea
beginning to shoot up out of the ground, is to hurry and stamp on it.
He is like the famous old gentleman who said: "I don't like artichokes
and I don't like people who like them. I myself have never been able
to bring myself to taste them."

As a typical specimen of "Uncle Joe's" treatment of a new legislative proposition, the student of American statesmanship is referred
to the *Congressional Record* for January 12, 1899.

The bill was a bill for changing the United States Commission of
Fish and Fisheries into the United States Commission for Fish, Fisheries, and Birds. It may have been a good bill or a bad one. That is
not the point. The object of interest just now is the mental route

"Uncle Joe" traveled in order to arrive at his almost inevitable goal of being against the proposition.

He had not been in Congress, he said, when the bill establishing the Fish Commission was passed. But there had been a Fish Commission for some time, and he was not in favor of disturbing it. It probably did valuable work, although he had heard that in some parts of the country it artificially heated the water in which it kept its fish. That didn't look right to him, but let it pass. Let fish be protected! Birds, however, were a different matter. He didn't know the difference between the economic value of birds on the one hand and fish on the other, but he thought that, at present, fish ought to be enough.

"As I look at this bill," he went on, "I see nothing in it. Gentlemen say we can withhold appropriations, but when we once begin to build aviaries, with all the expenses attending them, we do not know where the matter will stop. We do not know whether they will be heated with steam heat or hot water or some other arrangement which these scientific gentlemen may devise. When an aviary has been established in the district of one Representative, other Representatives will want aviaries established in their districts. We shall be unable to hold this expenditure in check when we get a lot of these scientific gentlemen, bird propagators, employed in this work throughout the length and breadth of the land, because each one of these gentlemen will have his friend or friends in the various districts."

Just how indiscriminate Mr. Cannon is in the use of his adjustable, reversible, universally obstructive, guaranteed-to-land-on-any-bill arguments may be judged from the fact that he had the almost inconceivable audacity to use them against the great Reclamation bill of 1902. They made him look on that occasion like a man impelling dried peas as engines of destruction against the hide of an elephant. The incongruity was pitiful.

The Reclamation bill was one of the few fundamentally important bills of the last quarter-century. Its consequences will be incalculable. It began the creation of what will amount to a new empire in the arid districts of the Rocky Mountains.

But Mr. Cannon treated the creation of a new western empire in the same petty spirit in which he had treated the creation of aviaries.

"This bill," he said, "is a mere opening wedge. If it were passed, Congress would be petitioned after a while to make grants of money, not only from the proceeds of the sales of public lands, but from the

Treasury itself. I am fearful," he remarked, "that they will come for a direct grant from the Treasury." This fearsome thought put him among the fifty-five lonesome congressmen who opposed the Reclamation bill. And it lost him forever all credit for the legislative policy which will add ten million sturdy farmers to the population of the United States without costing the national government a cent of real money.

They slander Mr. Cannon, however, who say that he is against new propositions because he is the tool of organized wealth. This puts the cart before the horse. Organized wealth finds Mr. Cannon acceptable because he is instinctively against all new propositions.

The fact that his obstructiveness is purely personal and temperamental is shown by the unremitting vigilance with which he opposes even those few occasional legislative innovations which are supported by the enlightened business interests of America.

As an illustration, the bill for the establishment of national reserved forests in the Appalachian and White Mountains will be sufficient.

The National Manufacturers' Association, the American Cotton Manufacturers' Association, the National Lumber Dealers' Association, the National Lumber Manufacturers' Association, the Carriage Builders' National Association, the National Slack Cooperage Association, the National Association of Box Manufacturers, and positively scores of other associations of an equally notorious degree of esthetic reform enthusiasm supported the bill.

A billion dollars of invested money was represented by the delegation which appeared before the Agricultural Committee this year in favor of the bill.

But "Uncle Joe" was against the bill just the same.

Yet if there ever was a cold, practical, bread-and-butter proposition, this is it.

It is not always so easy, however, to nail Mr. Cannon down to his opinions. When asked to express himself on a public question he frequently finds that his mind is a complete blank except for a very vivid recollection of a former acquaintance of his named "Eph."

"Eph" was an old [Negro] who used to live in Mr. Cannon's home town in Indiana when Mr. Cannon was a little boy. One day "Eph" and "Joe" went off together to see a menagerie that was visiting a neighboring village. They arrived finally in front of a cage in which there was a very black but very manlike ape.

"How is yo'?" said "Eph."

The ape said nothing.

"How is yo'?" repeated "Eph."

Still the ape said nothing.

"Dat's right, ol' man," shouted "Eph," as the ape's wisdom burst in upon him, "yo' jest keep yo' mouf shet. If yo' says a word dey'll put a hoe in yo' hand an' set yo' to raisin' co'n."

This affecting picture of the dangers of loquacity impressed Mr. Cannon deeply. He has never since allowed himself to say anything that would make the public set him to work in an agitation for a new idea. The first stage in his treatment of a new idea is silence. Not only has he never originated a new idea, but he has never even discussed one at its start.

The second stage is discussion without bias. A beautiful specimen from this status of his mental progress in any subject can be dug up from his Guilford College speech of last year. He was discussing woman suffrage. This is what he said:

"Why shouldn't our mothers, wives, and sisters vote? That is a question you hear. You will settle it down here in North Carolina just as we will up in Illinois."

Somewhat tentative! Perhaps even noncommittal!

The third stage is opposition. Many illustrations of this have been furnished, and many are still to come.

The fourth stage is reconciliation. It will be remembered that Mr. Cannon opposed the big appropriation for the Congressional Library. Six years afterward, in the Fiftieth Congress, he was advocating thoroughgoing liberality on behalf of the Congressional Library, and he disarmingly defended himself against the charge of inconsistency by remarking: "I guess I ought to have known more about it, but I didn't."

The fifth and last stage is enthusiasm. On the subject of insular possessions, for instance, his inevitable early dubiousness has now been warmed to the point of exclaiming, as he did last year at the University Club in Washington:

"Whether or not we liked their acquisition, now that we have those islands we will make all the appropriations necessary for them, and smile and——"

(At this point he assaulted his right palm with his left fist.)

"—say: 'By God! We like it!'"

. . . In the last congressional election Mr. Cannon mentioned the Pure Food bill and the Meat Inspection bill as magnificent legislative achievements to be enthusiastically credited to his Speakership. If he could swallow and assimilate those two obnoxious doses within six months after they were administered to him, there is nothing of which his political digestion is incapable.

Everybody remembers the kind of treatment the Meat Inspection and Pure Food bills had in the House in 1906 during the first session of the Fifty-ninth Congress. They were passed only at the point of the pen and the Big Stick. The press and the President, and not Mr. Cannon, were responsible for the success of those bills.

Mr. Cannon's habitual obstructiveness was somewhat veiled by the silence of the Speaker's chair, but it continued unabated, and even invigorated by its partial concealment. It would be difficult to find a newspaper correspondent, on the ground all the time and following legislative developments with a trained eye, who does not emphatically place the Speaker among the elements that had to be overcome before either bill could be enacted into law.

How well Mr. Cannon knows that he was really unfavorable to the Meat Inspection bill was let slip when he visited the last session of the Illinois State Legislature in order to lobby against the Illinois Direct Primary law. He urged the legislators to defy the Chicago newspapers. He had defied them, he said, when the Meat Inspection bill was up in Congress. And look! He was back again in Congress all right.

The fact is that "Uncle Joe" is dead set against all these latter-day extensions of Federal authority. He has said so repeatedly, and he showed it conclusively in his treatment of meat inspection and pure food.

At a public meeting in Danville, in the congressional campaign of 1906, he claimed personal credit for the Employers' Liability law which had passed Congress at its previous session, and unguardedly remarked:

"Had the Speaker been opposed, or even indifferent, to that bill it would have remained on the calendar with the thousands of other bills which failed for want of time to consider them."

Pure food owes nothing to Mr. Cannon, meat inspection owes nothing to him, except tardy and reluctant acquiescence in the inevitable. If he were a man like Foraker of Ohio he would now be publicly lamenting our national folly in allowing such laws to get written into the statute books. But, being himself, he stood up before his nominating convention in his district in 1906 and proudly said:

"The Railroad Rate law, the Free Alcohol law, the Consular Reform law, the Employers' Liability law, the Pure Food law, and the Meat Inspection law, all enacted at one session of Congress, make a record of legislation which has not been paralleled in many years."

The one vein of sentiment in Mr. Cannon's public career is his devotion to the Republican Party. As the Republican Party thinks, so thinks he. His absolute loyalty to it, no matter where it may lead him, may seem strange to younger men; but he is among those older men who can remember the year 1864, when the re-election of Abraham Lincoln seemed doubtful, and when the success of the Republican Party was the perpetuation of the Republic.

The Republican Party of 1908 is the same thing to "Uncle Joe" as the Republican Party of 1864. It was baptized into grace once for all by a baptism of fire and it remains today the only saved and regenerated party in the country. No matter what has to be done, let the Republican Party do it. If we have to have socialism, let socialism be introduced by the Republican Party. "Uncle Joe" would make quite a considerable preliminary fuss about socialism, but he wouldn't let the Republican Party go permanently out of office through resisting it too long.

In spite, however, of the coincidence between his convictions and those of his party, he can not, of course, help impressing his own character to a noticeable degree on the work done by the House of Representatives. Under his guidance the House is becoming the conservative, and the Senate, by comparison, the progressive branch of Congress. . . .

In Joseph G. Cannon of Illinois the United States now possesses the most stationary political object ever exhibited within its boundaries. Not reactionary. That implies movement. Just stationary, fixed, embedded, like a rock in a glacier. The Republican Party, like the glacier itself, slow, remorseless, irresistible, moves crunchingly onward, and carries Mr. Cannon with it. But it is not his motion. It is the glacier's. He remains personally motionless at the same relative point on the glacier's broad bosom.

The Republican Party has carried Mr. Cannon down to us intact from the period of the seventies, the period when he first touched national politics at Washington, the period when the national government first began to be submerged by private interests.

It was the dawn of a distinct era in American history. The stretch of years from the accession of Grant to the accession of Roosevelt is now acquiring, in retrospect, a definite, if not glorious, character as the era of the complete predominance of private over public interests in the United States.

It was an era in which, for the first time since independence, private men became more important than public men, and the Pennsylvania Railroad Company became more important than the State of Pennsylvania.

Mr. Cannon typified that era even in his private relations with his brother "Bill." "Bill" got to be a bigger man in Danville than "Joe." "Bill" was business. "Joe" was only politics.

But "Joe's" politics, of course, helped "Bill's" business just as politics everywhere was helping business, and being despised for it.

In the late nineties, the Illinois State Legislature passed a law designed to allow Mr. Yerkes of Chicago to get a street railway franchise for a longer term than twenty years. Twenty years had previously been the longest term possible. This law, known as the Allen Law, in memory of its chief advocate, was blown out of the statute books by a storm of popular anger before Mr. Yerkes could profit by it. But "Bill" Cannon was more strongly intrenched in Danville than Mr. Yerkes was in Chicago. He got an extension ordinance through the Danville City Council for his street railway before the Allen Law was repealed. It was the most scandalously venal law ever passed by an Illinois State Legislature. The Cannons were the only street-car owners who profited by it. Naturally, after all, "Charley" Allen, who introduced the bill and gave his name to it, was from the Cannon district. He was part of the Danville Republican machine.

Incidents like this do not bother Mr. Cannon. They do not stir him to a storm of anger. All that "Charley" Allen did was to make it possible to transfer public interests to private interests for a longer term than formerly. And that falls in line with Mr. Cannon's own conception of the general welfare, even when his own pocketbook is not concerned. He would reduce public enterprise to a minimum. He would swell private enterprise to a maximum.

"Sir," he said in the Forty-fifth Congress, "the function of the Federal government is to afford protection to life, liberty, and property. When that is done, then let every tub stand on its own bottom, let every citizen 'root hog or die.'"

And let him root into the public domain if he wants to. The more we give of the public domain to private enterprise, the better it will be, in the long run, for the country.

This is the reason why Mr. Cannon can appoint a man like Mondell of Wyoming to the chairmanship of the House Committee on Public Lands, a man who hates the public development of public lands, a man who yearns for their private exploitation, a man who is utterly out of sympathy with public national forests, a man who this very year has introduced bills for transferring the invaluable water-power of the streams on the public lands of the United States to private corporations on financial terms purely nominal and with no time limits at all, thus creating monopolies compared with which our present municipal monopolies would be Lilliputian.

If Mr. Cannon would write an autobiography, or if he would consent to having his conversation taken down, it would furnish a complete picture of the business era in the history of the American Republic from the time when public life died with the settlement of the slavery question to the time when it revived with the approaching settlement of the question of monopoly.

No reporter could ever listen to a more interesting story from more interesting lips. But those lips will never be opened for that purpose. They are too clearly a consistent part of a face which, while the most suggestive in America, is also the most secretive.

No face makes you want to know more. No face tells you less.

The short, stiff hair that ensemicircles its lower half gives it an appearance of combativeness, but equally an appearance of concealment. That uplifted, defiant beard seems to smile at interrogation. So does the long, cruel nose. So does the florid complexion which mendaciously gives the lie to long nights of eating, smoking, drinking, card-playing, and speech-making, and remains as florid as ever.

And the eyes! They are the most knowing eyes in any human head. But equally the most unspeaking. No reporter has ever got from them an even momentary flicker of self-revelation. They might as well have been forged at Pittsburgh out of real steel.

But, while they reveal nothing, they are, after all, the most vulnerable points in Mr. Cannon's countenance. The rest of it is as rugged as a medieval, rockbuilt fortress. The eyes are tender. More than tender. Sad. Even the word "sad" isn't enough. If the truth must be spoken, they are the most curiously and hauntingly pathetic eyes that any reporter ever interviewed. They would furnish an artist with his inspiration for a perfect portrait of disillusioned, inarticulate sorrow.

Why are they like that? They gaze at the world like two women from the deep recesses of fortress windows. Or, better, since there is nothing feminine about them, like two wounded soldiers, sick unto death.

Were they like that before his wife died? His steady poker-playing, which began after his wife's death, in an effort to forget her, might account, by itself, for that repelling, baffling look. So tragedy merges into comedy, and nobody will ever know, in Mr. Cannon's case, any more than in the case of the obscurest private citizen in America, where one ends and the other begins.

All that the reporter can see is the "Joe" Cannon who walks up and down the aisle of a campaign car singing camp-meeting hymns at the top of his voice, who stops to tell an indescribably filthy story, and who then ends up by exclaiming, with apparent deep reverence, as he did at Danville in a campaign speech in 1906:

"God bless the people of Danville; God bless the people of Illinois; God bless the 80,000,000 people who constitute the Republic."

That is one side of his public character—an intimate intermingling of religiosity and vulgarity. When he addressed the Illinois Republican State Committee in Chicago in 1906 he gave three minutes to acknowledging, perfunctorily, the value of the reforms of the last decade, and then thirty minutes to getting even with the reformers.

And he got fully even with them in just one simile. Most of them, he said, were like a discontented donkey he once knew. It was impossible to say whether they were braying because they were kicking or kicking because they were braying.

The more that remark is considered, the funnier it grows. But when the laugh of it has died away, the pathetic thought remains that a humorous derogatory simile is the greatest encouragement Mr. Cannon has given to the reforms of the last decade or of any other decade since he entered public life.

Collier's
May 30, 1908

MARK SULLIVAN

Comment About Congress

Books for an Old Man

W E HAVE ASSUMED a task which we conceive to be not only a
private kindness, but also not without dignity as a public service—the pointing out of those quiet pleasures which would make—
we use the potential mood with care—which would make a serene
old age in a substantial home on the outskirts of Danville, Illinois,*
preferable to the tumult and hurly-burly which are inevitable in an
assemblage of 391 somewhat boisterous men in a single room on Pennsylvania Avenue, Washington, District of Columbia. President Eliot
of Harvard University is at the present time engaged in compiling a
set which he aptly calls "five feet of books," a compilation of those
hundred volumes which, among all printed books, are of most worth.
The idea is full of subtle appeal. We wish Dr. Eliot would now address
himself to a more limited task. We would like to have from him a
list of, say, fifty books best adapted to a man of seventy-four who has
passed his years in arduous political life, but now sees an opportunity
for escape to quiet retirement and indulgence in those pleasures of
taste to which he has long denied himself. We should like a list which
would appeal powerfully to such a man, which would cause him to
recall long-forgotten aspirations for the charm of cultivation and learning—a list, the contemplation of which would help such a man to
make decision between the glamour and strife of politics on the one
hand, and, on the other, the fender and the book—a list so alluring
that it would brace him to resist the demand of the public that he
continue to serve him. As a start toward such a list, we suggest these
(the titles of acceptable additions to the list will be welcomed):

* Home of Joe Cannon.

Cicero: *De Senectute* (in the original)

Emerson: *The Over-Soul*

Wordsworth: *The Evening Walk*

These books and slippered immunity from the exactions of public life, long days of quiet in Danville, Illinois—these would appeal to us; we wish they would appeal to him.

Collier's
May 8, 1909

Again, 304 Days

In that long series of Congressional primaries next summer, which will stretch from the second Tuesday in April until the following November, the chief issue will be Cannon. It is inconceivable that, with the eyes of the country focused on this one issue, he should win. He would have been beaten last year but for the popularity of Taft at the head of the ticket. Every Republican Congressman that comes up for re-election must bear the burden of Cannon. Because of Cannon, district after district will be lost by the Republicans to the Democrats. They say that Uncle Joe is a man of pride. He has told his intimates that, even after he was elected Speaker in March, if his power of appointing the committees had been taken from him, he would have resigned. Those who like him say, too, that loyalty to his friends in Congress and devotion to his party are chief among the qualities that have made him powerful in the Republican organization. All these traits, if he really does possess them, call him to an act of self-sacrifice.

Collier's
June 12, 1909

The Climate of Japan

Whose is the pen that can paint the delights of a trip to Japan and a long, long rest among the flowers and lovely gardens of those gentle islands? From San Francisco to Tokyo is twelve slow settings of the sun, twelve days of quiet peace upon the long Pacific swell, each carrying a harassed man so much farther away from tumult and unlovely contention. How tired old eyes would freshen and brighten with long contemplation of the restful ocean! And, then, to see the soft colors of those islands rising from the sea! Weeks and weeks and weeks of rest among the cherry blossoms and the roses. Long afternoons on an easy chair, Ruskin or Wordsworth at hand to read, and, when reading tires, a lovely vista of soft green hills for the quickening eye to rest upon. The air is shot through and through with perfume; the very pores drink it hungrily in, and a cracked and grizzled old skin would assume again the soft pliancy of youth. In quiet lakes behind the hills, the swans float double, swan and shadow. In such a scene and such an air, anger, resentment, strife—all unlovely moods and malevolent impulses would fall away from the spirit like unlovely patches of old fleece from a sheep in spring. How a man would renew his youth! How long forgotten aspirations for beauty, sweetness, and serenity would lift their trampled heads and swell again with life. How far away and how humorously unworthy of effort, how like a half-forgotten nightmare would seem that huge room in Washington filled with three hundred and ninety-one turbulent men. For a man of seventy-four, at the end of a long life filled with fighting and scheming, whose age now calls him to physical repose and spiritual contemplation, how infinitely more desirable the climate of Japan, the scenery and the air of those gentle islands, than the harsh winters and the unlovely surroundings of Washington, District of Columbia, or Danville, Illinois.

Collier's
June 12, 1909

283 Days

From the date of this paper, it is 283 days until any change can be made in the complexion of the present Lower House of Congress. The second Tuesday in April, 1910, is the first day when any American citizen will have the opportunity to cast his ballot for a Member of Congress pledged to vote against CANNON for Speaker.

Collier's
July 3, 1909

THE STATE

CHRISTOPHER P. CONNOLLY was already a lawyer when he first turned his attention to writing and muckraking.

He was born in New York and moved to Montana at the age of twenty-one. There he was admitted to the bar, and eventually became an assistant district attorney, and later prosecuting attorney, of Butte, Montana. He prosecuted the first man to be hanged by the State of Montana.

Connolly began gathering his material for "The Story of Montana" while he was studying law under the late Senator Thomas J. Walsh of Montana.

The series started in the August 1906 issue of *McClure's*. "This is the first of a series of articles," said the editor's introduction, "which will tell fully and accurately the story of the personal and political feuds, the legal and business wars which have kept the State of Montana in turmoil from the beginning of the rivalry between Marcus Daly and William A. Clark, in the early '90s, up to the compromise of the legal and commercial differences between the Amalgamated Copper Company and F. A. Heinze, in the early part of the present year [1906]."

Although the story was read with interest, there were objections: "The man writing the story," said an editorial in the Great Falls *Daily Leader*, "is merely giving his factional side of it. Those on the other side are treated unjustly, and the facts are distorted to make points for those he favors and against those of the opposite faction." [42]

Connolly told the story of the clashes between lawlessness and the forces of order; the political, commercial and personal rivalries between Marcus Daly and William A. Clark; the purchase of the Montana legislature of 1899; the attempt to bribe the Montana Supreme Court, as well as the struggle of Heinze and Amalgamated Copper to control the state.

The series created more of a sensation outside of the state than within, probably because there was hardly "anyone throughout the length and breadth of Montana who wasn't at least aware of the major facts about the battle." [43] It was an old story to them.

"Montana had already been demoralized by easy money, open gambling, quick and unearned fortunes, low moral standards in the proletariat, subsidized newspapers, complacent representatives of the law. It might howl about bribery and conspiracy but it was not shocked." [44]

However, because of the national attention that was focused on Montana by the series, some of the "better element" in the state was undoubtedly concerned with the bad name Montana was getting elsewhere.

The New York *Herald Tribune* in its obituary on Connolly said, "His stories, which assailed the mining interests, created a nation-wide sensation." [45]

C. P. CONNOLLY

The Story of Montana

THE PLACER-MINES of Montana disgorged immense wealth. The greatest deposit of placer-gold, next to that of Alder Gulch, was in Last Chance Gulch, where Helena, the capital of the state, now stands. It was named "Last Chance" because it was the forlorn hope of the prospectors who discovered it. It produced sixty millions of gold. Placer-mining had its brief but flourishing day. The miners worked the placers out before they attempted quartz-mining because the placer-gold lies close to the surface, is easily accessible, and may be secured without draining expenditures of quartz-mining. Placer-mining is now practically extinct in Montana. And with the passing of the placers the story of the "Old West" drew to a close in Montana. The game of chance, with all its picturesque conditions, its appeal to the imagination, and its incidental bloodshed and violence, was played out, and organized industries took its place.

When the miners had exhausted the placer-beds, they naturally sought for the hidden veins, and quartz-mining—the extraction of the metals from within the mountains by the sinking of shafts—became in time the foremost industry of the Rockies. It was this form of mining that created in a day the millionaires of the West. The mere location of the surface outcrop, or apex of the vein, gave into the possession of the discoverer all the wealth between its walls, down as far as Chinese territory, without regard to the vein's devious wanderings. The refugee from eastern civilization who today lounges around the Montana gambling saloon, spurned like an ownerless dog, may tomorrow discover in the hills a mine worth millions, and become a power in affairs around him. On the other hand there are prospectors all through the West who spend precious years drilling through rock which every geologist condemns as hopelessly barren. The dream of

104

the prospector is unfading. He haunts the old cabin in the hills, living on flour and bacon; and only the grave snuffs out hope. "Let me have thirty dollars," said a prospector one day to a lawyer friend. "I must have powder and grub. I'll pay you back within a week. I've struck it rich. I'm within three feet of a million dollars." Two weeks later the lawyer, who had accommodated his friend, met him on the street. The prospector seemed anxious to avoid his creditor. "The last time I saw you, you were within three feet of a million dollars," remarked the lawyer. "What's the news now?" "Oh, h——," said the prospector, "I'm not within a million feet of three dollars."

It was the discovery of copper, however, that gave to Montana the name of the Treasure State. Around the Butte hill, which during the past fifteen years has produced one-third of the copper supply of the world, has centered one of the most fascinating conflicts, and at the same time one of the most corrupt political and commercial conflicts, known to history. This struggle between mining kings of limitless wealth made hundreds of men, and ruined thousands; it perverted the moral sense of entire communities; it placed scores of prominent men within the shadow of prison walls; it destroyed promising political careers, and checked worthy names from the scroll of state and national fame. It sent nondescripts afloat upon the sea of national politics, corrupted the machinery of justice to the core, and placed the law-making power of the state upon the auction block.

Fifty millions of dollars annually has been the average output of this marvelous deposit of copper which lies within six hundred acres of mountain—the area of a good-sized farm. Nine hundred millions of dollars in twenty years is the official government estimate of its product. Another hundred millions has doubtless failed of accounting, or has been lost to computation in the general riot of production. This was the prize around which was waged during later years the most prolonged and bitter struggle ever witnessed in American politics.

The richness of the Butte hill surpasses the treasure of Monte Cristo, and the story of the crimes and passions which seethed about it makes a narrative almost as romantic as the adventures of Edmond Dantes. Miners have packed their blankets on foot into Butte and within a year have ridden out in Pullman coaches, independently rich, bound for the alluring cities of the Pacific coast. Had the government of the United States withheld this strip of territory, instead of parting with it to its discoverers for five dollars an acre, it could have paid off the national debt. Its total output would have carried on the wars of Napoleon.

Inseparably linked with the discovery and development of this treasure trove of the hills is the name of Marcus Daly, one of the most remarkable men who ever came to the West, and one of the two great protagonists whose personal feud is a large part of Montana's history. Through the treasure of the Butte hill, Daly was suddenly elevated from the ranks of the miners to the most powerful sway any individual ever achieved over a western American community. No multimillionaire ever came into closer contact with all the elements of a turbid and unblending population or exerted such influence upon them. Around him were his old companions of the mining levels of the Comstock in Nevada, whom he had known in his early struggles. Daly was big-hearted and generous, and he assisted these cronies by giving them temporary leases on portions of his property, allowing them to enter the ground and take out wealth enough to live in luxury for the remainder of their days. Oftentimes he did not know or care how much they took. These men in turn emulated the generosity of their patron, and Butte in time became known for many an odd tale of extravagance, and many a touching story of charity.

Miles Finlen made a colossal fortune out of a lease given him by Marcus Daly. A few years ago, just before Christmastime, an old lady opened a little newsstand on one of the street corners of Butte. The weather was cold, and the woman looked pinched and depressed. Finlen happened along, bought an evening paper, and, pulling out a roll of bills, asked the old lady how much it would take to get her a comfortable room and pay her expenses through the winter. The old woman had never seen Finlen before and, somewhat dumfounded, said she didn't know. "Well," said Finlen, "here is three hundred dollars." "God bless you," said the old woman; "that will take me to California, where my cough will be better, and where I can be near my daughter."

The story of copper is largely woven around the passions, hatreds and ambitions of two men who by nature were antagonists—Marcus Daly and William A. Clark. To understand the story, one must understand the men. No two men of rival prominence in the world's affairs ever differed more strikingly in their whole physical and mental make-up. They would have been enemies had they never met, for each represented all that the other most despised and distrusted.

Clark was an undersized man, wiry of figure and rather delicately built. He was fond of art, a judge of good pictures, and had been from his boyhood a student. He had studied law in early life, had perfected himself in French, and had a smattering of other languages. From the beginning of his prosperity he traveled extensively and spent much of his time in Paris, where he had a residence. Inordinately vain, he loved the flattery and adulation of women. He was a Beau Brummel in the midst of the awkward inelegance of the West. His taste and cultivation made him conspicuous among the miner-millionaires of Montana, and his intelligence would have won for him the respect of all his fellows had it not been offset by a cold and treacherous temperament and a certain narrowness and selfishness which marked all his dealings with men. With all his wealth—and after his acquisition of the United Verde mine at Jerome, Arizona, it came to exceed Daly's by far—he had the reputation of being extremely close-fisted in his business relations and in his occasional contributions to public funds. This was true of him at all times, except when his own political interests seemed in jeopardy, or when Daly goaded him to the point of revenge. Even in politics he made himself unpopular by the bluntness of his bribes and his subsequent coldness toward those who had served him loyally. Men who had made personal sacrifices for him in politics often found it difficult to obtain ordinary business favors from him. His contributions to political committees were small.

Yet, withal, Clark had staunch and tried friends in those early days—some who were attached to him personally, others who looked jealously upon the growing power of Daly.

Daly resorted to bribery of a different sort. Vast sums of money left his purse which he must have known would find their way into questionable channels. In the capital fight of 1894 between Helena and Anaconda, he spent over a million dollars. But if he ever bribed men in high places, the fact never became public property, nor were such things even whispered, much less openly alluded to in the public press. Daly's popularity among the miners and businessmen of those sections of the state in which his vast interests lay, obviated the necessity of expending large sums of money to secure their political support.

Daly made a point of coming continually into personal contact with his miners. They might often be heard in eulogy of him. Clark directed his affairs largely from his office. He affected art and costly paintings. Daly found his recreation at his Bitter Root Ranch among his famous thoroughbreds. Clark sought political office. Daly was ambitious for the satisfying things that go with political power—outside of mere office-holding—the power to assist others politically, to win the gratitude of men for favors conferred, and to draw the good-will that goes out to the man who, though he has influence, has no ambition for office. . . .

"I know my shortcomings," said Daly. "In the Senate I would be out of my element. When the business magnates of the country cross the continent, they run their private cars into Anaconda to call on me. They respect me in my proper sphere. That is enough satisfaction for a man who started out in the world with as little capital as I had."

Daly was a man of medium height and stocky figure. A splendid, full-rounded head topped a well-knit body. His eye was marvelously clear, and his voice, in conversation, was low and mellow. His feet were small and his hands, despite the hardships of his early life, were delicate and shapely as a woman's. He had had no early advantages. He was born in Ireland and left that country when he was not yet fifteen. He sold newspapers in New York and later obtained employment as messenger in a mercantile or banking house in that city, where he saved enough money to take him by water to California. From there he drifted up to the Comstock in Nevada, and then went to Montana. He would have forced himself up through poverty and obscurity had he never discovered the Butte hill. No man was shrewder in his every-day intercourse with men. Few knew the real workings of his mind—he seemed to divine the mental processes of others. He did not belong to that race of poverty-stricken and superior men who, as Balzac said, can do everything for the fortunes of others but nothing for their own. . . .

Clark was reticent and exclusive—by nature rather than from policy. His manner had something of the dreamer. He lacked Daly's tremendous energy and personal magnetism. He lacked also his ready wit and the slashing force which accomplished big things on the stroke of the clock. But he was a man of quiet, earnest persistence and when forced to the wall, rarely gave up the struggle without showing fighting teeth and leaving a trail of havoc.

Clark had been a clerk for Robert W. Donnell, one of the early pioneers of Montana who accumulated a fortune as a merchant during the first gold excitements on the Rocky Mountains. Donnell opened a small banking house in Deer Lodge, Montana, and afterwards established the firm of Donnell, Lawson & Simpson, at 102 Broadway, New York, which failed in the Wall Street panic of 1884. When Robert W. Donnell was about to go to New York to establish his house there, he opened a branch house at Butte, taking into partnership W. A. Clark and another of his clerks, S. E. Larabee. Clark took charge of the Butte bank and acquired Donnell's interest after the failure of the New York house.

Donnell, Clark & Larabee had loaned, in the course of their banking business at Butte, some thirty thousand dollars to William L. Farlin, an intimate friend of Clark. Farlin had located several claims on the Butte hill, and one down below the town called the Trevonia. The Trevonia was promising. Farlin started to develop it and, in order to do so, borrowed the money from Donnell, Clark & Larabee at Butte.

When the loan came due, Farlin was unable to meet it, and in order to secure his friend Clark, placed all his mining property in Clark's hands with the understanding that Clark should work the properties to the best advantage, pay off the indebtedness, and restore the claims to Farlin. Instead of working the Trevonia, the most promising, Clark leisurely prospected the other claims—realizing nothing, of course—and at the expiration of his trusteeship claimed forfeit of everything Farlin owned. Larabee looked upon Clark's mineral holdings with distrust, and in a settlement between the two, took a band of valuable horses belonging to the firm in exchange for his half interest in the mines which had once belonged to Farlin. Clark thus became the sole owner of the interests which laid the foundation of his great fortune.

Marcus Daly went to Butte in 1876 as the representative of the Walker Brothers of Salt Lake City, large mining investors. He bought for Walker Brothers the Alice mine, afterwards one of the great silver mines of the state.

It was about 1880 that Daly became interested in the Anaconda mine, which lay lower down than the Alice, and near the foot of the Butte hill. He bought it for $30,000 from Michael A. Hickey, who, with his brother, Edward, and Charles X. Larabee, had located it on government ground. Hickey gave his discovery the name "Anaconda" because, when a soldier in the army of the Potomac, he had read one of Horace Greeley's editorials which said that McClellan was enveloping Lee's army "like a giant anaconda." The word lodged in Hickey's memory, and when he located his claim, he gave it the name which had quickened his fancy as a soldier. It has since become a name to conjure with in the copper world.

When Daly bought the Anaconda, it was, like the Alice, a silver property. George Hearst, the California mine-owner, father of William Randolph Hearst, was an early business associate of Daly's, and through Hearst, James B. Haggin and Lloyd Tevis became interested in the purchase of the Anaconda mine. This group of California capitalists was at the time negotiating for a now-forgotten mining property near Helena, seventy miles north of Butte. The experts sent by them from California reported favorably on the Helena property and unfavorably on the Anaconda. But Marcus Daly, though an unlettered miner, had the confidence of Hearst and Haggin, and his unfavorable report on the Helena property condemned it and led to their purchase, with Daly, of the Butte property.

When Daly discovered that the Anaconda was a copper mine, he believed that his theories of the Butte hill were verified. He was convinced it was one of the greatest copper deposits in the world. In mining, he was a genius. He had the intuition of a woman, the prescience of the seer. In his earlier career in Nevada he had studied rocks and soils, their forms and affinities, as men read books. He saw through the earth the dim signal-lights of the depths.

Nearly every mining engineer of note condemned the Butte hill, laughed at Daly, and called his theories absurd. Subsequently these authorities republished their textbooks to meet the new geological conditions which the unlettered miner had disclosed to the world.

The first move Daly made was to pull the pumps and close down the Anaconda. If this hill was the treasure house he foresaw, the race would be to the swift. Soon rumors were current that the Anaconda was a mare's nest and worthless. Daly's agents then bought up properties adjoining the mine for a song, and Daly and his friends became the owners of practically all that part of the Butte hill which they believed to be valuable. In the meantime, business in Butte was at a standstill.

When Daly had acquired the properties surrounding the Anaconda, he opened up the Butte hill. One must have a vivid imagination to picture to himself the growth of Butte from that time on during Marcus Daly's life. Fortunes were made and spent in a day. An army of men descended into the mines daily to strip them of their treasure; huge forests were despoiled of their timber to stull and shore up the excavations and protect the earth above—for these copper veins are often one hundred feet wide. Immense smokestacks began to vomit their clouds of smudge from scores of furnaces scattered over the hill; the moan and clank of huge pumps could be heard in the depths, forcing the water to the surface; the pound of hammers and the steady impact of drills sounded everywhere, while the earth trembled and bellowed with distant underground explosions. Great hollows, like cathedral naves, were scooped out, where the treasure had lain in the rock-ribbed earth. Horses and mules were blindfolded and lowered into the mines—where their hides, like the gray beards of the old miners, soon took on the greenish color of the copper which saturates everything below the surface. The Butte hill soon became a veritable underground city. . . .

The feud that shortened Daly's life and made of Clark's name a reproach, originated in Clark's inherent narrowness and in his jealousy of Daly. In politics both men were Democrats.

Had Clark been a bigger, broader, or manlier character, he would never have been compelled to resort to bribery to realize his political ambitions.

Probably the first event of any importance in this feud occurred in the late '70s. Daly was managing the Alice mine for the Walker Brothers of Salt Lake City. Clark, without request and without excuse, save the fact that Walker Brothers were neighboring bankers, wrote them a letter, saying that Daly's management of the Alice was extravagant and unbusinesslike. The Walker Brothers promptly remailed the letter to Daly.

After Daly had secured the cooperation of Haggin, Hearst and Tevis for the development of the Anaconda, Clark opened a correspondence with James B. Haggin, in which he used every stratagem to discredit Daly. The only result was that Haggin loosened his purse-strings the more, and Daly was finally given *carte blanche*.

There is no question that Clark made it a practice to refer to Daly slightingly, ridiculing his uncouthness and explaining his discovery of the Butte hill as an accident. These remarks were foolishly carried to Daly.

The first opportunity Daly had to take his revenge on Clark came in the congressional election of 1888. Montana was then a territory, not being admitted to the Union until a year later. The congressional representative from Montana was then but a territorial delegate, with a voice, but without vote in the House of Representatives. Clark had two overweening ambitions in life—to be considered one of the wealthiest men in the world, and to occupy a position of political prominence. His wealth made the nominating conventions of his party eager to encourage his candidacy for any office.

Clark was nominated for delegate in Congress in 1888 by the territorial Democratic convention. In order to insure Daly's support, a meeting of prominent Democrats was held during the campaign at the Democratic headquarters in Helena, and a promise was exacted from Daly that he would support Clark at the polls. Daly was certain to control the vote of three of the most populous counties in the Territory, and his support seemed all that was needed to assure Clark's success.

Thomas H. Carter, since twice elected United States Senator, was nominated by the Republicans as the candidate against Clark. He was a young lawyer, thirty-four years old, shrewd, able and diplomatic. Clark, with his wealth and Daly's support, would have been, ordinarily, invincible in any campaign; and with an unbroken series of Democratic victories behind him, his defeat was not considered for a moment. Carter, however, was elected by a five-thousand majority. Butte, Clark's home—even his own ward—repudiated him. Daly's strongholds gave Carter immense majorities, although Carter was practically a stranger to Daly. Clark suffered for the first time the sting of humiliation which he was to feel so often during his contests with Daly.

Witnesses of the struggle between these two antagonists saw a partial truce for the next few years. A year after Clark's defeat, Montana was admitted to the Union. Clark had been president of the convention which promulgated Montana's constitution. Far abler men took part in its deliberations, but Clark was a good presiding officer, and came out of the discussions of that body with honor and credit. After his defeat for Congress he had started out, nothing daunted, to master the rudiments of politics. He had learned the wisdom of "staying with" the things of his brain, the creations of his ambition. His persistence has always been one of his most effective weapons.

When the state was admitted, there was hatched the first of that series of political plagues, which, as a result of the relentless feud of these two men, for so long cursed Montana. The only Democrat elected on the state ticket was Joseph K. Toole, the candidate for governor. The legislature was in doubt. There were scenes of disorder and rumblings of a conflict, which was averted by the contending forces' agreeing to disagree. Two distinct legislative bodies were held without any attempt at the legislation which the new state so sadly needed after its thirty years of territorial dependence. The Democratic legislative branch sent to the United States Senate W. A. Clark and Martin Maginnis—the latter one of the able men of the state, and territorial delegate of Montana in Congress for twelve years. The Republican branch sent Col. Wilbur F. Sanders and Thomas C. Power. The seating of Sanders and Power was a foregone conclusion, and this was doubtless known to Daly, for he made no attempt to thwart Clark's ambition for this empty honor.

Sanders and Power drew lots and the short term of four years fell to the former. In 1893 Sanders' term expired, and all eyes were upon the legislature, which was politically doubtful. Neither Republicans nor Democrats had an absolute majority. The Populists, the disciples of the new political creed which was beginning to shake the West, held the balance of power, and with these Daly dickered and organized a Democratic-Populist majority.

For sixty days the legislature was in the throes of the Clark and Daly feud. Helena, the capital, was then, as it always had been, for Clark. Daly had no business interests in the town, was not well known personally, and many people there accused him of having dealt treacherously with Clark in the campaign of 1888.

Rumors of legislative corruption were rife. William Wirt Dixon was the principal Daly candidate opposed to Clark. Clark pursued, in this legislative campaign, those revolting tactics which provoked such bitter feeling against him. Men whose lives had been clean were corrupted not only by the use of money, but in worse ways. Questionable resorts were chartered and debaucheries ensued which shocked not only the high-minded but the indifferently scrupulous.

It was rumored that in several cases where Clark bought up legislators, the Daly forces paid a like amount to buy back their allegiance, or to get them to leave the state. Several Republicans voted for Clark during the session. On Saturday, February 11, 1893, five Republicans voted for him on joint ballot. A Republican caucus was then hastily called, and at this caucus one or two Republican deserters, who attempted to make rather lame explanations of their votes for Clark, were handled pretty roughly. All agreed that there should be no more Republican votes cast for Clark. The promise was kept the following legislative day, when Clark's total dropped to twenty-four. The Clark forces insisted that these votes were bound to them beyond the possibility of release, and that they were simply scattering them temporarily, awaiting the signal for concerted action. This proved true.

C. L. Coder, one of the Republican members who had voted for Clark, had told United States Senator W. F. Sanders, in the early days of the legislative session, that he had been offered a bribe by the Clark forces. Sanders met Coder in the lobby of the Helena Hotel after his vote had been cast for Clark. "I tell you, Coder," said Sanders, "that I have done my part with other men in ridding this country of road-agents and robbers. We accomplished that when we had to deal with sterner men than you are; and I tell you that this state will not hold the Republican who, in the presence of stalking bribery, votes for a Democrat."

Col. D. J. Tallant, of Cascade County, on Monday, February 20, made a speech in the joint assembly in which he said: "The very air surrounding this city seems to be foul and corrupt. For several weeks the vile odor of political corruption has tainted the atmosphere, and yet not a word has been said on the floor of this joint assembly on the subject."

On Wednesday, February 22, Coder, the representative from Fergus County whom Senator Sanders had publicly pilloried and branded as a bribe-taker, left Helena. He announced that his child was dying, but a telegram received the same day from a prominent citizen of Lewistown, near Coder's home, contradicted this statement, saying there was absolutely no sickness whatever in the Coder family.

As the session drew to a close, the excitement in the capital city was intense. There were no scenes like the thrilling ones of later years, when the war between these two millionaires reached its climax, and when Clark played with men's honor as with poker chips, and had his agents in the field buying up the public representatives like so many cattle on the hoof, driven into the market place, weighed, tested, marked and paid for. There were rumors of bribery, but no open admissions and defense of it as in later campaigns. The public realized that there was an irreconcilable conflict between these two powerful mining magnates from Butte, and that while Clark seemed to have the larger following in the state, Daly's home forces were more loyal, and Daly was by far the better general. Appeals from prominent Democrats throughout the country were sent to Clark and Daly, urging them to compromise their differences, and not to let slip the opportunity to elect a Democrat to the United States Senate. In response to these telegrams the followers of Judge W. W. Dixon, representing the Daly forces, offered to vote for any Democrat but W. A. Clark. Clark might have dictated the election of a United States Senator, but his temperament is sanguine, and his contests have always narrowed down to W. A. Clark or no one. This position was also the one assumed by his constituents, who felt that Clark's withdrawal would be a victory for Daly.

The last day of the session came. The legislature adjourned to the Auditorium in the heart of the city. The aisles and galleries were crowded. Three thousand people were present. Word had gone out from the Clark camp that everything was in readiness for the final

coup; that the earlier disappointments of the session—when the announcement had been made that Clark would be elected on certain
ballots—only made it the more certain that now Clark had secured a
final strangle-hold on his enemy. The people turned out in response
to these assurances, and Helena awaited the signal to celebrate Clark's
triumph. . . .

Clark sat in the front row of seats, just under the presiding officer,
ready with the manuscript of his speech of acceptance, so certain was
he of election. But he had not yet wholly mastered the game. He
bought only what he thought he needed, making no provision against
contingencies.

S. W. Graves, Republican, of Silver Bow County, said it was the
last day on which a senator could be elected. He thought it better for
the interests of Montana that a Democrat should be chosen in order
that he might be in accord with the administration at Washington.
"Traitor, traitor!" yelled Tallant, of Cascade. Beecher, another member, lifted his heavy cane to strike Tallant on the head. Representative Walkup caught the cane and wrenched it from Beecher's hand.

The result of the final ballot found Clark three votes short of the
number necessary to a choice.

Then came the climax of the session. E. D. Matts, state senator
from Missoula County, who sat beside Clark, rose and with vehement
eloquence, referred to what he called Clark's notorious bribery. In
tones that could be heard throughout the great hall, he denounced
his methods, while Clark sat, bowed and broken at his failure and
apparently unconscious of the words of the speaker or of the scene
about him. "I want to see no man representing this state in the
Senate," shouted Matts, pointing his finger at Clark, "who obtains
votes by force or fraud. I want to see a man elected to the United
States Senate who is not tainted by fraud, bribery or corruption." At
the end of his speech, Matts moved the final adjournment of the joint
session, the vote was carried, and Montana was without representation
in the United States Senate for four years.

The time soon came when not only all Democrats but all Republicans in the state were either Clark or Daly men, willing to sink
or swim with the fortunes of one or the other, and subordinating all
party prejudices to their allegiance to the war slogans of these two
mercenary chiefs.

Many incidents occurred in connection with this session which
illustrated Clark's and Daly's dissimilar methods of handling men.
A certain member of the legislature, from Jefferson County, voted

consistently, and without compensation, for his friend W. A. Clark. This member was a timber contractor. Shortly after the adjournment of the legislature, attachments aggregating $15,000 were threatened against him. He had large quantities of timber at a place called Bernice, and if this were attached and sold at a sacrifice, he would lose heavily. The timber was more than ample security for the amount of his debts. This legislator sought W. A. Clark at his Butte office, laid his exigency before him, and asked for a loan of $15,000, agreeing to pledge his timber as security. Clark curtly informed him that that kind of financiering was not in his line. The anxious timber contractor took train for Anaconda, twenty-eight miles away. He saw Daly, whom he had fought bitterly during the legislature, explained his predicament, and was promptly given, without security, $15,000.

The next struggle between Clark and Daly took place in the summer and fall of the following year, 1894. Helena had been, for a generation, the capital of the territory. The Constitutional Convention that sat in 1889 provided that the question of the permanent location of the seat of government should be submitted to the qualified electors of the state at the general election in 1892. No city received a majority of votes in 1892, but Helena, and Anaconda—Daly's home city, where his smelters were located—became rivals in 1894 for the permanent seat of government. . . .

The straggling mining-camp which became the city of Helena had its early growth high up in "Last Chance" gulch, and the town has since spread and widened over the clinging foothills. The early gold-seekers paused here to make one last stand against fate before quitting the scenes which had endeared to them the golden beauties of the West. Tired with wandering over the trackless earth in quest of gold, these Argonauts settled down to the building of permanent homes.

Culture and refinement soon developed. Helena, in time, had its mining kings, its cattle kings, its wealthy sheep men—liberal, democratic, and whole-souled—until it claimed to be the wealthiest community of its size on the globe. From the driving of the golden spike which completed the Northern Pacific Railroad in 1883, until 1890, Helena experienced that inflated growth common to western towns. Silver then began to decline, and with it the city that hitherto had manifested such impetuous energy. Butte became the commercial and financial center of the state, and left to Helena only its tradition of social supremacy and the capital which it was struggling to retain.

Marcus Daly, thrilled with the sense of his power, reached out for the possession of the capital, the last remnant of Helena's vanished splendors. From that time forth, his name was anathematized there. But for Clark, Daly's capital contest would have proved disastrous to the city. Clark became Helena's hero and to his fortunes her loyalty was pledged.

Anaconda was the home of the great Anaconda Copper Mining Company, with all its allied interests and concerns, its powerful influence and irresistible sway. Many people feared the clutch of this tremendous power upon the hearthstone of the state. Into the capital contest were dragged all the fierce hatreds of the Clark-Daly fight which had already begun to cast its sinister shadow over all public questions. The Helena Capital Committee, realizing the personal popularity of Marcus Daly, ignored him and attacked James B. Haggin, Daly's principal business partner, who was a man of the quiet, skullcap order, about whom little was known, except that he was rich, powerful and taciturn, and therefore easily a mark for public execration. Haggin was accredited with a controlling interest in the Homestake mining enterprises of the Black Hills. The Helena committee gathered into effective campaign material every act of that corporation hostile to the public good, and eloquently pictured these oppressions as the future heritage of Montana in the event of corporate influences capping the dome of its state house.

All through the summer of 1894 and the early stages of this campaign, Clark remained quiescent. Notwithstanding the fact that in the senatorial campaign of the year before, ex-Governor Samuel T. Hauser, a prominent Democratic candidate for senatorial honors, had withdrawn in Clark's favor under a promise from Clark to support Helena, Clark put in a large part of the summer of 1894 in the endeavor to secure Daly's future political support in exchange for his cooperation with Daly in the capital fight. Unsuccessful in this, a month before the election he threw overboard every pound of ballast and set his sails to the Helena breeze. He admitted before the Committee on Privileges and Elections of the United States Senate that he had spent $100,000 in the capital fight. John R. Toole, Marcus Daly's chief lieutenant in the capital fight, testified before the Helena grand jury, which pretended to investigate Clark's bribery scandals, to an expenditure in behalf of the Anaconda capital committee of $500,000; but Governor Hauser, in his testimony before the senatorial committee in Washington, gave the figures as over a million. Taking into consideration the vast sums of money which Daly afterwards gave away by farming out leases to his supporters, as rewards for their loyalty in this contest, it cost him, in round numbers, over $2,500,000, and Clark must have spent not less than $400,000. The vote of the state did not exceed 50,000 in that election. The cost of each vote would be, therefore, approximately $38.

In the early afternoon of the election day, an enthusiastic votary of Anaconda went down Main Street in Helena shouting, "Hurrah for Anaconda!" He was mobbed and then thrown into jail. Within an hour after his arrest, Daly chartered a special train in Butte and sent two of his ablest legal representatives, and some personal friends to Helena, to sue out a writ of habeas corpus in behalf of this stranger about whom he knew nothing except his enthusiasm. The man was released. Daly afterwards gave this election day furioso a lease on some Butte copper property which netted him $60,000; and then stopped his income only because he was squandering it in dissipation.

Helena won the capital fight by something like a 1,400 majority. Clark's money was a powerful ally, but the editorials of his Butte paper, *The Miner*, did even more. John M. Quinn, an editorial writer of dash and power, now a New York state senator from the sixteenth district, was then editor of *The Miner*. Quinn's editorials were striking in their clarion eloquence. There were thousands of voters who were not venal and who were not unfriendly to Daly, who yet hesitated to place the keeping of the great seal of the state in the possession of any corporation, and these the arguments of Clark's newspaper reached and converted. These men came out in the open and fought, not for Clark nor against Daly, but for the integrity of the state itself—young, full of promise, and dear to them as the home of brief but cherished traditions.

When the fight was won, Helena sent for Clark and Quinn and gave them the most royal ovation ever seen in the West. They unharnessed the horses from the carriage and hauled their heroes through the streets amid a carnival of fireworks that illuminated the mountain passes ten miles away. They placed the mock body of Daly, clad in funeral garments, in an improvised catafalque and jeered it through the streets—an insult Daly never forgot.

McClure's Magazine
September 1906

THE CITY

"You may have been an editor," said S. S. McClure to Lincoln Steffens. "You may be an editor. But you don't know how to edit a magazine. You must learn to."

Steffens was then managing editor on the *McClure's* staff, where he had come from his job as city editor of the *Commercial Advertiser*.

"How can I learn?" asked Steffens.

"Not here. You can't learn to edit a magazine here in this office," answered McClure.

"Where then can I learn? Where shall I go to learn to be an editor?"

"Anywhere else," responded McClure. "Get out of here, travel, go— somewhere. Go out in the advertising department. Ask them where they have transportation credit. Buy a railroad ticket, get on a train, and there, where it lands you, there you will learn to edit a magazine." [46]

McClure's magazine had a bill against the Lackawanna Railroad for advertising. Steffens got a ticket for Chicago. And there his saga of muckraking starts.

In his new assignment with *McClure's*, Steffens talked with writers, editors and leading citizens of Chicago to learn what they were interested in, and to get some of them to write for his magazine.

One of the men he talked with suggested that he go to St. Paul and interview Weyerhauser, the lumber baron.

Steffens went to St. Paul. Weyerhauser talked. He told how he obtained the lumber lands, how he used politics to get what he wanted, and how he justified his actions. But the lumber king had agreed to the conversation only if Steffens promised not to print any of it. The half-day interview was revealing, but Steffens had no story.

When he returned to Chicago, it was suggested that he go to St. Louis. "There's a man down in St. Louis; his name is Folk; he is raising the deuce of a row about bribery in the board of aldermen. We get the dust of it in the papers but no clear idea of just what it's all about." [47]

A day later Steffens was closeted with Joseph W. Folk in St. Louis. Folk told Steffens the story of his fight against the bribery that ruled St. Louis. "The local papers are backing me up now. . . . But they don't know yet what

I know," Folk told Steffens. "The ramifications of this thing, the direction the trails of evidence are taking, the character of the opposition I encounter— I'm afraid I'll soon be losing all local support." Since *McClure's* was published in New York, Folk felt that that magazine would not be "subject to the pulls and the threats of St. Louis." [48] Folk said he needed help, he needed publicity.

Steffens wrote *McClure's* that he had an article and was looking for the man to write it.

Folk then suggested Claude H. Wetmore, a St. Louis newspaperman. Wetmore agreed to do the article. But Wetmore was too close to the events and had left out some important facts. Steffens added to Wetmore's story some of what he himself had learned, and edited the article, inserting a few comparisons between the St. Louis situation and the Tweed machine in New York.

Wetmore insisted that Steffens sign the article with him so that Steffens could take the blame for his own insertions. Steffens agreed, and thus the first in a series of articles on "The Shame of the Cities" appeared.

His experience with the preparation of the initial article convinced Steffens that he must do future stories himself. From his conversation with Folk, he had evolved the premise "that bribery is not a mere felony, but a revolutionary process which was going on in all our cities and that, if I could trace it to its source, I might find the cause of political corruption and—the cure." [49]

What lay at the root of the corruption? Steffens gave one of his best answers to this question during a lecture in California. A clergyman asked the question of him. Steffens said: "Most people, you know, say it was Adam. But Adam, you remember, he said that it was Eve, the woman, she did it. And Eve said no, no, it wasn't she; it was the serpent. And that's where you clergy have stuck ever since. You blame that serpent, Satan. Now I come and I am trying to show you that it was, it is, the apple." [50]

After St. Louis, Steffens wrote about Minneapolis, Pittsburgh, Philadelphia, Chicago, New York. He turned his efforts to various states, where there too he found the same—civic corruption. His articles were so penetrating that there were times when they caused greater concern to a machine politician than did his opponent.

In 1904, Steffens' articles on the cities were published in a book titled *The Shame of the Cities*. It was—and is—a handbook on American city government.

Steffens, in his introduction to the book, said that the purpose of the articles as originally published in *McClure's* and in book form was "to sound for the civic pride of an apparently shameless citizenship." He did not blame politicians or businessmen or any one class: ". . . no one class is at fault," he wrote, "nor any one breed, nor any particular interest or group of interests. The misgovernment of the American people is misgovernment by the American people." [51] Behind every bribe taker, he found, is a bribe giver.

William Allen White, in reviewing the book, said: "Mr. Steffens . . .

has made an important step in the scientific study of government in America." [52]

Max Lerner, author and lecturer, contends that "if we valued our historical figures according to their usefulness in creating a richer and healthier American culture, men like . . . Lincoln Steffens . . . would be heroes to be celebrated in every school and college." [53]

Steffens did not offer remedies for the corruption he found. In the days of his muckraking, he felt that an interest in reform schemes would have kept him from the objectivity necessary to present the straight facts. He was concerned with ills, not with remedies.

But the results of his writing were felt. His article on St. Louis had a noticeable effect in encouraging Folk to pursue his municipal graft prosecutions in 1903. Arthur M. Schlesinger, Sr., Harvard University historian, notes that Folk was "incited by Steffens' articles" to carry on the prosecutions campaign "which raised him to the governorship of the state the following year." [54]

LINCOLN STEFFENS
(and CLAUDE H. WETMORE)

ex

Tweed Days in St. Louis

St. louis, the fourth city in size in the United States, is making two announcements to the world: one that it is the worst-governed city in the land; the other that it wishes all men to come there and see it. It isn't our worst-governed city; Philadelphia is that. But St. Louis is worth examining while we have it inside out.

There is a man at work there, one man, working all alone, but he is the Circuit (district or state) Attorney, and he is "doing his duty." That is what thousands of district attorneys and other public officials have promised to do and boasted of doing. This man has a literal sort of mind. He is a thin-lipped, firm-mouthed, dark little man, who never raises his voice, but goes ahead doing, with a smiling eye and a set jaw, the simple thing he said he would do. The politicians and reputable citizens who asked him to run urged him when he declined. When he said that if elected he would have to do his duty, they said, "Of course." So he ran, they supported him, and he was elected. Now some of these politicians are sentenced to the penitentiary, some are in Mexico. The Circuit Attorney, finding that his "duty" was to catch and convict criminals, and that the biggest criminals were some of these same politicians and leading citizens, went after them. It is magnificent, but the politicians declare it isn't politics.

The corruption of St. Louis came from the top. The best citizens—the merchants and big financiers—used to rule the town, and they ruled it well. They set out to outstrip Chicago. The commercial and industrial war between these two cities was at one time a picturesque and dramatic spectacle such as is witnessed only in our country. Businessmen were not mere merchants and the politicians were not mere grafters; the two kinds of citizens got together and wielded the power of banks, railroads, factories, the prestige of the city and the spirit of its citizens to gain business and population. And it was a close race. Chicago, having the start, always led, but St. Louis had pluck, intelligence, and tremendous energy. It pressed Chicago hard. It excelled in a sense of civic beauty and good government; and there are those who think yet it might have won. But a change occurred. Public spirit became private spirit, public enterprise became private greed.

Along about 1890, public franchises and privileges were sought, not only for legitimate profit and common convenience, but for loot. Taking but slight and always selfish interest in the public councils, the big men misused politics. The riffraff, catching the smell of corruption, rushed into the Municipal Assembly, drove out the remaining respectable men, and sold the city—its streets, its wharves, its markets, and all that it had—to the now greedy businessmen and bribers. In other words, when the leading men began to devour their own city, the herd rushed into the trough and fed also.

So gradually has this occurred that these same citizens hardly realize it. Go to St. Louis and you will find the habit of civic pride in them; they still boast. The visitor is told of the wealth of the residents, of the financial strength of the banks, and of the growing importance of the industries, yet he sees poorly paved, refuse-burdened streets, and dusty or mud-covered alleys; he passes a ramshackle firetrap crowded with the sick, and learns that it is the City Hospital; he enters the "Four Courts," and his nostrils are greeted by the odor of formaldehyde used as a disinfectant, and insect powder spread to destroy vermin; he calls at the new City Hall, and finds half the entrance boarded with pine planks to cover up the unfinished interior. Finally, he turns a tap in the hotel, to see liquid mud flow into wash basin or bathtub.

The St. Louis charter vests legislative power of great scope in a Municipal Assembly, which is composed of a Council and a House of Delegates. Here is a description of the latter by one of Mr. Folk's grand juries:

"We have had before us many of those who have been, and most of those who are now, members of the House of Delegates. We found a number of these utterly illiterate and lacking in ordinary intelligence, unable to give a better reason for favoring or opposing a measure than a desire to act with the majority. In some, no trace of mentality or morality could be found; in others, a low order of training appeared, united with base cunning, groveling instincts, and sordid desires. Unqualified to respond to the ordinary requirements of life, they are utterly incapable of comprehending the significance of an ordinance, and are incapacitated, both by nature and training, to be the makers of laws. The choosing of such men to be legislators makes a travesty of justice, sets a premium on incompetency, and deliberately poisons the very source of the law."

These creatures were well organized. They had a "combine"—a legislative institution—which the grand jury described as follows:

"Our investigation, covering more or less fully a period of ten years, shows that, with few exceptions, no ordinance has been passed wherein valuable privileges or franchises are granted until those interested have paid the legislators the money demanded for action in the particular case. Combines in both branches of the Municipal Assembly are formed by members sufficient in number to control legislation. To one member of this combine is delegated the authority to act for the combine, and to receive and to distribute to each member the money agreed upon as the price of his vote in support of, or opposition to, a pending measure. So long has this practice existed that such members have come to regard the receipt of money for action on pending measures as a legitimate perquisite of a legislator."

One legislator consulted a lawyer with the intention of suing a firm to recover an unpaid balance on a fee for the grant of a switchway. Such difficulties rarely occurred, however. In order to insure a regular and indisputable revenue, the combine of each house drew up a schedule of bribery prices for all possible sorts of grants, just such a list as a commercial traveler takes out on the road with him. There was a price for a grain elevator, a price for a short switch; side tracks were charged for by the linear foot, but at rates which varied according to the nature of the ground taken; a street improvement cost so much; wharf space was classified and precisely rated. As there was a scale for favorable legislation, so there was one for defeating bills. It made a difference in the price if there was opposition, and it made a difference whether the privilege asked was legitimate or not. But nothing was passed free of charge. Many of the legislators were saloonkeepers—it was in St. Louis that a practical joker nearly emptied the House of Delegates by tipping a boy to rush into a session and call out, "Mister, your saloon is on fire"—but even the saloonkeepers of a neighborhood had to pay to keep in their inconvenient locality a market which public interest would have moved.

From the Assembly, bribery spread into other departments. Men empowered to issue peddlers' licenses and permits to citizens who wished to erect an awning or use a portion of the sidewalk for storage purposes charged an amount in excess of the prices stipulated by law, and pocketed the difference. The city's money was loaned at interest, and the interest was converted into private bank accounts. City carriages were used by the wives and children of city officials. Supplies for public institutions found their way to private tables; one itemized account of food furnished the poorhouse included California jellies, imported cheeses, and French wines! A member of the Assembly caused the incorporation of a grocery company, with his sons and daughters the ostensible stockholders, and succeeded in having his bid for city supplies accepted although the figures were in excess of his competitors'. In return for the favor thus shown, he indorsed a measure to award the contract for city printing to another member, and these two voted aye on a bill granting to a third the exclusive right to furnish city dispensaries with drugs.

Men ran into debt to the extent of thousands of dollars for the sake of election to either branch of the Assembly. One night, on a street car going to the City Hall, a new member remarked that the nickel he handed the conductor was his last. The next day he deposited $5,000 in a savings bank. A member of the House of Delegates admitted to the grand jury that his dividends from the combine netted $25,000 in one year; a councilman stated that he was paid $50,000 for his vote on a single measure.

Bribery was a joke. A newspaper reporter overheard this conversation one evening in the corridor of the City Hall:

"Ah there, my boodler!" said Mr. Delegate.

"Stay there, my grafter!" replied Mr. Councilman. "Can you lend me a hundred for a day or two?"

"Not at present. But I can spare it if the Z———bill goes through tonight. Meet me at F———'s later."

"All right, my jailbird; I'll be there."

The blackest years were 1898, 1899, and 1900. Foreign corporations came into the city to share in its despoliation, and home industries were driven out by blackmail. Franchises worth millions were granted without one cent of cash to the city, and with provision for only the smallest future payment; several companies which refused to pay blackmail had to leave; citizens were robbed more and more boldly; payrolls were padded with the names of nonexistent persons; work on public improvements was neglected, while money for them went to the boodlers.

Some of the newspapers protested, disinterested citizens were alarmed, and the shrewder men gave warnings, but none dared make an effective stand. Behind the corruptionists were men of wealth and social standing, who, because of special privileges granted them, felt bound to support and defend the looters. Independent victims of the far-reaching conspiracy submitted in silence, through fear of injury to their business. Men whose integrity was never questioned, who held high positions of trust, who were church members and teachers of Bible classes, contributed to the support of the dynasty—became blackmailers, in fact—and their excuse was that others did the same, and that if they proved the exception it would work their ruin. The system became loose through license and plenty till it was as wild as that of Tweed in New York.

Then the unexpected happened—an accident. There was no uprising of the people, but they were restive; and the Democratic party leaders, thinking to gain some independent votes, decided to raise the cry "reform" and put up a ticket of candidates different enough from the usual offerings of political parties to give color to their platform. These leaders were not in earnest. There was little difference between the two parties in the city; but the rascals that were in had been getting the greater share of the spoils, and the "outs" wanted more than was given to them. "Boodle" was not the issue, no exposures were made or threatened, and the bosses expected to control their men if elected. Simply as part of the game, the Democrats raised the slogan, "reform" and "no more Ziegenheinism."

Mayor Ziegenhein, called "Uncle Henry," was a "good fellow," "one of the boys," and though it was during his administration that the city grew ripe and went to rot, his opponents talked only of incompetence and neglect, and repeated such stories as that of his famous reply to some citizens who complained because certain street lights were put out: "You have the moon yet—ain't it?"

When somebody mentioned Joseph W. Folk for Circuit Attorney the leaders were ready to accept him. They didn't know much about him. He was a young man from Tennessee; had been president of the Jefferson Club, and arbitrated the railroad strike of 1898. But Folk did not want the place. He was a civil lawyer, had had no practice at the criminal bar, cared little about it, and a lucrative business as counsel for corporations was interesting him. He rejected the invitation. The committee called again and again, urging his duty to his party, and the city, etc.

"Very well," he said, at last, "I will accept the nomination, but if elected I will do my duty. There must be no attempt to influence my actions when I am called upon to punish lawbreakers."

The committeemen took such statements as the conventional platitudes of candidates. They nominated him, the Democratic ticket was elected, and Folk became Circuit Attorney for the Eighth Missouri District.

Three weeks after taking the oath of office his campaign pledges were put to the test. A number of arrests had been made in connection with the recent election, and charges of illegal registration were preferred against men of both parties. Mr. Folk took them up like routine cases of ordinary crime. Political bosses rushed to the rescue. Mr. Folk was reminded of his duty to his party, and told that he was expected to construe the law in such a manner that repeaters and other election criminals who had hoisted democracy's flag and helped elect him might be either discharged or receive the minimum punishment. The nature of the young lawyer's reply can best be inferred from the words of that veteran political leader, Colonel Ed Butler, who, after a visit to Mr. Folk, wrathfully exclaimed, "D——n Joe! He thinks he's the whole thing as Circuit Attorney."

The election cases were passed through the courts with astonishing rapidity; no more mercy was shown Democrats than Republicans, and before winter came a number of ward heelers and old-time party workers were behind the bars in Jefferson City. He next turned his attention to grafters and straw bondsmen with whom the courts were infested, and several of these leeches are in the penitentiary today. The business was broken up because of his activity. But Mr. Folk had made little more than the beginning.

One afternoon, late in January 1903, a newspaper reporter, known as "Red" Galvin, called Mr. Folk's attention to a ten-line newspaper item to the effect that a large sum of money had been placed in a bank for the purpose of bribing certain Assemblymen to secure the passage of a street railroad ordinance. No names were mentioned, but Mr. Galvin surmised that the bill referred to was one introduced on behalf of the Suburban Railway Company. An hour later Mr. Folk sent the names of nearly one hundred persons to the sheriff, with instructions to subpoena them before the grand jury at once. The list included councilmen, members of the House of Delegates, officers and directors of the Suburban Railway, bank presidents and cashiers. In three days the investigation was being pushed with vigor, but St. Louis was laughing at the "huge joke." Such things had been attempted before. The men who had been ordered to appear before the grand jury jested as they chatted in the anterooms, and newspaper accounts of these preliminary examinations were written in the spirit of burlesque.

It has developed since that Circuit Attorney Folk knew nothing, and was not able to learn much more during the first few days; but he says he saw here and there puffs of smoke and he determined to find the fire. It was not an easy job. The first break into such a system is always difficult. Mr. Folk began with nothing but courage and a strong personal conviction. He caused peremptory summonses to be issued, for the immediate attendance in the grand jury room of Charles H. Turner, president of the Suburban Railway, and Philip Stock, a representative of brewers' interests, who, he had reason to believe, was the legislative agent in this deal.

"Gentlemen," said Mr. Folk, "I have secured sufficient evidence to warrant the return of indictments against you for bribery, and I shall prosecute you to the full extent of the law and send you to the penitentiary unless you tell to this grand jury the complete history of the corruptionist methods employed by you to secure the passage of Ordinance No. 44. I shall give you three days to consider the matter. At the end of that time, if you have not returned here and given us the information demanded, warrants will be issued for your arrest."

They looked at the audacious young prosecutor and left the Four Courts building without uttering a word. He waited. Two days later, ex-Lieutenant Governor Charles P. Johnson, the veteran criminal lawyer, called, and said that his client, Mr. Stock, was in such poor health that he would be unable to appear before the grand jury.

"I am truly sorry that Mr. Stock is ill," replied Mr. Folk, "for his presence here is imperative, and if he fails to appear he will be arrested before sundown."

That evening a conference was held in Governor Johnson's office, and the next day this story was told in the grand jury room by Charles H. Turner, millionaire president of the Suburban Railway, and corroborated by Philip Stock, man-about-town and a good fellow: the Suburban, anxious to sell out at a large profit to its only competitor, the St. Louis Transit Co., caused to be drafted the measure known as House Bill No. 44. So sweeping were its grants that Mr. Turner, who planned and executed the document, told the directors in his confidence that its enactment into law would enhance the value of the property from three to six million dollars. The bill introduced, Mr. Turner visited Colonel Butler, who had long been known as a legislative agent, and asked his price for securing the passage of the measure. "One hundred and forty-five thousand dollars will be my fee," was the reply. The railway president demurred. He would think the matter over, he said, and he hired a cheaper man, Mr. Stock. Stock conferred with the representative of the combine in the House of Delegates and reported that $75,000 would be necessary in this branch of the Assembly. Mr. Turner presented a note indorsed by two of the directors whom he could trust, and secured a loan from the German American Savings Bank.

Bribe funds in pocket, the legislative agent telephoned John Murrell, at that time a representative of the House combine, to meet him in the office of the Lincoln Trust Company. There the two rented a safe-deposit box. Mr. Stock placed in the drawer the roll of $75,000, and each subscribed to an agreement that the box should not be opened unless both were present. Of course the conditions spread upon the bank's daybook made no reference to the purpose for which this fund had been deposited, but an agreement entered into by Messrs. Stock and Murrell was to the effect that the $75,000 should be given Mr. Murrell as soon as the bill became an ordinance, and by him distributed to the members of the combine. Stock turned to the Council, and upon his report a further sum of $60,000 was secured. These bills were placed in a safe-deposit box of the Mississippi Valley Trust Co., and the man who held the key as representative of the Council combine was Charles H. Kratz.

All seemed well, but a few weeks after placing these funds in escrow, Mr. Stock reported to his employer that there was an unexpected hitch due to the action of Emil Meysenburg, who, as a member of the Council Committee on Railroads, was holding up the report on the bill. Mr. Stock said that Mr. Meysenburg held some worthless shares in a defunct corporation and wanted Mr. Stock to purchase this paper at its par value of $9,000. Mr. Turner gave Mr. Stock the money with which to buy the shares.

Thus the passage of House Bill 44 promised to cost the Suburban Railway Co. $144,000, only one thousand dollars less than that originally named by the political boss to whom Mr. Turner had first applied. The bill, however, passed both houses of the Assembly. The sworn servants of the city had done their work and held out their hands for the bribe money.

Then came a court mandate which prevented the Suburban Railway Co. from reaping the benefit of the vote-buying, and Charles H. Turner, angered at the check, issued orders that the money in safe-deposit boxes should not be touched. War was declared between bribe-givers and bribe-takers, and the latter resorted to tactics which they hoped would frighten the Suburban people into submission—such as making enough of the story public to cause rumors of impending prosecution. It was that first item which Mr. Folk saw and acted upon.

When Messrs. Turner and Stock unfolded in the grand jury room the details of their bribery plot, Circuit Attorney Folk found himself in possession of verbal evidence of a great crime; he needed as material exhibits the two large sums of money in safe-deposit vaults of two of the largest banking institutions of the West. Had this money been withdrawn? Could he get it if it was there? Lock-boxes had always been considered sacred and beyond the power of the law to open. "I've always held," said Mr. Folk, "that the fact that a thing never had been done was no reason for thinking it couldn't be done." He decided in this case that the magnitude of the interests involved warranted unusual action, so he selected a committee of grand jurors and visited one of the banks. He told the president, a personal friend, the facts that had come into his possession, and asked permission to search for the fund.

"Impossible," was the reply. "Our rules deny anyone the right."

"Mr.————," said Mr. Folk, "a crime has been committed, and you hold concealed the principal evidence thereto. In the name of the State of Missouri I demand that you cause the box to be opened. If you refuse, I shall cause a warrant to be issued, charging you as an accessory."

For a minute not a word was spoken by anyone in the room; then the banker said in almost inaudible tones:

"Give me a little time, gentlemen. I must consult with our legal adviser before taking such a step."

"We will wait ten minutes," said the Circuit Attorney. "By that time we must have access to the vault or a warrant will be applied for."

At the expiration of that time a solemn procession wended its way from the president's office to the vaults in the subcellar—the president, the cashier, and the corporation's lawyer, the grand jurors, and the Circuit Attorney. All bent eagerly forward as the key was inserted in the lock. The iron drawer yielded, and a roll of something wrapped in brown paper was brought to light. The Circuit Attorney removed the rubber bands, and national bank notes of large denomination spread out flat before them. The money was counted, and the sum was $75,000!

The boodle fund was returned to its repository, officers of the bank were told they would be held responsible for it until the courts could act. The investigators visited the other financial institution. They met with more resistance there. The threat to procure a warrant had no effect until Mr. Folk left the building and set off in the direction of the Four Courts. Then a messenger called him back, and the second box was opened. In this was found $60,000. The chain of evidence was complete.

From that moment events moved rapidly. Charles Kratz and John K. Murrell, alleged representatives of Council and House combines, were arrested on bench warrants and placed under heavy bonds. Kratz was brought into court from a meeting at which plans were being formed for his election to the national Congress. Murrell was taken from his undertaking establishment. Emil Meysenburg, millionaire broker, was seated in his office when a sheriff's deputy entered and read a document that charged him with bribery. The summons reached Henry Nicolaus while he was seated at his desk, and the wealthy brewer was compelled to send for a bondsman to avoid passing a night in jail. The cable flashed the news to Cairo, Egypt, that Ellis Wainwright, many times a millionaire, proprietor of the St. Louis brewery that bears this name, had been indicted. Julius Lehmann, one of the members of the House of Delegates, who had joked while waiting in the grand jury's anteroom, had his laughter cut short by the hand of a deputy sheriff on his shoulder and the words, "You are charged with perjury." He was joined at the bar of the criminal court by Harry Faulkner, another jolly good fellow.

Consternation spread among the boodle gang. Some of the men took night trains for other states and foreign countries; the majority remained and counseled together. Within twenty-four hours after the first indictments were returned, a meeting of bribe-givers and bribe-takers was held in South St. Louis. The total wealth of those in attendance was $30,000,000, and their combined political influence sufficient to carry any municipal election under normal conditions.

This great power was aligned in opposition to one man, who still was alone. It was not until many indictments had been returned that a citizens' committee was formed to furnish funds, and even then most of the contributors concealed their identity. Mr. James L. Blair, the treasurer, testified in court that they were afraid to be known lest "it ruin their business."

At the meeting of corruptionists three courses were decided upon. Political leaders were to work on the Circuit Attorney by promise of future reward, or by threats. Detectives were to ferret out of the young lawyer's past anything that could be used against him. Witnesses would be sent out of town and provided with money to remain away until the adjournment of the grand jury.

Mr. Folk at once felt the pressure, and it was of a character to startle one. Statesmen, lawyers, merchants, clubmen, churchmen—in fact, men prominent in all walks of life—visited him at his office and at his home, and urged that he cease such activity against his fellow townspeople. Political preferment was promised if he would yield; a political grave if he persisted. Threatening letters came, warning him of plots to murder, to disfigure, and to blackguard. Word came from Tennessee that detectives were investigating every act of his life. Mr. Folk told the politicians that he was not seeking political favors, and not looking forward to another office; the others he defied. Meantime he probed the deeper into the municipal sore. With his first successes for prestige and aided by the panic among the boodlers, he soon had them suspicious of one another, exchanging charges of betrayal, and ready to "squeal" or run at the slightest sign of danger. One member of the House of Delegates became so frightened while under the inquisitorial cross-fire that he was seized with a nervous chill; his false teeth fell to the floor, and the rattle so increased his alarm that he rushed from the room without stopping to pick up his teeth, and boarded the next train.

It was not long before Mr. Folk had dug up the intimate history of ten years of corruption, especially of the business of the North and South and the Central Traction franchise grants, the last-named being even more iniquitous than the Suburban.

Early in 1898 a "promoter" rented a bridal suite at the Planters' Hotel, and having stocked the rooms with wines, liquors and cigars until they resembled a candidate's headquarters during a convention, sought introduction to members of the Assembly and to such political bosses as had influence with the city fathers. Two weeks after his arrival the Central Traction bill was introduced "by request" in the Council. The measure was a blanket franchise, granting rights of way which had not been given to old-established companies, and permitting the beneficiaries to parallel any track in the city. It passed both houses despite the protests of every newspaper in the city, save one, and was vetoed by the mayor. The cost to the promoter was $145,000.

Preparations were made to pass the bill over the executive's veto. The bridal suite was restocked, larger sums of money were placed on deposit in the banks, and the services of three legislative agents were engaged. Evidence now in the possession of the St. Louis courts tells in detail the disposition of $250,000 of bribe money. Sworn statements prove that $75,000 was spent in the House of Delegates. The remainder of the $250,000 was distributed in the Council, whose members, though few in number, appraised their honor at a higher figure on account of their higher positions in the business and social world. Finally, but one vote was needed to complete the necessary two-thirds in the upper Chamber. To secure this a councilman of reputed integrity was paid $50,000 in consideration that he vote aye when the ordinance should come up for final passage. But the promoter did not dare risk all upon the vote of one man, and he made this novel proposition to another honored member, who accepted it:

"You will vote on roll call after Mr. ———. I will place $45,000 in the hands of your son, which amount will become yours, if you have to vote for the measure because of Mr. ———'s not keeping his promise. But if he stands out for it you can vote against it, and the money shall revert to me."

On the evening when the bill was read for final passage the City Hall was crowded with ward heelers and lesser politicians. These men had been engaged by the promoter, at five and ten dollars a head, to cheer on the boodling assemblymen. The bill passed the House with a rush, and all crowded into the Council Chamber. While the roll was being called the silence was profound, for all knew that some men in the Chamber whose reputations had been free from blemish were under promise and pay to part with honor that night. When the clerk was two-thirds down the list those who had kept count knew that but one vote was needed. One more name was called. The man addressed turned red, then white, and after a moment's hesitation he whispered "Aye"! The silence was so deathlike that his vote was heard throughout the room, and those near enough heard also the sigh of relief that escaped from the member who could now vote "No" and save his reputation.

The Central Franchise bill was a law, passed over the mayor's veto. The promoter had expended nearly $300,000 in securing the legislation, but within a week he sold his rights of way to "eastern capitalists" for $1,250,000. The United Railways Company was formed, and without owning an inch of steel rail, or a plank in a car, was able to compel every street railroad in St. Louis, with the exception of the Suburban, to part with stock and right of way and agree to a merger. Out of this grew the St. Louis Transit Company of today.

Several incidents followed this legislative session. After the Assembly had adjourned, a promoter entertained the $50,000 councilman at a downtown restaurant. During the supper the host remarked to his guest, "I wish you would lend me that $50,000 until tomorrow. There are some of the boys outside whom I haven't paid." The money changed hands. The next day, having waited in vain for the promoter, Mr. Councilman armed himself with a revolver and began a search of the hotels. The hunt in St. Louis proved fruitless, but the irate legislator kept on the trail until he came face to face with the lobbyist in the corridor of the Waldorf-Astoria. The New Yorker, seeing the danger, seized the St. Louisan by the arm and said soothingly, "There, there; don't take on so. I was called away suddenly. Come to supper with me; I will give you the money."

The invitation was accepted, and champagne soon was flowing. When the man from the West had become sufficiently maudlin the promoter passed over to him a letter, which he had dictated to a typewriter while away from the table for a few minutes. The statement denied all knowledge of bribery.

"You sign that and I will pay you $5,000. Refuse, and you don't get a cent," said the promoter. The St. Louisan returned home carrying the $5,000, and that was all.

Meanwhile the promoter had not fared so well with other spoilsmen. By the terms of the ante-legislation agreement referred to above, the son of one councilman was pledged to return $45,000 if his father was saved the necessity of voting for the bill. The next day the New Yorker sought out this young man and asked for the money.

"I am not going to give it to you," was the cool rejoinder. "My mamma says that it is bribe money and that it would be wrong to give it to either you or father, so I shall keep it myself." And he did. When summoned before the grand jury this young man asked to be relieved from answering questions. "I am afraid I might commit perjury," he said. He was advised to "Tell the truth and there will be no risk."

"It would be all right," said the son, "if Mr. Folk would tell me what the other fellows have testified to. Please have him do that."

Two indictments were found as the result of this Central Traction bill, and bench warrants were served on Robert M. Snyder and George J. Kobusch. The state charged the former with being one of the promoters of the bill, the definite allegation being bribery. Mr. Kobusch, who is president of a street-car manufacturing company, was charged with perjury.

The first case tried was that of Emil Meysenburg, the millionaire who compelled the Suburban people to purchase his worthless stock. He was defended by three attorneys of high repute in criminal jurisprudence, but the young Circuit Attorney proved equal to the emergency, and a conviction was secured. Three years in the penitentiary was the sentence. Charles Kratz, the Congressional candidate, forfeited

$40,000 by flight, and John K. Murrell also disappeared. Mr. Folk traced Murrell to Mexico, caused his arrest in Guadalajara, negotiated with the authorities for his surrender, and when this failed, arranged for his return home to confess, and his evidence brought about the indictment, on September 8, of eighteen members of the municipal legislature. The second case was that of Julius Lehmann. Two years at hard labor was the sentence, and the man who had led the jokers in the grand jury anteroom would have fallen when he heard it, had not a friend been standing near.

Besides the convictions of these and other men of good standing in the community, and the flight of many more, partnerships were dissolved, companies had to be reorganized, business houses were closed because their proprietors were absent, but Mr. Folk, deterred as little by success as by failure, moved right on; he was not elated; he was not sorrowful. The man proceeded with his work quickly, surely, smilingly, without fear or pity. The terror spread, and the rout was complete.

When another grand jury was sworn and proceeded to take testimony there were scores of men who threw up their hands and crying "Mea culpa!" begged to be permitted to tell all they knew and not be prosecuted. The inquiry broadened. The son of a former mayor was indicted for misconduct in office while serving as his father's private secretary, and the grand jury recommended that the ex-mayor be sued in the civil courts, to recover interests on public money which he had placed in his own pocket. A true bill fell on a former City Register, and more assemblymen were arrested, charged with making illegal contracts with the city. At last the ax struck upon the trunk of the greatest oak of the forest. Colonel Butler, the boss who has controlled elections in St. Louis for many years, the millionaire who had risen from bellows-boy in a blacksmith's shop to be the maker and guide of the governors of Missouri, one of the men who helped nominate and elect Folk—he also was indicted on two counts charged with attempted bribery. That Butler has controlled legislation in St. Louis had long been known. It was generally understood that he owned assemblymen before they ever took the oath of office, and that he did not have to pay for votes. And yet open bribery was the allegation now. Two members of the Board of Health stood ready to swear that he offered them $2,500 for their approval of a garbage contract.

Pitiful? Yes, but typical. Other cities are today in the same condition as St. Louis before Mr. Folk was invited in to see its rottenness. Chicago is cleaning itself up just now, so is Minneapolis, and Pittsburgh recently had a bribery scandal; Boston is at peace, Cincinnati and St. Paul are satisfied, while Philadelphia is happy with the worst government in the world. As for the small towns and the villages, many of these are busy as bees at the loot.

St. Louis, indeed, in its disgrace, has a great advantage. It was exposed late; it has not been reformed and caught again and again, until its citizens are reconciled to corruption. But, best of all, the man who has turned St. Louis inside out, turned it, as it were, upside down, too. In all cities, the better classes—the businessmen—are the sources of corruption; but they are so rarely pursued and caught that we do not fully realize whence the trouble comes. Thus most cities blame the politicians and the ignorant and vicious poor.

Mr. Folk has shown St. Louis that its bankers, brokers, corporation officers—its businessmen—are the sources of evil, so that from the start it will know the municipal problem in its true light. With a tradition for public spirit, it may drop Butler and its runaway bankers, brokers and brewers, and pushing aside the scruples of the hundreds of men down in blue book, and red book, and church register, who are lying hidden behind the statutes of limitations, the city may restore good government. Otherwise the exposures by Mr. Folk will result only in the perfection of the corrupt system. For the corrupt can learn a lesson when the good citizens cannot. The Tweed regime in New York taught Tammany to organize its boodle business: the police exposure taught it to improve its method of collecting blackmail. And both now are almost perfect and safe. The rascals of St. Louis will learn in like manner; they will concentrate the control of their bribery system, excluding from the profit-sharing the great mass of weak rascals, and carrying on the business as a business in the interest of a trustworthy few. District Attorney Jerome cannot catch the Tammany men, and Circuit Attorney Folk will not be able another time to break the St. Louis ring. This is St. Louis' one great chance.

But, for the rest of us, it does not matter about St. Louis any more than it matters about Colonel Butler et al. The point is, that what went on in St. Louis is going on in most of our cities, towns and villages. The problem of municipal government in America has not been solved. The people may be tired of it, but they cannot give it up—not yet.

McClure's Magazine
October 1902

THE WARD

THE FIRST WARD BALL was the personal property of two Chicago politicians. They dominated the ward for nearly half a century. They ran it to suit their own needs, and every year they threw a huge ball. An invitation was tantamount to a large contribution.

Through this annual event, which lasted for almost a decade, Michael "Hinky-Dink" Kenna and John "Bathhouse John" Coughlin enriched their political campaign treasuries by $50,000 each year. Kenna owned the Workingmen's Exchange on Clark Street. Coughlin was a former bathhouse attendant.

During their rule of the ward, they had "built an organization of saloonkeepers, gamblers, pimps, pickpockets and brothel owners who would help them, term after term, hold their City Council seats." [55]

The ball, held one year by Kenna and the other by Coughlin, was a frolicking, gaysome, gaudy affair at Chicago's Coliseum. Here the politician and the underworld, ladies of ill repute and gentlemen gamblers, enjoyed a bacchanalian revel or, as Will Irwin was to describe it: "The underworld sported in masks, while the upper world sat in boxes guiltily enjoying the show." [56]

A reform element in Chicago with the aid of the churches had been trying for some time to get the city to ban the ball. But each year the Mayor granted a permit for the event. The two aldermen, after all, were part of the city's administration, and though the Mayor was not in on the financial spoils accruing from the ball, his political party's coffers stood to profit.

While the permit for the 1908 ball was still going through the red tape formula, Alderman Coughlin, reported the Chicago Record-Herald, "was distributing privileged tickets among the councilmen. These tickets entitle the holder to admission without wardrobe charges, and, as the alderman put it, 'to all other privileges, including wine and song without taxation.' " [57]

A few days before the ball, Bathhouse John Coughlin ordered that all "regulars" of the First Ward come to the event in "full dress" and to be there at the opening of the party.

137

The Chicago *Daily Tribune* reported that the Monday night ball "will be a censored, tame affair compared with other years." [58] The *Tribune* also said it would list the names of the "responsible" persons who would attend the ball.

Kenna promised that there would be enough policemen there to see that order was maintained, and added: "We hope to have a fine crowd of representative men of Chicago, as we have had in the past." [59]

The day before the ball, a page-one headline of the Chicago *Record* said:

BOMB WRECKS HOUSE:
AIMED AT WARD ORGY

Inspector Wheeler of the police force told the newspapers he felt it was the work of "fanatical reformers." "The idea, apparently, is to frighten away those who plan to attend the affair tomorrow night. There *are* a lot of bad citizens connected with the so-called reform movement in Chicago. . . . How much the reform leaders in Chicago know about these bomb outrages, I can't say, but they had better take cognizance of the fact that they are under suspicion," said the Inspector.[60]

The bomb scare did not hold back the attendance.

On December 15, the day after the ball, the Chicago *Tribune* carried the headline:

LEVEE'S HORDES
STORM COLISEUM

The story read: "The Hon. Bathhouse Coughlin and the Hon. Hinky-Dink Kenna gave the social event of their lives last night—and the event was the crowning disgrace of Chicago. They packed the Coliseum so full of gentlewomen of no virtue and gentlemen attached to the aforesaid gentlewomen that if a great disaster, thorough in its work, had befallen the festive gathering there would not have been a second story worker, 'dip,' thug, plug ugly, porch climber, dope fiend, or scarlet woman remaining in Chicago."

Will Irwin attended the ball as a reporter for *Collier's*. He wrote in his autobiography, *The Making of a Reporter*, "I went to Chicago, established that the collectors for the First Ward machine were shaking down the department stores, the office buildings, the saloons, the gamblers, the madams of the bawdy houses, even the small prostitutes of the cribs— everyone who needed influence or 'protection'—for from two to five hundred tickets apiece."

He concluded that he "visited this cheap orgy and described it without comment in all its frowsy detail. And that was the last First Ward Ball." [61]

But it wasn't the last of the First Ward Balls. There was one more, the following year. But this one was a dull affair. The reform element of the city again protested angrily to the Mayor, and so great was the protest that the Mayor refused to issue a liquor license. The last "ball" was a benefit concert at the Coliseum where 3,000 people showed up.

WILL IRWIN

The First Ward Ball

"BATHHOUSE JOHN" COUGHLIN stood on the center floor of the great Coliseum, swept his eye over the outpouring of the moral sewers of Chicago, and waved his hand to the two bands, one in either gallery, as a signal that the Grand March of the First Ward Ball was to begin. Bathhouse John is a large, bull-necked Irishman of the John L. Sullivan type, the kind of Celt whose spirit responds, as a flower in rain, to polite public ceremonial. Over the white shirt front, which clothed his well-provisioned torso, he wore a red sash, with the inscription: "Grand Marshal." Eight and forty floor managers, selected either from the powers which rule in Chicago or the powers which rob Chicago—one does not know in which division to place many of them—scattered through the great dancing floor, arranging the couples into line. The bandmasters flourished their staves, and brass and wind struck into the key tune of the evening:

> Hail, hail, the gang's all right—
> What the hell do we care; what the hell do we care—

A movement surged through the tawdry maskers on the floor—they were singing. From end to end of the great hall ran the refrain—women of the half-world and of no world, all in the cheapest, dirtiest and most abbreviated costumes, hired, for two dollars and deposit, from professional costumers; scrubby little boys of the slums, patching out their Sunday clothes with five-cent masks that they might obey the rules of the floor; pickpockets, refraining, by the truce of the Devil which reigned that night, from plying their trade; scarlet women and the yellow men who live from and by them; bartenders; professional repeaters; small politicians; prosperous beggars; saloon bouncers; prize-fight promoters; liquor salesmen; police captains; runners for gambling

houses—all united in this hymn to the power that is in the First Ward
of Chicago:

> *Hail, hail, the gang's all right—*
> *What the hell do we care now?*

It was just striking midnight when Bathhouse John strode out before
the assembled couples to lead the grand march. For two hours the
sweepings and scourings had crowded into the Coliseum, the largest
assembly hall in the United States. At that very moment the police
were raiding the crowd without and closing the doors, for the hall was
packed to the danger point. That overflow crowd, shoving and rioting
to express their disappointment, filled the streets for a block either
way. Within, floor, gallery, passageways and boxes were choked. Those
boxes ran all the way about the dancing floor and only a step above it,
like the boxes at the horse show. They were reserved, mainly, either
for rich slummers or for the aristocracy of the ministers of dissipation.
The galleries held those who came not to revel but to look on. Along
the passageway behind the boxes moved a crowd which jammed into
knots at intervals, and untied itself with much mauling of women and
many fights. A policeman skated across the floor just as Bathhouse John
set off the grand march. He was shoving before him a young man who
lagged back and who threw out his knees very far in front as he walked.
The first serious fight of the evening was being bounced. As Bathhouse
John pranced down the floor at the head of the march, beating time to
the music with his outstretched hands, the tables in the boxes began
to blossom with the white and bronze seals of the brands of champagne
whose agents were the most liberal buyers that night. One, it appeared,
had anticipated the blossoming of the tables. From an end box re-
sounded a feminine shriek which rose above the bands, the singing, and
the shuffling feet. The woman who shrieked had risen and was pouring
Tenderloin billingsgate at some enemy on the floor. Her man hauled
her back and carried her away. The first drunk of the evening had
passed out.

They are not here strictly for the joy of it, these greasy revelers; let me
make that plain before I go further. Strictly, "Bathhouse John" Coughlin
and "Hinky-Dink" Kenna, aldermen of the First Ward, need money to
pay repeaters, colonizers, district leaders, and heelers—money for all the
expenses of keeping in line this, the richest graft district in the United
States. The annual ball is their way of collecting that money.

A month before, certain collectors, known for their works in the
Tenderloin, have visited every saloon, every brothel, every opium joint,
every dance hall, and certain favored business houses. They carry sheaves

of tickets—and lists. "A hundred and fifty tickets for yours this year," says the collector to the saloonkeeper. "What are youse giving us?" says the saloonkeeper. "It was only a hundred last year." "Yes, but look at all the business you done last year—things is coming the way of this corner." And a hundred and fifty it is—unless the saloonkeeper wishes to add a fourth fifty as the token of his esteem. "Mercy, a hundred tickets!" says the fat, marcelled woman in the mirrored room. "Why, it was only seventy-five last year—and my girls don't go any more, it is getting that common!" "You've got two more girls here than you had last winter, ain't you? Well, then." And a hundred it is. "Seventy-five tickets?" says the man at the roll-top desk. "Your ball is getting pretty tough, and the newspapers—" "You got a permit for a sign last year, didn't you? Huh?" And seventy-five it is. Lower and higher elements than these pay their tribute of fifty, a hundred, two hundred tickets— the dens from which footpads issue for their periodical raids on Chicago, the legitimate business houses which furnish supplies or service to the dark end of the First Ward. This bit of business conversation floated into my box from the door: "Say, the —— Carriage Company only took thirty tickets. Think of all the business they get hauling souses out of Twenty-second Street!" "Oh, well, they're a new concern—and the Bathhouse knows his business." Still other ways there are of making the First Ward Ball profitable.

Let us push the hands of the clock ahead for an hour, during which time the piles of empty champagne bottles in the boxes have grown and grown, during which the great Annex, where the common herd is served, has become a dump of empty beer bottles. In a box over by the northeast corner sits a little man, swaying gently under his load of champagne. Everything about him is slight—his legs, his shoulders, the lines of his drawn face. His skin is as white as his hair, and that is the color of fresh paper. He appears like a man who is struggling with a great hidden grief. You look a second time before you perceive that the mere mechanics of his face produce this effect. For his eyebrows are set slantwise, so that they rise at the inner corner above the nose, giving what actors call the "grief forehead." His large violet eyes are never still, even when the champagne has clouded them a little. One bejeweled hand rests on the edge of the box. Slender as it is, the soft, white flesh conceals every knuckle—it is a hand that has never been clenched.

The maskers on the floor, promenading between the crowded dances, nudge each other as they pass, and halt to stare. The ribboned com- mitteemen, as police captains, police-court lawyers, popular saloon- keepers and ward heelers, all stop to exchange the time of night. He answers them in a flat voice devoid of inflection, and in flat words devoid of individual turns of expression: "Sure. More here than there ever was before. Those damn reformers tried to blow the place up, and look what they got for it. Every big business house is represented here; all my friends are out." Where he sits is the royal box, for this is Hinky-Dink Kenna; and it is his ball. He will run for re-election next spring; so that the profits tonight—the guesses at these profits run from $60,000 up—all go to his campaign fund. Next year Bathhouse John, on the eve of his own re-election, will get the profits.

Drinking is in full swing now; the effects of it show not in any special joyousness, but in a sodden and dirty aspect of the whole place—floor, boxes and Annex, and especially that cellar café, where one drunk has already tried to undress a woman in a scarlet costume, and succeeded to the point of attracting police attention. No Latin verve and gaiety about it; not Mardi Gras, but Gin Lane. In passing, these public debaucheries with the English-speaking peoples seem always to accompany a bad conscience. A woman, wise in her generation, visited once a café where the peacock women of the half-world, the aristocracy of their craft, go to drink with their men. She looked over the Paris costumes, the complexions a little helped by art, the unsmiling eyes above the smiling faces. "If John the Baptist were to enter now," she said, "he would have these people groveling on the floor in three minutes." "Better than that," said the city politician who accompanied her—and he also was wise in his generation—"a good old Methodist exhorter would have them groveling in two minutes." Ten thousand "revelers" in floor and boxes and cafés getting joylessly drunk on champagne; five thousand spectators, come to see how the other half thinks that it lives, looking joylessly on!

The corner diagonally across from Hinky-Dink's is reserved, by some species of consent, for the select of the half-world. Here sit the wine agents. It is commonly believed that each agent must spend $1,500 for champagne of his own brand at the First Ward Ball. It is supposed, also, that a great deal of his own brand, which he buys in for cash, is "donated"—a delicate way of helping the cause without giving offense. In the struggle between white foil and bronze foil, one side is winning heavily. The agent of that brand sits in his box surrounded by pudgy blond women in diamonds and flowing feathers. As regularly as a minute gun, he "opens." Only then is there any expression on his face. With a little lightening of his eyes, he watches the cork fly to its zenith and fall; then his lids lower, and he goes on pouring for all visitors. A rival, less visited, is beginning to give it away to the populace. He and his assistant stand with their tall hats on the back of their heads, and pour and pour, and pass it out to the crowd, which grabs and jostles. This puts the appetite for free champagne into the small sewer rats, the saloon hangers-on who have been handed one of the graft tickets, all the little people of the floor. Whenever one uncorks a fresh bottle of wine in his box, a dozen fingers touch his elbow—"Hey, mister, give me a drink"—he is a pickpocket from the look of him. "Come over with one, boss"—the loud waistcoat, the cheap patent leather shoes, the ferret eyes in the young face too early tinting and falling into masses, mark him as one of those who live on cheap women of the underworld. "Give us a drink, pet"—she is a little woman in a man's suit, her eyes dull under her mask. She has found a glass somewhere, and she passes it over the edge of the box as she speaks. Though a page's costume is the favorite dress among the women—a costume greasy with the wearing of many previous maskers, and grimy with lying long on the shelves— hundreds of women have chosen to come in the borrowed clothes of men. Of those who do wear skirts, many walk with a free stride which betrays their sex. As for actual *Black Crook* tights—"We bars them," says Bathhouse John; "they're too indecent."

The rule "only maskers allowed on the floor" has become a dead letter. The units in that crowd which surged behind the boxes in the beginning are continually striving to get to the floor; once there, no one will throw them out. So the boxes which contain no women become points of attack for concerted rushes. Sometimes a floor manager, seeing the box-holders in trouble, comes through with a chair, and beats his constituents into order. More often the raiders, turning over table, champagne, and all in their rush, break through and whirl to the floor. These are mere spectators, who come to stare at the gaudy women and the sodden men in the boxes. Gradually, they delimit the dancing space; and gradually the dancers, getting more and more unsteady on their legs, turn their sole attention to getting drunk. A tall woman, dressed as a five-year-old boy, and carrying a tin pail and a sand shovel, goes from box to box wheedling the occupants into pouring champagne into her pail. When it is filled, she threads through the crowd, giving drinks to all comers. The very floor of the Annex is swimming in beer. The cellar café has become so unspeakably disorderly that a squad of policemen vanish into its depths; in five minutes they return, each policeman shoving before him his fighting drunk.

So it goes on, more and more noisy, more and more unsteady, more and more noisome, until half-past two. The early comers have left, but there is no diminution of the crowd. The people whose business keeps them until midnight in the Tenderloin have finished their work. They are sweeping in to take the vacant places, and to increase the sales of the white foil and the bronze. This year the reformers have threatened to make arrests if the sale of drinks does not stop promptly at three o'clock, according to law and license. The waiters pass from box to box with the admonition: "Order all the wine you want now; bar closes at three!" Later, they come back with sheaves of bottles for the grand, final, alcoholic burst of the evening. By half-past three, even the provident are drinking their last glasses; and Bathhouse John, waving to the musicians in the gallery, shouts: "Give 'em 'Home, Sweet Home.'" There is a flurry about the royal box. Hinky-Dink is going away. He steadies himself as he rises by the little hand without knuckles which moves all these dirty puppets of First Ward politics.

Five thousand drunken people at this hour of half-past three doing everything that a drunk does! In the box next to that of the most popular wine agent a woman has gone clean mad with liquor, as women do. She wears an extreme Directoire costume, with a large hat. The hat has fallen back on her shoulders, and her hair has tumbled down over it. As she stands on the table with outstretched arms, shouting loud obscenities to the crowd which collects to watch her, she bears a fearful resemblance to one of those furies of the French Revolution. Before her box lies a little flashily dressed man, dead drunk—groveling in the lees of the floor. No one pays more than passing attention to him. A telegraph messenger boy sways in the corner, very sick from free champagne. A woman in a bedraggled white evening dress hangs draped head down over the edge of her box, like clothes on a line. The two men and the other woman in her box are drinking a standing toast, oblivious of her. A woman in a page's costume passes another similarly dressed. She hurls a vivid insult as she passes; the other turns, spitting like a cat, and lays hold on her hair. The drunkards in the vicinity gather about them and cheer until the police break through and "bounce" them to the ladies' dressing room. An old-time wrestler, now a saloon bouncer, lolls over the edge of a box talking with a woman who sprawls across the table, regarding him with fishy eyes. A little scrubby boy, a pickpocket from the look of him, comes along in the blazing, nervous stage of drunkenness. He lurches against the rail and begins to address the woman. The bouncer wheels and hits him just once in the middle of the body. The scrubby boy shoots back like a cannon ball and brings up sprawling on the floor, where he lies kicking. The bouncer, taking no further look at him, goes on with the conversation. Four fat women sit in a corner box, drinking stupidly. Dressed gaudily in evening clothes, their laces, their white gloves, even their powdered complexions, are becoming grimy with the soot of drunkenness which falls over the great hall. Between them, on the table, stand seven empty champagne bottles and a monumental bouquet of wilting pink roses. They have been taking their pleasures very, very sadly. One nods drowsily; the others watch with eyes as hard and dead as pebbles the crowd which pays tribute to notoriety by stopping to stare. The pickpocket has recovered now; he picks himself up, reviles the bouncer at a safe distance, and staggers over to this box. Worming his way through the crowd, he halts at the rail and lays hold on the lace sleeve of the nearest woman. Expertly, she gets the lace out of his clutch; calmly, she puts her white-gloved hand in his face, sends him spinning back by a motion like the straight-arm in football, and goes on talking with her neighbor. An old man, blind drunk, comes down the hall brandishing a champagne bottle. A woman gets in his way; he hurls the bottle and strikes her on the shoulder. One spectator, more sober than the rest, complains to a policeman who stands grinning at the spectacle. "Oh, that's all right," says the policeman. "Can't you see he's drunk?"

At four o'clock, some merry drunkard, on his way out, smashes the box at the door and rings in a fire-alarm. The engines and the hook-and-ladder, plowing through the cabs and automobiles parked on the street, finish off the First Ward Ball for the year 1908.

I who had watched this for five hours, jostled to the door over drunken men, past drunken women, got clear of the crowd which still swayed and fought outside, clear of the parasites upon parasites who waited beyond, clear of the shouting newsboys with their early editions, clear of the soliciting nighthawk cabmen. The first breath of clean air struck me; I raised my face to it.

And suddenly I realized that there were stars.

Collier's
February 6, 1909

BUREAUCRACY

THE BALLINGER CONTROVERSY broke in 1909. It resulted from a charge hurled against the Secretary of the Interior, Richard A. Ballinger, by an investigator of the Field Division of the United States General Land Office, Louis R. Glavis.

The story, however, began three years earlier. In November 1906, President Theodore Roosevelt had withdrawn all the Alaskan coal lands from public entry. Up until that time about 900 claims, covering nearly 100,000 acres, had been filed. One of the most important claims pending was that of Clarence Cunningham, which consisted of thirty-three claims, including those of J. P. Morgan and the Guggenheims.

Glavis' first connection with these cases came in the fall of 1907 while he was in Seattle investigating other Land Office matters. He became suspicious about the Cunningham claims. It seemed to him that while these claims were listed individually, there were indications that they were arranged by interests who later would merge.

The law under which the government was to release the coal land was specific; it attempted to prevent a monopoly of the coal lands by limiting the amount of each claim, and provided that the claimant must use the land for himself.

The young investigator laid his suspicions before Ballinger, who at that time was Land Commissioner. Ballinger told Glavis to continue his investigation. Yes, some of the claimants were friends of his, but this should not deter the investigation, no matter where it would lead.

Within two weeks, however, Ballinger reversed himself and ordered the claims clear-listed, i.e., that they be recorded as valid claims. A protest from Glavis; the clear-listing was revoked; the study was again resumed by Glavis and a special agent.

In the meantime, in March 1908, Ballinger resigned as Commissioner of the Land Office. A few days before his resignation, he testified before the House Committee on Public Lands. Here he urged that the law be changed so that the technical violations could be overlooked and the Cunningham and other Alaska claims receive a patent to the Alaska coal fields. No action was taken. Glavis continued his investigation.

Then, in March 1909, a year after his resignation, President Taft appointed Ballinger Secretary of the Interior. Within a week after Ballinger took office, Glavis was directed to submit a complete report on the status of his investigation. A month later he was told that the investigation must be completed within sixty days. Despite his plea for more time on the grounds that his research had uncovered new facts which indicated fraud, the order for completion stood firm and he was told that another official in the Land Office was being sent to Seattle to take over his duties.

Overlooking protocol, Glavis turned to Gifford Pinchot, Chief Forester, for aid. Glavis recognized that he was breaking custom by going over the head of his superior to the head of another department, but he felt this was the only way he would be heard.

Pinchot, too, aware he was breaking protocol, gave the young clerk a letter of introduction to the President of the United States, to whom Glavis told his story.

The President studied the case. He then released to the press a copy of a letter he had written to Ballinger on September 13, 1909, in which he exonerated Ballinger and authorized the dismissal of Glavis.

The Taft letter said in part:

> Mr. Glavis's report does not formulate his charges against you and the others, but by insinuation and innuendo as well as by direct averment he does charge that each one of you while a public officer has taken steps to aid the Cunningham claimants to secure patents based on claims that you know or had reason to believe to be fraudulent and unlawful.
>
> I have examined the whole record most carefully and have reached a very definite conclusion. It is impossible for me in announcing this conclusion to accompany it with a review of the charges and the evidence on both sides. It is sufficient to say that the case attempted to be made by Mr. Glavis embraces only shreds of suspicions without any substantial evidence to sustain his attack.
>
> But when he makes a charge against his chief founded upon mere suspicions and in his statement he fails to give his chief the benefit of circumstances within his knowledge that would explain his chief's action as on proper grounds, he makes it impossible for him to continue in the service of the Government, and his immediate separation therefrom becomes a necessity.
>
> You are therefore authorized to dismiss L. R. Glavis from the service of the Government for filing a disingenuous statement, unjustly impeaching the official integrity of his superior officers.[62]

The matter might have rested there but for two facts: one, Pinchot was also concerned, and he came again to the defense of Glavis. Second, Glavis offered to *Collier's* an article on "The Whitewashing of Ballinger." He gave it to them with the "preliminary condition that nothing shall be paid for it," despite the fact that another magazine had offered him $3,000.[63]

Collier's had been watching the hassle between the Land Office investigator and the Secretary of the Interior. With the Glavis article, it stepped into the fracas.

In its December 18, 1909 issue, *Collier's* carried an unsigned article reportedly written by C. P. Connolly, "Can This Be Whitewashed Also?" While the Glavis article stirred the country to demand a Congressional investigation, the Connolly article forced the investigation.

About the same time, *Hampton's Magazine* carried several articles by John L. Mathews in which he discussed the economic situation underlying the controversy.

Biographer Henry F. Pringle, in his story of Taft, refers to the muckrakers in this campaign as "the Cassandras of woe and they wrote blistering attacks based on inaccurate information." [64]

On the other hand, A. T. Mason, McCormick Professor of Jurisprudence at Princeton University, writes that the "discussions in *Collier's* and *Hampton's* brought the conservation issue sharply to public attention and helped immeasurably in crystallysing opinion thereon." [65]

The case continued to make headlines; thus the *New York Times* of January 7, 1910:

PINCHOT DEFENDS
GLAVIS AGAINST TAFT

Forester Sends to the Senate a
Letter in Which He Asserts the
President Was Mistaken.

BALLINGER HELD IN RIGHT

Wickersham's Report Defends Him
Warmly, but Pinchot Stands Firm—
Taft, Angry, May Dismiss Him

The *New York Times* of January 8, 1910:

PINCHOT OUSTED;
PARTY WAR ON

President Dismisses Forester, Censuring
Him in Letter—Two Others
in Bureau Dropped.

REPUBLICANS BADLY SPLIT

Fights Between the Roosevelt Radical and the Conservatives
May Make Serious Breach

The House and Senate began to choose committee members for the investigation. The Senate had no difficulty, but in the House, Speaker Joe Cannon was having his problems, and during the debate to name the committee he was defeated by the combined voting of the Insurgents and the Democrats (see United States House of Representatives, page 84).

The hearings opened on January 26, 1910. Representing Pinchot were George Wharton Pepper and Nathan A. Smyth of the New York bar. Representing Glavis were Louis D. Brandeis, Boston lawyer who later was to become a member of the United States Supreme Court; Joseph P.

Cotton Jr., who was Undersecretary of State in the Hoover administration; and George Rublee of New York.

The committee, consisting of six Senators and six Representatives, of which seven were Republicans, four Democrats, and one Insurgent Republican, was in session for four months (January 26 through May 20) almost continuously from ten in the morning until five in the afternoon.

The investigating committee voted seven to five to sustain Ballinger. The majority, all Republicans, felt that nothing had been proven to show that Ballinger was anything but able, honorable and faithful in the performance of his office.

The report was signed by Knute Nelson, chairman; Frank P. Flint, George Sutherland, Elihu Root, Samuel W. McCall, Marlin E. Olmstead and Edwin Denby.

One minority report, signed by the dissenting Democrats Duncan U. Fletcher, William E. Purcell, Ollie M. James and James M. Graham, indicated that Ballinger was not fit to hold the office, and recommended that he be relieved of it. The other minority report, issued by E. H. Madison (Kansas Insurgent Republican), asserted that the Cunningham coal claims were not in the public interest, that the Glavis-Pinchot charges should be upheld, but that the Secretary should not be relieved of office.

Despite his exoneration, public opinion finally led to Ballinger's resignation on March 7, 1911.

But the story does not end here. Twenty-five years later, in May 1933, Secretary of the Interior Harold L. Ickes appointed Glavis to a Federal post to direct the investigations of the Interior Department.

Three months later, on August 4, the *New York Times*, in a story datelined Washington, D.C., reported: "To remove what the Interior Department termed 'an injustice allowed to stand for nearly a quarter of a century,' President Roosevelt restored the civil service status today of Louis R. Glavis, recently appointed Chief of the Division on Investigations of that department."

But in 1940, Secretary Ickes, who seven years earlier had named Glavis to the Federal position, re-examined the Ballinger case and reversed "his Bull Moose self" to say Ballinger was "not guilty."

In an article in the *Saturday Evening Post*, the "Old Curmudgeon" called Ballinger an American Dreyfus. He opened: "This article is by way of confession and penance. In writing it, I am hoping that a grave wrong may be righted." [66]

Whether Ballinger was an "American Dreyfus" or the issue in the case was conservation versus spoilation of natural resources, as Pinchot charged, the fact remains that the muckrakers brought the issue to the nation's attention and questioned the right of those in power to demand disciplined, unquestioned obedience from their subordinates.

ANONYMOUS*

ᘓᕼ

Can This Be Whitewashed Also?

THAT YOU MAY better understand how lids exist for the purpose of
being sat upon, we shall first summarize a little of the preceding
history of Alaska, showing how those who revealed the robber barons
at work were squelched then, even as now. Besides, it connects with the
present grabs in various interesting respects.

The Alaska Gold Mining Company, organized by Washington politicians, exploited Alaska with so high a hand that even Washington
gasped at the brazenness. Then the spoil was gold—now it is copper and
coal. Rex Beach told the story. Later he made its facts the foundation
for his novel, "The Spoilers." Speaking of the policy of suppression
which then controlled in Washington, he said: "You haven't heard of
it? Of course not. When the scandal came out, it was smothered, and
the public kept in ignorance. Criminals were pardoned, records expunged, thieves exalted to new honors." The wheels of justice at Washington were mysteriously clogged. The scheme, as originally planned
and for a long time successfully carried out, was to seize and operate,
in the interest of the Alaska Gold Mining Company, the rich Nome
placer mines owned by the unlettered but law-respecting prospectors.
It was proposed to steal these mines either by an adroitly worded act
of Congress—just as Ballinger tried to legalize the Cunningham claims
by having the laws amended—or, failing that, to confiscate them by
decisions of the Alaska courts, which were to be of their own making
and appointment—exactly as Ballinger sought to have his subordinates
create by the Pierce decision a special law for the Cunningham claims.
Alexander McKenzie of North Dakota was the captain of this filibuster-
ing enterprise. Donald R. McKenzie is one of the chief conspirators

* Reportedly written by C. P. Connolly.

in the present attempted steal. Alec McKenzie was backed and ably defended by the two Senators from North Dakota—McCumber and Hansbrough. Fred Dennett, the present Commissioner of the General Land Office, who figures actively in the Cunningham cases, was a former private secretary of Senator Hansbrough. He was clerk of the Senate Committee on Public Lands, of which Hansbrough was chairman, for several years immediately prior to becoming Special Land Agent in the West by appointment of Ballinger, then Commissioner of the General Land Office.

After all preparations had been perfected at the Washington end, spurious suits were brought in Alaska against the owners of most of the rich placers of Nome. McKenzie was appointed receiver of these claims by Arthur H. Noyes, his judge, and under protection of the United States troops proceeded to gut the mines under the eyes of the owners. He carried off the gold to his own vaults. When the facts became known, it was found that the stock of the Alaska Gold Mining Company was distributed generously throughout official circles in Washington. Judge Noyes denied appeals to the defeated litigants whose properties had been confiscated. Certified copies of the court record were filed with United States Attorney General Griggs. Griggs refused to take action.

Subsequently, in certain legal proceedings growing out of these outrages, Noyes, McKenzie and others were found guilty by the San Francisco Court of Appeals, and sentenced to imprisonment. McKenzie served only part of his sentence. While in jail he was, and for long after remained, a member of the Republican National Committee, and a powerful politician whose influence in Washington did not abate because of the little contretemps in his political affairs.

Whitewash has always been cheap. Senator McCumber of North Dakota said he had known McKenzie for twenty years. "I know him," he said, "to be a noble-hearted, generous, impulsive, sympathetic individual." Senator Hansbrough of the same state, in the Senate, referred to McKenzie as "a reputable man, an honest man, a man who in point of integrity is the peer of any man in this body"—language which pierces with strange light some of the recent fulsome eulogies which seem to be the only answer to present specific charges. When Senator Stewart of Nevada afterward exposed the whole crooked plot, tracing its trail from Washington to Nome and back, involving United States Senators and government officials, entire sections of his speech, exposing these same officials, were expunged by "Senatorial courtesy" from the *Congressional Record*.

Is there another Alaska conspiracy, this time to control the copper and coal? Will the public, remembering the past, be satisfied with star-chamber answers to this question?

It is common knowledge throughout Alaska and the West generally that the Morgan interests are allied with the Guggenheim mining interests, and that the same financial forces are allied with the Hill railroad interests. When Ballinger was nominated and elected Mayor of Seattle, he was put forward by the Hill political managers, ostensibly to put down certain local evils, but really to put the Hill forces in control of local politics. Ballinger supported Levi Ankeny, the railroad candidate who notoriously bought his seat in the United States Senate. An important detail of Ballinger's record to remember is his grant, as Secretary of the Interior, of the railroad right of way along the Des Chutes River in Oregon. Ballinger himself was an incorporator of the original Des Chutes Railroad, and was its vice-president and counsel. He is said to have disposed of his interest in this road to his partner at the time of his recent appointment as Secretary of the Interior. In the confession of S. A. D. Puter, king of the Oregon Land Fraud Ring, convicted by Heney, Puter charged that during Ballinger's short term as Commissioner of the General Land Office, Northern Pacific land patents by the wholesale were issued. He also stated that the General Land Office, under the Ballinger and Dennett administration, shut its eyes to glaring land frauds in Oregon.

As far back as August 13, 1907, Special Agent Horace T. Jones reported to Richard A. Ballinger, Commissioner of the General Land Office: "From the talk of different attorneys and individuals interested in the Alaska coal lands, I feel that the disposal of the lands all tends toward one direction, and that is: the Guggenheim companies. The papers here in Portland, Oregon, are full of the news that the Guggenheims are constructing railroads near Katalla, Alaska, for the purpose of taking out the oil, minerals, etc., and there is an advertisement in the said papers for the employment of two thousand men to go to Katalla, Alaska, and work for the Guggenheims." Katalla is the location of the Cunningham claims. Under date of December 1907, Cunningham's books show the receipt of $1,359.60 with this notation: "The above sum was received from Daniel Guggenheim [head of the Guggenheim syndicate], in full for expenses incurred on account of the examination of coal lands on his account."

. . . Commissioner Ballinger appeared before the House Committee on Public Lands and urged the passage of the Cale bill, which, had it passed, would have made the Cunningham claims legal. With Ballinger there appeared one Donald R. McKenzie. Found among the papers in the possession of former Special Agent H. K. Love, on whose favorable report Ballinger sought to have the Cunningham claims patented, was the following statement in an unsigned letter, dated Juneau, Alaska, March 10, 1908, and addressed to Hon. Oscar Foote of Seattle: "I have just received a copy of Mr. Cale's Coal bill. It seems all that Katalla interests could possibly wish. In fact, I think it was drafted by Judge McKenzie, who, with associates, has acquired large holdings there. It seems to open the whole proposition for corporate holding. The papers say that ex-Commissioner Ballinger urged before the committee the same bill; whether this [is true] or not, I don't know."

McKenzie, like his namesake and prototype in the placer story, is a well-known Washington lobbyist and an old-time political supporter of Senator Piles of Washington, Ballinger's friend. He is one of the beneficiaries of a town site of two thousand acres on Cordova Bay, Alaska, the terminus of the Guggenheim railroad. This town site was granted, through the efforts of Senator Piles of Washington, by the Sixtieth Congress, to McKenzie and two others, one of whom is ex-Governor John H. McGraw of Washington, former political manager for Senator Piles, and one of the committee of the Seattle Chamber of Commerce which recently, in answer to Glavis's article in this paper, gave Ballinger a glowing certificate of character and spoke of him as "a scrupulously honest man." On June 28 of the present year McKenzie brought S. W. Eccles of the Guggenheim syndicate, on his way to Alaska, to see Special Agents Glavis and Jones in Seattle, in order, as he stated, that Eccles might learn firsthand from them of the progress they were making with the Cunningham claims. At this interview McKenzie stated in the presence of these two officials that he and Eccles were particularly anxious to know when the matter would be submitted to the Commissioner of the General Land Office, since he, McKenzie, had assurances from the department that the cases would be given immediate attention as soon as reported.

In October 1908, in Portland, Oregon—after Ballinger had ceased all connection with the Land Office, and while the presidential campaign was on—Ballinger spoke to Glavis of the difficulty of raising campaign funds. He told Glavis that some of the Cunningham claimants had contributed freely in previous campaigns, but were unwilling to do so at that time on account of the investigation of their claims, and urged Glavis not to prosecute his investigations further until after election.

In his written report to President Taft at Beverly, Glavis stated that a number of the Alaska coal claimants "are men prominent in the

State of Washington, and many of them are personal friends of Mr. Ballinger." . . .

Clarence Cunningham lived at Wallace, Idaho, at the time he first became interested in the Cunningham claims. Wallace is the chief town of the Coeur d'Alene mining region. By a sort of financial manipulation, not here necessary to explain, the Guggenheims control the lead output of the Coeur d'Alenes. Wallace is the residence of Senator W. B. Heyburn of Idaho. Cunningham and Heyburn are, and have been for years, friends. In his affidavit, presented by Ballinger to Garfield, Cunningham says that certain of the claimants failed to come forward with their subscriptions and that these expenses were advanced by A. B. Campbell, another Cunningham claimant and a prominent Coeur d'Alene mine owner, who was subsequently reimbursed. John A. Finch, Campbell's mining partner, is also a claimant. Another is Charles Sweeney, Coeur d'Alene mine owner, who floated some Coeur d'Alene mines and sold them to Standard Oil interests. . . . It may interest the reader to know that court records in Seattle show that Ballinger's law firm represented the Standard Oil Company in three different suits.

Senator Heyburn was, at the time of his election to the United States Senate, the leading attorney at Wallace for some of the large Coeur d'Alene mine interests. After the hearing on the Cale bill Senator Heyburn, on April 23, 1908, introduced in the Senate another bill which would have legalized the Cunningham claims, and which would have passed but for the intervention of Secretary Garfield. In Washington Heyburn and Ballinger appear to have acted in concert. . . . It is unlawful for a United States Senator to act as attorney for persons interested in urging claims before the departments at Washington. It was for this offense that Senator Burton of Kansas and Senator Mitchell of Oregon were tried and convicted. Heyburn was elected Senator from Idaho January 13, 1903. In Cunningham's books, under date of September 1903, nine months after Heyburn's election as Senator, there is an entry which reads as follows: "Have agreed with W. B. Heyburn, in consideration for his services as attorney, to carry him for one claim of one hundred and sixty acres in the coal, free of cost to him, and he agrees to do all our legal work in procuring titles, etc., free of expense to us." When Cunningham, on September 4, 1908, made his affidavit, he knew these records were in possession of the department officials. Glavis had forwarded them with a letter calling attention to the Heyburn entry. Naturally, Cunningham, Ballinger and Heyburn, with Burton and Mitchell in mind, had a terrific scare. In his affidavit, prepared by Ballinger, Cunningham attempted to explain away many things. He quoted a letter from Senator Heyburn, dated October 20, 1905, to himself, in which Heyburn declares that he has frequently stated to Cunningham that he did not desire to be interested in the coal lands in Alaska, and now writes expressly to inform him again that he "does not desire to participate in, or be interested in any manner, directly or indirectly, in acquiring public lands." The letter contains 185 words. In those 185 words, this disclaimer is stated four different times, in four different ways. Was this letter written after Glavis got possession of Cunningham's records? And did Heyburn's withdrawal as an attorney have anything to do with the present employment of his nephew, John P. Gray of Wallace, as an attorney for the Cunningham claimants?

When Ballinger represented Cunningham, he represented all the Cunningham claims. Not only this, but the record is quick with the evidence of his employment by other Alaska coal claimants at different times. Under date of December 23, 1908, a little over two months before he took office as Secretary of the Interior, Ballinger wrote to the Register and Receiver of the United States Land Office at Juneau, Alaska, saying that he represented W. G. Whorf, whose entry was known as Coal Survey No. 315. On January 7, 1909, less than sixty days before Ballinger became Secretary of the Interior, M. A. Green, who represents another Alaska coal syndicate, wrote to John W. Dudley, Register of the Juneau, Alaska, Land Office: "I submitted this scrip to Judge Ballinger as my lawyer, and he has approved the same, saying it was regular in every way, so I bought it and paid for it, and am sending it forward to you at this time." Again, in this same letter, Green wrote: "I am expecting to go to Chicago the latter part of this month to meet Mr. McKenzie"—the same McKenzie who supported Ballinger's argument before the Committee on Public Lands in favor of the Cale bill—"and others interested in the Doughten ground, and shall expect to take up the work of perfecting their surveys and title as soon as possible." John Ballinger, a nephew of Achilles, now represents these interests. Under date of April 19, 1909—six weeks after Ballinger took the oath of office as Secretary of the Interior—Walter M. French of the law firm of Allen & French of Seattle, wrote John W. Dudley, Register of the Juneau Land Office: "Mr. Harriman, whom I represent, has on several occasions taken the matter of sale up with Judge Ballinger, whose firm represented the purchasers, and with Mr. Hartline, and the parties have at all times seemed to be in perfect accord." It is hard to keep track of them all, no doubt, and we must end the present list. On November 12, 1907, Glavis submitted a report to Ballinger as Commissioner of the General Land Office, in which he recommended a further investigation concerning a Soldier's Additional Application by Clarke Davis—who was represented by the Mr. Harriman referred to. Ballinger never replied to this phase of Glavis's report, either orally or in writing, but he did approve for patent, without further investigation, the Soldier's Additional Application.

The Seattle *Star* of May 18, 1907, had an article regarding the Alaska Petroleum & Coal Company, Clarke Davis's company. This article stated that the men prominent in the company, together with others interested in similar enterprises, had been endeavoring to secure the passage of an act of Congress which would enable their corporations to get possession of the coal lands. "All possible influence," said the *Star*, "has been brought to bear in Washington. Among those who went from Seattle to Washington on this mission was 'Dick' Ryan." Now notice. On the files of the Interior Department appears a letter of introduction from Ballinger to Secretary of the Interior Garfield under date of March 4, 1908, introducing "Richard S. Ryan of Alaska," and saying Mr. Ryan could "doubtless give" Mr. Garfield "valuable information." Doubtless he could, but it was not the kind of information on which Mr. Garfield was accustomed to act.

This disposes of the question of Ballinger's single employment by *one* claimant, so innocently stated by President Taft. Out of over a possible thousand lawyers in Seattle, Ballinger seems to have had a monopoly of syndicated Alaska coal clients. And who shall say that these clients were altogether lacking in sagacity?

Immediately after the statement in the President's letter that Ballinger did only a little work for one claimant is this further statement: "The evidence in respect to which you were consulted professionally was not secured by Mr. Glavis until after your resignation as Commissioner of the General Land Office." There is not even a "shred of suspicion" upon which to base this statement. The President was cruelly imposed upon, and he in turn unwittingly deceived the public.

The President also refers to the fact that Glavis was allowed to remain in charge of the claims, notwithstanding Ballinger was aware of his attitude as to their fraudulent character. As a matter of fact, the claims were not taken from Glavis, simply because it was feared he would do just what finally he did—go elsewhere for justice.

When Dennett was private secretary to Senator Hansbrough of North Dakota, Hansbrough was chairman of the Senate Committee on Public Lands, and in North Dakota was known as a Hill railroad senator.

Dennett owes his prominence in politics as much to Ballinger as to his former political connections. It is the belief in the State of Washington that he owes his present position also to Ballinger, because of his suppression of facts involving prominent citizens of Washington in public land frauds. On July 26 of the present year Glavis wrote to Dennett: "The investigation that was made at that time was disclosing a great deal of fraud among these coal claimants, and, as you were advised by telegram, we were uncovering a great deal of fraud which involved a great many prominent people in the State of Washington, as well as implicating a United States Senator. You, however, directed me to postpone taking further evidence."

A month previous to this Glavis had wired to Dennett asking if any admissions had been made to Dennett in Washington by Alaska coal claimants. Dennett replied by wire that no admissions had been made by claimants. Confronted personally with proofs of his mendacity, Dennett afterward admitted to Glavis, in the presence of another government agent, that these admissions had been made, and that he himself had worked for the legislation sought by these men, and had interviewed several congressmen in their behalf.

No more details today, but let us call attention to one incident that is understood to have been a disappointment (to put it mildly) to Theodore Roosevelt.

On June 26, 1909, Donald R. McKenzie, Ballinger's intimate associate and client, told Special Agents Jones and Glavis in Seattle that Secretary Garfield's attitude toward the Alaska coal claims, in which he and his friends were interested, was such "that they brought pressure to bear on Senators and Representatives to prevent his remaining in the Cabinet under President Taft." Are the same influences that kept Garfield out keeping Ballinger in? Will the President consider these facts in weighing the arguments now being pressed upon him by members of his Cabinet?

Or are the above circumstantially narrated events also nothing but "shreds of suspicion"?

Collier's
December 18, 1909

JOHN L. MATHEWS

☙

Mr. Ballinger and the
National Grab Bag

O UT OF THE DESERT of Central Oregon, down from a plateau 3,000 feet above sea level, flows the Des Chutes River, in many ways the most remarkable in America. Seeping out from a soil of volcanic ash, fed by the melting snows of distant mountain tops, it flows almost without variation from January to December. Its flood plane is not more than four feet above its low-water surface. From its head to its mouth it plunges precipitously. There is scarcely a foot along its course where a dam could not be installed for the profitable development of power. In one hundred miles its steady discharge of more than 5,000 second-feet provide for the creation of 1,000,000 electric horsepower—a greater energy than is possessed by any other river of this capacity in the world.

It has, besides this, another potential value for power; for though its banks are precipitous cliffs of basalt and of lava, though it lies sometimes more than a thousand feet below the rim of its gorge, the desert which sweeps away from this canyon to the Cascades on one side and to the John Day Valley and so to Idaho on the other, is as fertile and as ready for irrigation as the rich Horse Heaven country across the Columbia River in the State of Washington.

This Des Chutes River belongs to the people of the State of Oregon. Its banks and the adjacent desert (or such part of it as has not been given away, often on fraudulent land grants) belong to the people of the United States. The people of Oregon, more advanced in the direction of good water laws than the rest of us, and more vitally concerned because of this immense desert which covers the greater part of their map, have adopted a water law, recommended to them by their state engineer. This is the first clause:

"All the waters in the State of Oregon, from whatever source, belong to the public."

They have gone further and have provided that any person developing water power must do so on a limited franchise and pay an annual tax, which may amount to $2 per horsepower per year, the horsepower being defined by its minimum description in water, not by a generous measure in electric current. This amounts to practically $4 on the electric power when it reaches a market.

Under this law the water in the Des Chutes, developed for its power, should return an income of more than $2,000,000 a year to the State of Oregon. But let us consider for a moment its value from another standpoint. In the city of Spokane, Washington, is a typical General Electric power company, which has grabbed without return to state or nation the principal powers and reservoirs of the upper Spokane River. This company was financed by the sale of bonds, as is the common practice with water-power grabbers, and its plant cost about $8,000,000. The company charges the citizens of Spokane $40 for ten-hour power which it could afford to sell for $20. This high price is possible because of the cost of coal in Spokane. On this tremendous charge the Washington Water Power Company pays dividends of seven per cent on its $5,000,000 stock, water and all, interest on its $8,000,000 bonds, and has accumulated a surplus of about $300,000.

The only protection against the water-power grabbers which will be continually effective is public ownership. If the people of Oregon developed the Des Chutes they could afford to sell its power to themselves and even to their Washington neighbors for $20 for ten or $30 for twenty-four-hour horsepower, at which rate the river would return the state an income of $30,000,000 yearly, on an investment of probably $125,000,000.

This possible million horsepower represents the equivalent of one-fifth of the total country. It is far more than the State of Oregon will use for many decades. So let us suppose that she develops but half of it and uses part of that half to pump the remaining half of the water up to the desert for irrigation. The pumping would require only a small part of the developed power, so that a large balance could be sold.

The irrigating half of the stream would suffice to water not less than 400,000 acres of the Oregon uplands. Put into the ordinary crops of the northwestern irrigated lands this would produce not less than $80,000,000 annually in crops, and would support in comfort 40,000 families on the irrigated lands besides thousands more in the cities and villages which would grow up in that neighborhood.

I have gone at length into this Des Chutes case and the value of that water to the state through which it flows, because it is a fitting introduction to the story of the acts of Richard A. Ballinger as custodian of the national grab bag. Mr. Ballinger has unloosed the drawstrings of the grab bag just enough to allow the whole Des Chutes River to be pulled out by two of the most earnest grabbers of the Northwest— James J. Hill and the late Edward H. Harriman.

It needs but a glance at the map of Oregon and its neighbors to show one familiar with railway engineering that the Des Chutes Valley has a great value apart from its running water. It is of enormous strategic importance to the railway builders who wish to reach central Oregon. It is of even greater importance to those who wish to secure an economical line with low grades between San Francisco and the northern seaports. Because of this feature it early attracted the attention of Hill and Harriman. The old routes from San Francisco north circle the base of Mount Shasta after a heavy climb in each direction, and make travel and freight hauling slow and costly either way. To lessen this the Harriman lines have been for some years building an easterly division, but even this comes at last to the headwaters of the Willamette River and descends that stream to Portland and the Columbia.

At Portland, Harriman's domain ended and Hill's began. Hill could not cross and pass the rich gateway to western Oregon. Harriman could not advance upon Tacoma and Seattle. A couple of years ago Hill marched down the Columbia Valley with a short route to Portland known as the North Bank road, and in retaliation Harriman forced his way to Puget Sound. The war did not stop there. Balked at Portland, Hill was determined to seek a short cut through the great desert of central Oregon to California. Half a dozen routes were open, but all of them face steep grades and costly railroading except the Des Chutes. By this single river it is possible to build a railroad not exceeding 1 per cent in grade (that is, nowhere rising more than one foot in a hundred) from the Columbia to San Francisco. By this entrance, therefore, Hill determined to drive a wedge into the exclusively Harriman territory of central California and bring the southern magnate to terms.

Almost at the same moment Harriman advanced upon the gateway for a route northward toward Puget Sound and the Inland Empire cheaper for hauling than his existing lines. Porter Brothers, railway contractors representing in this deal the Hill interests, and John S. Stevens filed with the Secretary of the Interior a right of way up the Des Chutes. Immediately afterwards Harriman filed another. For many miles their traced railways were on the same side of the river and occupied the same ground. In one important particular they were exactly alike: they occupied the flood plane of the river, or were as slightly above it as circumstances would permit.

At President Roosevelt's instigation Secretary of the Interior Garfield made an investigation and discovered that the proposed railways would ruin the water power of the Des Chutes without any adequate return to the people. He therefore refused to grant the right of way until it should be so resurveyed that the railway tracks would be above the level of the dams and reservoirs necessary to develop the country.

The river banks are steep and high. The work of building a line high up in this canyon would not be vastly greater than building the lower line. Engineers have estimated that $500,000 extra money would carry them at high grade throughout without any extra gradient in the track. I discussed this point with Secretary Ballinger a short time ago, and he placed the cost higher than the estimate of engineers. "A million dollars, perhaps three or four times as much," was the Ballinger statement. On either basis, the amount it would cost the railroads is a bagatelle in comparison with the money loss each year to the State of Oregon.

The railroads refused to spend the money necessary to put their roadbeds higher up, and in this they were penny wise and pound foolish. If the Des Chutes could be developed along the lines I have suggested, the country would fill up with people, and the increased passenger and freight traffic would very soon wipe out the extra cost of construction.

The Hill and the Harriman interests played 'possum during the last days of Roosevelt and waited until his successor came into office. That happened on March 4, 1909. Their waiting was well rewarded. Within three weeks after he became Secretary of the Interior, Mr. Ballinger signed and approved the rights-of-way of the rival railway constructors. He approved them notwithstanding the fact that the rights-of-way conflicted with each other, without ruling on which side of the river they should go, without requiring that their conflicting locations be resurveyed. Also, he approved them without taking any measures whatever to preserve to the people of Oregon the enormous public resource contained in the running water. Mr. Ballinger was custodian of the banks of the river. He gave away this valuable property in such wise that its use will wreck the great heritage of the people of Oregon.

Meantime, the rival railroads are already engaged in a bitter, costly war. Tens of thousands of dollars have been lavished in counsel fees and court costs. Armies of workmen are deploying along the Des Chutes; I saw them last August engaged at close range in as bitter a fight as their employers, each gang expending more energy in hindering the work of the opponent than in prosecuting its own. Fist fights, battles with stones, these were part of the day's warfare. And in the end, little will be gained. The money that would have been required to elevate the tracks will be spent in warfare. Such is the rule of grab.

Before the invasion of the Des Chutes I called upon Secretary Ballinger in Washington and asked him if it were true that he had granted these permits. He was at first vexed that the matter was out, but quickly recovered himself.

"The permits are not granted, but they will be at once," he said.

"Is any reservation made about water power?" I asked.

"Only that at one point if the government ever desires to put in a dam the railroads must raise their tracks one hundred feet."

"What is your object in giving in to the railroads and letting them destroy this water power?"

Mr. Ballinger is not a large man. He has been questioned and quizzed about his troubles over conservation until he is no longer able to control his temper. He stepped away from his desk and paced rapidly up and down his office.

"See here. You don't understand this thing," he said. "You chaps who are in favor of this conservation program are all wrong. You are hindering the development of the West. These railroads are necessary to the country. And more than that, this whole big domain is a blanket —it is oppressing the people. The thing to do with it—" and here he stopped and faced me. "In my opinion the proper course to take with regard to this domain is to divide it up among the big corporations and the people who know how to make money out of it and let the people at large get the benefit of the circulation of the money."

It becomes necessary to quote this statement of Mr. Ballinger to make clear his position. It is not probable that he is corrupt, in the sense that a direct bribe could induce him to defraud the government. Mr. Ballinger is primarily an attorney who has received his training in representing large business interests, and it is entirely natural that his sympathies should be found on the side of corporations and capitalists when they come into conflict with the interests of the whole people as represented by the government.

It is worth while to examine briefly the history of the Public Domain and see how it came to be transferred into a grab bag and how there grew up men who believe that it is a grab bag to be emptied by everyone fortunate enough to be able to find the opening and insert his hand.

In Revolutionary times several of the colonies laid claim to lands running to the Mississippi, or to the Pacific, over the frontiers of which they had waged bitter war with the Indians and the French. All through the Revolution this frontier conflict was continued, and the British lost no opportunity of inciting the redskins to massacre. The heavy loss of life in defending the frontier was common to all. Its continuance appalled the struggling colonies, and the Legislature of Maryland demanded that if these lands were to be secured at the cost of the common blood they should be common lands, belonging to the nation and not to the several states.

Maryland's appeal won her neighbors. Colony after colony relinquished its claims to the country at large, until, when the nation was put upon its feet, there existed a great territory stretching west from the Alleghenies to the Pacific which, except for a number of colonial and royal grants antedating the Revolution, belonged to the nation.

That was the birth of the Public Domain, begot in bloodshed, a perpetual reminder of the hard struggles of our forefathers, a reward for their patriotism and unselfishness.

Then came those vast acquisitions that rounded out the great domain from the Mississippi River to the Pacific Ocean, including the Louisiana Purchase, which took from the treasury of the nation then a larger sum in proportion to its wealth than the whole Panama Canal project is taking from us now.

With this vast domain our nation in its youth started the most amazing campaign of expansion, through home-making, the world has ever seen. All the people of the world were invited to take up the farming land of the great West and become disciples of liberty, freedmen with their own land.

It was this that made America, but it was inevitable that this giving away of a great continent should excite the rapacity, the selfishness of many men who had no need for new homes, but who saw in the untillable areas opportunities for what they grew to call "development." Under the sanction of this phrase great timber grabbers swept away the vast timber lands of Michigan, Wisconsin and Minnesota, often carelessly setting fire to what they did not themselves cut off for lumber. Buying a few thousand acres, unscrupulous operators would use it as a cloak to steal the timber from the adjacent government lands; and so were built up many of the largest fortunes in the world.

What was done by the timber grabbers was done by the coal-mine grabbers, and by the men who fenced the grazing lands. They made tremendous fortunes, and the sight of these aggregations of wealth was welcomed by the pioneers in the West as a sign of development and an indication that they were approaching the civilization of the eastern states.

Able by the use of their money to command the strongest lawyers as well as to dominate socially, these grabbers of the Public Domain were powerful enough to build up not only a long series of court decisions supporting their claims and their actions, but a public opinion which condoned, if it did not defend; which came to regard, as they did, the grabbing of anything from the Public Domain as a process of "development" necessary to the prosperity of the new country. To call such affairs stealing would have been cause for ostracism and persecution a decade ago.

From the old-fashioned point of view it is of very little importance whether interior Oregon is ever irrigated, or whether the people of that state save and develop their water power. But it is of supreme importance that two railway magnates who desire to build railways—which will aid in developing the West, will absorb capital, will lead to uncut forests and unopened mines—have every facility to advance without regard to the result upon the public.

However, a revolution in this popular sentiment has taken place and the point of view of yesterday is not that of today. The people are beginning to insist that the laws passed to defend the Public Domain should defend it; should be obeyed; should not be ridden over rough-shod, or evaded by clever lawyer tricks. The Domain should not be a grab bag, but a treasure house in which the nation shall hold a vast store of riches to be developed economically for the public's good.

The Secretary of the Interior is custodian of the Public Domain. He is in control of the national grab bag. Therefore, it is of the greatest importance that we study and analyze the acts and the record of the man who holds this important position, so that we may determine whether his point of view is that of the grabbers or of the conservers. Sidelights on the man's business and professional life may help us in reaching a clearer understanding. . . . Let us look at him now in his relation to Alaska, a subject . . . very much connected with the trustification of our national resources.

The present movement in Alaska is the most tremendous attempt yet made by capitalists to obtain a monopolistic control of the natural resources remaining in the United States. Alaska, which we bought for $7,500,000, is the best bargain Uncle Sam's family has ever obtained. Its wealth is beyond computation. In gold a hundred million—two hundred million—no man can estimate it; the value may be two billion dollars. In timber, in agricultural land, in copper, the values run into the hundreds of millions of dollars. In coal the value is uncountable; it probably amounts to billions of dollars. The fisheries, already trustified, the sealeries controlled by Senator Elkins' trust, add to this return for our small investment.

To grab this vast treasure has stirred the pirate blood in many of our money kings till they would make any endeavor, legal or illegal, to obtain it.

The Guggenheims, smelter kings, first set eyes upon Alaska and obtained virtual monopoly of the navigation, railways and provision companies which control and direct the lives of those that work within the borders of the territory. Combining with J. Pierpont Morgan they fought for the copper empire of Alaska and secured such a wealth of deposits through methods we cannot here describe that their resources in Alaska are estimated to be worth $500,000,000. This half a billion dollars has been transferred from the national storehouse to theirs. There has been no reason for the transfer, save that the Guggenheims are strong, powerful grabbers. There has been no recompense to the people other than the government's nominal fees.

The Standard Oil-Amalgamated Copper interests, striving to secure for themselves hundreds of millions of copper in the Copper River country, fought the Guggenheims in Alaska for a long time. Opposing gangs of men hired to build impossible railways across glaciers, over morasses and through narrow gorges of rivers swollen by repeated floods, spent much of their time stalking and shooting their rivals. Often murder was done to advance the fight. At last Big Business triumphed over personal rivalry, and Morgan, Guggenheim, Standard Oil and Amalgamated signed a treaty of peace and directed their united energies toward grabbing everything of value in Alaska.

The cause of much of this trouble was the coal land of the Controller Bay region. Into the Pacific along the southern coast of Alaska flow two big rivers, the Susitna and the Copper, the one into Prince William

Sound, the other into Cook Inlet. Just to the east of Cook Inlet is
the town of Katalla and the body of water known as Controller Bay.
Copper River is the great inlet from the south to central Alaska and
the Yukon by river and by rail. At its head it comes close to the
Tanana, which flows into the Yukon. A railway runs by a treacherous
and difficult route from Katalla and from Cordova up the Copper River
to its principal rapids, and above that its glacier-fed waters support
steamboat navigation into the richest copper region yet discovered in
America. This copper, which "the interests" seek to control, is the
key to the prolongation of the Smelter Trust.

To smelt copper are needed two things: water power and coal,
principally coal.

Back of Controller Bay, beginning almost at tidewater and extending
inward until they are lost beneath the immense ice masses of Bering
and Martin's River Glaciers, extend the coal fields. Near the seashore
this coal, which crops out upon the surface, is of a soft, bituminous
character about the equal of the best Illinois fuel. A little farther back
is found an enormous amount of a semibituminous, coking coal, the
equal of Pocahontas, George's Creek, or any other first-class coking
coal of West Virginia. And beyond this again lies Carbon Mountain,
practically a great mountain of the finest anthracite in the world—
probably the largest known deposit of this valuable mineral.

The total value of these Controller Bay deposits (and they are but
a small part of the total Alaskan coal fields) is beyond calculation.
They have never been surveyed. The coal in sight on Carbon Mountain
is in four veins reaching to thirty feet in thickness and extending entirely around and through the mountain. What lies beneath the surface
no man knows. All this coal is within an hour of the ship side and
can be transshipped to San Francisco for less than Colorado coal can
climb the first range of mountains.

A vast quantity of this coal is well adapted for use in the vessels of
the Pacific Squadron, making these coal lands especially valuable to
the government. At present that squadron is supplied with coal from
the East.

In 1906, nine hundred mineral claims, aggregating about 150,000
acres, were pending against these Controller Bay deposits. These nine
hundred claims are still pending, for President Roosevelt in 1906
withdrew all the coal lands in Alaska from entry. Mr. Ballinger has
not yet questioned the President's authority to take this action. Among
these claims are included certain groups known as the Greene group,

the Alaska Petroleum and Coal Company group, the Alaska Development Company group, the Harriman group and the Cunningham group.

The first group of filings on this Alaskan land—and these are among the nine hundred awaiting patent—were made for the Alaska Development Company of Seattle, in 1902. They were of the worst type of "dummy entries." A contractor and a Katalla saloonkeeper picked the dummies and paid them $100 each to file on the claims and assign them to the Alaska Development Company. Later, when the government detected this fraud, members of the Alaska Development Company refiled on the same claims. These claims are believed to be under option to the firm of MacKenzie and Mann, the Canadian financiers said to represent the Standard Oil group, and owners of the Canadian Northern Railway. Standard Oil interests are involved in the Greene group, controlled by former Mayor Harry White, of Seattle, now of California, and by other Seattle men. The most serious charges made against Secretary Ballinger are in connection with various of these Alaskan coal claims. To understand the situation we need to examine the land laws which govern Alaska.

The general coal land law of 1873 provided that any person or association (the person being a citizen and with the usual qualifications) might enter for an individual 160 acres, or for an association 320 acres of coal lands not otherwise withdrawn or appropriated; and pay for it $10 an acre if it was more than fifteen miles from a railway, $20 if it was nearer. The law, however, does not limit this price, but says "not less than $20."

Another section of the same act provides that when any such association of not less than four persons has expended not less than $5,000 on improvements it may enter 640 acres embracing such improvements. Only one entry is allowed to each citizen and having made one he cannot sell that and make another. In determining disputed titles "continued good faith" is indicated as the proper guide. A "preference right of entry" is given by the improvement work. This is known as the "location," and by the rules the assessment work is required to be actually done to the opening of the mine. The right continues for one year.

In 1900 these laws were extended to Alaska. In 1904 the rules were amended to cover the unsurveyed districts and allow a claimant to lay out forty acres or a multiple of forty acres in a rectangle, with north and south boundaries, and to record and patent it under regulations.

The object of these various laws and regulations is to prevent a trust from securing control of an enormous tract of priceless mineral land at ten dollars an acre. The law expressly forbids an agreement among men to patent coal lands for the use of a corporation. Filings made under such an agreement are by that act void. After location and before entry, holders of Alaska claims up to 2,560 acres may combine them for mutual working . . . but no larger amount and no previous agreement is permitted.

In 1907 the Seattle *Star* blazoned forth on its front page an "exposé" of the Alaska Petroleum and Coal Company. This corporation, headed by Clarke Davis (according to the *Star* story—and it has never been gainsaid), a well-known and prosperous citizen of Seattle, had sought for oil in Alaska, and had failed to find it, but had found the now famous coal lands. Then a number of men who had organized the corporation filed, by power of attorney, upon these Alaska coal lands. Each took 160 acres, and all of them transferred their locations to the corporation. Then the corporation issued $5,000,000 of stock in one-dollar shares, basing the value on the ownership of the coal lands. Clarke Davis, said the *Star*, received one million shares for promotion work and for his own coal locations. Other shares were given to organizers of the corporation, and yet others were placed in the hands of men whose influence would be of value to the company. Many treasury shares were sold at prices ranging from seven cents to forty cents per share.

The *Star* created a sensation by announcing that under the law it is impossible to transfer titles to the location before entry, and that if any plan is entered into to do so the entry is refused and the land becomes again part of the Public Domain.

A prospectus was issued by the company and widely circulated through the mails. It stated that the company owned 1,920 acres of valuable coal lands in Alaska. Many people invested in stock. Failing legislation that would make their filings legal and give them title to the coal, the directors were in a dilemma. If they proved their claims and assigned them to the company, after taking oath that they were filing on them for their own use, they would be liable to prosecution by the government. And, on the other hand, if the company failed to get possession of the coal lands its officers might be liable to prosecution for the use they had made of the mails.

Mr. Ballinger was the attorney chosen to relieve this situation and to pilot the Alaska Petroleum and Coal Company through legal obstacles to a clear title. He went to Washington and did all in his power in two directions—one to secure the patenting of the lands in dispute, the other to secure broader laws for the use of corporations in grabbing Alaska.

The firm of Ballinger, Ronald & Battle, of which Mr. Ballinger was the senior partner until he became connected with the public service, is one of the leading legal forces of Seattle. In the Northwest, Ballinger, Ronald & Battle are generally recognized as the legal representatives of Standard Oil in Seattle.

Ballinger adds an agreeable personality to a keen knowledge of the law. He had been Mayor of Seattle and by a war on slot machines had made something of a reputation as a reformer. He had served the government as a lawyer on one or two occasions, and in various ways had attracted the attention of Roosevelt. In March 1907 the President appointed him Commissioner of the General Land Office in Washington. The unpleasant significance of this lies in the fact that Mr. Ballinger was thus in charge of the department which could refuse or consent to patent the Clarke Davis group of coal claims.

He took no action on the claims of his clients while he was Commissioner, but his appearance in Washington was immediately followed by the turning of Roosevelt's attention to the question of Alaska coal lands and a message to Congress asking the corporations be permitted to patent considerably larger areas. Ballinger appeared before the Committee on Public Lands for the House of Representatives, and urged the passage of such an act. In referring to the Clarke Davis situation he stated that to his own knowledge the men concerned had been guilty of merely technical violations of the law.

In the year 1907 a law *was* passed and presented to the President, but it was destined to go no further. While it was pending before President Roosevelt, however, Mr. Ballinger was actively at work for it.

Meetings were held in Seattle at which men prominent in northwestern business and political circles were present. Among others interested in these conferences were former Governor McGraw, of Washington; H. R. Harriman, an officer of the Alaska Petroleum and Coal Company, from whose connection it comes about that these are known as the Harriman claims; John Schram, president of the Washington Trust Company and a trustee of the Alaska Petroleum and Coal Company, and F. F. Evans, a mining broker. Mr. Ballinger was moved to leave his desk in the national capital and go to Seattle and there meet with the conferees. These men used their influence in urging James Garfield, then Secretary of the Interior, to aid in securing the signing of the bill.

Mr. Ballinger's friends in Seattle, and he has many of them, have assured me that they could see nothing improper in his thus pushing the claims of his former clients against the very department of the government with which he was officially connected. Indeed, some of his friends explained his participation to me—and they could see no objection to the situation—by the statement that Mr. Ballinger is, or has been, financially interested in 155,000 shares of the stock of the Alaska Petroleum and Coal Company.

But although the act of 1907 did not get past President Roosevelt, nevertheless, on the twenty-eighth of May 1908, there did go into effect a new law providing that locators who had, in good faith and for their own use, located prior to November 12, 1906, on coal lands in Alaska, might be allowed to combine their holdings to 2,560 acres (four square miles), and work them as a corporation.

This might be read in three ways: it might be construed to admit only those that had entered the lands before planning to combine; it might be construed to admit everybody even if their plan to incorporate were made before location; or it might take a middle course and include those that filed in good faith as individuals and then formed a corporation before entering for patent.

"We hoped," says a man very close to Ballinger, "to be able to give the statute the broadest possible interpretation so that all locators would be included. We hoped, in fact, to find in it a new rule for construing more broadly the old 640-acre statute."

In the meantime—in March 1908—Mr. Ballinger had resigned his position as Commissioner of the General Land Office. It may, therefore, have been due to his absence from the scene that this law, which Ballinger had helped to pass, contained a truly Rooseveltian last paragraph so strongly antitrust that the purpose of the law was lost. This paragraph, too long to quote, provides that if by any means whatever, tacitly or directly or in any indirect way or in any manner whatever the lands involved become concerned with, or the property of, or in any way connected with any agreement in restraint of trade or any *corporation* concerned in such an agreement, *the lands shall revert to the United States and the title become void.* It is said that Gifford Pinchot drafted this paragraph. Part of the coal lands lie in the Chugach Forest Reserve—which would give Mr. Pinchot good reason to take an interest in the legislation.

This antitrust paragraph daunted the promoters. Not a single claim has been pressed for entry under this antitrust act and the grabbers are pushing to have it repealed.

In March 1908, then, because his professional and business interests in Seattle demanded his time, Ballinger retired from the Commissionership and went home. He became immediately involved in another group of Alaska claims called the Cunningham group directly concerned with the Morgan-Guggenheim-Standard Oil combination and with the exploiting of Alaska.

Clarence Cunningham, a typical prospector who had tramped all over the Northwest, went up to the Controller Bay region in 1902 when others were hunting for gold, and examined the Carbon Mountain coal. He returned to Washington state, and pressed about among his friends with the news of the value and availability of this deposit and organized a syndicate to grab all they could of it and sell it out to bigger interests.

Into this Cunningham group came a number of men of wealth, and a few others who were acting as dummies. Each of these men gave Cunningham a power of attorney and with this he went to Alaska and filed on thirty-three claims, 5,280 acres of Carbon Mountain and adjacent coal lands, all richly underlaid with the fuel. It is alleged freely that the Cunningham group intended to form a corporation, to which their lands were to be sold, and that the corporation was to pass into the hands of the Guggenheims. But Roosevelt's last paragraph had prevented the execution of such a plan.

With the law against them, the Cunningham claimants turned to Ballinger. They presented to his attention their thirty-three claims, worth many millions of dollars, and sent Mr. Ballinger, who had just resigned the Commissionership, back to Washington to appeal to the Department of the Interior.

There is a law which to the common intellect seems to make that act of Ballinger's illegal. Section 190 of the revised statutes forbids *for two years after he has left the department,* any officer of a governmental department from practicing before that department in behalf of any claim which was pending during his term of office. It is designed to prevent department lawyers from being subsidized by corporations to resign and use their information against the government from which they have obtained it.

The Cunningham claims had been before the Land Office when Mr. Ballinger was Commissioner. Nevertheless, Attorney Ballinger soon appeared before his successor and pleaded to have the Cunningham claims passed to entry and patent. Attorney Ballinger's efforts in this case were not successful.

And then the presidential election came—and a few months later

Mr. Ballinger was occupying the position of Secretary of the Interior in Mr. Taft's Cabinet. And very soon after his installation in this honorable and important position he began to undo the work accomplished by Theodore Roosevelt. . . .

Bear distinctly in mind that I charge no corrupt motive in Mr. Ballinger's appearance in official Washington. That is, no corrupt motive in his mind or the President's.

In the Northwest charges are made that connect Postmaster General Frank Hitchcock—in his capacity of manager of the latest Republican national campaign—with the Guggenheim interests in an arrangement to secure the Interior portfolio for Mr. Ballinger. This may be partisan political gossip. It is very easy for interested parties to start such rumors, and very difficult for them to prove them.

Unquestionably Mr. Ballinger has strong political influences back of him. As I have shown, many powerful selfish interests would be more than willing to aid him in any ambition for high government position. But this would not prove that Mr. Ballinger was corrupt. As I have said, his talents as a lawyer have ever been employed by corporations or individuals who believe that the treasures of the Public Domain should become their private property. Mr. Ballinger is undoubtedly sincere and honest in his desires to further what he believes to be the legitimate interests of his clients. His point of view may be old-fashioned, but it is not likely that he can be proved guilty of corrupt acts.

When Mr. Ballinger was still Commissioner of the Land Office this peculiar train of events came to the attention of Louis R. Glavis, a special agent of the Department of the Interior. Glavis is young, enthusiastic, determined to follow the Roosevelt idea of protecting the public lands and of prosecuting graft to the end. His duties were to investigate claims offered for entry at the Government Land Offices. Many such claims are contested by rival applicants; many are fraudulent upon the face of them; and many, like these Cunningham claims, while apparently legal are believed to be really parts of a conspiracy to wrest property illegally from the Public Domain. It is the business of special agents to investigate these cases as fully as possible, and for that purpose Mr. Glavis was stationed at Portland, Oregon. From there, about two years ago, he sent a secret service agent named Smith to begin an investigation into the Cunningham claims. Then Glavis followed Smith almost immediately and so far as possible carried on the search for Cunningham evidence personally.

Some time ago the department, through the efforts of Mr. Taft, was awarded an extra appropriation of $1,000,000 to increase its staff and facilitate the movement of some 30,000 claims which had been delayed through the routine of the Land Office. Among these 30,000 claims were the Cunningham entries.

To expedite the work it was necessary to divide Mr. Glavis' district, and he was accordingly relieved of work at Portland and allowed to station himself at Seattle with practically nothing to occupy his attention but the alleged Alaskan coal frauds. He says that he saw a record belonging to Clarence Cunningham containing a list of those concerned in the Cunningham entry; the sums of money each was to receive for his land, when it was turned over to the eventual syndicate; and other evidence of a conspiracy to combine or trustify this big tract. This, with other evidence, was sent to Mr. Taft.

In addition to this evidence of the Cunningham plans, Mr. Glavis, feeling that his investigation was being interfered with, believed that he had stumbled upon evidence which indicated collusion between the officials of his department and the owners of these fraudulent claims, to facilitate the patenting. However, President Taft has made no comment whatever upon the Cunningham cases, but in his reply to Mr. Ballinger concerning the Glavis charges devotes himself to those of official collusion and dismisses them as unworthy of consideration because they are inferential, and because Glavis had not given Mr. Ballinger the inferential benefit of certain modifying circumstances.

President Taft dismissed Mr. Glavis from the government service, and thoroughly "whitewashed" his Secretary of the Interior. The speedy removal of the youthful inspector Glavis from the service emphasized the indorsement. So we have the "Pinchot-Ballinger Controversy." . . .

Hampton's Magazine
December 1909

PART FOUR

Poison——Beware!

PATENT MEDICINE

RETAIL SALES of patent medicines at the close of the nineteenth century were an estimated one hundred million dollars. The population of the United States at that time was eighty million.

The patent medicine producers were large advertisers, and as such influenced the editorial contents in many of the periodicals. If an editorial breathed one adverse word about patent medicines, the makers withdrew their advertising. For example, on November 10, 1906, *Collier's* reported: "We spoke out about patent medicines, and dropped $80,000 in a year."

The industry used all types of publications, newspapers and magazines, to advertise their products. Even the Socialist journal *Appeal to Reason*—which in the same issue * ran a boxed editorial announcement of the serializing of Upton Sinclair's *The Jungle*—carried the ad:

> Cancer Cured with soothing, balmy oils.
> Cancer, Tumor, Catarrh, Piles, Fistula, Ulcers,
> Eczema and all Skin and Womb diseases. Write for
> illustrated book. Sent free. Address Dr. Bye,
> cor. 9th and Broadway, Kansas City, Mo.

In many instances, however, the medicines were ineffectual. Some of the syrups contained as much as 80 per cent alcohol; many of the tonics used cocaine and morphine. Some of the medicines destroyed health, and made drunkards and dope addicts out of their users.

The most active magazines in the war against the patent medicine fraud were the *Ladies' Home Journal* and *Collier's*. Edward Bok, Mark Sullivan and Samuel Hopkins Adams were the leading writers in the field.

It was Edward Bok, editor of the *Ladies' Home Journal*, who started the original magazine reform push. Bok felt very strongly about the patent medicine evil and its alcoholic content. As early as 1892, he announced that his magazine would no longer accept patent medicine advertisements.

"Into this army of deceit and spurious medicines," wrote Bok in his autobiography, "the *Ladies' Home Journal* fired the first gun. Neither the public nor the patent medicine people paid much attention to the first

* February 4, 1905.

attacks. But as they grew, and the evidence multiplied, the public began to comment and the nostrum makers began to get uneasy." [67]

By 1904 Bok was writing editorials against patent medicines. He used the Women's Christian Temperance Union to fight periodicals which took ads for products containing a large percentage of alcohol.

Bok persuaded Mark Sullivan, who was just beginning a law practice in New York, to give up law and come to work for the *Ladies' Home Journal*. Sullivan's first assignment was to prepare an article on the patent medicine companies.

Sullivan started to collect data. He talked with people from the nostrum companies; he obtained letters which were written to the companies by men and women who were seeking help. These letters were being sold in bulk from one "patent medicine quack" operator to another.

One of the firms, the Lydia Pinkham Company, through its advertisements, invited women to write to Lydia Pinkham for advice, indicating that Miss Pinkham would answer personally. Sullivan went to the Pine Grove cemetery in Lynn, Massachusetts, and photographed the grave of Lydia Pinkham, who had died in 1883, twenty-three years earlier.

Sullivan also was able to obtain the minutes of a meeting of the Proprietary Medicine Association, the trade group of the patent medicine manufacturers. At this meeting its presiding officer, F. J. Cheney, maker of a catarrh cure, told how he incorporated in his contract with the press a clause which bound magazines and newspapers to fight any adverse legislation. Cheney said he had inserted in his contract with about 15,000 newspapers the clause: "It is hereby agreed that should your state, or the United States government, pass any law that would interfere with or restrict the sale of proprietary medicines, this contract shall become void." [68] Then, whenever a bill was introduced in legislatures to regulate patent medicines, Cheney would remind the newspapers in that state of the cancellation clause.

As a result of this discovery, Sullivan wrote an article entitled "The Patent Medicine Conspiracy Against Freedom of the Press."

Sullivan sent the article to Bok. "This article, however, was not adapted to the *Home Journal*; Bok's standard of length was short, two or three thousand words, and this article was long, about seven thousand words, and it was so tight-woven that it could not readily be cut. Bok, impressed by the article, wishing to see it printed, and eager to have other periodicals cooperate in his patent medicine crusade, took the article to *Collier's Weekly* and offered it to them for seven hundred dollars." [69] The article appeared in *Collier's* November 4, 1905, with no by-line.

A month earlier *Collier's* had started to print a series of articles by Samuel Hopkins Adams called "The Great American Fraud." [70]

In announcing the Adams series, *Collier's* said: "These articles, which have been written by Mr. Samuel H. Adams, after an investigation lasting several months, will not only describe the methods used to humbug the public into buying patent medicines through fake testimonials and lying statements published in the newspapers, but will show that a large number of the so-called 'tonics' are only cocktails in disguise, and that many of these nostrums are directly responsible for the making of drunkards and drug fiends." [71]

In his series, Adams would select a medicine, have it analyzed, study its advertising, its claims, and collect histories of people who used it.

Adams opened his first article with: "Gullible America will spend this year some seventy-five millions of dollars in the purchase of patent medicines. In consideration of this sum it will swallow huge quantities of alcohol, an appalling amount of opiates and narcotics, a wide assortment of varied drugs ranging from powerful and dangerous heart depressants to insidious liver stimulants; and, far in excess of all other ingredients, undiluted fraud. For fraud, exploited by the skilfulest of advertising bunco men, is the basis of the trade. Should the newspapers, the magazines, and the medical journals refuse their pages to this class of advertisements, the patent medicine business in five years would be as scandalously historic as the South Sea Bubble, and the nation would be the richer not only in lives and money, but in drunkards and drug fiends saved."

Will Irwin said of Adams: "We considered [him] a born muckraker." [72]

The *New York Times* in its obituary on Adams on November 17, 1958, wrote: "He became one of the foremost magazine writers investigating and exposing the evils of the early 20th century who came to be known as a 'muckraker.' His articles, piercing and denouncing the claims of patent medicines of those days, were an important cause of the subsequent enactment of the federal pure food and drug laws."

ANONYMOUS*

The Patent Medicine Conspiracy
Against Freedom of the Press

IN THE LOWER HOUSE of the Massachusetts Legislature one day last
March there was a debate which lasted one whole afternoon and
engaged some twenty speakers, on a bill providing that every bottle
of patent medicine sold in the state should bear a label stating the
contents of the bottle. More was told concerning patent medicines
that afternoon than often comes to light in a single day. The debate
at times was dramatic—a member from Salem told of a young woman
of his acquaintance now in an institution for inebriates as the end
of an incident which began with patent medicine dosing for a harmless
ill. There was humor, too, in the debate—Representative Walker held
aloft a bottle of Peruna bought by him in a drugstore that very day,
and passed it around for his fellow members to taste and decide for
themselves whether Dr. Harrington, the Secretary of the State Board
of Health, was right when he told the Legislative Committee that it
was merely a "cheap cocktail."

In short, the debate was interesting and important—the two qualities
which invariably ensure to any event big headlines in the daily newspapers. But that debate was not celebrated by big headlines, nor any
headlines at all. Yet Boston is a city, and Massachusetts is a state,
where the proceedings of the Legislature figure very large in public
interest, and where the newspapers respond to that interest by reporting
the sessions with greater fullness and minuteness than in any other
state. Had that debate been on prison reform, on Sabbath observance,

* This article was written by Mark Sullivan, but carried no by-line.

the early-closing saloon law, on any other subject, there would have been, in the next day's papers, overflowing accounts of verbatim report, more columns of editorial comment, and the picturesque features of it would have ensured the attention of the cartoonist.

Now why? Why was this one subject tabooed? Why were the daily accounts of legislative proceedings in the next day's papers abridged to a fraction of their usual ponderous length, and all reference to the afternoon debate on patent medicines omitted? Why was it in vain for the speakers in that patent medicine debate to search for their speeches in the next day's newspapers? Why did the legislative reporters fail to find their work in print? Why were the staff cartoonists forbidden to exercise their talent on that most fallow and tempting opportunity—the members of the Great and General Court of Massachusetts gravely tippling Peruna and passing the bottle around to their encircled neighbors, that practical knowledge should be the basis of legislative action?

I take it if any man should assert that there is one subject upon which the newspapers of the United States, acting in concert and as a unit, will deny full and free discussion, he would be smiled at as an intemperate fanatic. The thing is too incredible. He would be regarded as a man with a delusion. And yet I invite you to search the files of the daily newspapers of Massachusetts for March 16, 1905, for an account of the patent medicine debate that occurred the afternoon of March 15 in the Massachusetts Legislature. In strict accuracy it must be said that there was one exception. Anyone familiar with the newspapers of the United States will already have named it—the Springfield *Republican*. That paper, on two separate occasions, gave several columns to the record of the proceedings of the Legislature on the patent medicine bill. Why the otherwise universal silence?

The patent medicine business in the United States is one of huge financial proportions. The census of 1900 placed the value of the annual product at $59,611,355. Allowing for the increase of half a decade of rapid growth, it must be today not less than seventy-five millions. That is the wholesale price. The retail price of all the patent medicines sold in the United States in one year may be very conservatively placed at one hundred million dollars. And of this one hundred millions which the people of the United States pay for patent medicines yearly, fully forty millions goes to the newspapers. Have patience! I have more to say than merely to point out the large revenue which newspapers receive from patent medicines, and let inference do the rest. Inference has no place in this story. There are facts aplenty. But it is essential to point out the intimate financial relation between the newspapers and the patent medicines. I was told by the man who for many years handled the advertising of the Lydia E. Pinkham Company that their expenditure was $100,000 a month, $1,200,000 a year. Dr. Pierce and the Peruna Company both advertise much more extensively than the Pinkham Company. Certainly there are at least five patent medicine concerns in the United States who each pay out to the newspapers more than one million dollars a year. When the Dr. Greene Nervura Company of Boston went into bankruptcy, its debts to newspapers for advertising amounted to $535,000. To the Boston *Herald* alone it owed $5,000, and to so small a paper, comparatively, as the Atlanta *Constitution* it owed $1,500. One obscure quack doctor in New York, who did merely an office business, was raided by the authorities, and among the papers seized there were contracts showing that within a year he had paid to one paper for advertising $5,856.80; to another $20,000. Dr. Humphreys, one of the best known patent medicine makers, has said to his fellow members of the Patent Medicine Association: "The twenty thousand newspapers of the United States make more money from advertising the proprietary medicines than do the proprietors of the medicines themselves. . . . Of their receipts, one-third to one-half goes for advertising." More than six years ago, Cheney, the president of the National Association of Patent Medicine Men, estimated the yearly amount paid to the newspapers by the larger patent medicine concerns at twenty million dollars—more than one thousand dollars to each daily, weekly and monthly periodical in the United States.

Does this throw any light on the silence of the Massachusetts papers? Naturally such large sums paid by the patent medicine men to the newspapers suggest the thought of favor. But silence is too important a part of the patent medicine man's business to be left to the capricious chance of favor. Silence is the most important thing in his business. The ingredients of his medicine—that is nothing. Does the price of goldenseal go up? Substitute whiskey. Does the price of whiskey go up? Buy the refuse wines of the California vineyards. Does the price of opium go too high, or public fear of it make it an inexpedient thing to use? Take it out of the formula and substitute any worthless barnyard weed. But silence is the fixed quantity—silence as to the frauds he practices; silence as to the abominable stewings and brewings that enter into his nostrum; silence as to the deaths and sicknesses he causes; silence as to the drug fiends he makes, the inebriate asylums he fills. Silence he must have. So he makes silence a part of the contract.

Read the significant silence of the Massachusetts newspapers in the light of the following contracts for advertising. They are the regular printed form used by Hood, Ayer and Munyon in making their advertising contracts with thousands of newspapers throughout the United States.

. . . the contract made by the J. C. Ayer Company, makers of Ayer's Sarsaparilla [shows] at the top . . . the name of the firm, "The J. C. Ayer Company, Lowell, Mass.," and the date. Then follows a blank for the number of dollars, and then the formal contract: "We hereby agree, for the sum of .... Dollars per year, ... to insert in the ...., published at ...., the advertisement of the J. C. Ayer Company." Then follow the conditions as to space to be used each issue, the page the advertisement is to be on, and the position it is to occupy. Then these two remarkable conditions of the contract: "First—It is agreed in case any law or laws are enacted, either State or national, harmful to the interests of the J. C. Ayer Company, that this contract may be canceled by them from date of such enactment, and the insertions made paid for pro-rata with the contract price."

This clause is remarkable enough. But of it more later. For the present, examine the second clause: "Second—It is agreed that the J. C. Ayer Company may cancel this contract, pro-rata, in case advertisements are published in this paper in which their products are offered, with a view to substitution or other harmful motive, also in case any matter otherwise detrimental to the J. C. Ayer Company's interests is permitted to appear in the reading columns or elsewhere in the paper."

This agreement is signed in duplicate, one copy by the J. C. Ayer Company and the other one by the newspaper.

That is the contract of silence. . . . The same language [on a contract] bear[s] the name of the C. I. Hood Company, the other great manufacturer of sarsaparilla; and . . . again in identically the same words— for Dr. Munyon. That is the clause which, with forty million dollars, muzzles the press of the country. I wonder if the Standard Oil Company could, for forty million dollars, bind the newspapers of the United States in a contract that "no matter detrimental to the Standard Oil Company's interests be permitted to appear in the reading columns or elsewhere in this paper."

Is it a mere coincidence that in each of these contracts the silence clause is framed in the same words? Is the inference fair that there is an agreement among the patent medicine men and quack doctors each to impose this contract on all the newspapers with which it deals, one reaching the newspapers which the other does not, and all combined reaching all the papers in the United States, and effecting a universal agreement among newspapers to print nothing detrimental to patent medicines? You need not take it as an inference. I shall show it later as a fact.

"In the reading columns or elsewhere in the paper." The paper must not print it itself, nor must it allow any outside party, who might wish to do so, to pay the regular advertising rates and print the truth about patent medicines in the advertising columns. More than a year ago, just after Mr. Bok had printed his first article exposing patent medicines, a businessman in St. Louis, a man of great wealth, conceived that it would help his business greatly if he could have Mr. Bok's article printed as an advertisement in every newspaper in the United States. He gave the order to a firm of advertising agents and the firm began in Texas, intending to cover the country to Maine. But that advertisement never got beyond a few obscure country papers in Texas. The contract of silence was effective; and a few weeks later, at their annual meeting, the patent medicine association "Resolved"—I quote the minutes—"That this Association commend the action of the great majority of the publishers of the United States who have consistently refused said false and malicious attacks in the shape of advertisements which in whole or in part libel proprietary medicines."

I have said that the identity of the language of the silence clause in several patent medicine advertising contracts suggests mutual understanding among the nostrum makers, a preconceived plan; and I have several times mentioned the patent medicine association. It seems incongruous, almost humorous, to speak of a national organization of quack doctors and patent medicine makers; but there is one, brought together for mutual support, for cooperation, for—but just what this organization is for, I hope to show. No other organization ever demonstrated so clearly the truth that "in union there is strength." Its official name is an innocent-seeming one—"The Proprietary Association of America." There are annual meetings, annual reports, a constitution, bylaws. And I would call special attention to Article II of those bylaws.

"The objects of this association," says this article, "are: to protect the rights of its members to the respective trade-marks that they may own or control; to establish such mutual cooperation as may be required in the various branches of the trade: to reduce all burdens that may be oppressive; to facilitate and foster equitable principles in the purchase and sale of merchandise; to acquire and preserve for the use of its members such business information as may be of value to them; to adjust controversies and promote harmony among its members."

That is as innocuous a statement as ever was penned of the objects of any organization. It might serve for an organization of honest cobblers. Change a few words, without altering the spirit in the least, and a body of ministers might adopt it. In this laboriously complete statement of objects, there is no such word as "lobby" or "lobbying." Indeed, so harmless a word as "legislation" is absent—strenuously absent.

But I prefer to discover the true object of the organization of the "Proprietary Association of America" in another document than Article II of the bylaws. Consider the annual report of the treasurer, say for 1904. The total of money paid out during the year was $8,516.26. Of this, one thousand dollars was for the secretary's salary, leaving $7,516.26 to be accounted for. Then there is an item of postage, one of stationery, one of printing—the little routine expenses of every organization; and finally there is this remarkable item:

"Legislative Committee, total expenses, $6,606.95."

Truly the Proprietary Association of America seems to have several objects, as stated in its bylaws, which cost it very little, and one object—not stated in its bylaws at all—which costs it all its annual revenue aside from the routine expenses of stationery, postage, and secretary. If just a few more words of comment may be permitted upon this point, does it not seem odd that so large an item as $6,606.95, out of a total budget of only $8,516.26, should be put in as a lump sum, "Legislative Committee, total expenses"? And would not the annual report of the treasurer of the Proprietary Association of America be a more entertaining document if these "total expenses" of the Legislative Committee were carefully itemized?

Not that I mean to charge the direct corruption of legislatures. The Proprietary Association of America used to do that. They used to spend, according to the statement of the present president of the organization, Mr. F. J. Cheney, as much as seventy-five thousand dollars a year. But that was before Mr. Cheney himself discovered a better way. The fighting of public health legislation is the primary object and chief activity, the very *raison d'être*, of the Proprietary Association. The motive back of bringing the quack doctors and patent medicine manufacturers of the United States into a mutual organization was this:

here are some scores of men, each paying a large sum annually to the newspapers. The aggregate of these sums is forty million dollars. By organization, the full effect of this money can be got and used as a unit in preventing the passage of laws which would compel them to tell the contents of their nostrums, and in suppressing the newspaper publicity which would drive them into oblivion. So it was no mean intellect which devised the scheme whereby every newspaper in America is made an active lobbyist for the patent medicine association. The man who did it is the present president of the organization, its executive head in the work of suppressing public knowledge, stifling public opinion, and warding off public health legislation—the Mr. Cheney already mentioned. He makes a catarrh cure which, according to the Massachusetts State Board of Health, contains 14¾ per cent of alcohol. As to his scheme for making the newspapers of America not only maintain silence, but actually lobby in behalf of the patent medicines, I am glad that I am not under the necessity of describing it in my own words. It would be easy to err in the direction that makes for incredulity. Fortunately I need take no responsibility. I have Mr. Cheney's own words, in which he explained his scheme to his fellow members of the Proprietary Association of America. The quotation marks alone (and the comment within parentheses) are mine. The remainder is the language of Mr. Cheney himself:

"We have had a good deal of difficulty in the last few years with the different legislatures of the different States. . . . I believe I have a plan whereby we will have no difficulty whatever with these people. I have used it in my business for two years, and I know it is a practical thing. . . . I, inside of the last two years, have made contracts with between fifteen and sixteen thousand newspapers, and never had but one man refuse to sign the contract, and by saying to him that I could not sign a contract without this clause in it he readily signed it. My point is merely to shift the responsibility. We today have the responsibility of the whole matter upon our shoulders. As you all know, there is hardly a year but we have had a lobbyist in the different State Legislatures—one year in New York, one year in New Jersey, and so on." (Read that frank confession twice—note the bland matter-of-factness of it.) "There has been constant fear that something would come up, so I had this clause in my contract added. This is what I have in every contract I make: 'It is hereby agreed that should your State, or the United States Government, pass any law that would interfere with or restrict the sale of proprietary medicines, this contract shall become void.' . . . In the State of Illinois a few years ago they wanted to assess me three hundred dollars. I thought I had a better plan than this, so I wrote to about forty papers and merely said: 'Please look at your contract with me and take note that if this law passes you and I must stop doing business, and my contracts cease.' The next week every one of them had an article, and Mr. Man had to go. . . . I read this to Dr. Pierce some days ago and he was very much taken up with it. I have carried this through and know it is a success. I know the papers will accept it. Here is a thing that costs us nothing. We are guaranteed against the $75,000 loss for nothing. It throws the responsibility on the newspapers. . . . I have my contracts printed and I have this printed in red type, right square across the contract, so there can be absolutely no mistake, and the newspaper man can not say to me, 'I did not see it.' He did see it and knows what he is doing. It seems to me it is a point worth every man's attention. . . . I think this pretty near a sure thing."

I should like to ask the newspaper owners and editors of America what they think of that scheme. I believe that the newspapers, when they signed each individual contract, were not aware that they were being dragooned into an elaborately thought-out scheme to make every newspaper in the United States, from the greatest metropolitan daily to the remotest country weekly, an active, energetic, self-interested lobbyist for the patent medicine association. If the newspapers knew how they were being used as cat's-paws, I believe they would resent it. Certainly the patent medicine association itself feared this, and has kept this plan of Mr. Cheney's a careful secret. In this same meeting of the Proprietary Association of America, just after Mr. Cheney had made the speech quoted above, and while it was being resolved that every other patent medicine man should put the same clause in his contract, the venerable Dr. Humphreys, oldest and wisest of the guild, arose and said: "Will it not be now just as well to act upon this, each and every one for himself, instead of putting this on record? . . . I think the idea is a good one, but really don't think it had better go in our proceedings." And another fellow nostrum-maker, seeing instantly the necessity of secrecy, said: "I am heartily in accord with Dr. Humphreys. The suggestion is a good one, but when we come to put it in our public proceedings, and state that we have adopted such a resolution, I want to say that the Legislators are just as sharp as the newspaper men. . . . As a consequence, this will decrease the weight of the press comments. Some of the papers, also, who would not come in, would publish something about it in the way of getting square. . . ."

This contract is the backbone of the scheme. The further details, the organization of the bureau to carry it into effect—that, too, has been kept carefully concealed from the generally unthinking newspapers, who are all unconsciously mere individual cogs in the patent medicine lobbying machine. At one of the meetings of the Association, Dr. R. V. Pierce of Buffalo arose and said (I quote him verbatim): ". . . I would move you that the report of the Committee on Legislation be made a special order to be taken up immediately . . . that it be considered in executive session, and that every person not a member of the organization be asked to retire, so that it may be read and considered in executive session. There are matters and suggestions in reference to our future action, and measures to be taken which are advised therein, that we would not wish to have published broadcast over the country for very good reasons."

Now what were the "matters and suggestions" which Dr. Pierce "would not wish to have published broadcast over the country for very good reasons"?

Dr. Pierce's son, Dr. V. Mott Pierce, was chairman of the Committee on Legislation. He was the author of the "matters and suggestions" which must be considered in the dark. "Never before," said he, "in the history of the Proprietary Association were there so many bills in different State Legislatures that were vital to our interests. This was due, we think, to an effort on the part of different State Boards of Health, who have of late years held national meetings, to make an organized effort to establish what are known as 'pure food laws.' " Then the younger Pierce stated explicitly the agency responsible for the defeat of this public health legislation: "We must not forget to place the honor where due for our uniform success in defeating class legislation directed against our legitimate pursuits. The American Newspaper Publishers' Association has rendered us valued aid through their secretary's office in New York, and we can hardly overestimate the power brought to bear at Washington by individual newspapers." . . . (On another occasion, Dr. Pierce, speaking of two bills in the Illinois Legislature, said: "Two things operated to bring these bills to the danger line. In the first place, the Chicago papers were almost wholly without influence in the Legislature. . . . Had it not been for the active cooperation of the press of the State outside of Chicago, there is absolute certainty that the bill would have passed. . . . I think that a great many members do not appreciate the power that we can bring to bear upon legislation through the press.") But this power, in young Dr. Pierce's opinion, must be organized and systematized. "If it is not

presumptuous on the part of your chairman," he said modestly, "to
outline a policy which experience seems to dictate for the future, it
would be briefly as follows"—here the younger Pierce explains the
"matters and suggestions" which must not be "published broadcast over
the country." The first was "the organization of a Legislative Bureau,
with its offices in New York or Chicago. Second, a secretary, to be appointed by the chairman of the Committee on Legislation, who will
receive a stated salary, sufficiently large to be in keeping with such
person's ability, and to compensate him for the giving of all his time
to this work." "The benefits of such a working bureau to the Proprietary
Association," said Dr. Pierce, "can be foreseen: First, a systematic plan
to acquire early knowledge of pending or threatened legislation could be
taken up. In the past we have relied too much upon newspaper managers to acquaint us of such bills coming up. . . . Another plan would
be to have the regulation formula bill, for instance, introduced by some
friendly legislator, and have it referred to his own committee, where he
could hold it until all danger of such another bill being introduced were
over, and the Legislature had adjourned."

Little wonder Dr. Pierce wanted a secret session to cover up the
frank naïveté of his son, which he did not "wish to have published
broadcast over the country for very good reasons."

In discussing this plan for a legislative bureau, another member
told what in his estimation was needed. "The trouble," said he—I quote
from the minutes—"the trouble we will have in attempting to buy
legislation—supposing we should attempt it—is that we will never
know what we are buying until we get through. We may have paid the
wrong man, and the bill is passed and we are out. It is not a safe proposition, if we considered it legitimate, which we do not."

True, it is not legitimate, but the main point is, it's not safe; that's
the thing to be considered.

The patent medicine man continued to elaborate on the plans proposed by Dr. Pierce: "It would not be a safe proposition at all. What
this Association should have . . . is a regularly established bureau. . . .
We should have all possible information on tap, and we should have
a list of the members of the Legislature of every State. We should have
a list of the most influential men that control them, or that can influence them. . . . For instance, if in the State of Ohio a bill comes
up that is adverse to us, turn to the books, find out who are the members of the Legislature there, who are the publishers of the papers in
the State, where they are located, which are the Republican and which

the Democratic papers. . . . It will take money, but if the money is rightly spent, it will be the best investment ever made."

That is about as comprehensive, as frankly impudent a scheme of controlling legislation as it is possible to imagine. The plan was put in the form of a resolution, and the resolution was passed. And so the Proprietary Association of America maintains a lawyer in Chicago, and a permanent secretary, office, and staff. In every State capital in the United States it maintains an agent whose business it is to watch during the session of the Legislature each day's batch of new bills, and whenever a bill affecting patent medicines shows its head to telegraph the bill, verbatim, to headquarters. There some scores of printed copies of the bill are made and a copy is sent to every member of the Association—to the Peruna people, to Dr. Pierce at Buffalo, to Kilmer at Binghamton, to Cheney at Toledo, to the Pinkham people at Lynn, and to all the others. Thereupon each manufacturer looks up the list of papers in the threatened State with which he has the contracts described above. And to each newspaper he sends a peremptory telegram calling the publisher's attention to the obligations of his contract, and commanding him to go to work to defeat the anti-patent-medicine bill. In practice, this organization works with smooth perfection and well-oiled accuracy to defeat the public health legislation which is introduced by Boards of Health in over a score of states every year. To illustrate, let me describe as typical the history of the public health bills which were introduced and defeated in Massachusetts last year. I have already mentioned them as showing how the newspapers, obeying that part of their contract which requires them to print nothing harmful to patent medicines, refused to print any account of the exposures which were made by several members of the Legislature during the debate of the bill. I wish here to describe their obedience to that other clause of the contract, in living up to which they printed scores of bit-terly partisan editorials against the public health bill, and against its authors personally: threatened with political death those members of the Legislature who were disposed to vote in favor of it, and even, in the persons of editors and owners, went up to the State House and lobbied personally against the bill. And since I have already told of Mr. Cheney's authorship of the scheme, I will here reproduce, as typical of all the others (all the other large patent medicine concerns sent similar letters and telegrams), the letter which Mr. Cheney himself on the fourteenth day of February sent to all the newspapers in Massachusetts with which he has his lobbying contracts—practically every newspaper in the state:

TOLEDO, OHIO, Feb. 14, 1905

Publishers

——————, Mass.

Gentlemen:

Should House bills Nos. 829, 30, 607, 724, or Senate bill No. 185 become laws, it will force us to discontinue advertising in your State. Your prompt attention regarding this bill we believe would be of mutual benefit.

We would respectfully refer you to the contract which we have with you.

Respectfully,

CHENEY MEDICINE COMPANY

Now here is the fruit which that letter bore: a strong editorial against the anti-patent-medicine bill, denouncing it and its author in the most vituperative language, a marked copy of which was sent to every member of the Massachusetts Legislature. But this was not all that this one zealous publisher did; he sent telegrams to a number of members, and a personal letter to the representative of his district calling on that member not only to vote, but to use his influence against the bill, on pain of forfeiting the paper's favor.

Now this seems to me a shameful thing—that a Massachusetts newspaper of apparent dignity and outward high standing should jump to the cracking of the whip of a nostrum-maker in Ohio; that honest and well-meaning members of the Massachusetts Legislature, whom all the money of Rockefeller could not buy, who obey only the one thing which they look upon as the expression of the public opinion of their constituents, the united voice of the press of their district—that these men should unknowingly cast their votes at the dictate of a nostrum-maker in Ohio, who, if he should deliver his command personally and directly, instead of through a newspaper supine enough to let him control it for a hundred dollars a year, would be scorned and flouted.

Any self-respecting newspaper must be humiliated by the attitude of the patent medicine association. They don't ask the newspapers to do it—they order it done. Read again Mr. Cheney's account of his plan, note the half-contemptuous attitude toward the newspapers. And read again Mr. Cheney's curt letter to the Massachusetts papers: observe the threat, just sufficiently veiled to make it more of a threat; and the formal order, as from a superior to a clerk: "We would respectfully refer you to the contract which we have with you."

And the threat is not an empty one. The newspaper which refuses to aid the patent medicine people is marked. Some time ago Dr. V. Mott Pierce of Buffalo was chairman of what is called the "Committee on Legislation" of the Proprietary Association of America. He was giving his annual report to the Association. "We are happy to say," said he, "that though over a dozen bills were before the different State Legislatures last winter and spring, yet we have succeeded in defeating all the bills which were prejudicial to proprietary interests without the use of money, and through the vigorous cooperation and aid of the publishers. January 23 your committee sent out letters to the principal publications in New York asking their aid against this measure. It is hardly necessary to state that the publishers of New York responded generously against these harmful measures. The only small exception was the *Evening Star* of Poughkeepsie, New York, the publisher of which, in a very discourteous letter, refused to assist us in any way."

Is it to be doubted that Dr. Pierce reported this exception to his fellow patent medicine men that they might make note of the offending paper, and bear it in mind when they made their contracts the following year? There are other cases which show what happens to the newspaper which offends the patent medicine men. I am fortunate enough to be able to describe the following incident in the language of the man who wielded the club, as he told the story with much pride to his fellow patent medicine men at their annual meeting:

"Mr. Chairman and Gentlemen of the Proprietary Association," said Mr. Cooper, "I desire to present to you a situation which I think it is incumbent upon manufacturers generally to pay some attention to—namely, the publication of sensational drug news which appears from time to time in the leading papers of the country. . . . There are, no doubt, many of you in the room, at least a dozen, who are familiar with the sensational articles that appeared in the Cleveland *Press*. Gentlemen, this is a question that appeals to you as a matter of business. . . . The Cleveland *Press* indulged in a tirade against the so-called 'drug trust.' " . . . (The "drug trust" is the same organization of patent medicine men—including Pierce, Pinkham, Peruna, Kilmer, and all the well-known ones—which I have referred to as the patent medicine association. Its official name is the Proprietary Association of America.) "I sent out the following letter to fifteen [patent medicine] manufacturers:

GENTLEMEN:

Inclosed we hand you copy of matter which is appearing in the Cleveland papers. It is detrimental to the drug business to have this matter agitated in a sensational way. In behalf of the trade we would ask you to use your influence with the papers in Cleveland to discontinue this unnecessary publicity, and if you feel you can do so, we would like to have you wire the business managers of the Cleveland papers to discontinue their sensational drug articles, as it is proving very injurious to your business.

Respectfully,
E. R. COOPER

"Because of that letter which we sent out, the Cleveland *Press* received inside of forty-eight hours telegrams from six manufacturers canceling thousands of dollars' worth of advertising and causing a consequent dearth of sensational matter along drug lines. It resulted in a loss to one paper alone of over eighteen thousand dollars in advertising. Gentlemen, when you touch a man's pocket, you touch him where he lives; that principle is true of the newspaper editor or the retail druggist, and goes through all business."

That is the account of how the patent medicine man used his club on the newspaper head, told in the patent medicine man's own words, as he described it to his fellows. Is it pleasant reading for self-respecting newspaper men—the exultant air of those last sentences, and the worldly wisdom: "When you touch a man's pocket, you touch him where he lives; that principle is true of the newspaper editor . . ."?

But the worst of this incident has not yet been told. There remains the account of how the offending newspaper, in the language of the bully, "ate dirt." The Cleveland *Press* is one of a syndicate of newspapers, all under Mr. McRae's ownership—but I will use Mr. Cooper's own words:

"We not only reached the Cleveland *Press* by the movement taken up in that way, but went further, for the Cleveland *Press* is one of a syndicate of newspapers known as the Scripps-McRae League, from whom this explanation is self-explanatory:

OFFICE OF SCRIPPS-McRAE
PRESS ASSOCIATION

Mr. E. R. Cooper, Cleveland, Ohio:

Mr. McRae arrived in New York the latter part of last week after a three months' trip to Egypt. I took up the matter of the recent cut-rate articles which appeared in the Cleveland "Press" with him, and today received the following telegram from him from Cincinnati: "Scripps-McRae papers will contain no more such as Cleveland 'Press' published concerning the medicine trust—M. A. McRae." I am sure that in the future nothing will appear in the Cleveland "Press" detrimental to your interests.

Yours truly,
F. J. CARLISLE

This incident was told, in the exact words above quoted, at the nineteenth annual meeting of the Proprietary Association of America.

I could, if space permitted, quote many other telegrams and letters from the Kilmer's Swamp Root makers, from the Piso's Cure people, from all the large patent medicine manufacturers. The same thing that happened in Massachusetts happened last year in New Hampshire, in Wisconsin, in Utah, in more than fifteen states. In Wisconsin the response by the newspapers to the command of the patent medicine people was even more humiliating than in Massachusetts. Not only did individual newspapers work against the formula bill; there is a "Wisconsin Press Association," which includes the owners and editors of most of the newspapers of the state. That association held a meeting and passed resolutions, "that we are opposed to said bill . . . providing that hereafter all patent medicine sold in this State shall have the formulae thereof printed on their labels," and "Resolved, That the Association appoint a committee of five publishers to oppose the passage of the measure." And in this same state the larger dailies in the cities took it upon themselves to drum up the smaller country papers and get them to write editorials opposed to the formula bill. Nor was even this the measure of their activity in response to the command of the patent medicine association. . . . [A letter] was sent by the publisher of one of the largest daily papers in Wisconsin to the state senator who introduced the bill. In one western state, a Board of Health officer made a number of analyses of patent medicines, and tried to have the analyses made public, that the people of his state might be warned. "Only one newspaper in the State," he says in a personal letter, "was willing to print results of these analyses, and this paper refused them after two publications in which a list of about ten was published. This paper was 'The ———,' the editorial manager of which is in sympathy with the effort to restrict the sale of harmful nostrums. The business management interfered for the reason that five thousand dollars in patent medicine advertising was withdrawn within a week."

In New Hampshire—but space forbids. Happily there is a little silver in the situation. The Legislature of North Dakota last year passed, and the governor signed, a bill requiring that patent medicine bottles shall have printed on their labels the percentage of alcohol or of morphine or various other poisons which the medicine contains. That was the first success in a fight which the public health authorities have waged in twenty states each year for twenty years. In North Dakota the patent medicine people conducted the fight with their usual weapons, the ones described above. But the newspapers, be it said to their everlasting credit, refused to fall in line to the threats of the patent medicine association. And I account for that fact in this way: North Dakota is wholly a "country" community. It has no city of over twenty thousand, and but one of over five thousand. The press of the state, therefore, consists of very small papers, weeklies, in which the ownership and active management all lie with one man. The editorial conscience and the business manager's enterprise lie under one hat. With them the patent medicine scheme was not so successful as with the more elaborately organized newspapers of older and more populous states.

Just now is the North Dakota editor's time of trial. The law went into effect July 1. The patent medicine association, at their annual meeting in May, voted to withdraw all their advertising from all the papers in that state. This loss of revenue, they argued self-righteously, would be a warning to the newspapers of other states. Likewise it would be a lesson to the newspapers of North Dakota. At the next session of the Legislature they will seek to have the label bill repealed, and they count on the newspapers, chastened by a lean year, to help them. For the independence they have shown in the past, and for the courage they will be called upon to show in the future, therefore let the newspapers of North Dakota know that they have the respect and admiration of all decent people.

"What is to be done about it?" is the question that follows exposure of organized rascality. In few cases is the remedy so plain as here. For the past, the newspapers, in spite of these plain contracts of silence, must be acquitted of any very grave complicity. The very existence of the machine that uses and directs them has been a carefully guarded secret. For the future, be it understood that any newspaper which carries a patent medicine advertisement knows what it is doing. The obligations of the contract are now public property. And one thing more, when next a member of a State Legislature arises and states, as I have so often heard: "Gentlemen, this label bill seems right to me, but I can not support it; the united press of my district is opposed to it"—when that happens, let every one understand the wires that have moved "the united press of my district."

Collier's
November 4, 1905

SAMUEL HOPKINS ADAMS

The Great American Fraud

A DISTINGUISHED public health official and medical writer once made this jocular suggestion to me:

"Let us buy in large quantities the cheapest Italian vermouth, poor gin, and bitters. We will mix them in the proportion of three of vermouth to two of gin with a dash of bitters, dilute and bottle them by the short quart, label them 'Smith's Revivifier and Blood-Purifier; dose, one wineglassful before each meal'; advertise them to cure erysipelas, bunions, dyspepsia, heat rash, fever and ague, and consumption; and to prevent loss of hair, smallpox, old age, sunstroke, and near-sightedness, and make our everlasting fortunes selling them to the temperance trade."

"That sounds to me very much like a cocktail," said I.

"So it is," he replied. "But it's just as much a medicine as Peruna and not as bad a drink."

Peruna, or, as its owner, Dr. S. B. Hartman of Columbus, Ohio (once a physician in good standing) prefers to write it, Pe-ru-na, is at present the most prominent proprietary nostrum in the country. It has taken the place once held by Greene's Nervura and by Paine's Celery Compound, and for the same reason which made them popular. The name of that reason is alcohol. Peruna is a stimulant pure and simple, and it is the more dangerous in that it sails under the false colors of a benign purpose.

According to an authoritative statement given out in private circulation a few years ago by its proprietors, Peruna is a compound of seven drugs with cologne spirits. This formula, they assure me, has not been materially changed. None of the seven drugs is of any great potency. Their total is less than one-half of one per cent of the product. Medicinally they are too inconsiderable, in this proportion, to produce any effect. There remains to Peruna only water and cologne spirits, roughly in the proportion of three to one. Cologne spirits is the commercial term for alcohol.

Any one wishing to make Peruna for home consumption may do so by mixing half a pint of cologne spirits, 90 proof, with a pint and a half of water, adding thereto a little cubeb for flavor and a little burned sugar for color. It will cost, in small quantities, perhaps seven or eight cents per quart. Manufactured in bulk, so a former Peruna agent estimates, its cost, including bottle and wrapper, is about eight and one-half cents. Its price is $1.00. Because of this handsome margin of profit, and by way of making hay in the stolen sunshine of Peruna advertising, many imitations have sprung up to harass the proprietors of the alcohol-and-water product. Pe-ru-vi-na, P-ru-na, Purina, Anurep (an obvious inversion); these, bottled and labeled to resemble Peruna, are self-confessed imitations. From what the Peruna people tell me, I gather that they are dangerous and damnable frauds, and that they cure nothing.

What does Peruna cure? Catarrh. That is the modest claim for it; nothing but catarrh. To be sure, a careful study of its literature will suggest its value as a tonic, and a preventive of lassitude. But its reputation rests upon catarrh. What is catarrh? Whatever ails you. No matter what you've got, you will be not only enabled, but compelled, after reading Dr. Hartman's Peruna book, *The Ills of Life*, to diagnose your illness as catarrh, and to realize that Peruna alone will save you. Pneumonia is catarrh of the lungs; so is consumption. Dyspepsia is catarrh of the stomach. Enteritis is catarrh of the intestines. Appendicitis—surgeons, please note before operating—is catarrh of the appendix. Bright's disease is catarrh of the kidneys. Heart disease is catarrh of the heart. Canker sores are catarrh of the mouth. Measles is, perhaps, catarrh of the skin, since "a teaspoonful of Peruna thrice daily or oftener is an effectual cure" (*The Ills of Life*). Similarly, malaria, one may guess, is catarrh of the mosquito that bit you. Other diseases not specifically placed in the catarrhal class, but yielding to Peruna (in the book), are colic, mumps, convulsions, neuralgia, women's complaints, and rheumatism. Yet, "Peruna is not a cure-all," virtuously disclaims Dr. Hartman, and grasps at a golden opportunity by advertising his nostrum as a preventive against yellow fever! That alcohol and water, with a little coloring matter and one-half of one per cent of mild drugs, will cure all or any of the ills listed above is too ridiculous to need refutation. Nor does Dr. Hartman himself personally make that claim for his product. He stated to me specifically and repeatedly that no drug or combination of drugs, with the possible exception of quinine for malaria, will cure disease. His claim is that the belief of the patient in Peruna, fostered as it is by the printed testimony, and aided by the "gentle stimulation," produces good results. It is well established that in certain classes of disease the opposite is true. A considerable proportion of tuberculosis cases show a history of the Peruna type of medicines taken in the early stages, with the result of diminishing the patient's resistant power, and much of the typhoid in the Middle West is complicated by the victim's "keeping up" on this stimulus long after he should have been under a doctor's care. But it is not as a fraud upon the sick alone that Peruna is baneful; but as the maker of drunkards, also.

"It can be used any length of time without acquiring a drug habit," declares the Peruna book, and therein, I regret to say, lies specifically and directly. The lie is ingeniously backed up by Dr. Hartman's argument that "nobody could get drunk on the prescribed doses of Peruna."

Perhaps this is true, though I note three wineglassfuls in forty-five minutes as a prescription which might temporarily alter a prohibitionist's outlook on life. But what makes Peruna profitable to the maker, and a curse to the community at large, is the fact that the minimum dose first ceases to satisfy, then the moderate dose, and finally the maximum dose; and the unsuspecting patron, who began with it as a medicine, goes on to use it as a beverage, and finally to be enslaved by it as a habit. A well-known authority on drug addictions writes me:

"A number of physicians have called my attention to the use of Peruna, both preceding and following alcohol and drug addictions. Lydia Pinkham's Compound is another dangerous drug used largely by drinkers; Paine's Celery Compound also. I have, in the last two years, met four cases of persons who drank Peruna in large quantities to intoxication. This was given to them originally as a tonic. They were treated under my care as simple alcoholics."

Expert opinion on the nonmedical side is represented in the government order to the Indian Department, the kernel of which is this:

> In connection with this investigation, please give particular attention to the proprietary medicines and other compounds which the traders keep in stock, with special reference to the liability of their misuse by Indians on account of the alcohol which they contain. The sale of Peruna, which is on the lists of several traders, is hereby absolutely prohibited. As a medicine, something else can be substituted;

as an intoxicant, it has been found too tempting and effective. Anything of the sort under another name which is found to lead to intoxication you will please report to this office.

(Signed) C. F. LARRABEE, *Acting Commissioner*

Specific evidence of what Peruna can do will be found in the following report, verified by special investigation:

PINEDALE, WYOMING, Oct. 4.—(Special)—Two men suffering from delirium tremens and one dead is the result of a Peruna intoxication which took place here a few days ago. C. E. Armstrong of this place and a party of three others started out on a camping trip to the Yellowstone country, taking with them several bottles of whiskey, and ten bottles of Peruna, which one of the members of the party was taking as a tonic. The trip lasted over a week, the whiskey was exhausted, and for two days the party was without liquor. At last someone suggested that they use Peruna, of which nine bottles remained. Before they stopped the whole remaining supply had been consumed and the four men were in a state of intoxication, the like of which they had never known before. Finally, one awoke with terrible cramps in his stomach and found his companions seemingly in an almost lifeless condition. Suffering terrible agony, he crawled on his hands and knees to a ranch over a mile distant, the process taking him half a day. Aid was sent to his three companions. Armstrong was dead when the rescue party arrived. The other two men, still unconscious, were brought to town in a wagon, and are still in a weak and emaciated condition. Armstrong's body was almost tied in a knot and could not be straightened for burial.

Here is testimony from a druggist in a southern "no-license" town:
"Peruna is bought by all the druggists in this section by the gross. I have seen persons thoroughly intoxicated from taking Peruna. The common remark in this place when a drunken party is particularly obstreperous is that he is on a 'Peruna drunk.' It is a notorious fact that a great many do use Peruna to get the alcoholic effect, and they certainly do get it good and strong. Now, there are other so-called remedies used for the same purpose, namely, Gensenica, Kidney Specific, Jamaica Ginger, Hostetter's Bitters, etc."

So well recognized is this use of the nostrum that a number of the southern newspapers advertise a cure for the "Peruna habit," which is probably worse than the habit, as is usually the case with these "cures." In southern Ohio and in the mountain districts of West Virginia the "Peruna jag" is a standard form of intoxication.

A testimonial hunter in the employ of the Peruna Company was referred by a Minnesota druggist to a prosperous farmer in the neighborhood. The farmer gave Peruna a most enthusiastic "send-off"; he had been using it for several months, and could say, etc., etc. Then he took the agent to his barn, and showed him a heap of empty Peruna bottles. The agent counted them. There were seventy-four. The druggist added his testimonial. "That old boy has a 'still' on all the time since he discovered Peruna," said he. "He's my star customer." The druggist's testimonial was not printed.

At the time when certain Chicago drugstores were fighting some of the leading patent medicines, and carrying only a small stock of them, a boy called one evening at one of the downtown shops for thirty-nine bottles of Peruna. "There's the money," he said. "The old man wants to get his before it's all gone." Investigation showed that the purchaser was the night engineer of a big downtown building, and that the entire working staff had "chipped in" to get a supply of their favorite stimulant.

"But why should anyone who wants to get drunk drink Peruna when he can get whiskey?" argues the nostrum maker.

There are two reasons: one of which is that in many places the "medicine" can be obtained and the liquor can not. Maine, for instance, being a prohibition state, does a big business in patent medicines. So does Kansas. So do most of the no-license counties in the South, though a few have recently thrown out these disguised "boozes." Indian Territory and Oklahoma, as we have seen, have done so because of Poor Lo's predilection toward curing himself of depression with these remedies, and for a time, at least, Peruna was shipped in in unlabeled boxes.

United States District Attorney Mellette of the Western District of Indian Territory writes: "Vast quantities of Peruna are shipped into this country, and I have caused a number of persons to be indicted for selling the same, and a few of them have been convicted or have entered pleas of guilty. I could give you hundreds of specific cases of 'Peruna Drunk' among the Indians. It is a common beverage among them, used for the purposes of intoxication."

The other reason why Peruna or some other of its class is often the agency of drunkenness, instead of whiskey, is that the drinker of Peruna doesn't want to get drunk; at least she doesn't know that she wants to get drunk. I use the feminine pronoun advisedly, because the remedies of this class are largely supported by women. Lydia Pinkham's variety of drink depends for its popularity chiefly upon its alcohol. Paine's Celery Compound relieves depression and lack of vitality on the same principle that a cocktail does, and with the same necessity for repetition. I knew an estimable lady from the Middle West who visited her dissipated brother in New York—dissipated from her point of view, because she was a pillar of the W.C.T.U., and he frequently took a cocktail before dinner and came back with it on his breath, whereupon she would weep over him as one lost to hope. One day in a mood of brutal exasperation, when he hadn't had his drink and was able to discern the flavor of her grief, he turned upon her:

"I'll tell you what's the matter with you," he said. "You're drunk—maudlin drunk!"

She promptly and properly went into hysterics. The physician who attended diagnosed the case more politely, but to the same effect, and ascertained that she had consumed something like half a bottle of Kilmer's Swamp Root that afternoon. Now, Swamp Root is a very creditable "booze," but much weaker in alcohol than most of its class. The brother was greatly amused, until he discovered to his alarm that his drink-abhorring sister couldn't get along without her patent medicine bottle! She was in a fair way, quite innocently, of becoming a drunkard.

Another example of this "unconscious drunkenness" is recorded by the *Journal of the American Medical Association*: "A respected clergyman fell ill, and the family physician was called. After examining the patient carefully, the doctor asked for a private interview with the patient's adult son.

"'I am sorry to tell you that your father undoubtedly is suffering from chronic alcoholism,' said the physician.

"'Chronic alcoholism! Why, that's ridiculous! Father never drank a drop of liquor in his life, and we know all there is to know about his habits.'

"'Well, my boy, it's chronic alcoholism, nevertheless, and at this present moment your father is drunk. How has his health been recently? Has he been taking any medicine?'

"'Why, for some time, six months I should say, father has often complained of feeling unusually tired. A few months ago a friend of his recommended "Peruna" to him, assuring him that it would build him up. Since then he has taken many bottles of it, and I am quite sure that he has taken nothing else.'"

From its very name, one would naturally absolve Duffy's Malt Whiskey from fraudulent pretense. But it pretends to be a medicine and to cure all kinds of lung and throat diseases. It is especially favored by temperance folk. "A dessertspoonful, four to six times a day, in water, and a tablespoonful on going to bed" (personal prescription for consumptive), makes a fair grog allowance for an abstainer.

"You must not forget," writes the doctor in charge, by way of allaying the supposed scruples of the patient, "that taking Duffy's Malt Whiskey in small or medicinal doses is not like taking liquor in large quantities, or as it is usually taken. Taking it a considerable time in medicinal doses, as we direct, leads to health and happiness; while taken the other way, it often leads to ruin and decay. If you follow our advice about taking it, you will always be in the temperance fold, without qualm of conscience."

It has testimonials ranging from consumption to malaria, and indorsements of the clergy. . . . [Duffy's Pure Malt Whiskey] has its recognized place behind the bar, being sold by the manufacturers to the wholesale liquor trade and by them to the saloons, where it may be purchased over the counter for eighty-five cents a quart. This is cheap, but Duffy's Pure Malt Whiskey is not regarded as a high-class article.

Its status has been definitely settled in New York State, where Excise Commissioner Cullinan recently obtained a decision in the Supreme Court declaring it a liquor. The trial was in Rochester, where the nostrum is made. Eleven supposably reputable physicians, four of them members of the Health Department, swore to their belief that the whiskey contained drugs which constituted it a genuine medicine. The state was able to show conclusively that if remedial drugs were present, they were in such small quantities as to be indistinguishable, and, of course, utterly without value; in short, that the product was nothing more or less than sweetened whiskey. Yet the United States government has long lent its sanction to the "medicine" status by exempting Duffy's Pure Malt Whiskey from the Federal liquor tax. In fact, the government is primarily responsible for the formal establishment of the product as a medicine, having forced it into the patent medicine ranks at the time when the Spanish war expenses were partly raised by a special tax on nostrums. Up to that time the Duffy product, while asserting its virtues in various ills, made no direct pretense to be anything but a whiskey. Transfer to the patent medicine list cost it, in war taxes, more than $40,000. By way of getting a *quid pro quo*, the company began ingeniously and with some justification to exploit its liquor as "the only whiskey recognized by the government as medicine," and continues so to advertise, although the recent decision of the Internal Revenue Department, providing that all patent medicines which have no medicinal properties other than the alcohol in them must pay a rectifier's tax, relegates it to its proper place. While this decision is not a severe financial blow to the Duffys and their congeners (it means only a few hundred dollars apiece), it is important as officially establish-

ing the "bracer" class on the same footing with whiskey and gin, where
they belong. Other "drugs" there are which sell largely, perhaps chiefly,
over the bar, Hostetter's Bitters and Damiana Bitters being prominent
in this class.

When this series of articles was first projected, *Collier's* received a
warning from "Warner's Safe Cure," advising that a thorough investigation would be wise before "making any attack" upon that preparation.
I have no intention of "attacking" this company or any one else, and
they would have escaped notice altogether, because of their present
unimportance, but for their letter. The suggested investigation was not
so thorough as to go deeply into the nature of the remedy, which is an
alcoholic liquid, but it developed this interesting fact: Warner's Safe
Cure, together with all the Warner remedies, is leased, managed, and
controlled by the New York and Kentucky Distilling Company, manufacturers of standard whiskeys which do not pretend to remedy anything
but thirst. Duffy's Malt Whiskey is another subsidiary company of the
New York and Kentucky concern. This statement is respectfully submitted to temperance users of the Malt Whiskey and the Warner
remedies.

Hostetter's Bitters contain, according to an official state analysis, 44
per cent of alcohol; Lydia Pinkham appeals to suffering womanhood
with 20 per cent of alcohol; Hood's Sarsaparilla cures "that tired feeling" with 18 per cent; Burdock's Blood Bitters with 25 per cent; Ayer's
Sarsaparilla with 26 per cent; and Paine's Celery Compound with 21
per cent. The fact is that any of these remedies could be interchanged
with Peruna or with each other, so far as general effect goes, though
the iodide of potassium in the sarsaparilla class might have some effect
(as likely to be harmful as helpful) which would be lacking in the
simpler mixtures.

If this class of nostrum is so harmful, asks the attentive reader of
newspaper advertising columns, how explain the indorsements of so
many people of prominence and reputation? "Men of prominence and
reputation," in this connection, means Peruna, for Peruna has made a
specialty of high government officials and people in the public eye. In
a self-gratulatory dissertation the Peruna Company observes in substance that while the leading minds of the nation have hitherto shrunk
from the publicity attendant upon commending any patent medicine,
the transcendent virtues of Peruna have overcome this amiable modesty,
and one and all they stand forth its avowed champions. This is followed by an ingenious document headed "Fifty Members of Congress

Send Letters of Indorsement to the Inventor of the Great Catarrh Remedy, Pe-ru-na," and quoting thirty-six of the letters. Analysis of these letters brings out the singular circumstance that in twenty-one of the thirty-six there is no indication that the writer has ever tasted the remedy which he so warmly praises. As a sample, and for the benefit of lovers of ingenious literature, I reprint the following from a humorous member of Congress:

> My secretary had as bad a case of catarrh as I ever saw, and since he has taken one bottle of Peruna he seems like a different man.

> Taylorsville, N. C.   ROMULUS Z. LINNEY

The famous letter of Admiral Schley is a case in point. He wrote to the Peruna Company:

> I can cheerfully say that Mrs. Schley has used Peruna, and, I believe, with good effect.
> (Signed) W. S. SCHLEY

This indorsement went the rounds of the country in half-page blazonry, to the consternation of the family's friends. Admiral Schley seems to have appreciated that this use of his name was detrimental to his standing. He wrote to a Columbus religious journal the following letter:

> 1826 I STREET
> WASHINGTON, D.C.
> November 10, 1904

> EDITOR "CATHOLIC COLUMBIAN":
> The advertisement of the Peruna Company, inclosed, is made without any authority or approval from me. When it was brought to my attention first I wrote the company a letter stating that the advertisement was offensive and must be discontinued. Their representative here called upon me and stated he had been directed to assure me no further publication would be allowed, as it was without my sanction.
> I would say that the advertisement has been made without my knowledge or consent, and is an infringement of my rights as a citizen.
> If you will kindly inform me what the name and date of the paper was in which the inclosed advertisement appeared I shall feel obliged.

> Very truly yours,
> W. S. SCHLEY

Careful study of this document will show that this is no explicit denial of the testimonial. But who gives careful study to such a letter? On the face of it, it puts the Peruna people in the position of having forged their advertisement. Ninety-nine people out of a hundred would get that impression. Yet I have seen the testimonial, signed with Admiral Schley's name and interlined in the same handwriting as the signature, and I have seen another letter, similarly signed, stating that Admiral Schley had not understood that the letter was to be used for such advertising as the recipient based upon it. If these letters are forgeries the victim has his recourse in the law. They are on file at Columbus, Ohio, and the Peruna Company would doubtless produce them in defense of a suit.

One thing the public has a right to demand, in its attitude toward the proprietary medicines containing alcohol: that the government carry out rigidly its promised policy no longer to permit liquors to disguise themselves as patent medicines, and thereby escape the tax which is put upon other (and probably better) brands of intoxicants. One other demand it should make on the purveyors of these concoctions: that they label every bottle with the percentage of alcohol it contains. Then the innocent clergyman who writes testimonials to Duffy, and the W.C.T.U. member who indorses Peruna, Lydia Pinkham, Warner and their compeers, will know when they imbibe their "tonics," "invigorators," "swamp roots," "bitters," "nerve-builders" or "spring medicines," that they are sipping by the tablespoon or wineglassful what the town tippler takes across the license-paying bar.

Collier's
October 28, 1905

PURE FOOD

"DEAR, OH DEAR," said Mr. Dooley, "I haven't been able to ate annything more nourishin' thin a cucumber in a week. A little while ago no wan cud square away at a beefsteak with betther grace thin mesilf. Today th' wurrud resthrant makes me green in th' face. How did it all come about? A young fellow wrote a book." [73]

The young fellow was Upton Sinclair. The book: *The Jungle*.

Upton Sinclair commented after the book was published that "I aimed at the public's heart, and by accident I hit it in the stomach." [74]

The Socialist weekly, the *Appeal to Reason*, in 1904 offered to finance Sinclair with $500 during which time he would write a novel on the lives of the Packingtown workers.

Sinclair lived among the stockyard workers for seven weeks while he wrote *The Jungle*. He was not thinking of pure food when he described the preparation of meats. His primary intention was to describe the conditions under which the packinghouse workers labored.

The story appeared serially in *Appeal to Reason*, starting in early 1905.

The "novel" was offered to five book publishers and rejected the first four times. Sinclair was about to publish the book himself when Doubleday, Page & Co. finally accepted the manuscript and published it in book form in 1906. The book was an immediate success; it remained a best seller for a year and was translated into seventeen languages. It also became the center of a political controversy.

Sinclair, himself, was disappointed at the public's reaction. "I failed in my purpose," he wrote. "I wished to frighten the country by a picture of what its industrial masters were doing to their victims; entirely by chance I had stumbled on another discovery—what they were doing to the meat supply of the civilized world. . . ."

Though Mark Sullivan, many years after the publication of *The Jungle*, insisted that the book should not be considered muckraking because it was a "novel, fiction; and that these charges about conditions in the stockyards did not purport to have any more than the loose standard of accuracy that fiction demands for local color and background," Sinclair as late as 1958 considered it muckraking. [75]

Sinclair explained his method of developing the story: "I went out there and lived among the people for seven weeks. . . . I would sit in their [packinghouse workers] homes at night, and talked with them, and then in the daytime they would lay off their work, and take me around, and show me whatever I wished to see. I studied every detail of their lives. . . . I talked, not merely with workingmen and their families, but with bosses and superintendents, with night-watchmen and saloonkeepers and policemen, with doctors and lawyers and merchants, with politicians and clergymen and settlement-workers. . . . *The Jungle* is as authoritative as if it were a statistical compilation." [76]

Commenting on the book soon after its publication, Winston Churchill, then a prominent English writer, later Cabinet Member, and still later Prime Minister of England, wrote: "This terrible book . . . pierces the thickest skull and most leathery heart." [77]

Shortly after the publication of *The Jungle*, there was a clamor for reform. President Roosevelt appointed a commission to investigate the packers and their preparation of meats. Two New York social workers, Charles P. Neil and James B. Reynolds, were sent to Chicago by the President to investigate the charges. Their report vindicated Sinclair.

Muckraking magazines such as *Collier's* and *Success* began to clamor for a Pure Food Bill. In 1906, Congress passed the Pure Food and Drug Act and it became effective January 1, 1907, the law a direct product of muckraking.

UPTON SINCLAIR

The Jungle

... FROM THE ROOM where they kill the hogs, in each of the plants, go daily a certain number of carcasses marked with red tags: "U.S. Condemned." These hogs have been found to be tuberculous, which means that the flesh had ptomaines in it. These ptomaines are deadly poisons—and not germs which cooking can kill, but poisons, which will remain and [can] be fatal, no matter what may be done to the meat. The government requires that these carcasses be "tanked," that is, destroyed and turned into fertilizer; and it has stringent regulations as to exactly how it shall be done. The tanks are to be sealed at the bottom by a government employee, and the seals may not be removed, till certain things have been done to destroy the meat. And with these laws before them, the men found it quite impossible to convince any inquirer that these tanks were ever kept open, and the condemned meat, that was thrown in at the top, taken out at the bottom and made into sausage. Yet Jurgis met man after man who had seen this done with his own eyes, and some who had helped to do it. He grew interested, and found that the knowledge of it was an everyday, matter-of-fact thing among the men; and they would laugh, and tell how newspaper reporters and visiting wise men had demanded to know if they would make affidavit to it, and been answered, "Certainly, if you will go under bond to find me a job for the rest of my life."

Yet the visitors need not have given up in despair; there were plenty of other things they might have seen with their own eyes, if they were fairly lucky in dodging the "spotters" of the companies. It was quite easy, for instance, to be an eye witness of how the law regarding meat packed for shipment was heeded. Anyone can get this law from the Bureau of Animal Industries in Washington, and read how there must be an official inspector, with a force of assistants, wherever meat is packed and shipped; and that he shall examine each package, and then affix a numbered paper stamp, which he shall then cancel in a manner elaborately specified—so that the wavy lines of the cancellation shall run over each side of the stamp. The object of this is, of course, that the stamp shall be canceled after it is on the box and not before; and when the visitor has made sure of that, there are several thousands of employees in Packingtown who can tell him a dozen places to go and watch, while the foreman of the shipping-room goes over to the far-distant inspector's office and gets a big bunch of canceled stamps, and comes back and pastes one on each tightly nailed box of meat. There were men with whom Jurgis talked at the union meetings who had been working in the shipping-room for years, and had never seen that law complied with once in all the time.

There was never any inspection of meat at all after it left the killing-floor save by the packers themselves, and with meat intended for export. Jurgis asked why this was, and the men told him that there were some foreign countries in which the laws were enforced. For this reason all the best meat was sent abroad—it was impossible to get it in this country, not even the richest hotels and clubs could get it. The good went to France and England, and the very best to Germany, which was apparently the one country there was no deceiving. Germany had caused the packers no end of trouble—for which, with characteristic ingenuity, they had recouped themselves by putting out imitations of German meat for home markets! The great Anderson printing-plant made labels by the tens and hundreds of thousands, French, German, Italian, and what not; one of the men had some of them in his pocket and showed a whole set, for smoked and canned meats, labeled in brilliant colors: "August Bauer, Frankfurt am Main."

Jurgis heard of these things little by little, in the gossip of those who were obliged to perpetrate them. Every time you met a person from a new department, you heard of new swindles and new crimes. There was, for instance, a Lithuanian who was a cattle-butcher for the plant where Marija had worked, which killed meat for canning only; and to hear this man describe the animals which came to his killing-floor would have been worth while for a Dante or a Zola. It seemed that they must have agencies all over the country, to hunt out old and crippled and diseased cattle to be canned. On the prairies nearby, for instance, were hundreds of farms which supplied the city with milk; and all the cows that developed lumpy jaw, or fell sick, or dried up of old age—they kept them till they had a carload, which was twenty, and then shipped them to this place to be canned. Here came also cattle which had been fed on "whiskey-malt," the refuse of the breweries, and had become what the men called "steerly"—which means covered with boils that were full of matter. It was a nasty job killing these, for when you plunged your knife into them they would burst and splash foul-smelling stuff into your face; and when a man's sleeves were smeared with blood, and his hands steeped in it, how was he ever to wipe his face, or to clear his eyes so that he could see? It was enough to make anybody sick, to think that people had to eat such meat as this; but they must be eating it—for the canners were going on preparing it, year after year! . . . No doubt it was stuff such as this that made the "embalmed beef" that had killed several times as many United States soldiers as all the bullets of the Spaniards; only the army beef, besides, was not fresh canned, it was old stuff that had been lying for years in the cellars. . . .

Then one Sunday evening, Jurgis sat puffing his pipe by the kitchen stove, and talking with another fellow whom Jonas had introduced, and who worked in the canning-rooms at Anderson's; and then Jurgis learned a few things about the great and only Anderson's canned goods, which are a national institution. They were regular alchemists at Anderson's; they advertised a mushroom-catsup, and the men who made it did not know what a mushroom looked like. They advertised "potted chicken," and it was like the boardinghouse soup of the comic papers, through which a chicken had walked with rubbers on. Perhaps they had a secret process for making chickens chemically—who knows? said Jurgis's friend; the things that went into the mixture were tripe, and the fat of pork, and beef suet, and hearts of beef, and finally the waste ends of veal, when they had any. They put these up in several grades, and sold them at several prices; but the contents of the cans all came out of the same hopper. And then there was "potted ham" and "deviled ham"—de-vyled, as the men called it. "De-vyled" ham was made out of the waste ends of smoked beef that were too small to be sliced by the machines; and also tripe, dyed with chemicals so that it would not show white; and trimmings of hams and corned beef; and potatoes, skins and all; and finally the hard cartilaginous gullets of beef after the tongues had been cut out. All this ingenious mixture was ground up and flavored with spices to make it taste like something to the dear gullible public. Anybody who could invent a new imitation had been sure of a fortune from old Anderson, said Jurgis's informant; but it was hard to tell anything new to a man who even went out and gathered up carloads of cinders along the railroad tracks and brought them in and powdered them, to adulterate his bone fertilizers with!

Up to a year or two ago it had been the custom to kill horses in the yards—ostensibly for fertilizer; but after long agitation the newspapers had been able to make the public realize that the horses were being canned: now it was against the law to kill horses in Packingtown, and the law was really complied with—for the present, at any rate. Any day, however, one might see sharp-horned and shaggy-haired creatures running with the sheep—and yet what a job you would have to get the public to believe that a good part of what it buys for lamb and mutton is really goat's flesh!

There is another interesting set of statistics that one might gather as his acquaintance broadened in Packingtown, and that is the afflictions of the workers. When Jurgis had first inspected the packing-plants with Szedvilas, he had marveled while he listened to the tale of all the things that were made out of the carcasses of animals, and of all the lesser industries that were maintained there; now he found that each one of these lesser industries was a separate little inferno, in its way as horrible as the killing-floor, the source and fountain of them all. The workers in each of them had their own peculiar diseases; and the wandering visitor might be skeptical about all the swindles, but he could not be skeptical about these, for the worker bore the evidence of them about on his own person—generally he had only to hold out his hand.

There were the men in the pickle-rooms, for instance, where old Antanas had gotten his death; scarce a one of these that had not some spot of horror on his person. Let a man so much as scrape his finger pushing a truck in the pickle-rooms, and like as not he would have a sore that would put him out of the world; all the joints in his fingers might be eaten by the acid, one by one. Of the butchers and floormen, the beef-boners and trimmers, and all those who used knives, you could scarcely find a person who had the use of his thumb; time and time again the base of it had been slashed, till it was a mere lump of flesh against which the man pressed the knife to hold it. The hands of these men would be criss-crossed with cuts, until you could no longer pretend to count them or to trace them. They would have no nails—they had worn them off pulling hides; their knuckles were swollen so that their fingers spread out like a fan. There were men who worked in the cooking-rooms, in the midst of steam and sickening odors, by artificial light; in these rooms the germs of tuberculosis might live for two years, but the supply is renewed every hour. There were the beef-luggers, who carried two-hundred-pound quarters into the refrigerator-cars; this was a fearful kind of work, that began at four o'clock in the morning, and that wore out the most powerful men in a few years. There were those who worked in the chilling-rooms, and whose special disease was rheumatism; the time-limit that a man could work in the chilling-rooms was said to be five years. There were the wool-pluckers, whose hands went to pieces even sooner than the hands of the pickle-men; for the pelts of the sheep had to be painted with acid to loosen the wool, and then the pluckers had to pull out this wool with their bare hands, till the acid had eaten their fingers off. There were those who made the tins for the canned-meat; and their hands, too, were a maze of cuts, and any cut might cause blood-poisoning; some worked at the stamping-machines, and it was very seldom that one could work long at these at the pace that was set, and not give out and forget himself, and have a part of his hand chopped off. There were the "hoisters," as they were called, whose task it was to press the lever which lifted the dead cattle off the floor. They ran along upon a rafter, peering down through the damp and the steam. Old man Anderson's architects had not built the killing-room for the convenience of the hoisters, and so every few feet they would have to stoop under a beam, say four feet above the one they ran on; this got them into the habit of stooping, so that in a few years they would be walking like chimpanzees. No man who worked as a hoister had ever been known to reach the age of fifty years. Worst of any, however, were the fertilizer-men, and those who served in the rendering rooms. These could not be shown to the visitor—for the odor of the fertilizer-men would scare any ordinary visitor at a hundred yards, and as for the other men, who worked in tank-rooms full of steam, and in which there were open vats upon the level of the floor, their peculiar trouble was that they fell into the vats; and when they were fished out, there was never enough of them left to be worth exhibiting. Sometimes they would be overlooked for days, till all but the bones of them had gone out to the world as Anderson's Pure Leaf Lard!

Appeal to Reason
April 29, 1905

PART FIVE

People in Bondage

AFTER THE CIVIL WAR, with slavery officially ended, the Negro question lay dormant for years. The few writers who took up the problem at all wrote in the manner of preachers, in high-flung prose with moralistic overtones.

It was the northern reformer who finally gave an honest expression of the emancipated Negro's plight, and he did it through the muckraking magazines.

In January 1904, *McClure's* published Carl Schurz's "Can the South Solve the Negro Problem?" Four months later, McClure presented the southern viewpoint through Thomas Nelson Page and his article "The Negro: The Southerner's Problem."

Historian Louis Filler points out that "the value of the McClure articles lay in the fact that they opened the topic to inquiry and discredited the moralistic, eloquent, and otherwise futile studies that had formerly passed for serious opinion." [78]

It was Ray Stannard Baker, however, one of the founders of the McClure school of muckrakers, who was to approach the subject with a cold, scientific, reportorial logic.

McClure's sent him to report on lynching. After the first article appeared, President Theodore Roosevelt wrote Baker: "I think your last article in *McClure's* is far and away the best discussion of lynching that I have seen anywhere. You know how much I admire your treatment of labor matters; but upon my word I think this is even superior." [79]

About two years later, Baker completed a longer series of articles in *The American Magazine*. Entitled "Following the Color Line," Baker started with the 1906 riot in Atlanta and then described the rumors, the lawlessness, the murders, the fear, that runs rampant with a race riot.

In announcing this series, *The American Magazine* editorially pointed out that Baker would offer no solutions—that he would present, not an argument, but a view, a picture of conditions as they were which would serve to illuminate the whole situation. [80]

A competitive muckraking magazine, commenting on the Baker articles, said: "Final summary analysis of race prejudice is unanswerable." [81]

On the other hand, Arthur S. Link, historian, writing in 1955, calls

Baker's series "a pioneer study of prevailing racial attitudes, North and South." [82]

The country in the summer of 1908 was shocked by a race riot in Springfield, Illinois, the home of Abraham Lincoln. A mob made up of many of the town's "best citizens" rioted for two days, killing and wounding scores of Negroes and driving thousands of others from the city.

Reports of this riot appeared in newspapers and magazines. *The Independent* carried an article by a southerner, William English Walling, titled "The Race War in the North." Walling, a Socialist, in his article raised the challenge: "Either the spirit of the abolitionists, of Lincoln and of Lovejoy must be revived and we must come to treat the Negro on a plane of absolute political and social equality, or Vardaman and Tillman will soon have transferred the race war to the North." He concluded: "Yet who realizes the seriousness of the situation, and what large and powerful body of citizens is ready to come to their aid?"

One of the readers of Walling's article was Mary White Ovington. She was living in New York in a tenement in a Negro area, where she was making a study of Negro housing, employment opportunities, and health.

"My investigations and my surroundings led me to believe with the writer of the article that 'the spirit of the abolitionists' must be revived," wrote Mary White Ovington.[83]

She made contact with Walling. In the first week of January 1909 there was a meeting between Miss Ovington, Walling and Dr. Henry Moskowitz, who was associated with the administration of John Purroy Mitchell, mayor of New York City. It was then, in a little room of a New York apartment, that the National Association for the Advancement of Colored People was born.

This trio, with Oswald Garrison Villard, president of the New York Evening Post Company, issued the call for the association's organization.

The signers included Jane Addams, John Dewey, William Lloyd Garrison, Jr., Rabbi Emil G. Hirsch, Rev. John Haynes Holmes, Charles Edward Russell, Lincoln Steffens and Rabbi Stephen S. Wise, all notable educators or reformers. Ray Stannard Baker was not a signer.

Since the first articles on the Negro question appeared, the Negro problem is no longer only in the hands of philanthropic societies and well-wishers. It is an important social issue in its own right, affecting directly broader masses of the citizenry.

RAY STANNARD BAKER

The Clash of the Races in a Southern City

I ARRIVED in Atlanta, Georgia, on the first day of last November [1906]. The riot . . . had taken place about six weeks before, and the city was still in the throes of self-examination and reconstruction. Public attention had been peculiarly riveted upon the facts of race relationships not only in Atlanta but throughout the South, and all manner of remedies and solutions were under sharp discussion. If I had traveled the country over, I could not have found a more favorable time or place to begin following the color line.

I had naturally expected to find people talking about the Negro, but I was not at all prepared to find the subject occupying such an overshadowing place in southern affairs. In the North we have nothing at all like it; no question which so touches every act of life, in which everyone, white or black, is so profoundly interested. In the North we are mildly concerned in many things; the South is overwhelmingly concerned in this one thing.

And this is not surprising, for the Negro in the South is both the labor problem and the servant question; he is pre-eminently the political issue, and his place, socially, is of daily and hourly discussion. A Negro minister I met told me a story of a boy who went as a sort of butler's assistant in the home of a prominent family in Atlanta. His people were naturally curious about what went on in the white man's house. One day they asked him:

"What do they talk about when they's eating?"

The boy thought a moment; then he said:

"Mostly they discusses us culled folks."

The same consuming interest exists among the Negroes. A very large part of their conversation deals with the race question. I had been at the Piedmont Hotel only a day or two when my Negro waiter began to take especially good care of me. He flecked off imaginary crumbs and gave me unnecessary spoons. Finally, when no one was at hand, he leaned over and said:

"I understand you're down here to study the Negro problem."

"Yes," I said, a good deal surprised. "How did you know it?"

"Well, sir," he replied, "we've got ways of knowing things."

He told me that the Negroes had been much disturbed ever since the riot and that he knew many of them who wanted to go North. "The South," he said, "is getting to be too dangerous for colored people." His language and pronunciation were surprisingly good. I found that he was a college student, and that he expected to study for the ministry.

"Do you talk much about these things among yourselves?" I asked.

"We don't talk about much else," he said. "It's sort of life and death with us."

Another curious thing happened not long afterwards. I was lunching with several fine southern men, and they talked, as usual, with the greatest freedom in the full hearing of the Negro waiters. Somehow, I could not help watching to see if the Negroes took any notice of what was said. I wondered if they were sensitive. Finally, I put the question to one of my friends:

"Oh," he said, "we never mind them; they don't care."

One of the waiters instantly spoke up:

"No, don't mind me; I'm only a block of wood."

I set out from the hotel on the morning of my arrival to trace the color line as it appeared, outwardly, in the life of such a town.

Atlanta is a singularly attractive place, as bright and new as any western city. Sherman left it in ashes at the close of the war; the old buildings and narrow streets were swept away and a new city was built, which is now growing in a manner not short of astonishing. It has 115,000 to 125,000 inhabitants, about a third of whom are Negroes, living in more or less detached quarters in various parts of the city, and giving an individuality to the life interesting enough to the unfamiliar northerner. A great many of them are always on the streets, far better dressed and better-appearing than I had expected to see—having in mind, perhaps, the tattered country specimens of the penny postal cards. Crowds of Negroes were at work mending the pavement, for the Italian and Slav have not yet appeared in Atlanta, nor indeed to any extent anywhere in the South. I stopped to watch a group of them. A good deal of conversation was going on, here and there a Negro would laugh with great good humor, and several times I heard a snatch of a song: much jollier workers than our grim foreigners, but evidently not working so hard. A fire had been built to heat some of the tools, and a black circle of Negroes were gathered around it like flies around a drop of molasses and they were all talking while they warmed their shins—evidently having plenty of leisure.

As I continued down the street, I found that all the drivers of wagons and cabs were Negroes; I saw Negro newsboys, Negro porters, Negro barbers, and it being a bright day, many of them were in the street— on the sunny side.

I commented that evening to some southern people I met, on the impression, almost of jollity, given by the Negro workers I had seen. One of the older ladies made what seemed to me a very significant remark:

"They don't sing as they used to," she said. "You should have known the old darkeys of the plantation. Every year, it seems to me, they have been losing more and more of their carefree good humor. I some-times feel that I don't know them any more. Since the riot they have grown so glum and serious that I'm free to say I'm scared of them!"

One of my early errands that morning led me into several of the great new office buildings, which bear testimony to the extraordinary progress of the city. And here I found one of the first evidences of the color line for which I was looking. In both buildings, I found a sepa-rate elevator for colored people. In one building, signs were placed reading:

FOR WHITES ONLY

In another I copied this sign:

THIS CAR FOR
COLORED PASSENGERS,
FREIGHT, EXPRESS
AND PACKAGES.

Curiously enough, as giving an interesting point of view, an intelli-gent Negro with whom I was talking a few days later asked me:

"Have you seen the elevator sign in the Century Building?"

I said I had.

"How would you like to be classed with 'freight, express and pack-ages'?"

I found that no Negro ever went into an elevator devoted to white people, but that white people often rode in cars set apart for colored people. In some cases the car for Negroes is operated by a white man, and in other cases, all the elevators in a building are operated by colored men. This is one of the curious points of industrial contact in the South which somewhat surprise the northern visitor. In the North a white workman, though having no especial prejudice against the Negro, will often refuse to work with him; in the South, while the social prejudice is strong, Negroes and whites work together side by side in many kinds of employment.

I had an illustration in point not long afterward. Passing the post office, I saw several mail-carriers coming out, some white, some black, talking and laughing, with no evidence, at first, of the existence of any color line. Interested to see what the real condition was, I went in and made inquiries. A most interesting and significant condition developed. I found that the postmaster, who is a wise man, sent Negro carriers up Peachtree and other fashionable streets, occupied by wealthy white people, while white carriers were assigned to beats in the mill districts and other parts of town inhabited by the poorer classes of white people.

"You see," said my informant, "the Peachtree people know how to treat Negroes. They really prefer a Negro carrier to a white one; it's natural for them to have a Negro doing such service. But if we sent Negro carriers down into the mill district they might get their heads knocked off."

Then he made a philosophical observation:

"If we had only the best class of white folks down here and the industrious Negroes, there wouldn't be any trouble."

One of the points in which I was especially interested was the "Jim Crow" regulations, that is, the system of separation of the races in street cars and railroad trains. Next to the question of Negro suffrage, I think the people of the North have heard more of the Jim Crow legislation than of anything else connected with the Negro problem. I have seen, so far, no better place than the street car for observing the points of human contact between the races, betraying as it does every shade of feeling upon the part of both. In almost no other relationship do the races come together, physically, on anything like a common footing. In their homes and in ordinary employment, they meet as master and servant; but in the street cars they touch as free citizens each paying for the right to ride, the white not in a place of command, the Negro without an obligation of servitude. Street-car relationships are, therefore, symbolic of the new conditions. A few years ago, the Negro came and went in the street cars in most cities and sat where he pleased, but gradually Jim Crow laws or local regulations were passed forcing him into certain seats at the back of the car.

Since I have been here in Atlanta, the newspapers report two significant new developments in the policy of separation. In Savannah, Jim Crow ordinances have gone into effect for the first time, causing violent protestations on the part of the Negroes and a refusal by many of them to use the cars at all. Montgomery, Alabama, about the same time, went one step further and demanded, not separate seats in the same car, but entirely separate cars for whites and blacks. There could be no better visible evidence of the increasing separation of the races, and of the determination of the white man to make the Negro "keep his place," than the evolution of the Jim Crow regulations.

I was curious to see how the system worked out in Atlanta. Over the door of each car, I found this sign:

WHITE PEOPLE WILL SEAT FROM
FRONT OF CAR TOWARD THE BACK,
AND COLORED PEOPLE FROM REAR
TOWARD FRONT

Sure enough, I found the white people in front and the Negroes behind. As the sign indicates, there is no definite line of division between the white seats and the black seats, as in many other Southern cities. This very absence of a clear demarcation is significant of many relationships in the South. *The color line is drawn, but neither race knows just where it is.* Indeed, it can hardly be definitely drawn in many relationships, because it is constantly changing. This uncertainty is a fertile source of friction and bitterness. The very first time I was on a car in Atlanta, I saw the conductor—all conductors are white—ask a Negro woman to get up and take a seat further back in order to make a place for a white man. I traveled a good deal, but I never saw a white person asked to vacate a back seat to make place for a Negro. I saw cars filled with white people, both front seats and back, and many Negroes standing.

At one time, when I was on a car the conductor shouted: "Here, you nigger, get back there," which the Negro, who had taken a seat too far forward, proceeded hastily to do. Of course, I am talking here of conditions as they are in Atlanta. I may find different circumstances in other cities. . . .

No other one point of race contact is so much and so bitterly discussed among the Negroes as the Jim Crow car. I don't know how many Negroes replied to my question: "What is the chief cause of friction down here?" with a complaint of their treatment on street cars and in railroad trains.

Fundamentally, of course, they object to any separation which gives them inferior accommodations. This point of view—and I am trying to set down every point of view, both colored and white, exactly as I find it, is expressed in many ways.

"We pay first-class fare," said one of the leading Negroes in Atlanta, "exactly as the white man does, but we don't get first-class service. We don't know when we may be dislodged from our seats to make place for a white man who has paid no more than we have. I say it isn't fair."

In answer to this complaint, the white man says: "The Negro is inferior, he must be made to keep his place. Give him a chance and he assumes social equality, and that will lead to an effort at intermarriage and amalgamation of the races. The Anglo-Saxon will never stand for that." . . .

One result of the friction over the Jim Crow regulations is that many Negroes ride on the cars as little as possible. One prominent Negro I met said he never entered a car, and that he had many friends who pursued the same policy; he said that Negro street-car excursions, familiar a few years ago, had entirely ceased. It is significant of the feeling that one of the features of the Atlanta riot was an attack on the street cars in which all Negroes were driven out of their seats. One Negro woman was pushed through an open window, and, after falling to the pavement, she was dragged by the leg across the sidewalk and thrown through a shop window. In another case when the mob stopped a car the motorman, instead of protecting his passengers, went inside and beat down a Negro with his brass control lever.

I heard innumerable stories from both white people and Negroes of encounters in the street cars. Dr. W. F. Penn, one of the foremost Negro physicians of the city, himself partly white, a graduate of Yale College, told me of one occasion in which he entered a car and found there Mrs. Crogman, wife of the colored president of Clark University. Mrs. Crogman is a mulatto so light of complexion as to be practically undistinguishable from white people. Dr. Penn, who knew her well, sat down beside her and began talking. A white man who occupied a seat in front with his wife turned and said:

"Here, you nigger, get out of that seat. What do you mean by sitting down with a white woman?"

Dr. Penn replied somewhat angrily:

"It's come to a pretty pass when a colored man cannot sit with a woman of his own race in his own part of the car."

The white man turned to his wife and said:

"Here, take these bundles. I'm going to thrash that nigger."

In half a minute the car was in an uproar, the two men struggling. Fortunately the conductor and motorman were quickly at hand, and Dr. Penn slipped off the car.

Conditions on the railroad trains, while not resulting so often in personal encounters, are also the cause of constant irritation. When I came south, I took particular pains to observe the arrangement on the trains. In some cases Negroes are given entire cars at the front of the train, at other times they occupy the rear end of a combination coach and baggage car, which is used in the North as a smoking compartment. The complaint here is that, while the Negro is required to pay first-class fare, he is provided with second-class accommodations. Well-to-do Negroes who can afford to travel, also complain that they are not permitted to engage sleeping-car berths. Booker T. Washington usually takes a compartment where he is entirely cut off from the white passengers. Some other Negroes do the same thing, although they are often refused even this expensive privilege. Railroad officials with whom I talked, and it is important to hear what they say, said that it was not only a question of public opinion—which was absolutely opposed to any intermingling of the races in the cars—but that Negro travel in most places was small compared with white travel, that the ordinary Negro was unclean and careless, and that it was impractical to furnish them the same accommodations, even though it did come hard on a few educated Negroes. They said that when there was a delegation of Negroes, enough to fill an entire sleeping car, they could always get accommodations. All of which gives a glimpse of the enormous difficulties accompanying the separation of the races in the South.

Another interesting point significant of tendencies came early to my attention. They have just finished at Atlanta one of the finest railroad stations in this country. The ordinary depot in the South has two waiting rooms of about the same size, one for whites and one for Negroes. But when this new station was built the whole front was given up to white people, and the Negroes were assigned a side entrance, and a small waiting room. Prominent colored men regarded it as a new evidence of the crowding out of the Negro, the further attempt to give him unequal accommodations, to handicap him in his struggle for survival. A delegation was sent to the railroad people to protest, but to no purpose. Result: further bitterness. There are in the station two lunch rooms, one for whites, one for Negroes.

A leading colored man said to me:

"No Negro goes to the lunch room in the station who can help it. We don't like the way we have been treated."

Of course this was an unusually intelligent colored man, and he spoke for his own sort; how far the same feeling of a race consciousness strong enough to carry out such a boycott as this—and it is exactly like the boycott of a labor union—actuates the masses of ignorant Negroes, is a question upon which I hope to get more light. I have already heard more than one colored leader complain that Negroes do not stand together. And a white planter, whom I met in the hotel, said a significant thing along this very line:

"If once the Negroes got together and saved their money, they'd soon own the country, but they can't do it, and they never will."

After I had begun to trace the color line I found evidences of it everywhere—literally in every department of life. In the theaters, Negroes never sit downstairs, but the galleries are black with them. Of course, white hotels and restaurants are entirely barred to Negroes, with the result that colored people have their own eating and sleeping places, most of them inexpressibly dilapidated and unclean. "Sleepers wanted" is a familiar sign in Atlanta, giving notice of places where for a few cents a Negro can find a bed or a mattress on the floor, often in a room where there are many other sleepers, sometimes both men and women in the same room, crowded together in a manner both unsanitary and immoral. No good public accommodations exist for the educated or well-to-do Negro. Indeed, one cannot long remain in the South without being impressed with the extreme difficulties which beset the exceptional colored man.

In slavery time, many Negroes attended white churches and heard good preaching, and Negro children were often taught by white women. Now, a Negro is never (or very rarely) seen in a white man's church. Once since I have been in the South, I saw a very old Negro woman— some much-loved mammy, perhaps—sitting down in front near the pulpit, but that is the only exception to the rule that has come to my attention. Negroes are not wanted in white churches. Consequently, the colored people, who are nothing if not religious, have some sixty churches of their own in Atlanta. Of course, the schools are separate, and have been ever since the Civil War.

In one of the parks of Atlanta I saw this sign:

NO NEGROES ALLOWED
IN THIS PARK

A story significant of the growing separation of the races is told about the public library at Atlanta, which no Negro is permitted to enter. Carnegie gave the money for building it, and when the question came up as to the support of it by the city, the inevitable color question arose. Leading Negroes asserted that their people should be allowed admittance, that they needed such an educational advantage even more than white people, and that they were to be taxed their share—even though it was small—for buying the books and maintaining the building. They did not win their point, of course, but Mr. Carnegie proposed a solution of the difficulty by offering more money to build a Negro branch library, provided the city would give the land and provide for its support. The city said to the Negroes:

"You contribute the land and we will support the library."

Influential Negroes at once arranged for buying and contributing a site for the library. Then the question of control arose. The Negroes thought that inasmuch as they gave the land and the building was to be used entirely for colored people, they should have one or two members on the board of control. This the city officials, who had charge of the matter, would not hear of; result, the Negroes would not give the land, and the branch library has never been built.

Right in this connection: while I was in Atlanta, the Art School, which in the past has often used Negro models, decided to draw the color line there, too, and no longer employ them.

Formerly Negroes and white men went to the same saloons, and drank at the same bars, as they do now, I am told, in some parts of the South. In a few instances, in Atlanta, there were Negro saloon-keepers, and many Negro bartenders. The first step toward separation was to divide the bar, the upper end for white men, the lower for Negroes. Finally, after the riot, all Negro saloonkeepers were thrown out of business, and by the new requirement no saloon can serve both white and colored men.

Consequently, going along Decatur Street, one sees the saloons designated by conspicuous signs:

WHITES ONLY
COLORED ONLY

And when the Negro suffers the ordinary consequences of a prolonged visit to Decatur Street, and finds himself in the city prison, he is separated there, too, from the whites. And afterwards in court, if he comes to trial, two Bibles are provided; he may take his oath on one; the other is for the white man. When he dies he is buried in a separate cemetery.

One curious and enlightening example of the infinite ramifications of the color line was given me by Mr. Logan, secretary of the Atlanta Associated Charities, which is supported by voluntary contributions. One day, after the riot, a subscriber called Mr. Logan on the telephone and said:

"Do you help Negroes in your society?"

"Why, yes, occasionally," said Mr. Logan.

"What do you do that for?"

"A Negro gets hungry and cold like anybody else," answered Mr. Logan.

"Well, you can strike my name from your subscription list. I won't give any of my money to a society that helps Negroes."

Now, this sounds rather brutal, but behind it lies the peculiar psychology of the South. This very man who refused to contribute to the associated charities, may have fed several Negroes from his kitchen and had a number of Negro pensioners who came to him regularly for help. It was simply amazing to me, considering the bitterness of racial feeling, to see how lavish many white families are in giving food, clothing and money to individual Negroes whom they know. It is said that the southern housewife never serves hash; certainly I haven't seen so far a sign of it since I came down here. The adroit "made-over dishes" of economical New England are here absent, because nothing is ever left to make over. The Negro eats it up! Even bread here is not usually baked days ahead as in the North, but made fresh for every meal—the famous, delicious (and indigestible) "hot bread" of the South. A Negro cook often supports her whole family, including a lazy husband, on what she gets daily from the white man's kitchen. In some old families the "basket habit" of the Negroes is taken for granted; in the newer ones, it is, significantly, beginning to be called stealing, showing that the old order is passing and that the Negro is being held more and more strictly to account, not as a dependent vassal, but as a moral being, who must rest upon his own responsibility.

And often a Negro of the old sort will literally bulldoze his hereditary white protector into the loan of quarters and half dollars, which both know will never be paid back.

Mr. Brittain, superintendent of schools in Fulton County, gave me an incident in point. A big Negro with whom he was wholly unacquainted came to his office one day, and demanded—he did not ask, but demanded—a job.

"What's your name?" asked the superintendent.

"Marion Luther Brittain," was the reply.

"That sounds familiar," said Mr. Brittain—it being, indeed, his own name.

"Yas, sah. Ah'm the son of yo' ol' mammy."

In short, Marion Luther had grown up on the old plantation; it was the spirit of the hereditary vassal demanding the protection and support of the hereditary baron, and he got it, of course.

The Negro who makes his appeal on the basis of this old relationship finds no more indulgent or generous friend than the southern white man, indulgent to the point of excusing thievery and other petty offenses, but the moment he assumes or demands any other relationship or stands up as an independent citizen, the white men—at least some white men—turn upon him with the fiercest hostility. The incident of the associated charities may now be understood. It was not necessarily cruelty to a cold or hungry Negro that inspired the demand of the irate subscriber, but the feeling that the associated charities helped Negroes and whites on the same basis, as men; that, therefore, it encouraged "social equality," and that therefore it was to be stopped.

I shall have to ask the indulgence of the reader here . . . for getting away from the main-traveled road of my narrative. Sooner or later I promise solemnly to get back again, and not without the hope that I have illuminated some obscure by-way or found a new path through a thorny hedge.

Most of the examples so far given are along the line of social contact, where, of course, the repulsion is intense. They are the outward evidences of separation, but while highly provocative, they are not really of vital importance. Negroes and whites can go to different schools, churches and saloons, and sit in different street cars, and still live pretty comfortably. But the longer I remain in the South, the more clearly I come to understand how wide and deep, in other, less easily discernible ways, the chasm between the races is becoming. It takes forms that I had never dreamed of.

One of the natural and inevitable results of the effort of the white man to set the Negro off, as a race, by himself, is to awaken in him a new consciousness—a sort of racial consciousness. It drives the Negroes together for defense and offense. Many able Negroes, some largely of white blood, cut off from all opportunity of success in the greater life of the white man, become of necessity leaders of their own people.

And one of their chief efforts consists in urging Negroes to work together and to stand together. In this they are only developing the instinct of defense against the white man which has always been latent in the race. This instinct exhibits itself, as in the recent Brownsville case, in the way in which the mass of Negroes often refuse to turn over a criminal of their color to white justice; it is like the instinctive clannishness of the Highland Scotch or the peasant Irish. I don't know how many southern people have told me in different ways of how extremely difficult it is to get at the real feeling of a Negro, to make him tell what goes on in his clubs and churches or in his innumerable societies.

A southern woman told me of a cook who had been in her service for nineteen years. The whole family really loved the old [woman]: her mistress made her a confidant, in the way of the old South, in the most intimate private and family matters, the daughters told her their love affairs; they all petted her and even submitted to many small tyrannies upon her part.

"But do you know," said my hostess, "Susie never tells us a thing about her life or her friends, and we couldn't, if we tried, make her tell what goes on in the society she belongs to."

The Negro has long been defensively secretive. Slavery made him that. In the past, the instinct was passive and defensive; but with growing education and intelligent leadership it is rapidly becoming conscious, self-directive and offensive. And right there, it seems to me, though I speak yet from limited observation, lies the great cause of the increased strain in the South.

Let me illustrate. In the People's Tabernacle in Atlanta, where thousands of Negroes meet every Sunday, I saw this sign in huge letters:

FOR PHOTOGRAPHS, GO TO
AUBURN PHOTO GALLERY,
OPERATED BY COLORED MEN.

The old-fashioned [Negro] preferred to go to the white man for everything; he didn't trust his own people; the new Negro, with growing race consciousness, and feeling that the white man is against him, urges his friends to patronize Negro doctors and dentists, and to trade with Negro storekeepers. The extent to which this movement has gone was one of the most surprising things that I, as an unfamiliar northerner, found in Atlanta. In other words, the struggle of the races is becoming more and more rapidly economic.

One day, walking in Broad Street, I passed a Negro shoe store. I did not know that there was such a thing in the country. I went in to make inquiries. It was neat, well kept and evidently prosperous. I found that it was owned by a stock company, organized and controlled wholly by Negroes; the manager was a brisk young mulatto named Harper, a graduate of Atlanta University. I found him dictating to a Negro girl stenographer. There were two reasons, he said, why the store had been opened; one was because the promoters thought it a good business opportunity, and the other was because many Negroes of the better class felt that they did not get fair treatment at white stores. At some places—not all, he said—when a Negro woman went to buy a pair of shoes, the clerk would hand them to her without offering to help her try them on; and a Negro was always kept waiting until all the white people in the store had been served. Since the new business was opened, he said, it had attracted much of the Negro trade; all the leaders advising their people to patronize him. I was much interested to find out how this young man looked upon the race question. His first answer struck me forcibly, for it was the universal and typical answer of the businessman the world over, whether white, yellow or black:

"All I want," he said, "is to be protected and let alone, so that I can build up this business."

"What do you mean by protection?" I asked.

"Well, justice between the races. That doesn't mean social equality. We have a society of our own, and that is all we want. If we can have justice in the courts, and fair protection, we can learn to compete with the white stores and get along all right."

Such an enterprise as this indicates the new economic separation between the races.

"Here is business," says the Negro, "which I am going to do."

Considering the fact that only a few years ago, the Negro did no business at all, and had no professional men, it is really surprising to a northerner to see what progress he has made. One of the first lines he took up was—not unnaturally—the undertaking business. Some of the most prosperous Negroes in every southern city are undertakers, doing work exclusively, of course, for colored people. Other early enterprises, growing naturally out of a history of personal service, were barbering and tailoring. Atlanta has many small Negro tailor and clothes-cleaning shops.

The wealthiest Negro in Atlanta, A. F. Herndon, operates the largest barbershop in the city; he is the president of a Negro insurance company (of which there are four in the city) and he owns and rents some fifty dwelling houses. He is said to be worth $80,000, all made, of course, since slavery.

Another occupation developing naturally from the industrial training of slavery was the business of the building contractor. Several such Negroes, notably Alexander Hamilton, do a considerable business in Atlanta, and have made money. They are employed by white men, and they hire for their jobs both white and Negro workmen.

Small groceries and other stores are of later appearance; I saw at least a score of them in various parts of Atlanta. For the most part they are very small, many are exceedingly dirty and ill-kept; usually much poorer than corresponding places kept by foreigners, indiscriminately called "Dagoes" down here, who are in reality mostly Russian Jews and Greeks. But there are a few Negro grocery stores in Atlanta which are highly creditable. Other business enterprises include restaurants (for Negroes), printing establishments, two newspapers and several drugstores. In other words, the Negro is rapidly building up his own business enterprises, tending to make himself independent as a race.

The appearance of Negro drugstores was the natural result of the increasing practice of Negro doctors and dentists. Time was when all Negroes preferred to go to white practitioners, but since educated colored doctors became common, they have taken a very large part— practically all, I am told—of the practice in Atlanta. Several of them have had degrees from northern universities, two from Yale; and one of them, at least, has some little practice among white people. The doctors are leaders among their people. Naturally they give prescriptions to be filled by druggists of their own race; hence the growth of the drug business among Negroes everywhere in the South. The first store to be established in Atlanta occupies an old wooden building in Auburn Avenue. It is operated by Moses Amos, a mulatto, and enjoys, I understand, a high degree of prosperity. I visited it. A post office occupies one corner of the room; and it is a familiar gathering place for colored men. Moses Amos told me his story, and I found it so interesting, and so significant of the way in which Negro businessmen have come up, that I am setting it down briefly here:

"I never shall forget," he said, "my first day in the drug business. It was in 1876. I remember I was with a crowd of boys in Peachtree Street, where Dr. Huss, a southern white man, kept a drugstore. The old doctor was sitting out in front smoking his pipe. He called one little Negro after another, and finally chose me. He said:

" 'I want you to live with me, work in the store, and look after my horse.'

"He sent me to his house and told me to tell his wife to give me some breakfast, and I certainly delivered the first message correctly. His wife, who was a noble lady, not only fed me, but made me take a bath in a sure enough porcelain tub, the first I had ever seen. When I went back to the store, I was so regenerated that the doctor had to adjust his spectacles before he knew me. He said to me:

" 'You can wash bottles, put up castor oil, salts and turpentine, sell anything you *know* and put the money in the drawer.'

"He showed me how to work the keys of the cash drawer. 'I am going to trust you,' he said. 'Don't steal from me; if you want anything, ask for it, and you can have it. And don't lie; I hate a liar. A boy who will lie will steal, too.'

"I remained with Dr. Huss thirteen years. He sent me to school and paid my tuition out of his own pocket; he trusted me fully, often leaving me in charge of his business for weeks at a time. When he died, I formed a partnership with Dr. Butler, Dr. Slater and others, and bought the store. Our business grew and prospered, so that within a few years we had a stock worth $3,000 and cash of $800. That made us ambitious. We bought land, built a new store, and went into debt to do it. We didn't know much about business—that's the Negro's chief trouble—and we lost trade by changing our location, so that in spite of all we could do, we failed and lost everything, though we finally paid our creditors every cent. After many trials we started again in 1896 in our present store; today we are doing a good business; we can get all the credit we want from wholesale houses, we employ six clerks, and pay good interest on the capital invested."

I asked him what was the greatest difficulty he had to meet. He said it was the credit system; the fact that many Negroes have not learned financial responsibility. Once, he said, he nearly stopped business on this account.

"I remember," he said, "the last time we got into trouble. We needed $400 to pay our bills. I picked out some of our best customers and gave them a heart-to-heart talk and told them what trouble we were in. They all promised to pay; but on the day set for payment, out of $1,680 which they owed us we collected just $8.25. After that experience we came down to a cash basis. We trust no one, and since then we have been doing well."

He said he thought the best opportunity for Negro development was in the South where he had his whole race behind him. He said he had once been tempted to go north looking for an opening.

"How did you make out?" I asked.

"Well, I'll tell you," he said, "when I got there I wanted a shave; I walked the streets two hours visiting barbershops, and they all turned me away with some excuse. I finally had to buy a razor and shave myself! That was just a sample. I came home disgusted and decided to fight it out down here where I understood conditions."

Of course only a comparatively few Negroes are able to get ahead in business. They must depend almost exclusively on the trade of their own race, and they must meet the highly organized competition of white men. But it is certainly significant that even a few—all I have met so far are mulattoes, some very white—are able to make progress along these unfamiliar lines. Most southern men I met had little or no idea of the remarkable extent of this advancement among the better class of Negroes. Here is a strange thing. I don't know how many southern men have prefaced their talks with me with words something like this:

"You can't expect to know the Negro after a short visit. You must live down here like we do. Now, I know the Negroes like a book. I was brought up with them. I know what they'll do and what they won't do. I have had Negroes in my house all my life."

But curiously enough I found that these men rarely knew anything about the better class of Negroes—those who were in business, or in independent occupations, those who owned their own homes. They *did* come into contact with the servant Negro, the field hand, the common laborer, who make up, of course, the great mass of the race. On the other hand, the best class of Negroes did not know the higher class of white people, and based their suspicion and hatred upon the acts of the poorer sort of whites with whom they naturally came into contact. The best elements of the two races are as far apart as though they lived in different continents; and that is one of the chief causes of the growing danger of the southern situation. One of the first— almost instinctive—efforts at reconstruction after the Atlanta riot was to bring the best elements of both races together, so that they might, by becoming acquainted and gaining confidence in each other, allay suspicion and bring influence to bear upon the lawless elements of both white people and colored.

Many southerners look back wistfully to the faithful, simple, ignorant, obedient, cheerful, old plantation "darkey" and deplore his disappearance. They want the New South, but the old "darkey." That "darkey" is disappearing forever along with the old feudalism and the old-time exclusively agricultural life.

A New Negro is not less inevitable than a new white man and a

New South. And the New Negro, as my clever friend says, doesn't laugh as much as the old one. It is grim business he is in, this being free, this new fierce struggle in the open competitive field for the daily loaf. Many go down to vagrancy and crime in that struggle; a few will rise. The more rapid the progress (with the trained white man setting the pace), the more frightful the mortality.

American Magazine
May 1907

WILLIAM ENGLISH WALLING

❦

The Race War in the North

"L INCOLN FREED YOU, we'll show you where you belong," was one of the cries with which the Springfield [Illinois] mob set about to drive the Negroes from town. The mob was composed of several thousand of Springfield's white citizens, while other thousands, including many women and children, and even prosperous businessmen in automobiles, calmly looked on, and the rioters proceeded hour after hour and on two days in succession to make deadly assaults on every Negro they could lay their hands on, to sack and plunder their houses and stores, and to burn and murder on favorable occasion.

The American people have been fairly well informed by their newspapers of the action of that mob; they have also been told of certain alleged political and criminal conditions in Springfield and of the two crimes in particular which are offered by the mob itself as sufficient explanation why six thousand peaceful and innocent Negroes should be driven by the fear of their lives from a town where some of them have lived honorably for half a hundred years. We have been assured by more cautious and indirect defenders of Springfield's populace that there was an exceptionally criminal element among the Negroes encouraged by the bosses of both political parties. And now, after a few days of discussion, we are satisfied with these explanations, and demand only the punishment of those who took the most active part in the destruction of life and property. Assuming that there were exceptionally provocative causes for complaint against the Negroes, we have closed our eyes to the whole awful and menacing truth—that a large part of the white population of Lincoln's home, supported largely by the farmers and miners of the neighboring towns, have initiated a permanent warfare with the Negro race.

We do not need to be informed at great length of the character of this warfare. It is in all respects like that of the South, on which it is modeled. Its significance is threefold. First, that it has occurred in an important and historical northern town; then, that the Negroes, constituting scarcely more than a tenth of the population, in this case could not possibly endanger the "supremacy" of the whites, and, finally, that the public opinion of the North, notwithstanding the fanatical, blind and almost insane hatred of the Negro so clearly shown by the mob, is satisfied that there were "mitigating circumstances," not for the mob violence, which, it is agreed, should be punished to the full extent of the law, but for the race hatred, which is really the cause of it all. If these outrages had happened thirty years ago, when the memories of Lincoln, Garrison and Wendell Phillips were still fresh, what would not have happened in the North? Is there any doubt that the whole country would have been aflame, that all flimsy explanations and "mitigating circumstances" would have been thrown aside, and that the people of Springfield would have had to prove to the nation why they proposed to drive the Negroes out, to hold a whole race responsible for a handful of criminals, and to force it to an inferior place on the social scale?

For the underlying motive of the mob and of that large portion of Springfield's population that has long said that "something was bound to happen," and now approves of the riot and proposes to complete its purpose by using other means to drive as many as possible of the remaining two-thirds of the Negroes out of town, was confessedly to teach the Negroes their place and to warn them that too many could not obtain shelter under the favorable traditions of Lincoln's home town. I talked to many of them the day after the massacre and found no difference of opinion on the question. "Why, the niggers came to think they were as good as we are!" was the final justification offered, not once, but a dozen times.

On the morning after the first riot I was in Chicago and took the night train for Springfield, where I have often visited and am almost at home. On arriving in the town I found that the rioting had been continued throughout the night, and was even feared for the coming evening, in spite of the presence of nearly the whole militia of the state. Although we visited the mayor, military headquarters, the leading newspaper, and some prominent citizens, my wife and I gave most of our attention to the hospital, the Negro quarters and the jail.

We at once discovered, to our amazement, that Springfield had no shame. She stood for the action of the mob. She hoped the rest of the

Negroes might flee. She threatened that the movement to drive them out would continue. I do not speak of the leading citizens, but of the masses of the people, of workingmen in the shops, the storekeepers in the stores, the drivers, the men on the street, the wounded in the hospitals and even the notorious "Joan of Arc" of the mob, Kate Howard, who had just been released from arrest on $4,000 bail. [She has since committed suicide—Editor, *The Independent.*] The *Illinois State Journal* of Springfield expressed the prevailing feeling even on its editorial page:

> While all good citizens deplore the consequences of this outburst of the mob spirit, many even of these consider the outburst was inevitable, at some time, from existing conditions, needing only an overt act, such as that of Thursday night, to bring it from latent existence into active operation. The implication is clear that conditions, not the populace, were to blame and that many good citizens could find no other remedy than that applied by the mob. It was not the fact of the whites' hatred toward the negroes, but of the negroes' own misconduct, general inferiority or unfitness for free institutions that were at fault.

On Sunday, August 16, the day after the second lynching, a leading white minister recommended the southern disfranchisement scheme as a remedy for Negro (!) lawlessness, while all four ministers who were quoted in the press proposed swift "justice" for the Negroes, rather than recommending true Christianity, democracy and brotherhood to the whites. Even the governor's statement of the situation, strong as it was on the whole, was tainted in one place with a concession to Springfield opinion. He said that Burton, the first Negro lynched, was killed after he had incensed the crowd by firing into it to protect his home from incendiaries. But when Burton's home was attacked there had already been considerable shooting between the blacks and the whites. Moreover, according to his daughters, men had entered the house and threatened him with an ax and other weapons, while his firing of buckshot at random into a mob is by no means necessarily a murderous procedure. The governor made, then, an understatement of the character of the mob, suggesting that the Negroes had lost their heads and were accepting the mob's challenge to war. It is probable that Burton was defending not his home, but his life.

Besides suggestions in high places of the Negro's brutality, criminality and unfitness for the ballot we heard in lower ranks all the opinions that pervade the South—that the Negro does not need much education, that his present education even has been a mistake, that whites cannot live in the same community with Negroes except where the latter have

been taught their inferiority, that lynching is the only way to teach
them, etc. In fact, this went so far that we were led to suspect the
existence of a southern element in the town, and this is indeed the
case. Many of the older citizens are from Kentucky or the southern part
of Illinois. Moreover, many of the street railway employees are from
the South. It was a street railway man's wife that was assaulted the
night before the riots, and they were street railway employees, among
others, that led the mob to the jail. Even the famous Kate Howard had
received her inspiration, she told us, from the South. While traveling
with her brother in Texas and Arkansas she had observed enviously that
enforced separation of the races in cars and public places helped to
teach the Negro where he belonged. Returning home she had noticed
the growing boycott of Negroes in Springfield stores and restaurants,
participated in the alarm that "no white woman was safe," etc., and in
the demand for Negro blood. A woman of evident physical courage,
she held that it was time for the population to act up to their pro-
fessions, and by the cry of "cowards" is said to have goaded the mob
into some of the worst of its deeds. She exhibited to us proudly the buckshot wounds in her fleshy arms (probably Burton's), and said she relied
confidently on her fellow citizens to keep her from punishment.

This was the feeling also of the half hundred whites in the hospital.
It was, in fact, only three days after the first disturbance when they
fully realized that the lenient public opinion of Springfield was not the
public opinion of Illinois or the North, that the rioters began to
tremble. Still this did not prevent them later from insulting the militia,
repeatedly firing at their outposts and almost openly organizing a
political and business boycott to drive the remaining Negroes out.
Negro-employers continue to receive threatening letters and are dis-
missing employees every day, while the stores, even the groceries, so
fear to sell the Negroes goods that the state has been compelled to
intervene and purchase $10,000 worth in their behalf.

The menace is that if this thing continues it will offer automatic
rewards to the riotous elements and Negro haters in Springfield, make
the reign of terror permanent there, and offer every temptation to
similar white elements in other towns to imitate Springfield's example.

If the new Political League succeeds in permanently driving every
Negro from office; if the white laborers get the Negro laborers' jobs;
if masters of Negro servants are able to keep them under the discipline
of terror as I saw them doing at Springfield; if white shopkeepers and
saloonkeepers get their colored rivals' trade; if the farmers of neighboring
towns establish permanently their right to drive poor people out of

their community, instead of offering them reasonable alms; if white miners can force their Negro fellow workers out and get their positions by closing the mines, then every community indulging in an outburst of race hatred will be assured of a great and certain financial reward, and all the lies, ignorance and brutality on which race hatred is based will spread over the land. For the action of these dozen farming and four coal mining communities near Springfield shows how rapidly the thing can spread. In the little town of Buffalo, fifteen miles away, for instance, they have just posted this sign in front of the interurban station:

ALL NIGGERS ARE WARNED OUT OF TOWN BY MONDAY, 12 M. SHARP.
—BUFFALO SHARP SHOOTERS.

Part of the Springfield press, far from discouraging this new effort to drive the Negroes out, a far more serious attack on our colored brothers than the mob violence, either fails to condemn it in the only possible way, a complete denial of the whole hypocritical case against the Negro, or indirectly approves it. An evening paper printed this on the third day after the outbreak:

NEGRO FAMILY
LEAVES CITY
WHEN ORDERED.

The first Negro family routed from Springfield by a mob was the Harvey family, residing at 1144 North Seventh street, who were told Sunday morning to "hike," and carried out the orders yesterday afternoon. The family proved themselves obnoxious in many ways. They were the one Negro family in the block and their presence was distasteful to all other citizens in that vicinity.

The tone of this notice is that of a jubilant threat. As the family left town only the day after, not on account of the mob, but the standing menace, the use of the word "first" is significant.

We have not mentioned the Negro crimes which are alleged to have caused the disorders, as we are of the opinion that they could scarcely in any case have had much real connection either with the mob violence or the far more important race conflict that is still spreading geographically and growing in intensity from day to day.

The first crime is called a murder, resulting from an assault on a woman. An unknown Negro was discovered at night in the room of two young white girls. The father and mother and two sons were also at home, however, and there is every probability that it was no assault but a common burglary. The father attacked the Negro, was terribly cut up, and died. A few hours later a Negro was found sleeping not very far away, and the press claimed that there was every evidence that he was the criminal. However, Judge Creighton, a man respected by the whole community, saw cause to postpone the case, and it was this short delay of six weeks that was used by the enemies of the Negro in Springfield to suggest that the Negroes' political influence was thwarting the "swift justice" of the law.

The *State Journal,* ignoring the common sense of the situation, stated editorially that Ballard, the victim, "had given his life in defense of his child," and added significantly: "This tragedy was not enacted in the black belt of Mississippi or of Georgia," and further, twelve lines below, "Concerning him [the Negro] and the questions which arise from his presence in the community, it is well to preserve silence at the present time. The state of the public mind is such that comment can only add fuel to the feeling that has burst forth with general knowledge of the crime."

The writer has been rather cautious, but has he not succeeded in suggesting clearly enough to readers of the character we have mentioned (1) that the deed was to be connected in some way with the race question; (2) that the public mind as it was, and events, have since shown the world clearly what the writer must have known at that time was justified; and (3) in directing their attention to the South as a basis of comparison?

Then what was the second crime, which occurred six weeks later, early in the morning of August 15? This was an assault by a Negro on a white woman in her home. There is little doubt of the nature of the crime intended. But in this case there was far more doubt of the identity of the Negro arrested for the crime, who was of a relatively good character. However, the victim's portrait was printed and circulated among the crowd, first as an incentive to lynch the suspected Negro, then as a pretext for driving the Negroes out.

As we do not lay much emphasis on these or the previous crimes of Springfield Negroes, which were in no way in excess of those of the corresponding social elements of the white population, so we do not lay much stress on the frenzied, morbid violence of the mob. Mob psychology is the same everywhere. It can begin on a little thing. But Springfield had many mobs; they lasted two days and they initiated a state of affairs far worse than any of the immediate effects of their violence.

Either the spirit of the abolitionists, of Lincoln and of Lovejoy must be revived and we must come to treat the Negro on a plane of absolute political and social equality, or Vardaman and Tillman will soon have transferred the race war to the North.

Already Vardaman boasts that "such sad experiences as Springfield is undergoing will doubtless cause the people of the North to look with more toleration upon the methods employed by the southern people today."

The day these methods become general in the North every hope of political democracy will be dead, other weaker races and classes will be persecuted in the North as in the South, public education will undergo an eclipse, and American civilization will await either a rapid degeneration or another profounder and more revolutionary civil war, which shall obliterate not only the remains of slavery but all the other obstacles to a free democratic evolution that have grown up in its wake.

Yet who realizes the seriousness of the situation, and what large and powerful body of citizens is ready to come to their aid?

The Independent
September 3, 1908

PART SIX

High Finance

"MOTHER OF TRUSTS"

THE IDEA of publishing articles on trusts in *McClure's* magazine was that of its publisher, S. S. McClure. It was his intention to present a series on "the greatest American business achievements." [84]

Trusts and monopolies had been a topic of discussion in the United States since the end of the Spanish American War and the coming of prosperity. "The feeling of the common people," recalled McClure in his autobiography, "had a sort of menace in it; they took a threatening attitude toward the Trusts, and without much knowledge." [85]

At an editorial conference at *McClure's*, it was decided not to discuss trusts in the abstract but to take one trust, give its history, its effects, its method of operation.

As the Standard Oil Company was the most important trust at that time, the company was earmarked for study. It was the creation of one man—John D. Rockefeller—of whom McClure said: "There is no question that he is the Napoleon among business men." [86] To McClure and his editors, Standard Oil represented the "Mother of Trusts," and it acted as a model or an inspiration for others.

Ida Tarbell was already on the staff of *McClure's Magazine* when she was assigned to write the articles. She had lived for years in the heart of the Pennsylvania oil country. She was born not more than thirty miles from the first oil well, and its discovery shaped her father's life. She had grown up "with oil derricks, oil tanks, pipe lines, refineries, oil exchanges." [87]

Tragedy had hit her own household during the ten years that Standard Oil completed its monopoly. Her father's partner, "ruined by the complex situation shot himself, leaving [her] father with notes" to pay. In order for her father to pay these notes, he had to mortgage their home, which to him "in his modest economy was unsound and humiliating." [88]

In her research for the Standard Oil series, Miss Tarbell turned to records of Congressional investigations, state investigations, testimony of Mr. Rockefeller and other Standard Oil officials in suits brought against Standard Oil, and also information from those who had fought the "Mother of Trusts."

Through Mark Twain, Miss Tarbell met Henry Rogers, a top executive in Standard Oil, and a man whom she saw regularly for two years in her preparation of the series. Through Rogers she was able to meet and talk with other officials of the company.

Rogers and Miss Tarbell made a "bargain." She was to take up with him each case in the company's history as she came to it, and he in turn would give her documents, figures, explanations, and justifications—"anything and everything which would enlarge my understanding and judgment." [89]

In case of a disagreement, Miss Tarbell's judgment about these cases would prevail.

Her visits to Rogers ended when one of her articles disclosed that the shipments of independent oil companies "were interfered with, their cars side-tracked en route while pressure was brought on buyers to cancel orders. There were frequent charges that freight clerks were reporting independent shipments." [90]

Before the article appeared, Miss Tarbell told Rogers that she had come upon repeated charges that Standard Oil got reports of independent shipments from the railroad and that they stopped them.

"Do you have the help of railroad shipping clerks in the operation?" Miss Tarbell asked.

Rogers responded: "Of course we do everything we legally and fairly can to find out what our competitors are doing, just as you do in *McClure's Magazine*. But as for any such system of tracking and stopping, as you suggest, that is nonsense."

"Well," said Miss Tarbell, "give me everything you have on this point."

Rogers said he had nothing more than what he had already given her.

After the article in which she mentioned these charges was written, Rogers asked Miss Tarbell: "Where did you get that stuff?"

"Mr. Rogers," responded the reporter from *McClure's*, "you can't for a moment think that I would tell you where I got it. You will recall my efforts to get from you anything more than a general denial that these practices of espionage so long complained of were untrue, could be explained by legitimate competition. You know this bookkeeping record is true." [91]

There were no more interviews between the reporter and her company source.

Originally, "The History of the Standard Oil Company" was to be a three-article series, but before publication it was changed to six, and before the series was completed it ran to nineteen articles. It was published in book form in the fall of 1904. Though Ida Tarbell was already famous as a biographer before the appearance of *Standard Oil*, the series catapulted her into national fame and her name became a byword in many homes throughout the country. The author, however, was particularly interested to learn what kind of reception the book would get from the Standard Oil people.

A friend of hers reported to her that Rockefeller at one time thought of answering the McClure articles, but "it has always been the policy of the Standard to keep silent under attack and let their acts speak for themselves." [92]

Nevertheless, answers did come. For example, Elbert Hubbard of the Roycroft Shop of East Aurora, New York, wrote an essay on the virtues of the centralization of the oil industry by Standard. Miss Tarbell says in her autobiography that she had it "from various interested sources that five million copies were ordered printed in pamphlet form by the Standard Oil Company and were distributed by Mr. Hubbard." [93]

Hubbard wrote: "Up to this time, or until very recently, the Standard Oil company has declined to answer its assailants. . . . The Standard Oil company should have nailed a few of the Ida Tarbell fairy tales, ten years ago."

He went on to say: "Ida Tarbell . . . is an honest, bitter, talented, prejudiced and disappointed woman who wrote from her own point of view. And that view is from the ditch, where her father's wheelbarrow was landed by a Standard Oil tank-wagon. . . . She shot from cover, and she shot to kill. Such literary bushwhackers should be answered shot for shot. Sniping the commercial caravan may be legitimate, but to my mind the Tarbell-Steffens-Russell-Roosevelt-Sinclair method of inky warfare is quite as unethical as the alleged tentacled-octopi policy which they attack." [94]

When the book itself was published, most reviews were laudatory. The only voice of dissent came from a reviewer in *The Nation*, who wrote: "This book seems to have been written for the purpose of intensifying the popular hatred. The writer has either a vague conception of the nature of proof, or she is willing to blacken the character of Mr. John D. Rockefeller by insinuation and detraction. . . ." [95]

On the other hand, the magazine *Public Opinion* said: "The author never gets excited, however exciting her story may become; she sets forth the facts, and to a considerable extent leaves inference and conclusions to her readers. . . . It is, in effect, a liberal education in the fundamentals of the trust problem; it is the Blackstone of the literature that is growing up around this problem, in its entirety the most important of all in commercialized America." [96]

Will Irwin in his articles on the American newspapers in *Collier's* in 1911, more than half a decade later, wrote of the series: "Never was a contemporaneous history so temperately and accurately written."

From a vantage point of more than twenty-five years after its appearance, Professor Allan Nevins in his two-volume biography of John D. Rockefeller, published in 1940, refers to *The History of the Standard Oil Company* as "the greatest book produced by the muckraking movement . . . its most enduring achievement." [97]

"Readers today," wrote Dr. Nevins, "are likely to find . . . its sober, factual method difficult to read; and nine people out of ten who talk of the book actually know it only at second hand. But in 1902-4 the public had a background of knowledge which lent the articles a stirring interest." [98]

IDA M. TARBELL

The Rise of the Standard Oil Company

Strung along the banks of Walworth and Kingsbury Runs, the creeks to which Cleveland, Ohio, frequently banishes her heavy and evil-smelling burdens, there lay in the early sixties a dozen or more small oil refineries. Why they were there, more than two hundred miles from the spot where the oil was taken from the earth, a glance at a map of the railroads of the time will show. No railroad entered the region where oil was first discovered. To bring machinery for refineries to that distant and rugged locality was practically impossible. The simplest operation was to take the crude to the nearest manufacturing cities. Cleveland was one of these. Great as was its distance from the oil field, its advantages as a refining center more than balanced that. Cleveland commanded the entire western market. It had two trunk lines running to New York, both eager for oil traffic, and by Lake Erie and the canal it had for a large part of the year a splendid cheap waterway. Thus, at the opening of the oil business, Cleveland was destined by geographical position to be a refining center.

Men saw it, and hastened to take advantage of the opportunity. There was grave risk. The oil supply might not hold out. As yet there was no certain market for refined oil. But a sure result was not what drew people into the oil business in the early sixties. Fortune was running fleet-footed across the country, and at her garment men clutched. They loved the chase almost as they did success, and so many a man in Cleveland tried his luck in an oil refinery, as hundreds on Oil Creek were trying it in an oil lease. From the start the refineries

245

made money, even the rudest ones. Seeing this, and seeing, too, that the oil supply was probably permanent, men who loved the result rather than the gamble took up the business. Among these was a young firm of produce commission merchants. Both members of this firm were keen businessmen, and one of them had a remarkable commercial vision—a genius for seeing the possibilities in material things. This man's name was Rockefeller—John D. Rockefeller. He was but twenty-three years old at the time, but he had already got his feet firmly on the business ladder, and had got them there by his own efforts. Frugality had started him. It was the strongest trait of his character. Indeed, the only incident of his childhood preserved by biographers illustrates his love for saving. When he was eight years old, so the story runs, he raised a flock of turkeys—his earliest business venture. The flock was a fine one, for the owner had given it close care, and it was sold to advantage. A boy of eight usually earns to spend. This boy was different. He invested his entire turkey earnings at 7 per cent. It was the beginning of a financial career.

Five years after this turkey episode, when young Rockefeller was thirteen years old, his father moved from the farm in central New York, where the boy had been born (July 8, 1839), to Cleveland, Ohio. Here he went to school for three years. At sixteen he left school to become a clerk and bookkeeper. He was an admirable accountant—one of the early-and-late sort, who saw everything, forgot nothing, and never talked. His earnings he saved, waiting for an opportunity. In 1858 it came. Among his acquaintances was a young Englishman, M. B. Clark. Older by twelve years than Rockefeller, he had left a hard life in England when he was twenty, to seek fortune in America. He had landed in Boston in 1847, without a penny or a friend, and it had taken three months for him to earn money to get to Ohio. Here he had taken the first job at hand, as man-of-all-work, wood-chopper, teamster. He had found his way to Cleveland, had become a valuable man in the houses where he was employed, had gone to school at nights, had saved money. They were two of a kind, Clark and Rockefeller, and in 1858 they pooled their earnings and started a produce commission business on the Cleveland docks. The venture succeeded. Local historians credit Clark & Rockefeller with doing a business of $450,000 the first year, a figure that somewhat taxes credulity. However that may be, the firm prospered. The war came on, and as neither partner went to the front, they had full chance to take advantage of the opportunity for produce business a great army gives. A greater chance than furnishing army supplies, lucrative as most people found that, was in the oil business (so Clark and Rockefeller began to think), and in 1862, when an Englishman of ability and energy, one Samuel Andrews, asked them to back him in starting a refinery, they put in $4,000, and promised to give more if necessary. Now Andrews was a mechanical genius. He devised new processes, made a better and better quality of oil, got larger and larger percentages of refined from his crude. The little refinery grew big, and Clark & Rockefeller soon had $100,000 or more in it. In the meantime Cleveland was growing as a refining center. The business which in 1860 had been a gamble, was by 1865 one of the most promising industries of the town. There were thirty refineries, big and little, with a capacity of from 1,800 to 2,000 barrels of crude a day, and the refined shipments of the year amounted to nearly 200,000 barrels. It was but the beginning—so Mr. Rockefeller thought—and in that year he sold out his share of the commission business and put his capital into the oil firm of Rockefeller & Andrews.

In the new firm Andrews attended to the manufacturing. The pushing of the business, the buying and the selling, fell to Rockefeller. From the start his effect on the business was tremendous. He had the frugal man's hatred of waste and disorder, of middlemen and unnecessary manipulation, and he began a vigorous elimination of these from his business. The residuum that other refineries let run into the ground, he sold. Old iron found its way to the junk shop. He bought his oil directly from the wells. He made his own barrels. He watched and saved and contrived. The ability with which he made the smallest bargain furnishes topics to Cleveland story-tellers today. Low-voiced, soft-footed, humble, knowing every point in every man's business, he never tired until he got his wares at the lowest possible figure. "John always got the best of the bargain," old men tell you in Cleveland today, and they wince though they laugh in telling it. "Smooth," "a savvy fellow," is their description of him. To drive a good bargain was the joy of his life. "The only time I ever saw John Rockefeller enthusiastic," a man told the writer once, "was when a report came in from the Creek that his buyer had secured a cargo of oil at a figure much below the market price. He bounded from his chair with a shout of joy, danced up and down, hugged me, threw up his hat, acted so like a madman that I have never forgotten it."

He could borrow as well as bargain. The firm's capital was limited; growing as they were, they often needed money, and had none. Borrow they must. Rarely if ever did Mr. Rockefeller fail. There is a story handed down in Cleveland from the days of Clark & Rockefeller, produce merchants, which is illustrative of his methods.

One day a well-known and rich businessman stepped into the office and asked for Mr. Rockefeller. He was out, and Clark met this visitor. "Mr. Clark," he said, "you may tell Mr. Rockefeller, when he comes in, that I think I can use the $10,000 he wants to invest with me for your firm. I have thought it all over."

"Good God!" cried Clark, "we don't want to invest $10,000. John is out right now trying to borrow $5,000 for us."

It turned out that to prepare him for a proposition to borrow $5,000 Mr. Rockefeller had told the gentleman that he and Clark wanted to invest $10,000!

"And the joke of it is," said Clark, who used to tell the story, "John got the $5,000 even after I had let the cat out of the bag. Oh, he was the greatest borrower you ever saw."

These qualities told. The firm grew rich, and started a second refinery—William A. Rockefeller & Co. They took in a partner, H. M. Flagler, and opened a house in New York for selling their oil. Of all these concerns John D. Rockefeller was the head. Finally, in June 1870, five years after he became an active partner in the refining business, Mr. Rockefeller combined all his companies into one—the Standard Oil Company. The capital of the new concern was $1,000,000. The parties interested in it were John D. Rockefeller, Henry M. Flagler, Samuel Andrews, Stephen V. Harkness, and William Rockefeller.

The strides the firm of Rockefeller & Andrews made after the former went into it were attributed, for three or four years, mainly to this extraordinary capacity for bargaining and borrowing. Then its chief competitors began to suspect something. John Rockefeller might get his oil cheaper now and then, they said, but he could not do it often. He might make close contracts for which they had neither the patience nor the stomach. He might have an unusual mechanical and practical genius in his partner. But these things could not explain all. They believed they bought, on the whole, almost as cheaply and with as great, or nearly as great, economy. He could sell at no better price than they. Where was his advantage? There was but one place where it could be, and that was in transportation. He must be getting better rates from the railroads than they were. One of the rival refiners, of a firm long in the business, which had been prosperous from the start, and which prided itself on its methods, its economy, and its energy—Alexander, Scofield & Co.—went to the railroad companies' agents in 1868 or 1869. "You are giving others better rates than you are us," said Mr. Alexander, the representative of the firm. They did not attempt to deny it—they simply agreed to give him a rebate also. The arrangement was interesting. Mr. Alexander was to pay the open, or regular, rate on oil from the Oil Regions to Cleveland, which at the date was forty cents a barrel. At the end of each month he was to send to the railroad vouchers for the amount of oil shipped and paid for at forty cents, and was to get back from the railroad, in money, fifteen cents on each barrel. This concession applied only to oil brought from the wells. He was never able to get a rebate on oil shipped eastward. When he complained to the railroads he was told that if he would ship as large quantities as the Standard Oil Company he could have as good a rate.

Ship as large a quantity! It was a new principle in railroad policy. Were not the railroads public servants? Were they not bound, as common carriers, to carry ten barrels at the same rate per barrel as they did a hundred? If they were not, what was to become of the ten-barrel men? Could they live? Mr. Alexander remonstrated. The railroad agent was firm with Mr. Alexander. In all branches of business the heaviest buyer got the best rate; the railroad must regard this principle. It could not give him the same rate as Mr. Rockefeller unless he shipped as large amounts of oil, and he went back to his refinery knowing that he must do business with a handicap, nearly, if not quite, as great as his profit.

How had it happened that Rockefeller and his colleagues had secured this advantage so out of harmony with a railroad's obligation to the public? Nobody knew then. But ten years later the railroad man who granted them this privilege, and started them on the road by which, a few years later, they reached almost a complete monopoly of the oil business, stated the reasons for the discrimination in an affidavit which has never, to the writer's knowledge, been published. This man was General J. H. Devereux, who in 1868 succeeded Amasa Stone as vice-president of the Lake Shore Railroad. He came to this position at a moment when a lively contest was going on for the eastward oil traffic, and when the Pennsylvania Railroad, having the advantage, was claiming what General Devereux called a "patent right on the transportation of oil." The cheap rates which the Pennsylvania was giving, the wild speculations in both refined and crude, to which the officials of the Erie—Fiske and Gould—were lending aid, combined with the fact that a number of big and finely equipped refineries were going up in the Oil Regions, frightened the Cleveland refiners. Unless something was done, they told General Devereux, Cleveland would be destroyed as a refining center. Something was done—the Lake Shore ran its road still nearer to the heart of the Oil Regions, and began to give Rockefeller,

Andrews, & Flagler rebates on their crude oil. General Devereux's reason for making special rates to this firm and to no other, was that while all the other refiners expressed the fear that the advantages of refining on the Creek close to the oil supply were such that they might ultimately all have to move from Cleveland to the Oil Regions, Rockefeller and his associates promised to fight it out in Cleveland if the Lake Shore would handle their oil as cheaply as the Pennsylvania could. Why the railroad should not have quieted the fears of the other firms by the same assurance as it gave the Standard, General Devereux did not explain. This was the beginning. Two years later, in 1870, the Lake Shore made a broader contract with the Standard. The road had been carrying little oil eastward for the firm for some time. The rates they offered were not low enough, and the Standard firm was shipping principally by water; but this method was slow, and the way, for a portion of this year, was closed. Soon after the Standard Oil Company was formed, in 1870, Mr. Flagler, representing the firm, proposed that if General Devereux would give them a special through rate they would ship sixty carloads a day. The rate asked was considerably lower than the regular open rates, but the advantage of having a regular amount shipped daily was so great that the railroad company concluded that their profit would be greater than by serving all alike. It was evidently merely a question of which method paid better. The question of the railroad's duty as a public carrier was not considered. The Standard's arrangement with General Devereux, in 1870, gave them steady transportation the year round to the seaboard, at a rate cheaper than anybody else could get. It was equivalent to renting a railroad for their private use. Every Cleveland refiner was put out of the race by the arrangement. The refining business was so prosperous at the time the arrangement was made that suspicion was not at first aroused, but in a year's time the effect became apparent. Firms which had been making $10,000 to $20,000 a year found themselves making little or nothing. But why? That they did not see. The oil business in Cleveland was growing prodigiously. By 1870 the city had become the largest refining center in the United States, taking 2,000,000 barrels of crude oil from the region—one-third of the entire output of the Oil Regions. Instead of being destroyed by the competition of refineries built close to the wells, it was growing under the competition, but in spite of this growth only one firm—the Standard Oil Company—was making much money. This was puzzling and disheartening.

It would seem as if the one man in Cleveland who ought to have been satisfied with the situation in 1870 was Mr. Rockefeller. His organization, from his buyers on the Creek to his exporter in New York, was well-nigh perfect. His control of a railroad from the wells to the seaboard gave him an advantage nobody else had had the daring and the persuasive power to get. It was clear that in time he must control the entire Cleveland trade. But Mr. Rockefeller was far from satisfied. He was a brooding, cautious, secretive man, seeing all the possible dangers as well as all the possible opportunities in things, and he studied, as a player at chess, all the possible combinations which might imperil his supremacy. These twenty-five Cleveland rivals of his—how could he at once and forever put them out of the game? He and his partners had somehow conceived a great idea—the advantages of combination. What might they not do, if they could buy out and absorb the big refineries now competing with them in Cleveland? The possibilities of the idea grew as they discussed it. Finally they began tentatively to sound some of their rivals. But there were other rivals than these at home. There were the Creek refiners! They were there at the mouth of the wells. What might not this geographical advantage do in time? The Oil Regions, in the first years of oil production, had been an unfit place for refining because of its lack of connections with the outside world; now, however, the railroads were in, and refining was going on there on an increasing scale; the capacity of the region had indeed risen to nearly 10,000 barrels a day—equal to that of New York, exceeding that of Pittsburgh by nearly 4,000 barrels, and almost equaling that of Cleveland. The men of the oil country loudly declared that they meant to refine for the world. They boasted of an oil kingdom which eventually should handle the entire business and compel Cleveland and Pittsburgh either to abandon their works or bring them to the oil country. In this boastful ambition they were encouraged by the Pennsylvania Railroad, which naturally handled the largest percentage of the oil. How long could the Standard Oil Company stand against this competition?

There was another interest as deeply concerned as Mr. Rockefeller in preserving Cleveland's supremacy as a refining center, and this was the New York Central Railroad system. Let the bulk of refining be done in the Oil Regions, and that road was in danger of losing a profitable branch of business. For its own sake it must continue to support Cleveland—by which it meant the Standard Oil Company. The chief representative of the interest of the Central system in Cleveland was Peter H. Watson. Mr. Watson was an able patent lawyer, who served under the strenuous Stanton as an Assistant Secretary of War, and served well. After the war he had been made general freight agent of the Lake Shore and Michigan Southern Railroad, and later president of the branch of that road which ran into the Oil Regions. He had oil interests principally at Franklin, Pennsylvania, and was well known to all oil men. He was a business intimate of Mr. Rockefeller and a warm friend of Horace Clarke, the son-in-law of W. K. Vanderbilt, at that time president of the Lake Shore and Michigan Southern Railroad.

Two other towns shared Cleveland's fear of the rise of the Oil Regions as a refining center, and they were Pittsburgh and Philadelphia, and Mr. Rockefeller and Mr. Watson found in certain refiners of these places a strong sympathy with any plan which looked to holding the region in check. But while the menace in their geographical positions was the first ground of sympathy between these gentlemen, something more than local troubles occupied them. This was the condition of the refining business as a whole. It was unsatisfactory in many particulars. First, it was overdone. There was at that time a refining capacity of three barrels to every one produced, and this capacity was widely scattered. The result was, every now and then, ruinous underselling in order to keep or to secure a market. The export business was not what these gentlemen thought it ought to be. Oil had risen to fourth place in the exports of the United States in the twelve years since its discovery, and every year larger quantities were consumed abroad, but it was crude oil, not refined, which the foreigners were beginning to demand; that is, they had found they could import crude, refine it at home, and sell it cheaper than they could buy American refined. France, to encourage her home refineries, had even put a tax on American refined. Competition between the railroads was so keen that nobody could be sure what freight rates his neighbor was getting, and whether he might not any day secure a special advantage in transportation which would enable him to undersell. Then the speculation in crude oil caused wide variation in the cost of their product, as well as serious fluctuation in the refined market. In short, the business had all the evils of a young, vigorous growth. Its possibilities were still undefined, its future a mere guess. Time was bound to cure the evils in it, but the refiners were impatient of waiting.

In the fall of 1871, while Mr. Rockefeller and his friends were occupied with all these questions certain Pennsylvania refiners, it is not too certain who, brought to them a remarkable scheme, the gist of which was to bring together secretly a large enough body of refiners and shippers to compel all the railroads handling oil to give to the company formed special rebates on its oil, and drawbacks on that of others. If they could get such rates, it was evident that those outside of their combination could not compete with them long, and that they would become eventually the only refiners. They could then limit their output to actual demand, and so keep up prices. This done, they could easily persuade the railroads to transport no crude for exportation, so that the foreigners would be forced to buy American refined. They believed that the price of oil thus exported could easily be advanced 50 per cent. The control of the refining interests would also enable them to fix their own price on crude. As they would be the only buyers and sellers, the speculative character of the business would be done away with. In short, the scheme they worked out put the entire oil business in their hands. It looked as simple to put into operation as it was dazzling in its results. Mr. Flagler has sworn that neither he nor Mr. Rockefeller believed in this scheme. But when they found that their friend, Peter H. Watson and various Philadelphia and Pittsburgh parties, who felt as they did about the oil business, believed in it, they went in and began at once to work up a company—secretly. It was evident that a scheme which aimed at concentrating in the hands of one company the business now operated by scores, and which proposed to effect this consolidation through a practice of the railroads which was forbidden by their charters, although freely indulged in, and which was regarded as the greatest commercial scandal of the day, must be worked with fine discretion if it ever were to be effective.

The first thing was to get a charter—quietly. At a meeting held in Philadelphia late in the fall of 1871, a friend of one of the gentlemen interested mentioned to him that a certain estate then in liquidation had a charter for sale which gave its owners the right to carry on any kind of business in any country and in any way; that it could be bought for what it would cost to get a charter under the general laws of the state, and it would be a favor to the heirs to buy it. The opportunity was promptly taken. The name of the charter bought was the "Southern [usually written South] Improvement Company." For a beginning it was as good a name as another, since it said nothing.

With this charter in hand Mr. Rockefeller and Mr. Watson and their associates began to seek converts. In order that their great scheme might not be injured by premature public discussion, they asked of each person whom they approached a pledge of secrecy. Two forms of the pledges required before anything was revealed were published later. The first of these, which appeared in the New York *Tribune*, read as follows:

> I, A.B., do faithfully promise upon my honor and faith as a gentleman, that I will keep secret all transactions which I may have with the corporation known as the South Improvement Company; that,

should I fail to complete any bargains with the said company, all the preliminary conversations shall be kept strictly private; and, finally, that I will not disclose the price for which I dispose of my product, or any other facts which may in any way bring to light the internal workings or organization of the company. All this I do freely promise.

.........................Signed.

Witnessed by........................

A second, published in a history of the "Southern Improvement Company," ran:

The undersigned pledge their solemn words of honor that they will not communicate to any one without permission of (name of director of Southern Improvement Company) any information that he may convey to them, or any of them, in relation to the Southern Improvement Company.

....

.........................Witness.

That they met with encouragement is evident from the fact that, when the corporators came together on January 2, 1872, in Philadelphia, for the first time under their charter, and transferred the company to the stockholders, they represented in one way or another a large part of the refining interest of the country. At this meeting 1,100 shares of the stock of the company, which was divided into 2,000 shares of $100 each, were subscribed for, and 20 per cent of their value paid in. Just who took stock at this meeting the writer has not been able to discover. At the same time, a discussion came up as to what refiners were to be allowed to go into the new company. Each of the men represented had friends whom he wanted taken care of, and after considerable discussion it was decided to take in every refinery they could get hold of. This decision was largely due to the railroad men. Mr. Watson had seen them as soon as the plans for the company were formed, and they had all agreed that if they gave rebates all refineries then existing must be taken in.

Very soon after this meeting of January 2 the rest of the stock of the South Improvement Company was taken. The complete list of stockholders, with their holdings, was as follows:

William Frew, Philadelphia, Pa.	10 shares
W. P. Logan, Philadelphia, Pa.	10 "
John P. Logan, Philadelphia, Pa.	10 "
Chas. Lockhart, Pittsburgh, Pa.	10 "
Richard S. Waring, Pittsburgh, Pa.	10 "
W. G. Warden, Philadelphia, Pa.	475 "
O. F. Waring, Pittsburgh, Pa.	475 "

P. H. Watson, Ashtabula, Ohio 100   "
H. M. Flagler, Cleveland, Ohio 180   "
O. H. Payne, Cleveland, Ohio 180   "
Wm. Rockefeller, Cleveland, Ohio 180   "
J. A. Bostwick, New York, N. Y. 180   "
John D. Rockefeller, Cleveland, Ohio 180   "
                                                 ─────   "
                                                 2,000   "

Mr. Watson was elected president and Mr. Warden secretary of the new association. It will be noticed that the largest individual holdings in the company were those of W. G. Warden, of Philadelphia, and O. F. Waring, of Pittsburgh, each of whom had 475 shares. The company most heavily interested in the South Improvement Company was the Standard Oil Company of Cleveland, Messrs. J. D. Rockefeller, William Rockefeller, O. H. Payne, and H. M. Flagler, all stockholders of that company, each having 180 shares—720 in the company.

The organization complete, there remained contracts to be made with the railroads. Three systems were interested: the Central, which, by its connection with the Lake Shore and Michigan Southern, ran directly into the Oil Regions; the Erie, allied with the Atlantic and Great Western, with a short line likewise tapping the heart of the region; and the Pennsylvania, with the connections known as the Allegheny Valley and Oil Creek Railroad. The persons to be won over were W. H. Vanderbilt, of the Central; W. H. Clarke, president of the Lake Shore and Michigan Southern; Jay Gould, of the Erie; General G. B. Mc-Clellan, president of the Atlantic and Great Western; and Tom Scott, of the Pennsylvania. There seems to have been little difficulty in persuading any of these persons to go into the scheme. It was, of course, a direct violation of their charters as public carriers, but such violations had been in practice for at least four years in the oil business, and for a longer period in other industries. Under pressure or persuasion all of these roads granted special rates. For years they had been fighting bitterly for the oil trade, often cutting rates to get a consignment, until there was no profit in it. They were glad enough to go into any arrangement which guaranteed each a sure percentage of the business and gave them a profit on it. This the South Improvement Company did. They seem not to have agreed to the contracts until the company assured them that all the refiners were going in. The contracts they made were not on condition, however, that all were included. Three months after they were signed Congress investigated the great scheme. The testimony of the secretary of the company on this point before the Congressional committee is worth reading:

Q. You say you made propositions to railroad companies, which they agreed to accept upon the condition that you could include all the refineries?

A. No, sir; I did not say that; I said that was the understanding when we discussed this matter with them; it was no proposition on our part; they discussed it, not in the form of a proposition that the refineries should be all taken in, but it was the intention and resolution of the company from the first that that should be the result; we never had any other purpose in the matter.

Q. In case you could take the refineries all in, the railroads proposed to give you a rebate upon their freight charges?

A. No, sir; it was not put in that form; we were to put the refineries all in upon the same terms; it was the understanding with the railroad companies that we were to have a rebate; there was no rebate given in consideration of our putting the companies all in, but we told them we would do it; the contract with the railroad companies was with us.

Q. But if you did form a company composed of the proprietors of all these refineries, you were to have a rebate upon your freight charges?

A. No; we were to have a rebate anyhow, but were to give all the refineries the privilege of coming in.

Q. You were to have the rebate whether they came in or not?
A. Yes, sir.

"What effect were these arrangements to have upon those who did not come into the combination?" asked the chairman.

"I do not think we ever took that question up," answered Mr. Warden.

A second objection to making a contract with the company came from Mr. Scott, of the Pennsylvania road. "You take no account here," Mr. Scott told the secretary, W. G. Warden, who discussed the matter at length with him, "of the oil producer—the man to whom the world owes the business. You can never succeed unless you take care of the producer." Mr. Warden objected strongly to forming a combination with them. "The interests of the producers were in one sense antagonistic to ours; one as the seller and the other as the buyer. We held in argument that the producers were abundantly able to take care of their own branch of the business if they took care of the quantity produced." So strongly did Mr. Scott argue, however, that finally the members of the South Improvement Company yielded, and a draft of an agreement, to be proposed to the producers, was drawn up in lead pencil; it was never presented. It seems to have been used principally to quiet Mr. Scott.

The work of persuasion went on swiftly. By the eighteenth of January the president of the Pennsylvania road, J. Edgar Thompson, had put his signature to the contract, and soon after Mr. Vanderbilt and Mr. Clarke signed for the Central system, and Jay Gould and General McClellan for the Erie. The contracts to which these gentlemen put their names fixed gross rates of freight from all common points, as the leading shipping points within the Oil Regions were called, to all the great refining and shipping centers—New York, Philadelphia, Baltimore, Pittsburgh and Cleveland. For example, the open rate on crude oil to New York was put at $2.56. On this price the South Improvement Company was allowed a rebate of $1.06 for its shipments; but it got not only this rebate, it was given in cash a like amount on each barrel of crude shipped by parties outside the combination.

The open rate from Cleveland to New York was $2.00, and 50 cents of this sum was turned over to the South Improvement Company, which at the same time received a rebate enabling it to ship for $1.50. Again an independent refiner in Cleveland paid 80 cents a barrel to get his crude from the Oil Regions to his works, and the railroad sent 40 cents of this money to the South Improvement Company. At the same time it cost the Cleveland refiner in the combination but 40 cents to get his crude oil. Like drawbacks and rebates were given for all points—Pittsburgh, Philadelphia, Boston and Baltimore.

An interesting provision in the contracts was that full waybills of all petroleum shipped over the roads should each day be sent to the South Improvement Company. This, of course, gave them knowledge of just who was doing business outside of their company—of how much business he was doing, and with whom he was doing it. Not only were they to have full knowledge of the business of all shippers—they were to have access to all books of the railroads.

The parties to the contracts agreed that if anybody appeared in the business offering an equal amount of transportation, and having equal facilities for doing business with the South Improvement Company, the railroads might give them equal advantages in drawbacks and rebates, but to make such a miscarriage of the scheme doubly improbable, each railroad was bound to cooperate as "far as it legally might to maintain the business of the South Improvement Company against injury by competition, and lower or raise the gross rates of transportation for such times and to such extent as might be necessary to overcome the competition. The rebates and drawbacks to be varied *pari passu* with the gross rates."

The reason given by the railroads in the contract for granting these extraordinary privileges was that the "magnitude and extent of the business and operations" purposed to be carried on by the South Improvement Company would greatly promote the interest of the railroads and make it desirable for them to encourage their undertaking. The evident advantages received by the railroad were a regular amount of freight—the Pennsylvania was to have 45 per cent of the eastbound shipping, the Erie and Central each 27½ per cent, while westbound freight was to be divided equally between them—fixed rates, and freedom from the system of cutting which they had all found so harassing and disastrous.

It was on the second of January 1872 that the organization of the South Improvement Company was completed. The day before, the Standard Oil Company, of Cleveland, increased its capital from $1,-000,000 to $2,500,000, "all the stockholders of the company being present and voting therefor." These stockholders were greater by five than in 1870, the names of O. B. Jennings, Benjamin Brewster, Truman P. Handy, Amasa Stone, and Stillman Witt having been added. The last three were officers and stockholders in one or more of the railroads centering in Cleveland. Three weeks after this increase of capital Mr. Rockefeller had the charter and contracts of the South Improvement Company in hand, and was ready to see what they would do in helping him carry out his idea of wholesale combination in Cleveland. There were at that time some twenty-six refineries in the town—some of them very large plants. All of them were feeling more or less the discouraging effects of the last three or four years of railroad discriminations in favor of the Standard Oil Company. To the owners of these refineries Mr. Rockefeller now went one by one, and explained the South Improvement Company. "You see," he told them, "this scheme is bound to work. It means an absolute control by us of the oil business. There is no chance for any one outside. But we are going to give everybody a chance to come in. You are to turn over your refinery to my appraisers, and I will give you Standard Oil Company stock or cash, as you prefer, for the value we put upon it. I advise you to take the stock. It will be for your good." Certain refiners objected. They did not want to sell. They did want to keep and manage their business. Mr. Rockefeller was regretful, but firm. It was useless to resist, he told the hesitating; they would certainly be crushed if they did not accept his offer, and he pointed out in detail, and with gentleness, how beneficent the scheme really was—preventing the Creek refiners from destroying Cleveland, keeping up the price of refined oil, destroying competition, and eliminating speculation.

The perfection of the scheme, the inevitableness of the result, the persuasiveness of its advocate, the promise of great profits were different reasons for leading many of the refiners to succumb at once. Some of them took stock—more took money.

A few of the refiners contested before surrendering. Among these was Robert Hanna, an uncle of Mark Hanna, of the firm of Hanna, Baslington & Co. Mr. Hanna had been refining oil since July 1869. According to his own sworn statement he had made money, fully 60 per cent on his investment the first year, and after that 30 per cent. Some time in February 1872 the Standard Oil Company asked an interview with him and his associates. They wanted to buy his works, they said. "But we don't want to sell," objected Mr. Hanna. "You can never make any more money, in my judgment," said Mr. Rockefeller. "You can't compete with the Standard. We have all the large refineries now. If you refuse to sell, it will end in your being crushed." Hanna and Baslington were not satisfied. They went to see Mr. Watson, president of the South Improvement Company, and an officer of the Lake Shore, and General Devereux, manager of the Lake Shore road. They were told that the Standard had special rates; that it was useless to try to compete with them. General Devereux explained to the gentlemen that the privileges granted the Standard were the legitimate and necessary advantage of the large shipper over the smaller, and that if Hanna, Baslington & Co. could give the road as large a quantity of oil as the Standard did, with the same regularity, they could have the same rate. General Devereux says they "recognized the propriety" of his excuse. They certainly recognized its authority. They say that they were satisfied they could no longer get rates to and from Cleveland which would enable them to live, and "reluctantly" sold out. It must have been reluctantly, for they had paid $75,000 for their works, and had made 30 per cent a year on an average on their investment, and the Standard appraiser allowed them $45,000. "Truly and really less than one-half of what they were absolutely worth, with a fair and honest competition in the lines of transportation," said Mr. Hanna, eight years later, in an affidavit.

Under the combined threat and persuasion of the Standard, armed with the South Improvement Company scheme, almost the entire independent oil interest of Cleveland collapsed in three months' time. Of the twenty-six refineries, at least twenty-one sold out. From a capacity of probably not over 1,500 barrels of crude a day, the Standard Oil Company rose in three months' time to one of 10,000 barrels. By this maneuver it became master of over one-fifth of the refining capacity of the United States. Its next individual competitor was Sloan & Fleming, of New York, whose capacity was 1,700 barrels. The Standard had a greater capacity than the entire Oil Creek Regions, greater than the combined New York refiners. The transaction by which it acquired this power was so stealthy that not even the best-informed newspaper men of Cleveland knew what went on. It had all been accomplished in accordance with one of Mr. Rockefeller's chief business principles— "Silence is golden."

While Mr. Rockefeller was working out the "good of the oil business" in Cleveland, his associates were busy at other points. A little more time and the great scheme would be an accomplished fact. And then there fell in its path two of those never-to-be-foreseen human elements which so often block great maneuvers. The first was born of a man's anger. The man had learned of the scheme. He wanted to go into it, but the directors were suspicious of him. He had been concerned in speculative enterprises and in dealings with the Erie road which had injured these directors in other days. They didn't want him to have any of the advantages of their great enterprise. When convinced that he could not share in the deal, he took his revenge by telling people in the Oil Regions what was going on. At first the Oil Regions refused to believe, but in a few days another slip born of human weakness came in to prove the rumor true. The schedule of rates agreed upon by the South Improvement Company and the railroads had been sent to the freight agent of the Lake Shore Railroad, but no order had been given to put them in force. The freight agent had a son on his deathbed. Distracted by his sorrow, he left his office in charge of subordinates, but neglected to tell them that the new schedules on his desk were a secret compact, whose effectiveness depended upon their being held until all was complete. On February 26 the subordinates, ignorant of the nature of the rates, put them in effect. The independent oil men heard with amazement that freight rates had been put up nearly 100 per cent. They needed no other proof of the truth of the rumors of conspiracy which were circulating. . . .

McClure's Magazine
December 1902

STOCK MARKET

THOMAS LAWSON amassed $60,000 by the time he was sixteen. He lost this money in a "pool" speculation that was to have resulted in a gain of several hundred thousands of dollars for him.

At twenty, his bank account was close to six figures; in his early thirties he was worth a million dollars.

The son of a Nova Scotia carpenter, he left school at the age of twelve and went to work in Boston's Wall Street. His life centered on the Wall Streets of the country as his finances went up and down.

Lawson was to finance what Barnum was to show business. He was his own press agent. He knew every trick of publicity decades before press agentry became a profession in itself.

He reportedly said at one time: "My one instrument is publicity. It is the most powerful weapon in the world. With it I have been able to strike with some of the power which 80,000,000 Americans possess when they are wide awake and in earnest." [99]

Lawson was a lone guerrilla. His success in financial battles reaped rich rewards for himself as he drew closer to the heads of Standard Oil.

It was in association with Standard Oil that Lawson developed his scheme for the creation of a copper trust, and in 1899 the Amalgamated Copper was formally organized.

By 1904 Lawson had broken with the Standard Oil forces and started to issue his famous advertisements in newspapers denouncing what he called the "System."

A typical ad from the New York *Daily Tribune* of December 6, 1904 reads:

AMALGAMATED STOCKHOLDERS——WARNING

I advise every holder of Amalgamated stock to sell his holdings at once before another crash comes. Another slump may carry it to 33 again or lower.

It may go higher, but this is no affair of mine. From the moment of publication of this notice all those who have looked to me for advice must relieve me of further responsibility.

———

As the people who look to me for advice are scattered all over this country, I know of no other way than this to simultaneously notify them of what I have learned.

———

Boston, December 6, 1904   THOMAS W. LAWSON

At the time Lawson broke with Standard Oil, the editor of *Everybody's Magazine* approached him to write a series of articles.

They wanted the inside story, sort of a "true confession." Until Lawson's agreement to write the story, "no big man in the financial world had ever consented to tell the inside" [100] of the workings of finance.

The editors did not have very much difficulty in getting Lawson to accept the offer. He made one stipulation, however: he would receive no fee, but the magazine would spend $50,000 to advertise the series. *Everybody's* agreed to this. Lawson himself spent five times that amount before the series was completed.

In an ad in the New York *Post*, June 21, 1904, announcing "The Story of Amalgamated Copper," Mr. Lawson told his motives for the series: "I have unwittingly been made the instrument by which thousands upon thousands of investors in America and Europe have been plundered. I wish them to know my position as to the past, that they may acquit me of intentional wrongdoing; as to the present, that they may know that I am doing all in my power to right the wrongs that have been committed; and as to the future, that they may see how I propose to compel restitution."

In an introductory article, he explained he was not taking issue with men, but rather with a principle; that the good or the evil these men had done were the products of a condition and not of their individuality, and that "if not one of them had ever been born the same good and evil would today exist. Others would have done what they did, and would have to answer for what has been done, as they must. So I say the men are merely individuals; the 'System' is the thing at fault, and it is the 'System' that must be rectified." [101]

His series went on to explain interlocking directorates and dummy agents; he attacked some of the most discussed, feared and admired men in the country, but always went beyond them to explain the "System."

One of the most sensational chapters cited the bribing of the Massachusetts legislature in 1896 by Henry M. Whitney, Boston electric-street-railway-system magnate.

"In the charges and assertions of Mr. Thomas W. Lawson," editorially commented *The Independent*, "there is a curious mixture of truth, exaggeration and misrepresentation. . . . From the beginning a certain plausibility was imparted even to his most sensational charges by settled public opinion as to certain men whom he attacked. . . .

"This plausibility," the magazine continued, "has been enhanced by the failure of powerful accused men to prosecute Mr. Lawson (a millionaire) for assertions that, if false, are clearly libelous." [102]

Public Opinion announced in its January 5, 1905 issue that in two weeks it would begin a series of articles on "The Truth About Frenzied Finance" by Denis Donohoe, financial editor of the New York *Commercial*.

This series, however, was more concerned with disclosing the unsavory record of Lawson than with repudiating his assertions.

The editors in introducing the series wrote: "We have never believed in Mr. Lawson's sincerity of purpose. We have long been acquainted with certain phases of his character, as shown in incidents in his career . . . which seemed to us effectually to preclude any such confidence in him." [103]

C. C. Regier, writing twenty-seven years later in his thesis on the muckrakers, said that nowhere in the entire muckraking movement "do we find a better example of mixed motives and confused results. Lawson undoubtedly wished to pay off an old score, and it is possible that he used the sensation his articles caused to advance his personal interests in the stockmarket. On the other hand, there was a strange streak of altruism in the man, a sort of messianic eagerness to deliver the common people from what he regarded as their bondage." [104]

As for the results of the series, Regier contends that "the articles had less effect than Lawson thought, but undoubtedly they did some harm and more than a little good." [105]

Allan Nevins, in his biography of Rockefeller, asserts that here and there Lawson's story was "exaggerated," but "his indictment of the 'System' of organized speculation and thimble-rigging which made Amalgamated Copper possible was perfectly sound." [106]

Writing in 1955, Arthur S. Link, professor of history at Northwestern University, says, "there can be no doubt that his series contributed to the public demand for control of the stock market that culminated in the Pujo committee's investigation of 1913." [107]

During the Pujo investigations, nine years after he had written "Frenzied Finance," Lawson began a series of articles in *Everybody's* titled "The Remedy" in which he proposed certain reforms to the stock market.

Professor Filler says: "It might have given Lawson some satisfaction to know that it ["The Remedy"] was 20 years ahead of its time, and that the Securities and Exchange Commission, operating under the Securities Act of 1933, would provide many of the safeguards which he had demanded." [108]

Commenting on Lawson's death in 1925, *The Nation* wrote: "It is significant of the kind of fame attained by Thomas Lawson that when he died on February 8 middle-aged Americans had forgotten that he was still alive and the younger generation was unaware that he had ever lived. Yet the edition of *Everybody's Magazine* in 1904 which contained the first installment of 'Frenzied Finance' was exhausted within three days. . . ." [109]

THOMAS W. LAWSON

Frenzied Finance

(THE STORY OF AMALGAMATED)

AMALGAMATED COPPER was begotten in 1898, born in 1899, and in the first five years of its existence plundered the public to the extent of over one hundred millions of dollars.

It was a creature of that incubator of trust and corporation frauds, the State of New Jersey, and was organized ostensibly to mine, manufacture, buy, sell and deal in copper, one of the staples, the necessities, of civilization.

It is a corporation with $155,000,000 capital, 1,550,000 shares of the par value of $100 each.

Its entire stock was sold to the public at an average of $115 per share ($100 to $130), and in 1903 the price had declined to $33 per share.

From its inception it was known as a "Standard Oil" creature, because its birthplace was the National City Bank of New York (the "Standard Oil" bank), and its parents the leading "Standard Oil" lights, Henry H. Rogers, William Rockefeller, and James Stillman.

It has from its birth to present writing been responsible for more hell than any other trust or financial thing since the world began. Because of it the people have sustained incalculable losses and have suffered untold miseries.

But for the existence of the National City Bank of New York, the tremendous losses and necessarily corresponding profits could not have been made.

I laid out the plans upon which Amalgamated was constructed, and, had they been followed, there would have been reared a great financial edifice, immensely profitable, permanently prosperous, one of the world's big institutions.

264

The conditions of which Amalgamated was the consequence had their birth in Bay State Gas. To explain them I must go back a few years.

In 1894 J. Edward Addicks, of Delaware, Everywhere, and Nowhere, the Boston Gas King, invaded the gas preserves of the "Standard Oil" in Brooklyn, N.Y., and the "Standard Oil," to compel him to withdraw, moved on his pre-empted gas domains in Boston, Mass.

In 1894 a fierce battle was raging in Boston between Gas King Addicks and Gas King Rogers, and the very air was filled with denunciation and defiance—bribery and municipal corruption—and King Addicks was defeated all along the line and in full retreat, with his ammunition down to the last few rounds.

Early in 1895 I took command of the Addicks forces against "Standard Oil."

In the middle of 1895 the Addicks troopers had the "Standard Oil" invaders "on the run."

In August 1895 Henry H. Rogers and myself came together for the first time at his house in New York, and we practically settled the Boston gas war.

At the beginning of 1896 we actually settled the gas war, and "Standard Oil" transferred all its Boston gas properties ($6,000,000) to the Addicks crowd.

In October 1896 the Bay State Gas outfit passed from the control of Addicks and his cohorts into the hands of a receiver, and growing out of this receivership and accumulated complications, "Standard Oil," in November 1896, regained all of its old Boston companies, and in addition all of the Addicks companies, with the exception of the Bay State Gas Company of Delaware.

By 1896 I formulated and perfected the plans for "Coppers," a broad and comprehensive project, having for its basis the buying and consolidating of all the best-producing copper properties in Europe and America, and educating the world to their great merits as safe and profitable investments.

In 1897 I laid these plans before "Standard Oil."

In 1898 "Standard Oil" were so far educated to my plans on "Coppers" as to accept them.

In 1899 Amalgamated, intended to be the second or third section of "Coppers," was suddenly shifted by "Standard Oil" into the first section, and with a full head of steam ran out of the "City Bank" Station, carrying the largest and best trainload of passengers ever sent to destruction on any financial trunk line.

In 1899, after the allotment of the Amalgamated public subscription, the public for the first time, in a dazed and benumbed way, realized it had been "taken in" on this subscription, and a shiver went down America's financial spinal column.

In 1900, after the price of Amalgamated had slumped to 75 instead of advancing to 150 to 200, as had been promised, the "Standard Oil"-Amalgamated-City Bank Fraternity called Wall Street's king of manipulators, James R. Keene, to the rescue, and under his adroit handling of the stock in the market Amalgamated was sent soaring over its flotation price of 100.

In 1901 Boston & Montana and Butte & Boston, after long delay, drew out of the Standard Oil Station as the second section of Amalgamated, carrying the biggest load of investors and speculators to what was at that time confidently felt would be Dollar Utopia; and the price of the enlarged Amalgamated fairly flew to 130. These were the stocks which I had originally advertised would be part of the first section of the consolidated "Coppers," and which, after Amalgamated had been run in ahead of them, I advertised would follow in due course.

In the latter part of 1901 President McKinley was assassinated, and the great panic which would have ensued was averted by the marvelous power of J. Pierpont Morgan.

Then the Amalgamated dividend, without warning and in open defiance of the absolute pledges of its creators, was cut, and the public, including even James R. Keene, found themselves on that wild toboggan whirl which landed them battered and sore at the foot of a financial declivity.

This, briefly, is the tortuous course of Amalgamated, and it is along this twisting, winding, up-alley-and-down-lane way I must ask my readers to travel if they would know the story as it is.

Twenty-six Broadway, New York City, is the home of the Standard Oil. Its countless miles of railroads may zigzag in and out of every state and city in America, and its never-ending twistings of snaky pipe lines burrow into all parts of the North American continent which are lubricated by nature; its mines may be in the West, its manufactories in the East, its colleges in the South, and its churches in the North; its headquarters may be in the center of the universe and its branches on every shore washed by the ocean; its untold millions may levy tribute wherever the voice of man is heard, but its home is the tall stone building in old New York, which by the name "26 Broadway" has become almost as well known wherever dollars are made as is "Standard Oil."

Wall Street and the financial world know that there are two "Standard Oils," but to the public there is no clear distinction between Standard Oil, the corporation which deals in oil and things which pertain to the manufacture and transportation of oil, and "Standard Oil," the giant, indefinite system which sometimes embraces all the "Standard Oil" group of individuals and corporations and sometimes only certain of the individuals.

This giant creature, "Standard Oil," can best be described so that the average man will understand it as a group of money-owners—some individuals and some corporations—who have a right to use the name "Standard Oil" in any business undertakings they engage in. The right to use the name is of priceless value, for it carries with it "assured success."

Standard Oil, the seller of oil to the people, transacts its business as does any other corporation, but as it plays no part in my story, I shall not hereafter touch upon its affairs, but confine myself, wherever I use the name "Standard Oil," to the larger and many times more important "System."

There are only three men who can lend the name "Standard Oil," even in the most remote way, to any project, for there is no more heinous crime in the "Standard Oil" decalogue than using the name "Standard Oil" unauthorizedly. The three men are Henry H. Rogers, William Rockefeller and John D. Rockefeller. Sometimes John D. Rockefeller uses the name alone in projects in which Mr. Rogers and William Rockefeller have no interest. Mr. Rogers or William Rockefeller seldom, if ever, use the name in projects with which neither of the other two is associated. Sometimes, but not often, John D. and William Rockefeller use the name in connection with projects of their own in which Mr. Rogers has no interest. Mr. Rogers and John D. Rockefeller, I believe, never are associated in projects in which William Rockefeller has no interest. Mr. Rogers and William Rockefeller frequently use it in connection with their joint affairs in which John D. Rockefeller has no interest, and during the past ten years it has been used more in their undertakings than in all others.

There are eight distinct groups of individuals and corporations which go to make up the big "Standard Oil":

1. The Standard Oil, seller of oil to the people, which is made up of many subcorporations by actual ownership or by ownership of their stock, or bonds. Probably no person other than Henry H. Rogers, William Rockefeller and John D. Rockefeller knows exactly what the assets of the Standard Oil corporation are, although John D. Rocke-

feller, Jr., son of John D. Rockefeller, and William G. Rockefeller, the able and excellent business son of William Rockefeller and the probable future head of "Standard Oil," are being rapidly educated to this great secret. In this first institution all "Standard Oil" individuals and estates are direct owners.

2. Henry H. Rogers, William Rockefeller and John D. Rockefeller, active heads, and included with them their sons.

3. A large group of active captains and first lieutenants, men who conduct the affairs of the different corporations or sections of corporations in which some or all of the "Standard Oil" are interested. Many of these are the sons or the second generation of others who held like positions in Standard Oil's earlier days, and of these Daniel O'Day and Charles Pratt are fair examples.

4. A large group of captains retired from active service in the Standard Oil army, who only participate in a general way in the management of its affairs, and whose principal business is looking after their investments. These men are each worth from $5,000,000 or $10,000,000 to $50,000,000 or $75,000,000. The Paynes and the Flaglers are fair illustrations of this group.

5. The estates of deceased members of this wonderful "Standard Oil" family, which are still largely controlled by some or all of the prominent "Standard Oil" men.

6. "Standard Oil" banks and banking institutions, and "the system" of national banks, trust companies and insurance companies of which the "Standard Oil" has by ownership and otherwise practically absolute control. The head of this group is James Stillman, and it is when they are called into play in connection with "Standard Oil" business that he is one of the Standard Oil leaders, second to neither Mr. Rogers nor either of the Rockefellers.

7. The "Standard Oil" army of followers, capitalists and workers in all parts of the world, men who never require anything more than the order, "Go ahead," "Pull off," "Buy," "Sell," or "Stay where you are," to render as absolute obedience and enthusiastic cooperation as though they knew to the smallest detail the purposes which entered into the giving of the order.

8. The countless hordes of politicians, statesmen, law makers and enforcers, who, at home or as representatives of the nation abroad, go to make up our political structure, and judges and lawyers.

To the world at large, which looks on and sees this giant institution move through the ranks of business with the ease and smoothness of a creature one-millionth its size and without noise or dissension, it would seem that there must be some wonderful and complicated code of rules which guide and control the thousands of lieutenants and privates who conduct its affairs. This is partially true, partially false. Its governing rules are as rigid as the laws of the Medes and Persians, yet so simple as to be easily understood by anyone.

First, there is a basic law, from which no one—neither the great nor the small—is exempt. In substance it is: "Every 'Standard Oil' man must wear the 'Standard Oil' collar."

This collar is riveted onto each one as he is taken into "the band," and afterward can only be removed with the head of the wearer.

Here is the Code. The penalty for infringing the following rules is instant removal:

1. Keep your mouth closed, as silence is gold, and gold is what we exist for.

2. Collect our debts today. Pay the other fellow's debts tomorrow. Today is always here, tomorrow may never come.

3. Conduct all our business so that the buyer and the seller must come to us. Keep the seller waiting; the longer he waits the less he'll take. Hurry the buyer, as his money brings us interest.

4. Make all profitable bargains in the name of "Standard Oil," debatable ones in the names of dummies. "Standard Oil" never goes back on a bargain.

5. Never put "Standard Oil" trades in writing, as your memory and the other fellow's forgetfulness will always be re-enforced with our organization. Never forget our Legal Department is paid by the year, and our land is full of courts and judges.

6. As competition is the life of trade—our trade; and monopoly the death of trade—our competitors' trade, employ both judiciously.

7. Never enter into a "butting" contest with the government. Our government is by the people and for the people, and we are the people, and those people who are not us can be hired by us.

8. Always do right. Right makes might, might makes dollars, dollars make right, and we have the dollars.

All business of the great "Standard Oil" system is dealt with through two great departments. Mr. Rogers is head of the executive and William Rockefeller the head of the financial department. All new schemes, whether suggested by outsiders or initiated within the institution, go to Mr. Rogers. Regardless of nature or character, he must first take them under advisement. If good enough to run the gantlet of his tremendously high standard, the promoter, after he has set forth his plans and estimates, hears with astonishment these words:

"Wait until I go upstairs. I'll say yes or no upon my return."

And upon his return it is almost always "yes." If the project, however, does not come up to his exacting requirements, it is turned down without further ado or consultation with any of his associates.

Those intimate with affairs at 26 Broadway have grown curiously familiar with this expression, "I am going upstairs." "Upstairs" means two distinct and separate things. When a matter in Mr. Rogers' department is awaiting his return from "upstairs," it means he has gone to place the scheme before William Rockefeller, on the thirteenth floor, and laying a thing before Mr. Rockefeller by Mr. Rogers consists of a brief, vigorous statement of his own conclusions and a request for his associate's judgment of it. Mr. Rockefeller's strong quality is his ability to estimate quickly the practical value of a given scheme, and his approval means he will finance it, and William Rockefeller's "say-so" is as absolute in the financing of things as is Mr. Rogers' in passing upon their feasibility. It does not matter whether it is an undertaking calling for the employment of $50,000 capital or $50,000,000 or $500,-000,0000. Mr. Rockefeller's "yes" or "no" is all there is to it. He having passed on it, Mr. Rogers supervises its execution.

The other "upstairs" is one that is heard each weekday except Saturdays during the summer months. At 26 Broadway, just before eleven o'clock each day, there is a flutter in the offices of all the leading heads of departments from Henry H. Rogers down, for going "upstairs" to the eleven o'clock meeting is the one all-important event in each "Standard Oil" man's mind every working day in the year.

In the big room, on the fifteenth floor, at 26 Broadway, there gather each day, between the hours of eleven and twelve o'clock, all the active men whose efforts make "Standard Oil" what "Standard Oil" is, and there also meet and mingle with the active heads the retired captains when "they are in town." Around a large table they sit. Reports are presented, views exchanged, policies talked over, and republics and empires made and unmade. If the Recorders in the next world have kept complete minutes of what has happened "upstairs" at 26 Broadway, they must have tremendously large fireproof safes. It is at the meeting "upstairs" that the melons are cut, and if one of the retired captains should be asked why he was in such a rush to be on hand each day when in town, and he were in a talkative mood—which he would not be—he would answer: "They may be cutting a new melon, and there's nothing like being on hand when the juice runs out."

If a new project has been started—an Amalgamated Copper, for instance—it is at one of these meetings that the different "Standard Oil" men are informed for the first time that the project, about which they have read or heard much outside, is far enough along for them to participate in it. Each is told what size slice he may have if he cares for any, and it is a very exceptional thing for anyone to ask for more than he has been apportioned, and an unheard-of thing for anyone to refuse to take his slice, although there is absolutely no compulsion in the connection.

The success of "Standard Oil" is largely due to two things—the loyalty of its members to each other and to "Standard Oil," and the punishment of its enemies. Each member before initiation knows its religion to be reward for friends and extermination for enemies. Once a man is within the magic circle he at once realizes he is getting all that anyone else on earth can afford to pay him for like services, and still more thrown in for full measure. The public has never heard of a "Standard Oil" man leaving the ranks. I know of but one case, a very peculiar one. . . . While a "Standard Oil" man's reward is always ample and satisfactory, he is constantly reminded in a thousand and one ways that punishment for disloyalty is sure and terrible, and that in no corner of the earth can he escape it, nor can any power on earth protect him from it.

"Standard Oil" is never loud in its rewards nor its punishments. It does not care for the public's praise nor for its condemnation, but endeavors to avoid both by keeping "its business" to itself.

In connection with the gas settlements I made with "Standard Oil," it voluntarily paid one of its agents for a few days' work $250,000. He had expected at the outside $25,000. When I published the fact, as I had a right to, "Standard Oil" was mad as hornets—as upset indeed, as though it had been detected in cheating the man out of two-thirds of his just due, instead of having paid him ten times what was coming to him.

In the great Thing known to the world as "Standard Oil," the foremost example of a "system" . . . there are three heads, Henry H. Rogers, William Rockefeller, and John D. Rockefeller. All the others are distinctively lieutenants, or subordinate workers, unless possibly I except James Stillman, who from his peculiar connection with "Standard Oil" and his individually independent position, should perhaps be placed in the category of heads.

Someone has said: "If you would know who is the head of a family, slip into the home." The world, the big, arbitrary, hit-or-miss, too-much-in-a-hurry-to-correct-its-mistakes world, has it that the master of

"Standard Oil" is John D. Rockefeller, and John D. Rockefeller it is to all but those who have a pass-key to the "Standard Oil" home. To those the head of "Standard Oil"—the "Standard Oil" the world knows as it knows St. Paul, Shakespeare, or Jack the Giant-killer, or any of the things it knows well but not at all—is Henry H. Rogers. John D. Rockefeller may have more money, more actual dollars, than Henry H. Rogers, or all other members of the "Standard Oil" family, and in the early days of "Standard Oil" may have been looked up to as the big gun by his partners, and allowed to take the hugest hunks of the profits, and to have so handled and judiciously invested them as to be at the beginning of the twentieth century the richest man on earth, but none of these things alters the fact that the big brain, the big body, the Master of "Standard Oil," is Henry H. Rogers.

If you should happen to take station at the entrance of 26 Broadway and watch the different members of the "Standard Oil" family as they enter the building, you will exclaim once and only once: "There goes the Master!" And it will be Henry H. Rogers.

The big, jovial detective who stands all day long with one foot resting on the sidewalk and one on the first stone step, will make oath he shows no different sign to Henry H. Rogers than to a Rockefeller, a Payne, a Flagler, a Pratt or an O'Day; yet watch him when Mr. Rogers passes up the steps—an unconscious deference marks his salutation—the tribute of the soldier to the commanding general.

Follow through the door with the sign, "Henry H. Rogers, President of the National Transit Co.," on the eleventh floor, and pass from the outer office into the beautiful, spacious mahogany apartment beyond with its decorations of bronze bulls and bears and yacht-models, the walls covered with neatly framed autograph letters from Lincoln, Grant, "Tom" Reed, Mark Twain and other real, big men, and it will come over you like a flash that here, unmistakably, is the *sanctum sanctorum* of the mightiest business institution of modern times. If a single doubt lingers, read what the men in the frames have said to Henry H. Rogers, and you will have proof positive that these judges of human nature knew this man, not only as the master of "Standard Oil," but also as a sturdy and resolute friend whose jovial humanity they had recognized and enjoyed.

Did my readers ever hear of the National Transit Company? Very few have—yet the presidency of it is the modest title of Henry H. Rogers. When the world is ladling out honors to the "Standard Oil" kings, and spouting of their wondrous riches, how often is Henry H. Rogers mentioned? Not often, for he is never where the public can get a glimpse of him—he is too busy pulling the wires and playing the buttons in the shadows just behind the throne. Had it not been that the divinity which disposes of what men propose, compelled this man, as he neared the end of his remarkable career, to come into the open on Amalgamated, he might never have been known as the real Master of "Standard Oil." But if he is missing when the public is hurrahing, he is sufficiently in evidence when clouds lower or when the danger-signal is run to the mast-head at 26 Broadway. He who reads "Standard Oil" history will note that, from its first day until this day, whenever the bricks, cabbages, or aged eggs were being presented to "Standard Oil," always was Henry H. Rogers' towering form and defiant eye in the foreground where they flew thickest.

During the past twenty years, whenever the great political parties have lined up for their regular once-in-four-years tussle, there would be found Henry H. Rogers, calm as a race-track gambler, "sizing up" the entries, their weights and handicaps. Every twist and turn in the pedi-grees and records of Republicans and Democrats are as familiar to him as the "dope sheets" are to the gambler, for is he not at the receiving end of the greatest information bureau in the world?

A "Standard Oil" agent is in every hamlet in the country, and who better than these trained and intelligent observers to interpret the vary-ing trends of feeling of their communities? Tabulated and analyzed, these reports enable Rogers, the sagacious politician, to diagnose the drift of the country far ahead of the most astute of campaign managers. He is never in doubt about who will win the election. Before the con-test is under way he has picked his winner and is beside him with generous offers of war expenses.

Whenever labor howled its anathemas at "Standard Oil," and the Rockefellers and other stout-hearted generals and captains of this band of merry money-makers would begin to discuss conciliation and retreat, it was always Henry H. Rogers who fired at his associates his now famous panacea for all "Standard Oil" opposition, "We'll see Standard Oil in hell before we will allow any body of men on earth to dictate how we shall conduct our business!" And the fact that "Standard Oil" still does its business in the Elysian field of success, where are neither sulphur nor the fumes of sulphur, is additional evidence of whose will it is that sways its destinies.

An impression of the despotic character of the man and of his man-ner of dispatching the infinite details of the multitudinous business he must deal with daily may be gathered from seeing Henry H. Rogers at one of the meetings of the long list of giant corporations which number him among their directors. Surrounded though he be by the elite of all financialdom, the very flower of the business brains of America, you will surely hear his sharp, incisive, steel-clicking, "Gentlemen, are we ready for the vote, for I regret to say I have another important and unavoidable meeting at——" You look at your watch. The time he mentions is twelve, or, at the most, fifteen minutes away. There is no chance for discussion. Cut-and-dried resolutions are promptly put to the vote, and off goes the master to his other engagement, which will be disposed of in the same peremptory fashion.

At a meeting of the directors of "financed" steel, during the brief reign of its late "vacuumized" president, Charlie Schwab, an episode occurred which exhibited the danger of interfering with Mr. Rogers' iron-clad plans. The fact that the steel throne was many sizes too large for Schwab had, about this time, become publicly notorious, but Carnegie and Morgan on the surface, and Standard Oil beneath, were so busy preparing their alibis for the crash which then was overdue, that they had neither time nor desire to adjust themselves on the seat.

In advance Mr. Rogers made his invariable plea for quick action on a matter before the board, when Schwab, with the tact generated by the wabbling of a misfit Wall Street crown chafing a generous pair of ears, blurted out: "Mr. Rogers will vote on this question after we have talked on it."

In a voice that those who heard it say sounded like a rattlesnake's hiss in a refrigerator, Rogers replied: "All meetings where I sit as director vote first and talk after I am gone."

It is said, and from my knowledge of these and after events I believe with truth, that this occurrence was the spark that started the terrific explosion in United States Steel, for not long afterward some unknown and mysterious power began that formidable attack on Steel stocks which left Wall Street full of the loose ears, eyes, noses, breastbones and scalps of hordes of financial potentates and their flambeau carriers. Whether or not this is absolutely the case, no man, of course, can positively state, but I can vouch for the fact that about this time Mr. Rogers, when talking "Steel" affairs with intimates, displayed a most contemptuous bitterness against "King Charlie" and certain of his associates.

At sixty-five Henry H. Rogers is probably one of the most distinguished-looking men of the time; as tall, as straight, as well-proportioned, and as supple as one of the beautiful American elms which line the streets of his native town. He was born in Fairhaven, a fishing town just over the bridge from the great whaling port, New Bedford. He comes of stalwart New England stock; his father was a sea captain, and his lot, like that of most of the sons of old New England seaport towns, was cast along those hard, brain-and-body-developing lines which, beginning in the red village schoolhouse, the white meeting house, and the yellowish-grayish country store, end in unexpected places, often, as in this instance, upon the golden throne of business royalty.

Mr. Rogers' part in the very early days of Standard Oil was that of clerk and bookkeeper. He makes no secret that when he had risen to the height of $8 a week wages he felt as proud and confident as ever in after life when for the same number of days' labor it was no uncommon occurrence to find himself credited with a hundred thousand times that amount.

All able men have some of God's indelible imprints of greatness which stand out more strongly than others. This man's every feature bespeaks strength and distinction. When he walks, the active swing of his figure expresses power—realized, confident power. When at rest or in action his square jaw tells of fighting power, bulldog, hold-on, never-let-go fighting power, and his high, full forehead, of intellectual, mightily intellectual power; and they are re-enforced with cheekbones and nose which suggest that this fighting power has in it something of the grim ruthlessness of the North American Indian. The eyes, however, are the crowning characteristic of the man's physical make-up.

One must see Mr. Rogers' eyes in action and in repose to half appreciate their wonders. I can only say they are red, blue, and black, brown, gray, and green; nor do I want my readers to think I put in colors that are not there, for there must be many others than those I have mentioned. I have seen them when they were so restfully blue that I would think they never could be anything but a part of those skies that come with the August and September afternoons when the bees' hum and the locusts' drone blend with the smell of the new-mown hay to help spell the word "Rest."

I have seen them so green that within their depths I was almost sure the fish were lazily resting in the shadows of those sea-plants which only grow on the ocean's bottom; and I have seen them as black as that thunder-cloud which makes us wonder: "Is He angry?" And then again I have seen them when they were of that fiery red and that glinting yellow which one sees only when at night the doors of a great, roaring furnace are opened.

There is such a kindly good will in these eyes when they are at rest that the man does not live who would not consider himself favored to be allowed to turn over to Henry H. Rogers his pocketbook without receiving a receipt. They are the eyes of the man you would name in your will to care for your wife and children's welfare. When their animation is friendly one would rather sit and watch their merry twinkle as they keep time to his inimitable stories and nonduplicatable anecdotes, trying to interpret the rapid and incessant telegraphy of their glances, than sit in a theater or read an interesting book; but it is when they are active in war that the one privileged to watch them gets his real treat, always provided he can dodge the rain of blazing sparks, and the withering hail of wrath that pours on the offender. To do this requires real nerve, for it is only a nimble, stout-hearted, mail-covered individual that can sustain the encounter.

I have seen many forms of human wrath, many men transformed to terrible things by anger, but I have never seen any that were other than jumping-jack imitations of a jungle tiger compared with Henry H. Rogers when he "lets 'er go"—when the instant comes that he realizes someone is balking the accomplishment of his will.

Above all things Henry H. Rogers is a great actor. Had his lot been cast upon the stage, he might easily have eclipsed the fame of Booth or Salvini. He knows the human animal from the soles of his feet to the part in his hair, and from his shoulder-blade to his breastbone, and like all great actors, is not above getting down to every part he plays. He is likely also to so lose himself in a role that he gives it his own force and identity, and then things happen quite at variance with the lines. The original Booth would come upon the stage the cool, calculating, polished actor, but when well into his part was so lost that it was often with difficulty he could be brought back to himself when the curtain fell. Once while playing Richard III, at the old Boston Museum, Richmond, by whom he was to be slain, made the thrust at the ordained moment which should have laid him low, but instead, Booth in high frenzy parried it, and with the fiendishness of the original Richard, step by step drove Richmond off the stage and through the wings, and it was not until the police seized Booth, two blocks away, that the terrified duke, who had dropped his sword and was running for dear life, was sure he would ever act again.

When in the midst of his important plans, it is doubtful whether Henry H. Rogers realizes until the guardians of the peace appear where the reality begins and the acting should end. His intimate associates can recall many times when his determination to make a hit in his part has caused other actors cast with him to throw aside their dummy swords and run for their lives.

The entire history of "Standard Oil" is strewn with court scenes, civil and criminal, and in all the important ones Henry H. Rogers, the actor, will be found doing marvelous "stunts." "Standard Oil" historians are fond of dwelling on the extraordinary testifying abilities of John D. Rockefeller and other members of the band, but the acrobatic feats of ground and lofty tumbling in the way of truth in the parts which they have given when before the blinking footlights of the temples of justice are as Punch and Judy shows to a Barnum three-ring circus compared to Henry H. Rogers' exhibitions.

His "I will tell the truth, the whole truth and nothing but the truth, so help me God" sounds absolutely sincere and honest, but as it rings out in the tone of the third solemnest bell in the chime, this is how it is taken down in those unerring shorthand notes of the recording angel and sent by special wireless to the typewriter for His Majesty of the Sulphur Trust: "What I tell *shall be* the truth and the whole truth, and there *shall be* no truth but that I tell, and God help the man or woman who tells truth different from my truth." The recording angel never missed catching Henry H. Rogers' court oaths in this way, and never missed sending them along to the typewriter at Sulphurville, with this postscript: "Keep your wire open, for there'll be things doing now!"

At the recent but now famous sensational Boston "Gas Trial," Henry H. Rogers in the role of defendant was the principal witness. I sat in court five hours and a half each day, as day after day he testified, and watched, as the brightest lawyers in the land laid their traps for him in direct and cross-examination, to detect a single sign of fiction replacing truth, or going joint-account with her, or where truth parted company with fiction, and I was compelled, when he stepped from the witness stand, to admit I had not found what I had watched for. This, too, when I was equipped with actual knowledge and black-and-white proofs of the facts. Weeks before the trial began Mr. Rogers knew that Attorney Sherman L. Whipple, one of the great cross-examiners of the time, had made his boast he would break through the "Standard Oil" magnate's heretofore impenetrable bulwarks, and when he entered the courtroom for the first time and let his eagle eye sweep the lawyers, the laymen, and the judge until it finally rested on Whipple, the glance was as absolute a challenge and a defiance as ever knights of old exchanged.

I followed Mr. Rogers on the witness stand and was compelled to give testimony the direct opposite of that which he had given, and at one time, as I glanced at the row of lawyers who were in "Standard Oil's" hire, I felt a cold perspiration start at every pore at the thought of what would happen if I even in a slight detail got mixed in my facts. Then I fully realized the magnificence of Mr. Rogers' acting, for not once in all the hours I had sat and watched him could I detect a single evidence of cold or hot perspiration coming from his pores.

Yet away from the intoxicating spell of dollar-making this remarkable man is one of the most charming and lovable beings I have ever encountered, a man whom any man or woman would be proud to have for a brother; a man whom any mother or father would give thanks for as a son, a man whom any woman would be happy to know as her husband, and a man whom any boy or girl would rejoice to call father. But once he passes under the baleful influence of "The Machine," he becomes a relentless, ravenous creature, pitiless as a shark, knowing no law of God or man in the execution of his purpose. Between him and coveted dollars may come no kindly human influences— all are thrust aside, their claims disregarded, in ministering to this strange, cannibalistic money-hunger, which, in truth, grows by what it feeds on.

In describing one head of "Standard Oil," I have necessarily used many words because nature cast him in a most uncommon and chameleonlike mold. The other two require less of my space, for neither is cast in an unusual or remarkable mold.

John D. Rockefeller, however great his ability or worldly success, can be fully described as a man made in the image of an ideal money-maker and an ideal money-maker made in the image of a man. A footnote should call attention to the fact that an ideal money-maker is a machine, the details of which are diagrammed in any of the blueprints already in circulation.

With William Rockefeller it is different. When I read in my Bible that God made man in His own image and likeness, I find myself picturing a certain type of individual—a solid, substantial, sturdy gentleman with the broad shoulders and strong frame of an Englishman and a cautious, kindly expression of face. And that is the most fitting description I can give of William Rockefeller. A man of few, very few words and most excellent judgment—rather brotherly than friendly, clean of mind and body; and if I have not given you the impression of a good, wholesome man made in the image of his God, I have done William Rockefeller a greater wrong than an honest man can afford to do another.

. . . I will give two pictures of events, which to my mind aptly illustrate those all-important features of the "Standard Oil" institution, "upstairs," "generosity," and Rogers the Master, showing how the "Standard Oil" mind is impressed with the importance of the first and the flexibility of the second, and that all rules and principles may be suspended or waived at the behest of Rogers the Master.

Before Amalgamated was launched, in bringing together the different properties of which it was composed, I negotiated for the acquisition of the Parrot mine, the majority of whose stock was held by certain old and wealthy brass manufacturers in Connecticut. They had never seen any of the Rockefellers, nor Henry H. Rogers, but getting the deal into shape took us several months before it was finally arranged, and they became familiar with the great "Standard Oil" institution. So much so that the chief of the owners—to whom was delegated the duty of turning over the securities to my principals—looked forward with much eagerness to the time when he must necessarily meet these mysterious and important personages. Finally the day came, and at precisely a quarter of eleven I let him into one of the numerous private offices which are a part of Mr. Rogers' suite. He had under his arm a bundle of papers representing the stocks which he was to exchange for the purchase money, amounting to $4,086,000, and, I think, fully expected that in their examination, the receipting for so large an amount of money, and in the general talkings over, which he, of course, thought must be a necessary part of the delivery, the greater part of the day would be taken up. It took me some six or seven minutes to get him located, and it was close onto five minutes of eleven when Mr. Rogers stepped into the room. I was well into the introduction, when out came Mr. Rogers' watch, and with what must have appeared to the visitor as astonished consternation:

"I do hope you will excuse me," he exclaimed in the middle of a hand shake, "but, my gracious, I am overdue upstairs," and he bolted.

His place was taken fifty seconds after by Mr. Rogers' secretary, who in less than five minutes had exchanged a check of $4,086,000, made out to herself and endorsed in blank, for the bundle of stocks, and in another minute I was ushering the old gentleman into the elevator.

When he came to on the sidewalk he got his breath sufficiently to say: "Phew! I thought my trade was a big one, but that friend of yours, Rogers, must have had some other fellow upstairs who was going to turn in $40,000,000 of stuff, because he did appear dreadfully excited!"

The great Anaconda mine and affiliated properties, previous to the creation of the Amalgamated, were owned by J. B. Haggin, Lloyd Tevis, and Marcus Daly. The control of the properties and their opera-

tions were absolutely vested in Marcus Daly, and he alone knew where
the lean veins ended and the fat ones began. For many years he had
kept a close guard over the very fat ones, never letting his right eye
know what the left one saw when he was examining them. For deep
down in his mind Marcus Daly cherished a dream—a dream of immense
riches, and it was to be realized in a simple enough way. He would
get together the millions to buy out his partners on the basis of a
valuation of the "ore in sight," then in supreme ownership himself
reap untold profits out of the milling of the plethoric veins he had been
so careful to leave unworked. The immense natural endowments of
the Anaconda rendered this easy enough, for even the lean veins "in
sight" contained a vast store of copper and gold and silver.

Just about the time the world awaited the first section of "Coppers"
which I had advertised should consist of the rich Boston and Montana,
and Butte and Boston properties, it "happened" that Mr. Rogers "met"
Marcus Daly. The result of the conjunction of the two personalities—
the wholesouled, trusting miner and the fascinating and persuasive
master of Standard Oil—was decisive; the miner confided his dreams
and his aspirations to the magnate, who at once magnificently undertook
to realize them. The trade was almost instantly made. Mr. Rogers
would buy the properties of Daly, Haggin and Tevis, at "in sight"
prices, and Daly would be his partner, but the partnership must remain
secret until the purchase was consummated.

The ownership of the Anaconda Company at the time consisted of
1,200,000 shares, and the purchase of a few shares over the majority
at the "in sight" lean-vein valuation of $24,000,000 would carry the
turnover of the management and the control. It took but a very brief
time to get together the other properties which were finally included
in the first section of Amalgamated. They consisted of the Colorado,
Washoe and Parrot Mining Companies and timber, coal and other
lands, and mercantile and like properties situated in the State of
Montana, for which Mr. Rogers paid in round figures $15,000,000,
*a total of $39,000,000 for what within a few days after purchase was
capitalized at $75,000,000 in the Amalgamated Company.*

No one but Henry H. Rogers, William Rockefeller, myself, and
one lawyer knew the actual figures of the cost, although a number of
the members of the different groups, including Marcus Daly, the silent
partner, were sure they were in the secret.

As soon as the properties were secured, they were capitalized for
$75,000,000 as the Amalgamated Copper Company and were im-
mediately offered for sale to the public. It will thus be seen that the

profit on this section alone was $36,000,000, probably the largest actual profit ever made by one body of men in a single corporation deal, yet so nicely does "Standard Oil" discriminate in dispensing its generosity that in this case those who received the $36,000,000 profit refused to deduct from it $77,000 of expenses connected with the formation of the company, thereby compelling it to start $77,000 in debt. This was something Marcus Daly never forgave and to the day of his death he repeatedly referred to the act as the personification of corporation meanness.

In the organization of the Amalgamated Corporation certain individuals and institutions, for various considerations, were entitled to some share in the profits of the deal. First there was Marcus Daly who knew what the major portion of the property had cost and was a silent partner in the winnings as he knew them. The Amalgamated Company was organized in and floated on the public from the City Bank, and so James Stillman, its head, who is also one of the inner circle of "Standard Oil" chiefs, should participate. Something was due also to J. Pierpont Morgan & Co., and to Frederick Olcott, president of the Central Trust Company of New York, who were on the board of directors. On the board of directors, too, was Governor Flower, of the banking and brokerage house of Flower & Company, who had acted as fiscal agents for the corporation at its formation. Nor must I forget the Lewisohn Brothers, who had been induced to turn in all their copper business at actual cost, to be incorporated in the United Metals Selling Co., a part of the Amalgamated scheme, but not included in the corporation, and every one of these had elaborate assurances that he was in on the cellar floor.

This is what actually occurred. Before Mr. Rogers and William Rockefeller let anyone at all in, they built a superbly designed water-, air- and light-proof structure (particularly light-proof), consisting of five floors, each one being the exact duplicate of the $39,000,000 one upon which they, and they only, stood. Marcus Daly alone was ushered in on the first floor, elevated just a few million dollars above their own. James Stillman and Leonard Lewisohn, of Lewisohn Brothers, were admitted to the next one, the $50,000,000 floor. In other words, Mr. Stillman and Mr. Lewisohn were given an unnamed percentage, the percentage to be arranged later by Mr. Rogers, in all profits above actual cost, and such actual cost was called $50,000,000 and was arrived at by adding the $11,000,000 of secret profits to the actual $39,000,000 cost. Then J. P. Morgan & Co., Frederick Olcott, Governor Flower, and one or two of the dearest friends and closest associates, were let in on the $60,000,-

ooo floor—were given an unnamed percentage, the percentage to be arranged by Mr. Rogers, in all profits above actual cost, and such actual cost was called $60,000,000, and was arrived at by adding the $21,000,000 of secret profits to the actual $39,000,000 cost. Then the selected ones from the eight different groups of "Standard Oil" were all allowed to move in to the fifth, or underwriters' floor, which was affirmed to be $70,000,000 cost; and then, as a solid phalanx, all the different floor-dwellers marched upon the dear public at $75,000,000, in the front ranks of which were all those of the eight groups of the Standard Oil army that had not already been admitted to any of the secret floors.

Right here the crime of Amalgamated was born, not so much the legal crime but the great moral crime. . . .

In the ethics of Wall Street the heinousness of this transaction is not in the fact that the public was compelled to pay $36,000,000 profit to a few men who had invested but $39,000,000—and, as I shall show when I approach this part of my story, the $39,000,000 did not even belong to them—but in the fact that Mr. Rogers and Mr. Rockefeller had given to their associates what, in the vernacular of "the Street," is termed "the double cross."

The everyday people, the millions who do not know Wall Street— realm of the royal American dollar—Wall Street, its sidewalks inlaid with gold coin and paved from curb to curb with solid gold bricks— Wall Street, lined with huge money-mills, where hearts and souls are ground into gold dust, whose gutters run full to overflowing with strangled, mangled, sandbagged wrecks of human hopes which, in a never-ending stream, it pours into the brimming waters of the river at its foot for deposit at the poorhouses, insane asylums, states' prisons, and suicides' graves, that the grim flood washes in its daily ebb and flow—the everyday people I know will not take in the blackness of this transaction at this stage of my story, but before it is ended I will lay this and many more of an equally black nature before them in such ABC simplicity that all can read the portent as clearly as the Prophet Daniel read the writing on the wall in the banquet hall of Belshazzar.

Everybody's Magazine
August 1904

INSURANCE

When Thomas Lawson started his series on "Frenzied Finance," he had no intentions of getting into any lengthy discussion on insurance.

He did, however, in his introductory chapter, note that: "This 'System' is a process or a device for the incubation of wealth from the people's savings in the banks, trust, and insurance companies, and the public funds." *

In one of his chapters, as a means of illustrating how the "System" works, Lawson cited the tie-in with life insurance companies. Specifically, he mentioned the New York Life Insurance Company.

Immediately he was bombarded with letters from readers asking for more details and explanations.

One reader wrote to Lawson: "I have been astounded beyond measure at the revelations you make in your second article regarding the New York Life Insurance Company, because I have two policies in that concern which I am keeping up for the protection of my family. . . . Do you really believe the officers of the company personally profited from using the 'cash on hand' of the company?"

Lawson answered: "I desire to emphasize that the New York Life Insurance Company, which I cited, is no different from the Equitable and the Mutual Life, or many of the other large companies. They are links . . . in the device by which dollars are 'made,' by which the savings of the people are sucked from the people to the 'System,' the 'Private Things.' " [110]

And so insurance became part of Lawson's muckraking articles in *Everybody's Magazine*.

The Era Magazine, in October 1904, announced the start of a series of its own on a theme which "touches so vitally the business affairs and home interests, the family ties and affections of every man and woman . . . a theme involving questions of great wrongs committed in the broad light of day by a coterie of men in the highest public and social stations, whose high handed methods had been so long unheeded and unchecked they were emboldened to acts of the greatest financial tyranny."

John W. Ryckman, the editor of *The Era*, stressed, however, that there was no question about the solvency of the insurance companies, nor any dispute with the benefits of life insurance.

* *Everybody's Magazine*, July 1904.

"The revelations we shall make concern rather the persistent disregard by the companies of the equitable rights of their policyholders; the with-holding of enormous amounts of divisible surplus; their coalition with Wall Street in support of the most audacious schemes of speculation and their defiance of salutary legal requirements." [111]

Lawson complimented Ryckman on the magazine's exposures on life insurance as being "valuable, and I congratulate you upon them. Rest as-sured it will give me great pleasure to see that *The Era* is given full credit, should I make use of any of the important figures it has collected." [112]

Two months after Lawson's series on "Frenzied Finance" started, he pur-chased space in the advertising columns of *Everybody's* to run a department called "Lawson and His Critics," in which he answered letters from readers on insurance.

In that department in December 1904, Lawson proclaimed: "I am going to cause a life insurance blaze that will make the life insurance policyholders' world so light that every scoundrel with a mask, dark-lantern and suspicious-looking bag will stand out so clearly that he cannot escape the consequences of his past deeds, nor commit new ones."

As a result of Lawson's exposures, wrote Terence O'Donnell in *History of Life Insurance*, "the comparatively placid insurance pool at last began to show troubled ripples, the seepage of numberless lapsations became evident and there became evident the first roiling that in time became so muddy it required the historic exposures of the Armstrong Investigation to restore clarity to insurance again." [113]

Indications that not all was going well at the Equitable Life Assurance Society became apparent in January 1905. Equitable's president, James W. Alexander, and James Hazen Hyde, son of the founder of Equitable, were engaged in a battle for control of the company.

Furthermore, there was concern over young Hyde's expensive escapades which reached its zenith with the famous "French Ball," a $12,000 extrava-ganza banquet for the French Ambassador paid for from the Equitable treasury as an expense of advertising.

For a time the struggle for control over Equitable was a family affair carried on in closed meetings in the directors' room. Eventually, however, the dispute flared wide open.

In his articles Lawson called for an extension of voting privileges to stockholders. The New York *World* called for a legislative investigation.

The Governor of New York appointed a committee to investigate not only Equitable, but other big life insurance companies. William W. Arm-strong of Rochester was named chairman of the committee and Charles Evans Hughes, later to be Governor of New York and a Supreme Court Justice of the United States, its chief counsel. The committee held fifty-seven public hearings from September 6 to December 30, 1905.

Hughes showed during the investigation that life insurance funds had been used for speculation, for influencing legislation, for personal profit as well as for political funds.

He showed that "large sums have also been expended in the attempt to influence public opinion through the press by the insertion of so-called 'reading notices,' that is to say, by disguised advertising and by payments to newspaper correspondents and news writers for presumably similar services."

"As a result of Hughes's investigation," wrote Mark Sullivan, "two vice-presidents of one company and the president and two vice-presidents of another were indicted. All the presidents and most of the other high officials of the three big companies resigned or were forced out. The members of the finance committee of the New York Life Insurance Company who had sanctioned contributions to political campaign committees paid back to the company $148,000 out of their own pockets, fifteen men giving about $10,000 each. James Hazen Hyde reimbursed the Equitable for the expenses of the dinner to the French Ambassador and for other expenditures deemed unjustifiable." [114]

The report itself resulted in changes in insurance practices.

During and after the Armstrong investigation, other magazines also muckraked insurance. *World's Work* published late in 1905 and early 1906 a series of six articles under the by-line "Q.P."

McClure's started a series in May 1906 on "The Story of Life Insurance" written by Burton J. Hendrick.

At the height of the Armstrong investigation, *Collier's* commented on both the investigation and Lawson's series: "It is a striking irony that his [Lawson's] own importance for the moment should fade before events which he assisted in bringing forth." [115]

But some historians pin a medal of honor on Lawson and the other muckrakers for their contribution in exposing the malpractices of life insurance companies. In 1925 Arthur Schlesinger wrote: "The mismanagement of the great New York insurance companies, charged by leading Muckrakers, led to a legislative investigation in 1905, which first brought Charles E. Hughes, one of the attorneys for the state, to favorable national attention." [116]

Allan Nevins, writing in 1940, said: "His [Lawson's] statement that three great insurance companies . . . were an integral part of the 'System,' helped precipitate the much-needed insurance investigation." [117]

THOMAS W. LAWSON

Lawson and His Critics

THE NEW YORK LIFE INSURANCE COMPANY is no different from the Equitable and the Mutual Life, or many of the other large companies. They are links in the chain of the "System"—necessary links in the device by which dollars are "made," by which the savings of the people are sucked from the people to the "System," the "Private Things."

The insurance companies use the billions the people have placed with them to buy or create banks and trust companies, the stocks of which are a large part of their assets. They then use these banks and trust companies, which exist because of the people's savings, in stock gambling enterprises, speculations as unsafe and as frenzied as those of the wildest plunger of Wall Street. I will give one illustration:

The New York Life Insurance Company's directors and managers created the New York Security and Trust Company. $1,000,000 capital; $500,000 surplus—in all, $1,500,000. $150 per share, of which the insurance company held about two-thirds. The Trust Company soon secured deposits to the extent of about $50,000,000, and these it loaned out by "financing" new and old enterprises. Among them was the New Hampshire Traction. The Trust Company flourished. Its stock advanced in price to over $1,300 per share, or over $13,000,000, and its different speculative ventures prospered exceedingly. New Hampshire Traction kept pace with the rest and simultaneously with them bounded upward in value until the amount of this stock owned by the Trust Company represented a value of between $5,000,000 and $6,000,000. There came a time when the directors of the New York Life Insurance Company decided to dispose of their stock in the Trust Company, and did so to a syndicate composed of their own members, headed by John

D. Rockefeller, at $800 per share. Afterward the stock disposed of at $800 per share advanced to over $1,300, or, with the third which had not been owned by the insurance company but by the "insiders" and their friends, to a total of over $13,000,000. Then came the slump, and the price of the New Hampshire Traction fell to twenty-five cents on the dollar, and the Trust Company's stock to less than $600.

If in all the histories of the wildcats of the wild catteries of Wall Street a wilder case of "frenzied finance" can be discovered, I don't know it, and yet this is only one of many I could quote, selected at random. Boiled down, it means that what was bought at $150 went to $1,400 and back to $590, and that it changed hands at $800 before it got to $1,400, and that the plunger in this transaction, which made this plunging possible, was one of the most conservative life insurance companies in America.

Policyholders in the three great life insurance companies may argue: "The man who is known to us policyholders as the real head of the New York Life is John A. McCall, its president. All that you may say about the 'System's' votaries being in control may be so, but we depend on the integrity and the character of this one man to protect our interests. He is our representative, not the 'System's,' and our savings are surely safe in his strong hands."

There is the point. In the great insurance corporations that are "one-man run," the hundreds of thousands of policyholders have but one protection. This, notwithstanding the protection of the state laws, the guardianship of the Insurance Department of the various states, and the provisions of the company's charter and bylaws.

However impregnable may seem the safeguards which the law has built round the administration of our great insurance companies, the fact absolutely is that the honesty of "the one man" is the one potent protection policyholders may depend on. The others may be juggled with as are the rules of the Stock Exchange, which say in thunder tones, "All within our sacred walls is honest and honorable," when in reality if the microbes of dishonor and dishonesty generated within Stock Exchange walls each busy week of every year should be collected and disseminated throughout the land they would give typhoid of the soul to our eighty millions of Americans. So it becomes the duty of every policyholder to find out by such tests as he can apply, "Is 'the one man' who runs our company an honest man or is he a dishonest man?" If "the one man" stands their tests, if he emerges from their ordeal clean, strong, honest, as they believed, then they may rest awhile in patience. But if he is revealed as dishonest, then it behooves the policyholders of that company to take measures for the protection of their interests. The welfare and happiness, perhaps the very lives of their mothers, their wives, and their children depend on their action.

I was recently waited upon by an important man.

"Lawson, what are you doing in life insurance?" he asked.

"Giving facts about the life insurance branch of a 'System' which is foully plundering the people," I answered.

"What are you trying to do?"

"Educate the millions of life insurance policyholders to their present peril; after they are educated, arouse them to quick, radical action."

"What are you going to do?" he asked.

"I am going to cause a life insurance blaze that will make the life insurance policyholders' world so light that every scoundrel with a mask, dark-lantern and suspicious-looking bag will stand out so clearly that he cannot escape the consequences of his past deeds, nor commit new ones."

"Have you figured the consequences to yourself?"

"Having no interest in what the consequences may be to myself in performing what I have decided is a sacred duty, I have not."

"Let me show them to you. First let me ask, do you intend to confine your criticisms to the New York Life Insurance Company?"

"I intend to bring out the facts, particularly as to the New York Life, the Mutual Life, and the Equitable Life; and, so far as in my power lies, as to every other life insurance company in America that is connected with the 'System.' "

"Are you actuated by any selfish motives—again, revenge, or friendly interest in certain life insurance companies or banks or trust companies?"

"My only interest is to perform a duty in righting a startling wrong, and I would not undertake the terrible task if I could possibly avoid it."

"I am sent to ask you these questions, to find out whether, if you are only seeking to serve the policyholders, and the insurance companies can absolutely prove to you that your making public your facts will cause terrible destruction to policyholders' interests, you will consent to forego the life insurance branch of your story?"

"I know the facts. I have calmly, and I believe intelligently, reviewed the effects of their being given to the world, and have concluded that the damage to policyholders and the people would, in any circumstances or conditions, be greater because of my not doing what I have decided to do than by my doing it. Therefore I will not in any circumstances consent to stop until I have laid before the world those things I consider it should know."

"Well and good. Let me show you what you are up against. The Equitable, the New York Life, and Mutual Life Insurance Companies, and their affiliated institutions and individuals, are today by all odds the greatest power in the world, greater by all odds than any power that can possibly be gathered together from those outside themselves, a power so great that the effort of no man nor party of men outside themselves can possibly prevail against their wishes."

"Stop where you are for a minute," I answered, "and let me run over to you what I know I am up against, and then you can judge whether I appreciate the difficulties of my task:

"First, the three companies I have named have absolute possession of property and money in the form of assets of over $1,000,000,000—more than half the combined assets of all the insurance companies of America—and indirectly, through their affiliated institutions, of an additional sum, the aggregate of which is much greater than the assets of all the national banks of America and the great financial institutions of Europe, such as the Banks of England, France and Germany. The three have a ready cash surplus of almost $200,000,000, which is greater than the combined capital of the four greatest institutions of Europe—the Banks of England, Russia, France and Germany. The income of these three companies is, each year, $100,000,000 greater than the combined capitals of the Banks of England, Russia, France and Germany—or about $250,000,000, $200,000,000 of which is taken each year from their policyholders in the form of premiums. Yet from out of this income there is returned to their policyholders each year in dividends less than $15,000,000, and in total payments of all kinds not over $100,000,000. And yet these three companies pay out each year in what they call expenses to keep the concerns running $50,000,000, paying to the officers of the companies $3,000,000 in salaries, almost $1,000,000 to their lawyers, and a number of millions in various forms of advertising.

"Second, the three companies are absolutely steered and controlled from a common center, and the men who do the steering and controlling are the 'System's' foremost votaries, Henry H. Rogers, William Rockefeller, James Stillman, and J. Pierpont Morgan through George W. Perkins, a partner in J. Pierpont Morgan & Co. Mr. Rogers, vice-president of the Standard Oil Company, is a trustee of the Mutual Life and a director in one of the largest trust companies owned by the three great insurance companies, the Guaranty Trust Company of New

York. William Rockefeller, vice-president of the Standard Oil Company, is a trustee of the Mutual Life and director in the National City—the 'Standard Oil'—Bank. James Stillman is a trustee of the New York Life, and president of the National City—the 'Standard Oil'—Bank of New York. George W. Perkins, partner of J. Pierpont Morgan & Co., is vice-president and trustee of the New York Life and a director in the National City—the 'Standard Oil'—Bank; while John A. McCall, the president of the New York Life, is a director in the National City—the 'Standard Oil'—Bank.

"These great institutions own a majority of the capital stock or have absolute control of a number of the leading banks and trust companies of New York and elsewhere; and such ownership shows conclusively the linking together of the three great insurance companies. For instance, the Equitable owns more than a majority of the stock of the Mercantile Trust Company of New York, of a book value of about $4,500,000 and a market value of almost $13,000,000; and of the Equitable Trust of New York, of a book value of $5,500,000 and a market value of $9,000,000; and of the Bank of Commerce of New York, of a book value of about $8,000,000 and a market value of over $9,000,000; and in the directory of the Mercantile Trust of New York and Equitable Trust is E. H. Harriman, one of the leading 'Standard Oil' men and one of the active votaries of the 'System,' while in the directory of the Bank of Commerce are the president of the Mutual Life and seven other trustees of the Mutual Life and three of the trustees of the New York Life.

"The Mutual Life owns stock of the Bank of Commerce, of a book value of $4,500,000 and a market value of $7,500,000; of the United States Mortgage & Trust Company, of a book value of $2,000,000 and a market value of $4,500,000; and of the Guaranty Trust Company of New York, a book value of $1,250,000 and a market value of $5,500,000. The directors of the United States Mortgage & Trust Company consist of eight trustees of the Mutual Life, including its president, and two trustees of the Equitable Life, while in the Guaranty Trust directory is the president of the Mutual Life, Henry H. Rogers, and E. H. Harriman, 'Standard Oil' votary and director in the Equitable.

"In addition to these financial institutions, the Mutual Life has about $20,000,000 of its funds invested in the stock of twenty-five other trust companies and national banks, while the Equitable has about $10,000,000 invested in some fifteen other trust and banking institutions.

"Third, the absolute control of the three great companies, and through them of their subsidiary financial institutions, while supposed to be in the hands of the policyholders, is entirely beyond their regulation, as all policyholders of the three companies give over complete control of their companies to the 'System' through the following machinery: the control of the New York Life rests absolutely in President McCall, that of the Mutual Life with President McCurdy. Originally these men were elected to office by policyholders' proxies, voted by the great general agents; but so immeasurable has been the growth of these corporations that only rebellion among policyholders on an international scale could oust from power the McCalls and the McCurdys. The control of the Equitable Life rests in the $100,000 of capital stock which is almost entirely owned by the men who elect themselves to manage the company.

"Therefore you will see that I fully comprehend that this power, which you claim to be, and which undoubtedly is, the greatest on earth, is absolutely, for all practical purposes, in the hands of three men, and that anyone who attempts to do anything contrary to what this power allows will find himself opposed by practically unlimited money, which can be used first to corrupt all sources of help, including state insurance-law enforcers, and then to keep such corruptions from the policyholders by subsidizing the press. In other words, you see that I fully comprehend that I, or any man or any body of men, would be absolutely helpless in an attempt to correct present evils unless we could do two things: first, show to the policyholders of the great insurance companies that they are absolutely in the hands and at the mercy of 'one man,' and next, that this 'one man' is unscrupulous."

My charge that the directors of the great life insurance corporations of America use the funds of the companies they control in stock speculation for their personal benefit is but one contention in my argument against the character of their management. Here I formally add another charge: it is that in the placing of loans, in the purchase of properties and securities, and in the underwriting of enterprises, there are enormous profits made, directly and indirectly, which are pocketed by individuals and are never shown on the books of the corporation.

The basis of life insurance is security. A policyholder pays his premium to enable the corporation accepting it to make good its contract with him when death or time matures it. The vast sums in the possession of the three great companies are accumulated to safeguard their policyholders and should be invested only in securities of tried and solid worth, which will bring in no more nor less than the going rate of interest. There must be no experiments and, above all, no speculation.

But what do we find? The positions of managers and manipulators of these huge hoards of the people's money have become the greatest financial prizes of the day. New and ingenious methods of graft have been devised in connection with them. The vast revenues of the insurance companies have become the "System's" most potent instrument in working its will in the stock world. Their investments, largely in the securities of properties or corporations in which the "System's" votaries have large interests, are fertile sources of profit to the "insiders." The groups of banks and trust companies affiliated with them are the medium through which access to the coveted insurance funds is obtained, for these institutions are allowed by law to use money for speculative purposes, which the insurance concerns are prohibited from doing.

The immense opportunities for profit afforded by the control of these great money hoards are taken advantage of in various ways. Let me illustrate one or two of them. Rogers, Rockefeller, Stillman and Morgan buy the capital stock of three railways at a fair valuation, say, $20,000,000 apiece, $60,000,000 for the three. Owning all, or nearly all, the stock, they can put its price on the stock exchanges to any figure they desire, say, $60,000,000 for each railway, or $180,000,000 in all. They proceed to deposit the stocks of the three roads in a trust company, issuing against them $180,000,000 of what they call "bonds." An "underwriting" syndicate is then organized. This is composed of certain individuals and corporations who agree that when these bonds are offered to the public at $180,000,000, the portion the public does not buy, they (the "underwriters") will purchase on the basis of $120,000,000; in other words, they guarantee the sale of the bonds at $180,000,000. In return they "make" on all the bonds sold the difference between the price to them, $120,000,000, and the price the public pays, $180,000,000. Let us assume that the public takes up the issue greedily and the full price, $180,000,000, has been secured. The original owners, Rogers, Rockefeller, etc., have made $60,000,000, the difference between the first cost and $120,000,000, the cost to the "underwriters," while the "underwriters" have made $60,000,000, the difference between $120,000,000 and the $180,000,000, the cost to the people. In looking over the list of subscribers to these bonds, you will note that the largest purchases have been made for the great insurance corporations and the banks and trust companies owned or controlled by them and the "System." If, in the instance I am using for illustration, a president or vice-president of one of the great insurance companies is known to be willing to subscribe for, say, $10,000,000 for his insurance company; $5,000,000 for his principal trust company, which is owned by the insurance company; $1,000,000 apiece for five other banks and trust companies, also owned or controlled by the insurance company; and can influence five other affiliated institutions to subscribe for $1,000,000 apiece, he controls, as will readily be seen, a purchasing power of $25,000,000, and is sought for as an underwriter, if he is not already an owner. For this $25,000,000 which his institutions buy he "draws down," as his personal profit, 33⅓ per cent "under-writers'" commission, or over eight millions of dollars.

In taking this amount, he is not *robbing* his insurance company, in the common acceptance of the term in this era of "frenzied finance," though he has absolutely appropriated to himself a profit which belongs to it and not to him.

It must not be supposed that such transactions as this I have outlined are conducted in the simple ABC fashion I have set down here for purpose of illustration. No "one man" appears through any deal. The purchases and sales are usually made through dummies, and the final recipient of the "made millions" carefully conceals all the phases of his participation.

Let us take another type of transaction. An insurance company owns two adjoining pieces of unimproved city real estate, for which it paid $250,000 apiece, but which are now worth $500,000 each. The directors of the corporation formally decide to dispose of these holdings, and sell the first piece to a trust company, which is owned or con-trolled by the insurance company. One of the "System's" dummies or an officer or director of the corporation agrees to take the other at the same price. This is a perfectly legitimate transaction, and the insurance company shows a half million profit on its investment. The next step is this. On its piece the trust company erects a $2,000,000 building, procur-ing the money from the insurance company at a low rate of interest. Thereupon the value of the adjoining piece bought by the "System's" votary jumps 50 per cent, so he has made $250,000 without risking a dollar. At the same time there have been several other profitable trans-actions between institutions and individuals. The agent who disposed of the two pieces of real estate and who is "in" the transaction receives a generous commission for making the sales; the trust company's representative has his own "draw-down," and there are further com-missions to the agents who borrow and loan the money and control the erection of the building.

My readers may well ask, Are these merely illustrations, or do such things really take place? I unqualifiedly reply that deals similar to these have occurred repeatedly and that the principle and procedure set forth are the rule and not exceptional. Here is a minor episode of which I have personal knowledge. A well-known man made direct application to the Mutual Life Insurance Company for a loan of $400,000 on a valuable city business block which he owned. He was told that the corporation had no funds available for that purpose. The refusal was authoritative and definite. A few days later a lawyer and real estate agent came to his office and said to him: "I'm informed that you want $400,000 on your property. I can let you have it, or $500,000 if you need that much."

"Good," said the would-be borrower, "I will take it. Whose money is it?"

"The Mutual's."

"My dear fellow," said the would-be borrower, "how can that be? I was there at the office a few days ago and was assured I could not have the money."

"That's all right," was the answer. "Of course you could not get the money. The right party did not see the right party. D'ye understand?"

He understood.

All this is preliminary to treating the case of the Prudential Insurance Company. I want to say here that I do not know the corporation, any of its officers, nor anyone interested in the control or management of it, and personally have never had the slightest connection with its officers. I desire to prove through an outsider, someone of unquestioned authority, that the great insurance companies are part of the "System" and are engaged in manipulating the stock market with the funds their policyholders put in their hands as a sacred trust. In so far as the Prudential is concerned, rank and unsound as are the transactions I am about to speak of, my investigations have proved to me that this insurance corporation is only as a baby carriage to a runaway automobile compared with the three great representatives of the "System," the New York Life, the Mutual, and the Equitable. Certain critics have accused me of being unduly emphatic in my strictures on the doings of the corporations of which I am treating. I will confess to a secret amusement at being able, in this instance, to quote the language of one of the most conservative insurance officials in America, Frederick L. Cutting, for many years Insurance Commissioner for the State of Massachusetts.

The Prudential Life Insurance Company has $2,000,000 capital stock. The stock is owned and the company absolutely controlled by a few men. This capital of $2,000,000 represents only $91,000 paid in in cash; the balance has been derived from stock dividends; that is, profits that have been made out of policyholders. In addition to this enormous amount there has been paid 10 per cent in cash dividends annually, so that for every thousand dollars paid in, the stockholders hold $22,000 of stock, upon which they receive annually $2,200, or, as Commissioner Cutting puts it, "each year for ten years the stockholders have received in cash dividends more than twice the original investment." I commend to the policyholders of the Prudential and other insurance corporations, and to other honest men, these tremendous figures; every $1,000 invested turned into $22,000, not in a gold or diamond mine, but in a life insurance company where every dollar comes from the policyholder who is supposed to pay in only enough to insure a promised payment plus provision for honest expense.

The Prudential Company owned the stock of the Fidelity Trust Company, the capital of which was $1,500,000, and the directors came before Commissioner Cutting and informed him that they proposed to double up the stock of the Fidelity Trust Company to $3,000,000; that the new $1,500,000 at a par value of $100 was to be sold for $750 per share; that the new stock was to be bought by the Prudential Company and the Equitable Company; and that with the proceeds of the sale, the Trust Company was to buy a control of the Prudential Company from its directors. The motive of this transaction was as follows: the set of men who absolutely controlled the Prudential, with its sixty millions of assets belonging to its policyholders, proposed to control it for all time, but without tying up $7,000,000 of their own money in the business. In other words, they desired to eat their pudding and yet have it for continuous re-eating, and had found a way to accomplish this heretofore impossible feat.

By this plan the men who controlled the Prudential Company, and thereby the Trust Company, at the time the plan went into force, would forever continue to manage and control both institutions, although not one of them held a policy or any investment in the insurance company beyond the one share of stock required by law to qualify as director.

If this scheme had been consummated it would have borne to "frenzied finance" the same relationship that perpetual motion does to mechanics. By it a few men could gamble forever with the entire assets of the policyholders of this corporation for their own personal benefit. If my readers will imagine the same scheme applied to several other great insurance companies and the men controlling them, the "System's" votaries, they will recognize the "System's" ideal world, with all the people in a condition of ideal servitude. However, this ingenious plan was forestalled because there happened to be in control of the life insurance affairs of Massachusetts one of those old-fashioned relics of American honesty—a man who thought more of the interests of the people intrusted to his care than of the prospect of innumerable "made dollars" which might have been his had he proved more amenable. It is regrettable that he was not able to deprive the conspirators of their power to juggle with the property of the corporation, for only two weeks later they developed and executed an alternative device which practically accomplished the result which the Massachusetts authorities had declared illegal and the courts of New Jersey had enjoined.

Everybody's Magazine (later reprinted in book form, titled
Frenzied Finance)
1905

RAILROADS

THE RAILROADS—the first large-scale business to develop in this country—grew up too fast for the laws of the country to keep up with them. By the turn of the century, they had consolidated their power and integrated their lines. Any legislative action to control them, which had been passed in the 1880s and 1890s, was now a mere mockery.

The transcontinental rail lines were completed in the eighties; by 1890 there were 167,000 miles of railroad, by 1900 there were 198,964 railroad miles; in 1910, 249,992.

The railroad controlled the life of the West and Midwest. It could settle the destiny of a town by either passing through it or by-passing it. The farmer was absolutely dependent on it since the railroad was his only means of shipping his crops to market and bringing back the manufactured goods.

Frank Norris hit on a likely metaphor when he called the railroads "the Octopus." This octopus told the farmer what he could charge for his grain and cattle; it set the price of land; it influenced legislation and was responsible for political corruption. It showed favoritism in setting rates, and rebates were a normal part of its operation.

Farmers through their Granges demanded state regulation, and the first state regulatory laws which are known as "Granger Laws" were passed between 1869 and 1874 by Illinois, Minnesota, Iowa and Wisconsin.

Most other states were to pass such laws in the next decade. These laws generally prohibited rate discrimination, outlawed the consolidation of railroads running parallel lines and set maximum rates.

The railroads objected to such legislation on two grounds: first, that state regulation of railroad rates is in violation of the "due process law"; and second, that most railroad traffic was interstate—hence not under the jurisdiction of the individual state.

When Congress passed the Interstate Commerce Act in 1887, Federal control of railroads was officially initiated. Among the provisions of this act was the outlawing of special rates and rebates. Also, higher rate charges for short hauls over long ones were made illegal.

The enforcement of the law was placed in the hands of the Interstate Commerce Commission, which was in reality only a fact-finding board.

If it wanted to enforce any of its findings, it had to press the matter in the courts.

The abuses of the railroads continued. The railroads evaded the laws and the courts practically always ruled in their favor.

Laws to restrain railroads were openly flouted. "As late as 1906, Roosevelt credited Harriman with saying that 'he could buy a sufficient number of Senators and Congressmen or State Legislators to protect his interests, and when necessary he could buy the Judiciary.' " [118]

U.S. Senator Robert Marion LaFollette of Wisconsin fought the railroads and demanded new legislation; the popular magazines hammered away at this issue; and to them was added the strong ally of President Roosevelt, who urged Federal legislation for a more effective regulation of the railroads.

The muckrakers brought the issues to the public. B. O. Flower in *The Arena* pinpointed the issues before LaFollette came to Washington. Passes, rebates, accidents and deaths on the railroads, as well as the evils of the private car, were "exposed."

Ellery Sedgwick, who never considered himself a muckraker, nevertheless wrote about the accident and death rates in *Leslie's*, and "to the future editor of *The Atlantic Monthly*, and to his magazine *Leslie's*, must go credit for a campaign which did much to bring government regulation of the railroads." [119]

Mark Sullivan wrote an article on "The Way of a Railroad" [120] in which he muckraked the "courtesy pass," an early twentieth-century form of "payola," and in his hands as well as in those of other muckrakers, the pass became "a symbol of railroad misrule." [121]

Ray Stannard Baker wrote on the railroads for both *Collier's* and *McClure's*. In *Collier's* he wrote "Railroads and Popular Unrest," [122] and in *McClure's* a series of articles on "Railroads on Trial."

In announcing the Baker series, *McClure's* proclaimed: "Charges of the utmost seriousness have been, for a long time, and are now being preferred against the men who control and operate the railroads of the country. They are at this moment upon trial, not merely because President Roosevelt has called a special session of Congress to decide whether these men have properly conducted the large interests intrusted to their care, but they are on trial before the higher court of public opinion." [123]

Baker wrote to President Roosevelt, asking him if he would like to see the proofs of his first article. The President responded that he would like to see the proofs "not because of any good I can do you, but because I have learned to look to your articles for real help." [124]

The proofs were mailed and within days the President wrote to Baker again: "I haven't a criticism to suggest about the article. You have given me two or three thoughts for my own message."

The first article in the series started in November 1905, and its sights were set on rates, then on rebates; an article on the private car and the beef trust followed; then came an article on the private car and the fruit industry. Finally, an "exposure" of "How Railroads Make Public Opinion."

In December 1905, Roosevelt in a message to Congress called for "government supervision and regulation of rates charged by the railroads." This was followed shortly by the introduction of a bill by Representative Hepburn of Idaho in the House of Representatives.

The Hepburn Act, which was passed May 18, 1906, gave the Interstate Commerce Commission authority to regulate rates; extended its jurisdiction to cover storage and terminal facilities, sleeping cars, express companies, and pipe lines; and it forced the railroads to give up their interests in steamship lines and coal companies. Free passes were abolished, except for railway employes, the clergy and some charitable workers.

Baker's "scholarly and convincing indictment of railroad malpractices" strengthened "President Roosevelt's hand in the battle to enlarge the powers of the Interstate Commerce Commission." [125]

The Independent asserted that passage of the Hepburn Act was "due chiefly to the men with the muckrake."

RAY STANNARD BAKER

Railroads on Trial

All free governments, whatever their name, are in reality governments by public opinion and it is on the quality of this public opinion that their prosperity depends. . . . With the growth of democracy grows also the fear, if not the danger, that this atmosphere may be corrupted . . . and the question of sanitation becomes more instant and pressing. Democracy in its best sense is merely the letting in of light and air.

JAMES RUSSELL LOWELL

T HE PEOPLE are today making up their minds on the railroad problem; out of their present decision will grow laws, and those laws will shape the destiny of the nation. It becomes of incalculable importance, then, to know where the information upon which we now base our thinking is coming from. Are the sources clear? Is the information true?

Railroad owners were undisguisedly astonished last winter by the force of the public demand for railroad legislation; it drove the Esch-Townsend bill through the House of Representatives almost without opposition. Such a measure threatened the existing unrestrained private control of railroad corporations and endangered the prestige of the men who own them.

Though the popular bill was stopped at the doors of an unwilling Senate, the railroad men knew that unless public opinion was modified, other legislation, perhaps more drastic, would be sought when Congress convened this winter. Accordingly they undertook to counteract or modify the swelling force of unfriendly opinion and to create in its place a more favorable regard. Since Congress adjourned last spring, they have been engaged in what is undoubtedly the most sweeping campaign for reaching and changing public thought ever undertaken in this country. No investigation into the meanings of the railroad problem as it now presents itself in this country can be regarded as complete, which does not take cognizance of these remarkable activities.

Consider the conditions. A great cloud had come up out of the West; it was black with complaints against railroad injustice and represented the undoubted sentiments of the people, it owed its expression largely to certain shippers and business organizations. And finally it was voiced by President Roosevelt, and definite legislation was demanded.

But the people, however vigorous their demands for reform, are undisciplined and unorganized. They are torn by petty local interests and they are busy. To make the giant bestir himself the issues must be made very clear and the feeling must be deep. By presenting new information, new issues, new arguments, it is therefore evident that a publicity organization may either convince or confuse public opinion so that it does not settle with undivided mind upon definite demands and stick to them until reforms are attained.

Railroad men have a perfect right, of course, in common with all other citizens, to present facts and arguments to the people. The more true publicity there is the better, for the public mind should not only be made up, but made up right. But the people have a duty to inquire concerning the sources of the information they are getting; they are entitled to know, when a man is presenting an argument, whether he represents himself or is paid by someone else. It is one thing to inform the public mind; another thing to deceive it. And finally the people have not only a right but a duty to inquire if the facts which they are receiving are true facts. Perhaps there was never before in our history such need of intelligent discrimination and analysis upon the part of the people as there is at this moment; it is a sort of supreme test of the nation: whether we know enough, whether we are brave enough, to deserve a real democracy.

Wall Street, accordingly, with characteristic thoroughness, organized a campaign; and a committee of three men was appointed to direct operations: Samuel Spencer, president of the Southern Railroad; F. D. Underwood, president of the Erie; and David Wilcox, president of the Delaware & Hudson.

Upon Mr. Spencer fell the main responsibility of the work, and for several reasons. In the first place, he had for years made his headquarters in Washington, the central office of the Southern Railroad, where he naturally formed the acquaintance of many senators and congressmen; and he had come to know all the by-paths of legislative activity. An experienced, agreeable, discreet man, he was well fitted for the task. To him the railroads of the country, sharing the burden, contributed all the necessary money. The extent of the various enterprises of the organization will enable us to form some idea of how large a sum was required.

Several channels exist through which public opinion may be reached: newspapers, and magazines, perhaps, first of all; speeches, lectures, and sermons; books; conventions; investigations.

The fountainhead of public information is the newspaper. The first concern, then, of the railroad organization was to reach the newspapers.

For this purpose a firm of publicity agents, with headquarters in Boston, was chosen. Their business was not extensive, but both members of the firm were able and energetic; and both had had a thorough training in the newspaper business. They had represented high-class clients; notably Harvard University.

Immediately the firm expanded. It increased its Boston staff; it opened offices in New York, Chicago, Washington, St. Louis, Topeka, Kansas—Kansas being regarded as especially threatening—and it employed agents in South Dakota, California and elsewhere. I can, perhaps, give the clearest idea of the scope of the work by describing the activities of a single branch office—that in Chicago.

The firm occupies rooms in the Orchestra Building on Michigan Avenue. Its employees in Chicago alone number forty-three. Foremost among these are a corps of experienced newspaper men.

To this office comes every publication of any sort within the Chicago territory—every little village paper in Nebraska, Wisconsin, Illinois, and other states. All of these are carefully scanned by experienced readers and every article in any way touching upon the railroad question is clipped out and filed. But the bureau does not depend upon the papers alone. Traveling agents have visited every town in the country and have seen, personally, every editor, the circulation of his paper, whether he is prosperous or not, his political beliefs, his views on the trust problem, on the liquor question, even on religious subjects, the peculiar character of his paper, whether devoted mostly to local news, or whether expressing vigorous editorial opinions. Moreover, there are notations dealing with peculiar industrial and commercial interests of each town—its weaknesses and its strength. In short, reading some of the cards in this catalogue I could almost see the little villages out in the Mississippi Valley, see the country editor in his small office, and understand all his hopes, fears, ambitions.

Possessed of this knowledge, how adroitly and perfectly the well-equipped publicity agents can play upon each town and influence each editor! Every card bears also, in columns, a list of numbers. Every number refers to an article sent out by the firm. Most of these articles are especially prepared by the staff writers for a certain town, or a group of towns. There is no confused firing of wasteful volleys; each shot is carefully aimed. It is really interesting material often mingled with valuable matter on other subjects, and the country editor, like every editor, is eager for the good things. In cases I know of the railroads have employed very able correspondents at state capitals, or at Washington, who sent daily or weekly letters on various subjects, but never failing to work in masked material favorable to the railroads. Often, perhaps usually, the editor has no idea of where this material comes from. It apparently drops out of the blue heavens like a sort of manna—for these publicity agents are careful not to advertise the fact that they are in any way connected with the railroads.

Having sent out an article to an editor, the readers closely watch his paper, and when it appears, the number in the card catalogue is checked in red. A glance at a card, therefore, will instantly reveal how many and what sort of railroad articles every paper in the country is publishing, how railroad information is running high in one community and low in another—whether a paper is "good" or "bad" from the standpoint of the railroads.

This card catalogue is well named in the office "The Barometer." It is certainly as good an indicator of the atmosphere of railroad opinion in the country as could possibly be devised. It gives the observer, indeed, an impression of hopeless perfection. What chance have feeble, unorganized outsiders to make and register public opinion in the face of such a machine?

Does it get results? Indeed it does. One of the members of the firm told me with pride of the record in Nebraska. In the week ended June 5 [1905] last, the newspapers of that state published exactly 212 columns of material unfavorable to the railroads, and only two columns favorable. Eleven weeks later, after a careful campaign, a week's record showed that the papers of Nebraska had published 202 columns FAVORABLE to the railroads and FOUR unfavorable. A pretty good barometric condition!

But the work is by no means confined to the offices. If an editor is found to be radically anti-railroad, as frequently happens in the West, an agent goes about among shipping and commercial organizations of the town and stirs up public opinion against the editor. Now, shippers and businessmen generally are peculiarly subject to railroad influence or discrimination. A very little thing will put them wrong with the railroad. Consequently, when the railroad asks a favor that costs nothing—like the signing of a petition, or the writing of a letter— why, they are inclined to yield and avoid trouble. Moreover, it is of familiar knowledge that the politicians in many towns are pro-railroad. Usually one or more of the prominent lawyers are retained by the railroads, and there is always the local railroad staff to be counted upon.

All these forces are so cunningly marshaled that the recalcitrant editor is "smoked out" by his own people.

Now, I have no evidence that this particular firm of publicity agents had any "corruption fund" or that they PAID editors to support the railroad cause. Moreover, I do not believe, knowing something of the character of the men, that they have done it in any instance. Their position was this: they owned a publicity machine—a highly intelligent one. They sold its services to the railroads and thereafter they sent out railroad arguments just as they would have sent out baking-powder arguments if they had been employed by a baking-powder company— without wasting a moment's thought apparently as to what effect their action might have upon the public welfare.

Two points must be emphasized. In the first place, these agents conducted their operations secretly. It is a principle that the attorney must declare what client he defends. If these agents had appeared frankly before the court of public opinion as railroad employees, no one could have quarreled with them; and they would have deceived no one. And why, if the railroad men have a really good argument, should they not make it openly and frankly?

In the second place, against such an organization as this, supplied with unlimited money, representing a private interest which wishes to defeat the public will, to break the law, to enjoy the fruits of unrestrained power, what chance to be heard have those who believe that present conditions are wrong? The people are unorganized, they have no money to hire agents, nor experts to make investigations, nor writers to set forth the facts attractively. The result is that the public gets chiefly the facts as prepared by the railroad for their own defense. The case is exactly that of the rich litigant who goes before the court with lawyers, experts, and unlimited money to combat the poor litigant who must appear without lawyers or experts whom he has no money to hire. And in this case the rich litigant represents the few thousand railroad owners and those powerful shippers who are favored by railroad discrimination, and the poor litigant is the great unorganized public. . . .

Besides the direct preparation of articles for newspapers, these publicity agents send out enormous numbers of publications in pamphlet and book form.

Now, it is a good thing for the people to have all these arguments; provided THEY KNOW THE SOURCE FROM WHICH THE ARGUMENTS COME and provided THE OTHER SIDE HAS AN EQUAL OPPORTUNITY TO PRESENT ITS CASE. Editors, professors in colleges, prominent lawyers, clergymen and other public men, anyone, indeed, who is likely to have even a little influence in his community, have been supplied with much of this railroad literature. Most of the pamphlets are not on their face railroad arguments at all, but are seemingly perfectly dispassionate and unprejudiced discussions of the problem. I have a collection of fifty-six such books and pamphlets, all different, issued within the last few months. The literature varies all the way from a cloth-bound book of 486 pages to a leaflet of four pages. Since I began my present series of articles on the railroad question I have had at least thirty copies of one of them, a small book prepared by H. T. Newcomb of Washington, called *Facts About the Railroads,* sent to me from various parts of the country by people who wanted to know where it came from, and whether or not it was a railroad publicity pamphlet. These various publications are planned to reach every interest. One is addressed to the farmers, called *The Farmer and His Friends,* another is for workers, another is a book of 206 pages for lawyers, discussing the legal aspects of the question, with careful summaries of decisions. There are many pamphlets for editors, containing reprints from editorials published by papers in various parts of the country—SOME OF THEM HAVING BEEN ORIGINALLY WRITTEN IN THE OFFICE OF THE PUBLICITY AGENTS and sent out to the newspapers. . . .

McClure's Magazine
March 1906

PART SEVEN

The Church

It is not enough that men give money, they must give themselves: and the same is true of the churches.

RAY STANNARD BAKER, "The Godlessness of
New York," *American*, June 1909

A FRANCHISE was granted to Trinity in 1697 by the English kingdom for a parish church to be located at the head of Wall Street for "the use and in behalf of the inhabitants from time to time inhabiting and to inhabit within our said city of New York, in communion of our said Protestant Church of England, as now establisht by our laws." The franchise specified that this should be the "sole and only parish church in the city of New York." Eight years after this, the church was given a grant of land which later became the great bulk of its holdings. In 1788, after the separation of the United States from England, the corporation name changed from "Protestant Church of England" to "Protestant Episcopal Church in the State of New York."

By 1788, the corporation had three churches: Trinity, which was the church proper, and two chapels: St. George's on Beekman Street and St. Paul's on Vesey Street. The city and the number of people grew. By 1793 Christ Church, a separate and rival congregation, was created. It was refused admission to the Convention because Trinity was by franchise the "sole and only parish" in the city. Later, however, St. Mark's, first a Trinity chapel, was set apart as a separate church and Trinity gave some land, and then followed other separate churches, to which Trinity gave both her blessings and some land.

The land originally given Trinity developed as the city grew, and by the early twentieth century was rich with all types of property. That part used for church and educational purposes was not taxed. Along much of their other property, particularly that surrounding the church proper at the head of Wall Street, a horde of tenements had sprung up, and Trinity was reaping huge financial benefits.

The downtown neighborhood started to change and the wealthy moved uptown. In 1852 Trinity Corporation appropriated $230,000 to build Trinity chapel on West Twenty-fifth Street. In 1890 St. Agnes on West Ninety-second Street was built for $500,000. At the same time, the corporation discontinued its missionary work downtown. In 1909 Trinity summarily tried to close St. John's, one of its oldest chapels in downtown New York, with close to 500 members, on the theory that it didn't pay and they could use the money elsewhere to better advantage.

This brought forth a comment from Dr. John P. Peters, rector of St. Michael's Protestant Episcopal Church, New York: "The appropriation granted for the maintenance of St. John's was counted as a benevolent dole given to the poor; the similar appropriations to the well-to-do congregations of Trinity and St. Agnes were regarded as their right. The well-to-do congregations had representatives in the Corporation, the poor congregations had none. In principle, the methods of the insurance scandal were repeated here." [126]

The Trinity tenement properties were notorious for their squalor and filth; they were breeding places for disease, particularly tuberculosis. Hundreds of rickety firetraps; sanitation limited to backyard sheds. Trinity fought each new improvement law—one case even going to court, where they lost and eventually had to comply by installing tap water on each floor of a tenement building.

Originally, the muckrakers had focused their attention on national and business affairs. Eventually, however, they began to study local conditions and it was not long before Trinity with its tenement housing came under the muckrake.

Ray Stannard Baker's "The Case Against Trinity" in *The American Magazine*, July 1909, indicted Trinity Church for the way it ran its holdings, and its autocracy over its chapels. He criticized the church in that it failed to live up to its duty, but made it clear that it was the institution he was criticizing, and not religion. This particular article was part of a series Baker did for the magazine on "The Spiritual Unrest" which was published in 1908 and 1909.

In April-May 1908, Charles Edward Russell told the story of "Trinity: Church of Mystery," in *Broadway* (later *Hampton's*) *Magazine*.

Russell in his autobiography says: "The series, with its photographs of conditions and its array of indubitable facts, started a cyclone of resentment, particularly in our highest social circles.

"The Reverend Morgan Dix, chief pastor of Trinity, died in the midst of the engagement and it was poignantly suggested that grief and chagrin over the attacks upon his corporation had caused his death." [127]

Everybody's in July 1908 published Russell's "The Tenements of Trinity Church." In introducing the article, *Everybody's* editors wrote that it "aims to describe the actual condition of some of these Trinity tenements and to give an idea of their relation to the health and security of the city. It also raises a very great and interesting question: whether the good wrought by the charitable and philanthropic enterprises of Trinity equals the evil wrought by the tenements that finance the charities."

In answer to letters of criticism which appeared in *Everybody's* after Russell's article, Russell wrote an article titled "Trinity's Tenements—The

Public's Business," in which he stated that the public was minding its own business, as it was told to do by a reader, whom Russell took to be a Trinity trustee. It is up to the public, wrote Russell, to take care of the public health. In this respect, the fact that the tenements are laden with germs makes it its business. On a business basis, since the tenement properties are depressed, taxes are low, and the rest of New York's citizens must make up the difference.[128]

In his book *The Battle with the Slum*, Jacob Riis said, "Trinity, the wealthiest church corporation in the land, was in constant opposition as a tenement house landlord, and finally, to save a few hundred dollars, came near upsetting the whole structure of tenement law that had been built up in the interest of the toilers and of the city's safety with such infinite pains." [129]

Twenty-five years after his articles on Trinity appeared, Russell wrote in his autobiography: "The smoke of battle finally cleared away. Trinity had the usual vindication, the wickedness of the muckraker was satisfactorily demonstrated and all was once more peace. Then Trinity began quietly to pull down its objectionable tenements." It is estimated that in the next three years after the articles some scores of these "filthy old barracks disappeared from the face of the earth." [130]

In April 1910, *Hampton's* editorialized: "We are as ready to praise as to attack. Therefore, we are glad to announce, upon reliable authority, that Trinity Corporation has torn down, since the publication of these articles [about two years previously] about four blocks of its miserable tenements in New York City, and is showing a disposition to clean up at least a part of its property."

CHARLES EDWARD RUSSELL

The Tenements of Trinity Church

O N THE LOWER West Side of New York City, in the old Eighth
Ward and not far from the docks, is a place called Hudson
Park, where in certain poor piles of sand the little children of the
tenements sometimes come to play.

It is not much of a park; a little slice of rescued city space, a mere
glimpse of open sky, a part of a city block without the usual hideous
city houses and set with weary trees, uncertain grass, some rigid
benches—no more than that. In the center, a curious and unreasonable
depression adorned with some doubtful classicism, and at the rear the
sand piles where the chalk-faced children play. That is all.

And yet you, looking upon it, poor and forlorn as it is, feel in your
heart an impulse to fall upon your knees there in the reek of the
filthy street and utter gratitude for even so much. All about you to the
south blink the frowsy, scaly, slatternly, bleary, decayed and crumbling
old houses, leering from dirty windows like old drunkards through blood-
shot eyes; the broken shutters awry like deformities, the doors agape like
old, toothless mouths. All about is the hell of the West Side tenement-
house region, and compared with its outward and visible signs, this
maidenhood of Hudson Park, albeit ill-clad and gawky, is something
sweet. You think back upon the years of dreary struggle and contest
and argument and travail that were required to secure this little island
of sanity in the mad region around you, and wonder to yourself if we
are all perfectly crazy that we tolerate such things.

Drunken, disreputable, decayed, topsyturvy old houses, the homes
of thousands of families and the breeding places for so many children
that are to carry on the world's work—who owns these terrible places?
Who draws the wretched profit of their existence?

311

Trinity Church, holder of one of the greatest estates in New York or in the country, owns many of them. This is the heart of her possessions: street after street is lined with her properties. Here is Clarkson Street, on the south of the tiny park—she owns a dozen tenement properties there; Varick Street, crossing Clarkson at right angles—she owns sixty-six tenement properties there; West Houston, noisome and dilapidated—she owns fifty-one tenement properties there; upper Greenwich Street—she owns sixty-five tenement properties there; Charlton Street, a dreary place—she owns twenty-six tenement properties there; Canal Street toward the North River—she owns forty-seven tenement properties there; Hudson Street—she owns 138 tenement properties there. You do not think well of the appearance of Vandam Street; Trinity owns forty-one tenement properties there. You think Barrow Street down here looks ancient and seedy; Trinity owns twenty-two tenement properties there. Wherever you walk in this dreadful region, you find something that Trinity owns, and, as a rule, it is something that you know she ought not to own.

For this is the state to which have come certain cabbage fields and swamplands once (in the earliest days of New York) bestowed upon the church by the careless hand of the good Queen Anne; this is the Jans farm of the ancient days; this is the wealth that the sheer growth of New York has made for Trinity; and this is the fortune that by the managers of this remarkable church is guarded with a strange secrecy and care. It owns in the city property worth, according to different estimators, from $39,000,000 to $100,000,000, from which it draws an enormous revenue, the amount of which is never made public. For many years no investigator has been able to obtain any more definite knowledge of these matters than that this is the wealth of Trinity which she holds for good purposes.

What? Expressed in wretched, rotten, old tenement houses? Yes. Expressed in hundreds of such tenement houses.

I have before me the testimony of a very eminent authority about tenement houses, and she says that confirmed tenement house dwellers are as a class sickly, anemic, lethargic, and show unmistakable tendencies toward constitutional weakness. Tuberculosis has a strong hold upon them; the effect of tenement house life is such that the third generation of tenement house dwellers (if you can conceive of a third generation) is usually of an inferior mentality, without intelligent interest in anything, leads dull and vacant lives, and furnishes recruits for the reformatory and the state prison.

It appears, therefore, that while the charities established by Trinity since 1857 * are trying to lead men upward, the Trinity tenements, with an irresistible force, are crushing men downward; and we are therefore presented at once with a very memorable spectacle of the contradictions and inconsistencies of this our mortal state.

Because the tenement, speaking generally, works ill, Trinity's tenements must be a matter of grave concern to us all, Trinity's tenements must work more than common ill, for they are the worst tenements in New York.

One reason why they are the worst is that they were never designed for tenements at all.

They are the residences that a century ago began to show from St. John's Park northward the growth of the young city. Two-story and basement houses, most of them, they were planned in every case to be the homes each of a single family. You can imagine, then, the results when, with an amazing parsimony in repairs and alterations, these same houses are made to shelter five or six families. But unless you have been there, you cannot possibly imagine the horrible dirt and neglect and slovenliness that are spread over so many of these places.

Is it not strange? No, it is not strange; it is only a part of a yellow wizardry that in many ways gives to the management of Trinity Corporation an aspect furtive and mysterious, that seems to impel it to many courses inconsistent with candor and to bewitch many good men engaged in the conduct of its affairs. Profit, much profit, very great profit, lies in property of this sort; it yields much to the golden stream. These are houses that old-time tenants built on land let from Trinity on short leases. When the leases expired, Trinity, following a consistent and profitable policy, refused to grant renewals—to the late tenants. It also refused to purchase the house that the tenant had built. The tenant, therefore, was confronted with this situation: he could tear his house down brick by brick and cart it away to the dump or the river; or he could abandon it (as it stood) to Trinity, sometimes for nothing, sometimes for a nominal sum. These are houses, therefore, in which the investment of Trinity was almost nothing, possibly an average of $200 each, and now from these same houses she gathers $40 or $50 a month for rent, paying out nothing for repairs.

Some of these houses are brick, some are wooden. Very few of them are fit under any circumstances for any human habitation. Not one of them is fit for human habitation as at present it is inhabited.

---

* Trinity was investigated in 1857 by a Committee of the State Senate. One result was a report severely condemning the church for its apparent indifference to charitable enterprises and religious benevolence.

Tastes differ. I know that the vestry of Trinity would be terribly shocked at a suggestion that the corporation should make money by administering arsenic to people, or carbolic acid, or deadly nightshade. But the vestry or the standing committee that represents it in these matters has no objection whatever to making money for the corporation by maintaining poisonous tenements.

As between tuberculosis and arsenic, where lies the choice?

Suppose now we turn us from these reflections (which may be supposed to threaten the sacred basis of the social edifice) and see how the facts stand. We will imagine that we guide a party of inquiring and well-fed tourists to whom the tenement house is merely a name, comfortable and genial tourists, that sleep o'nights. We take you first into one of the tenement houses that blink out disreputably about the little park and gather much income for Trinity, a tenement house in Clarkson Street near Hudson. It presents to the street a dirty brick front, scaly, like its fellows, and long demanding paint. Come inside and see how you like it. Four floors there are, three of them made into dwellings for families, two dwellings on a floor. An old house, very old, very poorly built, very flimsy, very ramshackle. Everything about it seems going to decay. The halls are narrow, dark, dirty, and smell abominably. The stairways are narrow, wooden and insecure. On the second and third floors are interior bedrooms that have no natural light nor ventilation, and must therefore, according to the Board of Health, be a prolific breeding place for the germs of tuberculosis. A horrible, mephitic odor and the dampness that clings about old cellars and sunless courts seem to strike against you with a physical impact. You know that in this heavy and sickly air is no place to rear men and women.*

The only sanitation for the families dwelling in this dreadful house is to be found in wooden sheds in the back yard. It is of a nature that one might expect to see in Chinese cities, but never in the foremost city of America. The back yard is a horror into which you set your foot with an uncontrollable physical revulsion against the loathsome contamination. It has much rubbish, it is vilely unkempt, it seems to exude vileness. The water supply in the house consists of one common tap for each floor, placed in the hall. Formerly even these primitive conveniences did not exist, and the overwrought women that live in these houses were obliged to carry in pails up the steep stairs the water supply, each for her household. The water tap on each floor was com-

---

* I am pleased to state that this particular building has now been sold to the city and is about to be demolished.

manded by the new Tenement House Law, and it was this feature of the law that Trinity most opposed.

In the rear, reached by a narrow passage, is another tenement house, a four-story brick building, occupied, when I was there, by seven families. If the front tenement is bad, what shall we say of the tenement in the rear? Whatever is abominable in the one is more abominable in the other. The gloom is worse, the ventilation is worse, the aspect of dreary decay and neglect is worse. Some of the dwellers in the front house can get air and light; most of the dwellers in the rear house can get very little of either. When the building was new and clean, it might have been a tolerable place in which to house horses—temporarily; say for a day. It was never, at any time, a tolerable place in which to house human beings. For fifty or sixty years it has been unfit for anything except burning. How would you like to draw an income from the maintaining of such a place? You would want to have the money disinfected before it touched your hand, would you not? Lest into your presence it bear some odor of the rear tenement, or some bacteria from the interior bedrooms, or from the filthy courts.

Come, then, into the filthy little back yards at the rear of No. 20 Clarkson Street, and, looking over the rotting fences, you may discover a peculiarity of many of the houses in this region. The front walls are of brick; the rear and side walls are wooden. On the wooden walls the clapboards sag and sway and are falling off, the ancient laths and plaster are exposed beneath. Window panes are broken out. On one of the days when I was there, a bitter day in December, an icy wind blew through these apertures. I went into some of the living rooms. There were women and children around the fire in the one stove that cooked for them and gave them heat. They were trying to keep warm— with coal they bought by the pailful at the rate of $16 a ton. They paid $5.50 a month for the two miserable rooms—one with light, the other without.

And what kind of people are these that dwell in such quarters? "Foreigners, likely, only lately recruited from the hives of Naples or Palermo, and finding even these habitations not much worse than those to which they have been accustomed." So you think. But these are not foreigners. These are Americans; respectable and industrious Americans. They are old-time residents of the Eighth Ward, most of them; their fathers lived there, they were born there; with that fatuity that is so common and still so hard to explain, they cling to the familiar regions of their youth. And not the least pathetic part of the unfortunate situation is the struggle they make against their environment, the painful effort to keep their poor little rooms neat and tidy; the cherished old pictures on the dismal walls, and the handful of ornaments on the shelf. You cannot crush out the instincts of the race by two decades in a tenement house; but you can in four, or five, good gentlemen of the vestry.

The good gentlemen of the vestry have strong and steady nerves; they are not easily worried; they are not likely ever to die of heart failure. I know that they have large and well-grounded philosophies and rest steadfastly upon the belief that a Special Providence watches over the tenement house region. I know this must be so because otherwise they would never be able to sleep, under the terror that the condition of their tenement houses must inspire. Of all the tinder-boxes in New York these houses are the worst. If some of them had been designed for the express purpose of trapping and destroying human beings, by no possibility could they have been more ably arranged to that end.

The old wooden walls, the old wooden stairways, the old wooden floors, dry as powder, inflammable as oil, are only a part of the peril. The one access to, the one exit from, the rear tenement is usually through a narrow passage, or a tunnel, maybe three feet wide, sometimes with wooden sides and top; sometimes above it is part of the front house.

In the event of a fire, these tunnels would become almost at once impassable. Thereupon the people in the overcrowded rear tenements would have no conceivable chance to escape. Many of them could not even get down to the ground floor, because some of the houses have no fire escapes. Yes, I know the law provides that there shall be such things, but here are houses on Trinity property to which this law seems never to have been applied. There are no fire escapes on the houses at Nos. 32, 34, and 36 Clarkson Street, for instance. I suppose that technically this is not Trinity's fault; but narrow old wooden stairs, dry old tinder walls, an overcrowded building, and no fire escapes! Yes, I think the vestrymen have good nerves; they cannot be susceptible to carking care.

And how about the rest of us that are not obliged to lead our lives in such surroundings, but are still our brothers' keepers? I know that there is a belief more or less widespread among us that tenement house dwellers do not have feelings like ours. They are differently constituted, their fibers are different, their ganglia are of another material; so by a merciful provision they do not feel the pangs of poverty nor mind dirt, darkness and squalor. We should mind such things, but these people do not, because of some great difference in their physical and mental make-up. In fact, they are said to be very happy in the station to which Providence has assigned them, and we really should let them live on in their cellars and back rooms so long as tuberculosis and typhoid will allow.

I know this view must be correct, because I have heard it urged by very learned and wise persons, and I make a point of not disputing eminent authority. Still, I should think that even to persons of a very different fiber indeed the sensation of burning to death would be painful, and most of us would prefer not to derive an income from tinder-box houses that are without fire escapes.

I can only suppose, therefore, that about this matter Trinity Corporation has implicit faith in the idea of a Special Providence.

The Special Providence went off watch on the night of March 29, 1896, and the tinder-box at No. 374 Hudson Street exploded into flame; for it seems an inaccuracy of speech to say that one of these places merely takes fire. Of course the wooden stairway was unusable, and the unfortunate and trapped inhabitants were driven to throw themselves from the windows. Four of them, two men and two women, were killed; about a dozen were badly injured. I gather from this that while the fiber of people that live in tenements is different from the fiber of the rest of us, it is not sufficiently different to prevent such people from being burned, nor from having their bones broken if they fall far enough.

It was also not different enough to prevent some of the survivors from grieving over the loss of their relatives and from suing Trinity as the responsible cause of that loss. So the whole story was turned up in the courts. But I have been unable to find that anything ever came of these actions. Somehow, nothing usually comes of a suit against Trinity.

Bearing in mind what happened at No. 374 Hudson Street, I should think the vestry might at times feel a slight uneasiness. No. 374 Hudson Street was a fireproof structure compared with some of the other properties. At Nos. 192½ and 192¾ Varick Street, for instance, is an ancient, sorry-looking structure of wood, three stories high, and there is no fire escape at either number. What the inmates would do in case that tinder-box were fired, I do not know; burn with the tinder, I suppose. The fire escapes that exist on some of the other houses are makeshifts. Perhaps an adult man or a woman of average weight could get upon one without fetching the whole thing away, but I do not see how. Why worry? The houses have never burned. Hence let us conclude that they never will burn.

But we tourists of the well-fed and better orders resume our excursion among the habitations of the lowly, and here are some of the places we enter; no better and no worse than others. Human beings actually live in these places; many human beings; and pay for the privilege.

No. 265 West Houston Street. Brick, three stories and basement, four families, rear fire escape, dirty back yard sanitation in two wooden sheds in the yard, water in halls. An interior bedroom on top floor, where an old woman says, "That's all right; we get too much air in the winter."

No. 368 Hudson Street. Brick, three stories, fire escapes in rear, small yard, sanitation in wooden sheds, interior bedroom.

No. 342 Hudson Street. Three stories, rotten wood in front, half wood, half brick in rear; a dilapidated old shack. Fire escape in front, house occupied by three families and two stores. Dirty little yard heaped with rubbish, sanitation in old wooden sheds.

You say, why don't they [the tenants] move elsewhere? Yes, to Staten Island maybe, or to Yonkers or Poughkeepsie, all admirably adapted to be places of residence. Dear soul, so long as Trinity offers a tenement at $5.50 a month somebody (in the conditions of life that we create and maintain) is certain to live in it. But how does that excuse Trinity? In what way does that clear her of the moral responsibility for the chalk-faced children that are growing up in the terrible places she owns?

The children! Ah, well, I was coming to them. I have now in mind some pictures that stand out above the others of the horrible things I saw in my wanderings here. I remember one place: a tiny and scantily stocked store in front, the living room of the family next, and beyond that a wretched wooden shed used as a bedroom. A little girl lay sick on a bed against the further side of the shed. The old mattress she lay upon was filthy, the old blanket that covered her was filthy, the floor was filthy, the walls were bare, the room was a cold, cheerless hole, almost dark, for the one window that opened upon the filthy back yard admitted hardly any light. The child lay close by the thin wooden wall of that shed, and on the other side of that wall were the reeking back yard and things I must not speak about. She lay there in that choking and fetid atmosphere, and a constitution enfeebled by years of such existence was still battling for her life.

What kind of children do you think will develop in such an atmosphere, supposing them to escape the mercy of death? The only times in their lives when they can breathe anything but mephitis is when they can get into the roaring streets, and when they get into the roaring streets the trucks and cabs run them down or the police chase them off the block. Imagine the eighteen growing years of a life spent among the damp and dripping walls of some of these places, with the nauseating rubbish of the neglected back yard for a prospect and the darkness of filthy halls and stairways for a companion. Do you think it in any way wonderful that some lives thus led and thus trained should turn to crime? If you wished to rear a criminal, do you think you could devise a better training place? . . .

So runs this extraordinary story. Many strange features pertain to it. The managing forces of Trinity control a very great property. The real owners of that property are the communicants of the church. For ninety-four years none of the owners has known the extent of the property, nor the amount of the revenue therefrom, nor what is done with the money. Every attempt to learn even the simplest fact about these matters has been baffled. The management is a self-perpetuating body, without responsibility and without supervision. All these are strange conditions. But stranger than all is this: that a Christian church should be willing to take money from such tenements as Trinity owns in the old Eighth Ward.

Everybody's Magazine
July 1908

PART EIGHT

Prisons

EXPOSURE OF prison conditions during the era of the muckrakers was in most instances accomplished by specialists in the field. The one exception was Charles Edward Russell, who as a muckraker contributed to the literature of exposure in varied fields, including that of prison conditions.

The muckraking magazines carried a number of articles which decried the inhuman conditions found in prisons. For example, *The Arena* in 1904 published an article by Dr. G. W. Galvin of the Emergency Hospital in Boston on "Inhuman Treatment of Prisoners in Massachusetts." The article excited protest and produced some amelioration of the conditions in the Massachusetts penitentiaries.

A letter to *Everybody's Magazine* from an ex-prisoner, telling about his experience in the Georgia prison system, initiated Russell into the field of prison muckraking. *Everybody's* sent him to investigate the man's accusations. "A Burglar in the Making" resulted.

In announcing "A Burglar in the Making," *Everybody's* editor noted: "For apparent reasons, the man's identity must be carefully guarded here; but all the essentials of the narrative are exactly as recited. Many of them Mr. Russell has been able to verify from his own observations; the others can be accepted upon faith. They reveal clearly the shameful system by which the State of Georgia surrenders for profits the solemn duty of correcting her wrongdoers. . . ." [131]

Prior to the Civil War, convicts in Georgia were kept in a prison, but after the war, with an upsurge of crime, penitentiary facilities were inadequate to house all the convicts, so the state adopted the policy of leasing prisoners to contractors. At first it was on public works projects; later this was changed so that the state could lease them to private individuals for a period of five years. In 1879, the state started to lease the convicts to three companies under an agreement to run for a period of twenty years. These companies were to pay the state $500,000 in twenty annual installments for the use of the convicts.

Eighteen years later a law was passed to the effect that when the companies' contracts expired (in two years), the convict leasing system would be amended.

Under the law, a prison commission was appointed to obtain a prison farm where the old, the young and the sick would be housed apart from the hardened criminals. Convicts with sentences of five years and under were to be sent to a chain gang; those with sentences of more than five years were to be leased to contractors. The contractor paid $100 a year for the more "desirable" convicts, the others went to the highest bidders.

Russell made this system the target for his articles.

In the November 1908 issue of *Everybody's*, its publishers commented: "Georgia didn't waste any time finding fault with us for calling attention to the spot on her pretty gown. Georgia cleaned the spot off quicker'n scat —that's Georgia—and, looking up smiling, said, 'What was that last remark of yours?' We didn't really kill the bear—Georgia did it. . . . All we did was to criticize. . . . We are proud to have had a little share in the good work."

That same issue quoted a Georgia citizen as saying that Russell's article was "the spark that set off the powder that is now exploding in the legislative halls of the state of Georgia."

And there was an explosion in the Georgia legislature. The hearings made page-one news.

At one session, reported the Atlanta *Constitution*, a member of the legislature, Judge Covington, spoke against leasing convicts and "appealed to the sentiments of his hearers. He painted with words a picture of the camp life, the beating of the convicts, and worked the house up to a considerable pitch . . . with the orator's skill he mixed wit with wisdom and eased the house off when it became too tense in its attentions." [132]

In the meanwhile, many Georgia newspapers editorialized against the leasing system:

The Atlanta *Constitution*: "The legislature now involved in serious discussion of the convict problem, should approach its solution with the determination that the state shall get away, just as far away from the iniquitous and barbaric lease system as the conditions which confront it will permit." [133]

"Georgia's fair name has been trailed in the dirt in magazines and elsewhere too long. If the charges are true, it is time to call a halt . . ." said the Americus *Times Recorder*.[134]

The Cordele *Rambler* said: "We have been advertised to the world as allowing all kinds of cruelty, graft and corruption, and nothing short of an investigation will place us in good standing again . . ." [135]

Hearings continued, and headlines proclaimed:

CONVICTS BEATEN TO DEATH,
SAY WITNESSES UNDER OATH
Revolting Stories of Cruelty at
Prison Camps Told In-
vestigating Committee

200 to 300 floggings
monthly at one camp,
testifies employee

"Men were treated with unmerciful severity, given tasks beyond their powers of physical endurance, and whipped when they sank under the strain of the ordeal," [136] testified a witness.

One contractor admitted he made between $200,000 and $300,000 during the five years of his contract with the state in leasing convicts.

But the lower and upper houses of the legislature could not reach agreement on how to handle the leasing situation. The upper house wanted complete repeal of the leasing system. The lower house desired amendments.

The Atlanta *Constitution* compared the efforts of the legislature to pass a new convict bill with the "flounderings of the 'Prairie Ball' ":

> She heaved and she sot
> She sot and she heaved
> And high her rudder flung
> And every time she heaved and sot
> A deeper leak she sprung.

The regular session of the legislature adjourned with no action on the problem. But it did call for a special session to discuss the convict bill. At this session, several weeks later, once again there was "floundering," but eventually a bill was passed which satisfied both houses and was signed by the governor.

The new law provided that the governor and the prison commission might lease for one year any "overs" after cities, municipalities and state institutions had been accommodated with their needs for convict labor.

"The law does not 'unconditionally' terminate the lease system upon March 3, 1909 as repeatedly demanded by the upper house. However, it takes a long step toward that much needed result," reported the Atlanta *Constitution*.[137]

CHARLES EDWARD RUSSELL

A Burglar in the Making

H E HAD STOLEN the $300, there was no doubt about that, and now he sat in the Atlanta court room and listened while his lawyer pleaded in his behalf, urging his youth and inexperience and previous good record, since there was so little else to urge, and trying to break or mitigate in some way the force of the cold, pitiless, indubitable testimony that had bound chains upon him while he sat there.

Young he was, true enough; his look still ingenuous, his face fair and fresh and boyish. You could well understand that, as the lawyer said, droning on interminably and hopelessly, his antecedents and training had been good; he was no familiar and hardened criminal. But he had stolen the $300; and in a place of trust. His employer's cash drawer had been in his charge, he had become fascinated with that devil's own game that is called playing the races; he had stolen again and again: with open eyes he had broken the law; now upon his head were to fall the consequences.

At last the droning lawyers ceased to drone; the judge charged briefly and in curt, keen sentences, each a slash at the young man's frail hopes; the jury retired. The young man sat there very pale, his dry lips apart, his pulses beating visibly in his neck, his fingers fumbling incessantly on his hat brim. He had not long to wait—the jurors' retirement was merely for form's sake; they gave the expected verdict, and the young man stood there, shivering, to take his sentence. Four years.

With obvious hopelessness the lawyer made the usual dilatory motions. It appeared that the young man was without friends or funds, his parents were dead, the court had been obliged to appoint counsel for his defense, there was for him no stay, no appeal, no arrest of judgment.

325

The sheriff's officer put his hand upon the young man's shoulder and led him gently away. He walked like one in a dream.

That afternoon they started for the farm near Milledgeville that the State of Georgia provides for the reception of its convicted lawbreakers, for it has no penitentiary nor prison. The next day, shaved and shorn and clothed in the stripes that are the badge of the convicted wrong-doer, he found himself standing in a long line of other men similarly clad, black men and white men, placed on exhibition, while an agent for the contractors passed along and appraised their muscles and esti-mated their worth.

He was making selections, this man, for the forces to be drafted to a convicts' camp, where the contractor should have his will of them. For the State of Georgia, having no penitentiary nor prison nor other means of caring for its offenders, practices upon them a very strange device. It sells them for the terms of their sentences into the hands of private and irresponsible persons, and it was for these persons that the man was now going up and down the line, selecting the likeliest and choicest. Fifty years before, on another spot near at hand, another man had gone similarly up and down another line, making similar selections for service. But the service of fifty years ago had been called slavery, and the service of this day was called contract labor, and with this difference of names a great and splendid state had managed in some way to salve its con-science.

But the man did not choose George, the new-made thief from At-lanta; not George, who was thin and weak and waxen; not George, whom the doctor had certified to have a valvular disease of the heart: therefore he went back to the plain, rough sleeping quarters and the plain, simple duties of the farm. He had food, poor in quality and scanty in quantity, but he lived; and not being hardened nor sullen, he reflected at times upon the huge folly that had brought him to this situation and the inevitable fact that he had wrought his misfortune upon himself. He reflected upon these things and had no disposition to complain of his lot; but he did wish, with a yearning that was at first a wholly novel sensation and gradually grew toward a passion, that in some way he could obliterate the past and forget it.

In the jail back in Atlanta some kind of missionary or chaplain or Salvation Army worker, he knew not what, had talked with him and told him that, with his youth and his capabilities, he had every chance to reform his life and redeem his errors and recover the world's respect. At the time he had pushed aside the suggestion, because in his misery and chill terror it had been but as a senseless drumming in his ears;

but now he recalled it, and it began to form some vague sense of hope or promise in his heart. Perhaps he could start over again. The man in the next cell at Atlanta had told him that he would always be a criminal; that, once a man got down, the world was leagued to keep him down; that police and courts and law would hedge him in and compel him to add crime upon crime. He had cared little then, because somehow a vague idea of being an outcast and defying everybody rather appealed to him so long as the man talked, and seemed romantic, and like the brave spirits he had admired in books he had read and plays he had seen; but out here at the convict farm the thing looked very different. He saw day by day drift by him the battered old hulks of professional criminals, and the sight inevitably revolted him and shook the spirit of bravado. He did not want to end like these men, and after a while he made up his mind that when he got out he would try the missionary's advice. He had still a chance in the world. And then one day an older man, and one whose business was to say to him anything else framable in words rather than this, came to him, leering, and said:

"You're Big Bill's pal, ain't you? You're in the bank-sneak line, ain't you?"

George said:

"I never heard of Big Bill, and I'm not in any line."

"Aw, go on," said the man, "don't give me none of that. Think I ain't fly? I seen you pinched many's the time. Think you can fool anybody here? I guess not. You're smooth all right enough, but you needn't play them games here: we're on to you."

A few days later the same man came upon George sitting with his head in his hands, thinking.

"Framin' up a yeggman's job?" asked the man.

"I was thinking what I can do to keep straight when I get out of here," said George.

The man croaked with evil laughter. "Keep straight! You won't keep straight. Do you suppose anybody ever came in here and kept straight afterward? You're a crook now, if you never were before, and a crook you'll stay till the end of your days. There ain't power enough in all this country to make you anything else."

George could write, and very many of his fellow prisoners could not, for 39.10 per cent of the convicts in Georgia are illiterate (the state apparently preferring chain gangs to schools), so he fell into the way of writing letters home for the others. They told him what they wanted to say and he said it. He had no idea what became of these letters, and it never occurred to him that he was in any way responsible for the sentiments that he transcribed at dictation. One day he wrote for a prisoner a letter wherein some complaint was made about the food and other matters at the farm, not necessary to go into here. The next day a prison officer, holding in his hand this letter, stalked angrily up.

"You wrote that, didn't you?" he said, shoving the letter into the boy's face.

"Why, yes," said George. "I wrote it for this prisoner. What's the matter?"

"You wrote this about the food and these other things, didn't you?"

"Why, yes; but he dictated it: it wasn't my letter."

"You're a liar," said the officer. "You put him up to kick."

"I didn't, really I didn't," said the boy.

"You're a liar and a sneak," said the officer, "and now you'll get what's coming to you."

The next day the prisoners were lined up for the slave mart, and George was promptly chosen.

He was taken to a convicts' camp at a place that I shall call Gehenna. That is not its name on the map, but it will do well enough for our purposes. It was one of many convict camps; some better, some worse. The company that had bought of the State of Georgia this particular batch of slaves was engaged in making brick. Its camp was remote from the cities and ordinary ways of men; nobody knew what went on there, and nobody cared.

It was morning when George, with a fresh detail of purchased slaves, arrived at Gehenna. With the first glance at the camp, a chill struck to his heart; there was something most forbidding about the wild and desolate spot, made more hideous with the ragged, dirty structure and the black chimneys of the brickyard. In one corner was a high stockade with guard pens about it and men with rifles on guard, within the stockade were wretched, dark, dilapidated and most filthy huts in which other men were doomed to sleep and eat. About the factory yard were men at work, in the broad stripes of the convict, some preparing the clay, some wheeling the yellow, damp, new bricks to the furnaces to be baked. George noticed that all these men were very badly clad, and some went almost naked. Beyond the brick kiln the land sloped into a swamp, a promising breeding place for disease.

George and the others of the new gang were led to one of the filthy sheds, where they received a breakfast of one slice of boiled salt pork and one piece of greasy corn bread. There were no knives nor forks, and George took the pork into his fingers. He felt something move under his fingers. He looked sharply at the pork. He saw what it was that had moved. It was worms.

Struggling hard with himself, he managed to swallow a little of the corn bread (after he had carefully examined it), and with the rest of the gang he was marshaled into the yard. His work was to wheel loads of those fresh, clayey, yellow bricks from the place where they had been shaped to the place where they were to be baked. When he went the first time to the place where the bricks were shaped, he was amazed to see that the persons engaged in removing the bricks from the drying belt were women. He remembered then that the State of Georgia has no prison for convicted women, and that they are rented to slave brokers just as the men slaves are rented. The work that these women were doing seemed very laborious: with bent backs they must toil hour after hour, lifting the heavy bricks and piling them. A man with a rifle stood and watched the women. They regarded him with manifest terror. If for an instant he turned away, they were wont to stand up and straighten their backs and draw in long breaths of air.

From the place where bricks were shaped to the place where bricks were burned there wound through the yard a path about four hundred feet long. George was told that by this path he must take upon the wheelbarrow each time from fifty to seventy bricks and that he must deliver at the furnaces not fewer than 105 loads in the day, sixty loads from sunrise to noon and forty-five loads from the end of the noon hour to sunset. He was also told that his work would be checked up every few hours, and that if he were found to be falling behind he would with good reason be sorry. This is the substance of the information conveyed to him: I need not quote the words. Each of the unbaked bricks weighed between five and six pounds. That made usually a wheelbarrow load of more than three hundred pounds. George weighed 110 pounds and he had been certified by the prison doctor to have heart disease.

He has not proceeded far with that first day's work when he has an opportunity to learn exactly what are the good reasons for regretting a failure to complete an apportioned task. There is a commotion in the yard, and two of the guards appear, leading forward a convict to a place where a great barrel lies on its side. A big, authoritative man comes forward and gives orders. The convict is stripped. Then he is bent over the barrel. Two Negroes hold his arms and his head. Two others hold his legs. He begs and pleads and struggles. The Negroes hold him fast. Another man stands by with an instrument. It is made of sole leather about three inches wide, three feet long, and three-eighths of an inch thick. It has a stout wooden handle. The man lifts the instrument high in the air. He brings it down, *swish!* upon the naked man on the barrel. The man on the barrel screams aloud with sudden agony. He does not shout nor exclaim, he screams a horrible shrill scream of unutterable pain.

The other man raises the instrument and brings it down, *swish!* again. Again the man on the barrel screams. A blow and a scream: a blow and a scream. Presently it is a blow and a sob: the man on the barrel is crying. Again a moment, and his blood trickles down his side; he is screaming, sobbing, crying now—and bleeding. The blows fall upon his bruised and bloody back; he wriggles and twists about; the Negroes can hardly hold down his head and his legs; the other men stand and gaze; the guards hold their rifles; and from the bluest of skies the soft sun of Georgia looks upon the frightful scene, and the sweet spring air from the southern woods blows over it.

But the man has done wrong: he has committed a fault.

Yes: from sunrise to noon he has wheeled fifty-seven loads of fresh brick; the regulations of this hell on earth require that in such a time he shall wheel sixty loads. So, having thus transgressed, power and law and justice as administered in the State of Georgia exact from him this penalty until he screams and cries and sobs—and bleeds.

He walks with difficulty, this offender against the majesty of the State of Georgia and its slave contracts. George notices his limping gait and thinks it arises from the punishment the offender has earned. But day after day George notices that the offender walks always with the same difficulty. Then George learns that the offender is a cripple; he has chronic rheumatism in his back. So that is why he offends concerning the three loads missing from his tally between sunrise and noon. He is lame, he is no longer young, about fifty-five, George thinks; he cannot with ease wheel three-hundred-pound loads. So thereupon the State of Georgia by means of the slave contractors that it tolerates quickens his movements with three feet of sole leather, well laid on.

So grinds on the first day. For dinner they have each a piece of boiled salt pork, a piece of greasy corn bread. Although he is nearly famished, having worked all morning in the open air, George looks upon the food before him, and at the recollection of his breakfast his stomach revolts upon him and he turns sick and faint. But he gulps down the corn bread and, at last, turning the salt pork to the light and shredding it with his fingers, he manages for sheer hunger's sake to swallow a little of it. The rest is begged by the hungry man next to him. For supper he has boiled salt pork and a piece of corn bread. He learns then that the State of Georgia does not furnish these viands: they are provided at the sole charge and cost of the company to which his slave labor has been sold.

A light begins to dawn upon him. He perceives that he is no concern of the State of Georgia and no concern of the company to which he has been sold. Between the two he is the lost and forgotten outcast and pariah. The state turns him over to the company and does not care; the company can get all the convicts it wants and does not care. Nobody cares. Why, then, should the convict care what war he makes upon the society that has thrust him into a pit and left him there?

The days that followed that first day were to George like days in a madman's dream. He must learn to face the salt pork and its animated contents; he must harden himself against the daily whippings, he must harden himself against the incessant brutality, vile smells, and abominable sights. While all else is being hardened in him, shall his soul escape? At night he crawls sore and weary into his horribly bestenched prison house, where whites and Negroes, young and old, veteran criminal and novice, decent and vile, herd together indiscriminately. Every few days his stomach, which, however his mind may fare, will not become accustomed to the salt pork and greasy corn bread, rebels and rejects the poisonous stuff, and then he works on in the sun ready to drop of weakness and weariness.

Once he falls in a faint at his task and his companions in misery carry him to his filthy bunk, and even the camp doctor admits that he can work no more that day. And so he lies there, and a million insects that inhabit his bed crawl over him and feed upon him, and for weakness he can hardly lift his hand to brush them from his face. So he lies there two days, three days, four days, five days, delirious part of the time, happily unconscious part of the time. The doctor comes and glances at him and goes his way; the slave contractor's agent looks in at the door and curses him. There is one person that seems to feel a spark of human interest in him. She comes in at noon and gives him a drink and lays her hand on his head and straightens the pillow and chases away the insects. She is one of the convict women that pile brick down there at the drying-place.

At last he comes back from the shadowland where he has strayed, and the insects drive him to his feet, and he puts on the broad stripes and staggers into the yard. And then his wheelbarrow is put into his hands again and he begins to wheel brick. But they do not exact of him that day nor for many days the 105 loads. Even in the brickyards of Gehenna there is a limit to brutality. Or maybe it would be ill if in such a way he should die on the slave contractor's hands. Long afterward he learns that in the nearby town some church society or Salvation Army or someone else had learned that there was a very sick convict and had sent him invalid's food and chickens to be made into broth. But he never received them. He knew why. And if the agents of society practiced theft upon him, why should he not practice theft upon society?

Many were the horrible sights he witnessed and shuddered at in those days before the crushing of the system had atrophied in him the last nerve of conscious revolt and he had arrived at the state in which he did not care. Three times in one day he saw that same old man whipped, the man that had rheumatism in his back: three times, and for no fault but for failing to make the required number of loads. After the third whipping he was too sore to move and had to be helped to his cot. His rheumatism was very bad, but he lay on his filthy bunk with no covering but a cotton sheet, and between the chinks of the wretched wall of that hut the night wind blew sharply upon him. The rags wherewith he was clad scarcely covered him; his rheumatism grew worse; it was in his legs now as much as in his back. To see him struggling along the path with his barrow of heavy brick was a pitiable sight, but after a time George didn't notice it. He was sinking into a lethargy of indifference. He had learned to eat his salt pork now— sometimes. And when he could not, his companions would beg it of him.

The whippings went on. Nobody cared, except those that were whipped. George learned after a time that the men in charge were obliged by the rules to report to the State Prison Commissioners every case of punishment, with the cause thereof and the name of the person punished, but in fact not one case in twenty was ever so reported. He knew that because, writing a neat hand he was employed to copy the reports and had monthly before him the evidence of the dereliction.

The deputy warden that represented the state in charge of the camp was also in the pay of the company, which paid him three times as much as the state paid him and to which his obligation was in the same proportion. To the contracting company his use seemed to be to extract from the convicts the utmost labor at the least cost. To the state his duty was much vaguer. The contracting company was obliged by its contract to feed and clothe the slaves; the function of the state seemed to be that it kept the convicts from running away. Simply that and nothing more. Nowhere appeared the slightest suggestion that any of these unfortunates were men—men, made in the divine image and in spite of our follies and weaknesses and sins like our own, still men to be pitied and helped and reformed and redeemed.

There were rules, George found, of the most beautiful and humane character, rules evidently designed by kind-hearted men to prevent cruelty and to secure some measure of comfort to the convicts, but all the rules were merely a jest among the persons in charge of the camp; no one pretended to observe them. Thus, it was prescribed that the contracting company should furnish ample food of good quality, good and sufficient clothing, good and clean beds. All these rules were as if they had never existed. In that remote and seldom-visited spot the deputy warden was the unquestioned master and seemed to have no limit to his sway except the interest of the contractor.

All the conditions seemed framed and designed to make life wretched for the victims of this terrible system. In the beginning the contractor had bought the labor of the convicts for $11 a head for each year. Now competitive bidding had increased the price to $225 a head a year, and even more, and besides the contractor bore the expense of feeding and clothing. That he might secure a profit on such a bargain it was necessary that the men should be driven through long hours to the utmost capacity of their endurance. And that was why the deputy warden was on the contractor's payroll.

Once in a long time an inspector from the State Prison Department came to visit the camp, but his coming was invariably known in advance, and the men were set to work to clean up the barracks and whitewash the stockade; and when the inspector came, for that one meal the men had decent food, and the whip was out of sight. The inspector went among the convicts to receive complaints, but a deputy warden or a yard boss went with him everywhere, listening to every word said to him, and the convicts knew too well what would be the consequences to them of any complaint. They were in a trap.

In the middle of George's second year, the term of the old rheumatic sufferer expired. He had made a faultless prison record, for there is one gleam of mercy in this system of evil in that the whippings for insufficient work are not allowed to be entered against a convict's record. Therefore, the old man had earned for good behavior eleven months' commutation. He knew it and was filled with joy as the day of his freedom drew near. The Prison Commission in Atlanta looked over his record and found it good, and the customary order was sent for his release. But he was not released. Instead, he served out his full time, and for eleven months longer he toiled with his heavy wheelbarrow up and down the path, battened upon scraps, and endured the lash. Another kind of man would have complained, or his friends would have complained for him. This old man was ignorant, friendless, helpless— and a criminal. So he bore his lot and went forth at last with another sense of injury burning at his wronged heart.

Some incidents came to vary the monotony of horror, the whippings, the tugging at the wheelbarrow, the struggle to and fro in the hot sun or the cold rains. Old faces disappeared as men died or as time won for them an exit from the doors of hell; new faces appeared as fresh relays of slaves were brought up to feed the insatiable contract. At rare intervals other events broke upon the stupor in which they dragged out their days. One of the prisoners had a mistress, a prostitute of Atlanta, who came sometimes to the camp to see her lover, and then the extraordinary liberties allowed to this couple awoke a loathsome comment through the camp. And once a convict stood for a moment by the marge of the swamp, looking at the bright sunlight as it lay on the hills far away, and then plunged suddenly into the water. Instantly blazing rifle shots awoke the echoes, and guards ran and shot and shouted; an hour passed in excitement until, covered with mud, the fugitive was dragged back, to be beaten first and then loaded with heavy shackles that for weeks he must wear.

And once there was something else. All day the man that was working next to George complained of terrible pains in his chest and stomach. Some instinct of fast-perishing decency must have revived in George, for he called a guard's attention to the case. A yard boss came and looked the man over and ordered him back to work. He toiled in agony, holding, when he could, his hand to his side. At last he fell in a faint. They carried him to his bunk and that night he died. His death was entered as due to sunstroke. It was no sunstroke; the time was the fall, and the weather was cool. But what of truth shall the records bear that are made in such a place?

Some of the men got pneumonia and died of it. Sometimes they stood for hours to their knees in icy water while they worked in the swamp. Always they were ill clad, ill nourished, and in no state to withstand the cold. The contractor furnished shoes as well as clothes, and the shoes were rotten and worthless even when they were new, and went quickly to pieces, so that in winter men with bare protruding toes walked in the slush. Some had no underclothes, some had no socks. One received a letter from a friend announcing that a supply of shoes and socks was about to be sent to him. Some days later he received one pair of socks but no shoes. Afterward he noticed a guard that wore socks of a pattern like his and good shoes. But he said nothing. He had no desire for the heavy shackles nor for more beatings than fell naturally to his lot.

The time wore by and George came to the end of his term. He had learned to be as sullen, as defiant, as hardened, as reckless as the indurated men about him. When at last the doors opened to set him free, a guard said to him:

"Well, I suppose you are going to yegg it." And George said:

"By God, I am."

He did. He went back to Atlanta and turned burglar.

And was he the only man that went forth from those gates resolved to prey upon the society that had preyed upon him? I think not. Was he the only man that ever learned at Gehenna the terrible lessons of desperation and revenge that are taught daily in that most perfect academy of crime? I think not, by some thousands. Then how shall we justify to ourselves the system that makes criminals and turns them loose to do evil among us and then catches and brands still deeper the very criminals it has made?

Convicts. I know it. Most of them Negroes. I know it. Convicts and Negroes, we have decided, are outside the pale of humanity, having no souls, nor rights nor feelings. I know it. The convict must be punished—society has so decreed; he has done ill, he has brought his retribution upon himself. I know it. Then why bother? What is all this to us?

Much: it is very much to us for three reasons. In the first place, if it had been a horse or a dog that had been thus beaten and maltreated in the name of the State of Georgia, a million voices would have been raised in vehement protest, a million hands would have been stretched out to shield the victim. It is ill for us all, ill for our common humanity that to anything in the shape of a man we should do that which we should not endure to have done to a brute. And this is true, soul or no soul, rights or no rights.

In the second place, for all these things the world at large must pay too dearly.

In the third place, there is back of the whipper and his dreadful thong, back of the screaming man on the barrel, back of the armed guard and the dreary stockade and the contract slaver, a typical American story that holds the glass up to us and shows exactly what spectacle we present to the world when we are engaged in our favorite national pursuit of dosing the symptoms of an evil instead of cutting out their source.

This is a story of "regulation" as a cure for social wrongs. It is also a

story of how we fare and how our victims fare under the beautiful
political system by which we are enabled to shoulder our civic re-
sponsibilities from one to another and to go smugly and undismayed
about our private aims and personal profit, no matter who is
wronged. . . .

For the whole system of leasing convicts, in other words for the whole
system of convict slavery, the great majority of the people of Georgia
have only abhorrence. Of the hideous things the system involves they
know little or naught, but on general principles and because they are
a humane and kindly people, they abhor it. Against their will it was
forced upon them; they never chose it nor wanted it nor approved of
it. They have always loathed it; if a proposal to abolish the system
could be submitted to a popular vote, it would carry five to one. At any
time for many years such a proposal would have carried. And yet this
hateful thing continues.

Why? For two reasons: first, the people of Georgia, being, like the
people of the rest of the United States, cursed and clogged with representative instead of popular government, have no direct control of
their own affairs; and, second, the system is profitable to very powerful
interests. So far these interests have frustrated every attempt to end
the abomination. Therefore, and for these familiar reasons, behold it
still persisting in spite of all the indictments of its horrors that cry
aloud against it and in spite of the plain evidence that it is of no avail
in this world, truly none except to break hearts and maim bodies and
ruin souls. And these profitable interests are able to maintain this system of hell in the midst of one of the most enlightened and progressive
commonwealths in the Union.

Incidentally, the history of this matter involves a very curious illustration of another trait of ours, to wit, our quacksalving device of changing
names and disguises.

Ten or twelve years ago, when the Populists were powerful in Georgia,
they took up convict leasing and declared in their platform their intention to annihilate the business. The people of Georgia showed such a
disposition to respond to this program that the ruling powers were
alarmed and hastened to make a concession to popular sentiment. So
ten years ago the system of making leases was gravely abolished. Thereafter "convict leasing" did not exist in Georgia—according to the ruling
powers. Instead of leases there were "contracts," and, though no conceivable difference resulted in any essential particular, the change of
name afforded to some persons that soothing relief for the conscience

that we all are too ready to accept when civic duty interferes with our interest.

But however the thing may be named, lease or contract or what not, the fact remains that the state does give over to private, unauthorized and irresponsible persons the care, control and labor, and therefore the punishment, of its offenders; and that to the private persons thus most improperly endowed with one of the most solemn and perplexing functions of state, the sole interest lies in extracting the greatest possible amount of labor at the least possible cost. Under such a system the most terrible conditions, multiple and irremediable, are absolutely assured. It makes little difference and can make little that the present Prison Commissioners are honest, faithful, zealous and kindly; it makes little difference that to the very utmost of their power, and unceasingly, they strive to remedy every abuse that is brought to their attention; it makes little difference that the legislature repeatedly investigates the condition of the victims of these contracts. The whole thing is utterly and incurably and hopelessly evil. Nothing does nor can affect the great fatal fact that from the labor of the state's culprits private persons make gains, that the extent of such gains depends upon the amount of labor that the culprits can be forced to perform, and that the culprits are and must be practically at the mercy of those that buy such labor.

For the year ending May 31, 1907, the State of Georgia had 2,464 convicts, of whom 1,890 were contracted into servitude to various private persons and corporations, and 574 were employed on the county roads. In 1906 the number was 1,773 to the contractors and 571 on the county roads. From the labor of these culprits thus sold to private persons, the state in 1906 received $333,463.84 and in 1907 $353,455.55. These profits are the sole returns from a system that multiplies criminals, breeds brutality, encourages crime, and puts upon one of the fairest states in the Union a hideous blot. If the profits were a thousand times as great, they would be dear at that price.

Everybody's Magazine
June 1908

PART NINE

Labor

WORKMEN'S

COMPENSATION

THE EDITOR of *Everybody's Magazine* in a note preceding William Hard's
article "Making Steel and Killing Men" asks three questions.* But these
questions are asked after presenting certain comments by the superintendent
of a steel mill and reports from the records of the Chicago coroner's
office. The comments:

"The English idea with regards to blast furnaces is to run moderately
and save the lining," Charles S. Price, superintendent of the Cambria
Steel Works at Johnstown, Pennsylvania, is quoted as saying. "What do
we care for the lining? We think that a lining is good for so much iron,
and the sooner it makes it the better."

From the records of the Chicago coroner's office, the editor cites the
statistic: "Forty-six men were killed in accidents last year [1906] in the
South Chicago plant of the United States Steel Corporation. There was
no great casualty. The largest number killed at any one time was four. Two
other accidents accounted for two men apiece. All the rest were killed
singly. During the course of the year, therefore, there were 41 separate
accidents that resulted in the destruction of the one valuable thing in the
world, human life."

The editor now asked his three questions: "Have we in America the
same attitude toward human beings that we have toward the linings of
blast furnaces? Do we think that a man is good for so much iron and
steel, and the quicker he makes it the better? Must he then go to the
graveyard just as the lining of the blast furnace goes to the junk heap?"

Several years after the publication of "Making Steel and Killing Men," and
another article by Mr. Hard, "The Law of the Killed and Wounded," [138]
Everybody's Magazine, in an editorial roundup on what the magazine had
accomplished, cited these articles as "unquestionably influencing much of the
humanitarian legislation of the past few years." The editor asked his readers

* November 1907.

to "wade through" the list of articles which the editor considered "our apology for being alive." [139]

Several months after six girls were burned to death and nineteen others died as a result of jumping from fourth-floor windows in a Newark factory fire, Mary Alden Hopkins in *McClure's Magazine* showed that the loss of life was mainly due to defective doors and fire escapes.

She concludes that article with: "If an employer has provided broad, easily accessible fire escapes, and enough of them, if he has provided interior staircases constructed in a flame-proof manner; if he has provided interior fire-alarms, and has taken enough interest in the safety of his people to establish a fire drill, then he has at least given his employees a chance for their lives." [140]

Soon thereafter, safety committees were named in factories, safety rules formulated and continuous inspection decreed. Here again the muckrakers detailed the problems and their exposures sparked the movement for safety, which resulted in legislative action in the various states.

By 1912, thirteen states had passed Workmen's Compensation laws. By 1917, about forty states had enacted such regulations.

Probably the greatest contribution to labor legislation during the fifteen-year period ending 1917, were these Workmen's Compensation laws.

WILLIAM HARD

Making Steel and Killing Men

T<small>HE</small> S<small>OUTH</small> C<small>HICAGO</small> plant of the United States Steel Corporation stretches along the shore of Lake Michigan for a distance of about two miles northward from the broad mouth of the Calumet River.

This plant, as you see it from the deck of a yacht out in the lake, is just an opaque mass of smoke, thirty million dollars' worth of smoke. You may descry, it is true, certain dim outlines of multitudinous buildings, like the faint surmises of a dream. You may be diverted by the long rows of slender smokestacks, rearing their heads through the smoke and standing shoulder to shoulder at rigid attention as if they were about to salute. You may be thrilled by the three thin, wavering tongues of flame that spurt up from the throats of the Bessemer converters and fight their way through the thick layers of their imprisonment, like fleeting spirits, to the clear air above. But these things are mere modifications of the central theme, which is smoke, a mountain of smoke, or, rather, a cave of smoke. For the mountain is hollow, and in its interior ten thousand men are at work.

Here, in the smoke on the north bank of the Calumet, forty-six men performed their final earthly act last year. Here, at the edge of the plant, just inside the high white board fence, stands the company's private hospital, with fifty beds, a chief surgeon, two assistant surgeons, an interne, and three nurses. Here, in the inquests held in the undertakers' shops in the neighborhood of the plant, the United States Steel Corporation, in the person of the Illinois Steel Company, was censured six times last year by coroner's juries. Here, at the time when ten men were injured in the pig-casting department, the Building Department of the City of Chicago was forced to intervene and to admonish the company that "a little diligent thought and precaution on your part would minimize the occurrence of such accidents." Here the number of the dead, who are reported to the coroner, furnishes the only clue to the number of the merely burned, crushed, maimed and disabled, who are reported to nobody.

But let us make an estimate (and it will have to be a rough one, for there are no local statistics) of the number of men burned and crushed and maimed and disabled in the plant of the Illinois Steel Company last year, as compared with the number of men actually killed.

The best statistics on such subjects are those of the German government, which, as it has established a system of compulsory insurance, is in a position to know exactly what is happening in the manufacturing establishments within its jurisdiction.

From these statistics (covering a period of twelve years) it appears that for every man killed in Germany there were eight who suffered a permanent disability of either a partial or a total character. It further appears that for every man killed, four were disabled temporarily, which, in the German statistics, means for at least thirteen weeks.

If the law of averages is the same in Chicago as it is in Berlin (and there is no reason to suppose that it isn't), the record of casualties at the South Chicago plant of the United States Steel Corporation would read as follows:

Dead 46
Disabled temporarily (for at least 13 weeks).... 184
Disabled permanently 368
    Total................................ 598

The record of the long battle in the cave of smoke on the north bank of the Calumet River for the year 1906 would therefore present 598 killed and wounded men to the consideration of a public which would be appalled by the news of the loss of an equal number of men in a battle in the Philippines.

And it should be remembered that the estimate here given does not include any of those men who suffered injuries which disabled them for a period of less than the thirteen weeks above mentioned. If such cases were included, the total number of casualties would be enormously increased. Minor accidents are far more numerous than those of a serious nature. The total number of all accidents, major and minor, at the plant of the Illinois Steel Company would certainly be more than twice as large as the number of major accidents which we have already computed.

If, therefore, 598 men were involved last year in major accidents, entailing, at the least, a disability of thirteen weeks each, there must have been at least 1,200 men who were involved in accidents of all kinds. Doctors who have been employed in the hospital of the Illinois Steel Company place the number even higher. They have said that there are at least 2,000 accidents every year. But many of these accidents extend only to the painful scorching of a leg. If the figure be kept at 1,200, it will be a conservative estimate, including only those injuries that may be legitimately regarded as being of material consequence.

Here, then, is the record of one American industrial establishment for one year! It is not an establishment that enjoys any pre-eminence in heartlessness. If it were, there would be no use in writing an article about it. The exceptional proves nothing. But the plant in South Chicago is just an American plant, conducted according to American ideals. Its officials are men whom one is glad to meet and proud to know. And yet in the course of one year in their plant they had at least 1,200 accidents that resulted in the physical injury, the physical agony, of human beings.

Must we continue to pay this price for the honor of leading the world in the cheap and rapid production of steel and iron? Must we continue to be obliged to think of scorched and scalded human beings whenever we sit on the back platform of an observation car and watch the steel rails rolling out behind us? Is this price necessary, or could we strike a better bargain if we were shrewder and more careful?

A partial answer to these questions will suggest itself as we go along. We shall learn something by leaving general statistics at this point and by descending to particular individual instances. When the American Institute of Social Service tells us that 536,165 Americans are killed or maimed every year in American industry, our minds are merely stunned. But the specific case of Ora Allen, on the twelfth day of December 1906 has a poignant thrust that goes through the stunned mind to the previously untouched recesses of the heart.

Ora Allen is Inquest 39,193 in the Coroner's Office in the Criminal Court Building downtown. On the twelfth of last December he was a ladleman in the North Open Hearth Mill of Illinois Steel Company, twelve miles from downtown, in South Chicago. On the fifteenth he was a corpse in the company's private hospital. On the seventeenth his remains were viewed by six good and lawful men at Griesel & Son's undertaking shop at 8946 Commercial Avenue.

The first witness, Newton Allen, told the gist of the story.

On the twelfth of last December Newton Allen was operating overhead Crane No. 3 in the North Open Hearth Mill of the Illinois Steel Company. Seated aloft in the cage of his crane, he dropped his chains and hooks to the men beneath and carried pots and ladles up and down the length of the pouring-floor.

That floor was 1,100 feet long, and it looked longer because of the dim murkiness of the air. It was edged, all along one side, by a row of open-hearth furnaces, fourteen of them, and in each one there were sixty-four tons of white, boiling iron, boiling into steel. From these furnaces the white-hot metal, now steel, was withdrawn and poured into big ten-ton molds, standing on flatcars. When the molds were removed, the steel stood up by itself on the cars in the shape of ingots. These ingots, these obelisks of steel, cooled to solidity on their outsides, but still soft and liquid within, were hauled away by locomotives to other parts of the plant.

It was a scene in which a human being looks smaller than perhaps anywhere else in the world. You must understand that fact in order to comprehend the psychological aspect of accidents in steel mills.

On the twelfth of last December, Newton Allen, up in the cage of his 100-ton electric crane, was requested by a ladleman from below to pick up a pot and carry it to another part of the floor. This pot was filled with the hot slag that is the refuse left over when the pure steel has been run off.

Newton Allen let down the hooks of his crane. The ladleman attached those hooks to the pot. Newton Allen started down the floor. Just as he started, one of the hooks slipped. There was no shock or jar. Newton Allen was warned of danger only by the fumes that rose toward him. He at once reversed his lever, and, when his crane had carried him to a place of safety, descended and hurried back to the scene of the accident. He saw a man lying on his face. He heard him screaming. He saw that he was being roasted by the slag that had poured out of the pot. He ran up to him and turned him over.

"At that time," said Newton Allen, in his testimony before the jury, "I did not know it was my brother. It was not till I turned him over that I recognized him. Then I saw it was my brother Ora. I asked him if he was burned bad. He said no, not to be afraid—he was not burned as bad as I thought."

Three days later Ora died in the hospital of the Illinois Steel Company. He had told his brother he wasn't "burned bad," but Ira Miltimore, the doctor who attended him, testified that his death was due to a "third-degree burn of the face, neck, arms, forearms, hands, back, right leg, right thigh, and left foot." A third-degree burn is the last degree there is. There is no fourth degree.

But why did the hook on that slag pot slip?

Because it was attached merely to the rim of the pot, and not to the lugs. That pot had no lugs. It ought to have had them. Lugs are pieces of metal that project from the rim of the pot, like ears. They are put there for the express purpose of providing a proper and secure hold for the hooks. But they had been broken off in some previous accident and they had not been replaced. On the twelfth of last December the ladleman had been obliged to use the mere rim, or flange, of the pot, and with that precarious attachment the pot had been hoisted and carried.

"Is it dangerous to carry a pot by its flange?" asked the deputy coroner.

"It is," said Newton Allen, "but it is the duty of the ladleman to put the hooks on the pot. I work on signal from him."

Mike Skiba, the ladleman, being summoned, testified that he had attached the hooks to the pot by the flange, but that he had no orders against attaching them in that way.

John Pfister, the boss ladleman, Mike Skiba's superior, said, on oath: "I have no orders not to raise the slag pots when the lugs are broken off."

George L. Danforth, the superintendent of the North Open Hearth Mill, an expansive man, who might himself have been killed on the occasion in question, because his duties oblige him to frequent all parts of the mill, testified that "pots have been raised in the manner described for three or four years and this was the first time that one of them has fallen."

What did the jury think? It thought as follows:

"We, the jury, believe that slag pots should not be handled without their lugs, and we recommend that the lugs be replaced before the pots are used in the future."

So came to an end the case of Ora Allen, burned to death by the slag from a pot that was being hoisted by his brother. Was it a necessary tragedy? Was all that agony, all the horror that filled the soul of Ora Allen's brother when he turned him over and recognized him, was all that wait of three days for death in the hospital, a necessary incident in the production of steel? The coroner's jury evidently did not think so, although such a jury is notably reluctant to utter a censure.

As I read the testimony and afterwards looked at that gigantic, that deafening and hypnotizing North Open Hearth Mill, my mind was carried back to the American locomotive engineer who astonished Mr. Kipling when he was on his first visit to this country. The train was just starting across a trestle that looked as if it were ready to crumble away, on the slightest provocation, into the mountain torrent beneath. Mr. Kipling remonstrated, and the engineer, in reply, gave utterance to the whole philosophy of American business life. He said:

"We guess that when a trestle's built it ought to last forever. And sometimes we guess ourselves into the depot. And sometimes we guess ourselves into hell."

The company will tell you, very straightforwardly and very honestly, that it is impossible to prevent the men from being reckless, that it is beyond human power to prevent the men from hooking up slag pots by their flanges. The men get in a hurry and they become careless.

There is a good deal of truth in this observation, as I shall show later. The men do get careless and, under our outdated but unrepealed laws, the carelessness of a ladleman, resulting in the death of a fellow ladleman, will relieve the company from all money liability for that ladleman's death. It is impossible that men in steel mills should not grow careless. It is part of the inevitable psychological consequence of working next to a three-mouthed monster with sixty-four tons of boiling metal in its insides. But suppose, just suppose, that instead of being relieved from all money liability by the carelessness of a ladleman toward a fellow ladleman, suppose, just suppose that the company had to pay a flat fine of $20,000 every time a ladleman was killed. Do you think that any slag pot would ever be raised by its flange?

That is the real question. And the answer is, No. The United States Steel Corporation has too much ability, it has done too many wonderful, too many almost impossible things, to fail in such a project of prevention. But the cold fact is that there is no adequate incentive to the prevention of carelessness among employees. There is a perfectly adequate incentive to the prevention of laziness. The lazy employee is discharged. Let society once provide the capable intellect of the United States Steel Corporation with a sufficient reason for preventing carelessness, and it will be the one best bet of the age that there will be no more carelessness in any of the United States Steel Corporation plants.

The forty-six men who were killed last year in the South Chicago plant of the United States Steel Corporation went to their deaths by a large number of different and divergent routes. Twelve of them were killed in the neighborhood of blast furnaces. One of them was hurled out of life by a stick of dynamite. Three of them were electrocuted. Three of them were killed by falls from high places. Four of them were struck on their heads by falling objects. Four of them were burned to death by hot metal in the Bessemer Converter Department, where, as in the Open Hearth Department, iron is transformed into steel. Three of them were crushed to death. One of them was suffocated by the gas from a gas-producer. One of them was thrown from an ore-bridge by a high wind. One of them was hit by a red-hot rail. One of them, Ora Allen, was scorched to death by slag. And ten of them were killed by railroad cars or by railroad locomotives.

This last fact seems most extraordinary, most inexplicable, until an inspection of the plant is made. There are about one hundred and thirty miles of track in that plant, broad-gauge track, narrow-gauge track, stretching across open spaces, wiggling between dead walls, swerving around corners, darting through buildings, running in twenties, running in couples, climbing up to the mouths of the Bessemer converters, descending to the level of the lake shore, creeping across the Calumet down and away to Indiana.

And there are cars, cars carrying coke, cars carrying limestone, cars carrying ladles of liquid iron, cars carrying pots of hot slag, cars carrying ingots of red steel.

And there are locomotives, all kinds of locomotives, all the way from the through freight locomotive that can haul eighty cars of coke, to the little "dinky" locomotive that looks like a toy and that hauls the steel ingots from the Bessemer and Open Hearth Departments to the rail mill, the slabbing mill, the blooming mill, the billet mill, and the structural-shape mill.

At the south end of the plant there is a high bridge that spans a series of switching-tracks. Elsewhere the men go across at grade. There are danger signs, but it is useless to expect a Slovenian who has worked all day in the heat and glare and stress of a blast furnace to pay much attention to a danger sign, especially if he doesn't know how to read, which he usually doesn't. There will be more bridges and a few subways in the South Chicago plant of the United States Steel Corporation before that corporation is many years older. As things stand today, the men have come to expect the danger signs to be supplemented by the puffing and clanging of the locomotive and by the cries of the engineer.

This point of view was admirably illustrated by a man who was injured not long ago but who fortunately recovered. He described his accident succinctly as follows:

"No choo choo! No ling ling! No God damn you get out of the way! Just run over!"

The only death-dealing force that exceeded the railroad last year in the Illinois Steel Company plant was the blast furnace.

There are eleven blast furnaces in the plant. Each of them is a fire-brick and cast-iron giant a hundred and fifty feet high and containing from six hundred to a thousand tons of tumultuous material. When you feed it at its top with coke, limestone, and iron ore, you cannot tell exactly what is happening inside it, until from the tapping hole at its base, you withdraw the pure iron and the refuse that is called slag. Its digestive tract is too long and too well concealed. A blast furnace is like a human being. When it is in trouble you have to make a diagnostic guess from the outside.

On the ninth of last October, at about ten o'clock in the evening, Walter Stelmaszyk, a sample-boy, went to one of the blast furnaces to get a sample of iron to take to the laboratory. He stood at one of the entrances to the platform. The bright, liquid iron was running out of its tapping hole and flowing in a sparkling, snarling stream along its sandy bed to the big twenty-ton ladle that stood beside the platform on a flatcar. Walter Stelmaszyk stood still for a moment and gazed at the scene. It was well for him that he hesitated. Suddenly there came a flash, a roar and a drizzle of molten metal. Milak Lazich, Andrew Vrkic, Anton Pietszak, and Louis Fuerlant lay charred and dead on the casting-floor.

What was the cause of the accident?

The expert witnesses, employed around the blast furnace, all agreed that the hot metal had come in contact with water.

And how did it come in contact with water?

Here, again, the expert witnesses were in agreement.

About two months before the accident, the keeper of the furnace had called the attention of the foreman to a little trickling of water around the tapping hole. An examination was made and it was found that some of the firebrick at one side of the tapping hole had fallen out. The foreman reported this fact to his immediate superior. But the firebrick was not replaced. Patches of fire clay were substituted for it. These patches were renewed from time to time. They wore out very rapidly.

On the night of the ninth of October, according to all the experts at the trial, the fierce molten iron ate its way through the fire clay and came in contact with a water coil. The union of the hot iron with the water resulted in the explosion and in the sacrifice of four human lives.

It is true that no similar accident had ever before happened. The company did not mean to kill those men. I am making no such foolish charge. But, as in the case of Ora Allen, I ask the question whether or not the company would exercise a stricter surveillance over the recklessness of its foremen and workingmen if it had a stronger pecuniary incentive. In other words, if the company were offered a prize of a million dollars for getting through a year without one single fatal accident, would it then allow patches of fire clay to be used as a substitute for firebrick around the tapping hole of any furnace in its plant? Would it not find a way to prevent such makeshift methods effectually and finally?

When the accident had happened, the water in the coil just next to the place where the fire clay had been eaten away and where the explosion had originated was shut off. The man who shut it off was a pipe fitter, G. H. Hunter.

"In your opinion," said the deputy coroner, "would it have been safe to run the furnace before this accident with the water a little bit further away from the tapping hole?"

"No, sir."

"Is the furnace running that way now?"

"Yes, sir."

"Is it safe now?"

"No, sir, not as safe as it was when the water was running."

And it was while the water was running that the accident happened and that the four men were killed. Before the accident the furnace was evidently in a dangerous condition. After the accident it was apparently in a still more dangerous condition!

How can the Illinois Manufacturers' Association think, when such evidence, given under oath, is public property, that the State of Illinois or the United States of America will continue to regard the killing and maiming of employees as an entirely private matter between those employees and the company in whose service they were slaughtered or injured? All sentiments of humanity offer an invulnerable negative to that proposition. And so also, as I shall show later, do all considerations of enlightened selfishness.

The total number of men killed last year by blast furnaces in the plant of the Illinois Steel Company was twelve. Not all of these men were burned to death. Some were struck by flying objects and some were asphyxiated by the gas which constantly escapes from the pores of a blast furnace and which can sometimes be seen, burning with a ghastly blue flame, along the crevices between the bricks.

I am perfectly willing to admit that it is exceedingly difficult to prevent all exhibitions of recklessness even in cases in which the company has provided certain measures of precaution. This is intended to be a fair article. It would do no permanent good unless it were fair. And recklessness is certainly a psychological characteristic of men in steel plants. All tradition teaches them to be reckless. The very example of their superiors teaches them to be reckless. The assistant superintendent of the plant that the Illinois Steel Company maintains at Joliet stepped on an unprotected gear and lost his leg just after he had warned his men not to be guilty of any such culpable negligence of their own safety. I am willing to admit the existence of culpable negligence altogether apart from the negligence of the company. And not only that, but I am also willing to give a specific illustration.

I was standing one day on the platform of a blast furnace. All at once, unexpectedly, I heard the four whistles that indicate danger. There was a "hang" in the furnace. The whirling, eddying mass of ore, coke and limestone in the high interior of that furnace had got caught somewhere, somehow, and was refusing to come down. When it did come down, there would be a crash, and, perhaps, an explosion.

I ran and got behind a brick pillar. On coming into the plant that morning I had signed a piece of paper, just the same kind of piece of paper that every visitor signs, saying that I would not hold the Illinois Steel Company responsible for anything that might happen to me. I reflected that nobody would profit by my demise. But observe what the other men around that blast furnace did!

I could see them as I peered out from behind my brick pillar. Those of them who were already in front of the furnace looked up at it with an expression of profound curiosity on their faces. Two other men who had been standing at the back of the furnace ran all the way around it and came out in front! There they all stood, hurling their mute interrogatories at the crafty, reticent volcano that might nevertheless the next moment hurl forth an indignant answer at their heads!

In a steel mill there is still another element besides recklessness to be considered. It is this:

Most steel men have come up from the ranks. They have themselves risked their lives. They have become hardened to scenes that chill the blood of the fresh observer.

Most steel men in the United States today (and I am talking of steel men, not financiers) have themselves leaped those flaming streams of angry metal, have themselves dodged the red-hot, writhing steel snakes that hiss through the big cast-iron rolls of the rail mill on their way to the straightening beds, have themselves fallen dizzy to the ground with the gaseous breath of the blast furnace stoves in their lungs.

Steel is War. When it is finished it brings forth, for the victors, Skibo Castles and Peace Conferences. But while it is in process it is War.

The superintendent of the South Chicago plant of the United States Steel Corporation is a young man named Field, William A. Field. I investigated his career.

When he came to the South Chicago plant from Kentucky via Stevens Institute, his first day's work lasted twenty-four hours. When he had worked twelve hours, his foreman said to him: "Run home now and get a bit to eat and be back here as soon as you can." He came back and worked twelve hours longer.

Today they have a fiendish institution at the South Chicago plant called the twenty-four-hour shift. Eighteen hundred men in that plant work for twenty-four hours without stopping, on every alternate Sunday. They begin on Sunday morning and work through without a pause till Monday morning at seven o'clock. In order to keep awake, some of the men cultivate a keen intellectual interest in the mechanical processes about them. Others swallow chewing tobacco. It is a frightful stretch of time. But William A. Field not only worked that twenty-four-hour shift on his own account when he was sculling ladles (which means cleaning the slag out of them) but, even after being promoted from that menial employment, he has worked seventy-two hours at a stretch without sleeping, and has worked one hundred and sixty-eight hours without any other kind of sleep than that which can be gathered from a hard chair in a dark corner.

What is the use of talking to a man like that about the severity of a twenty-four-hour shift? When two sheets in the steam pipe in the pump room of the rail mill were blown out and three men and a boy were killed, Field worked from Sunday evening to Wednesday evening without ever closing his eyes. And then he spent the rest of Wednesday evening at the opera. And when the rail mill at Joliet was frozen up by a cold winter, Field stayed in the mill a whole week, with a chair for a bed, and kept that mill from complete stagnation at the cost of seven nights' sleep and also at the cost, in all probability, of three or four years of his life.

On one occasion Field was knocked twenty feet by a stray crowbar and experienced some difficulty in recovering. On another occasion the top of his hat was shaved neatly off by a hot rail which just missed shaving off his scalp. On still another occasion he walked off a dock into the Calumet River and was pulled out just in time.

I admire such a man. There is no man I admire more. But I deny that he constitutes a good judge of ordinary human safety for ordinary human beings. He is an exceptional man who enjoys an exceptional reward. He therefore risks his life and becomes superintendent. The ordinary man risks his life and does not become superintendent. It is for him that measures of safety are demanded. His only possible reward is a continuance of the life that God has given him.

Nevertheless, if you want to understand the psychology of a man like Field, just stand in front of the three converters in the Bessemer Department. There they swing and sway and tip, shaped like the enormous, mythical eggs attributed to that strange and never-yet-discovered bird called the roc by the Oriental authors of the *Arabian Nights*. It is only the roc that could have laid such eggs. They contain fifteen tons apiece. They receive iron. They produce steel. The metal within them, tossed by currents of compressed air, boils and bubbles. When they tip over, to discharge their burdens into the ladles beneath, they fill the whole building with fluttering sparks and thick, whirling fumes which vary in color from light gray to deep orange. The clothes of the men in this department are filled with fine holes burned in them by the sparks. When the ladles are filled, the boiling metal exudes queer little tender blue flames all over its white surface. The men call this weird display "the devil's flower garden." With less apparent poetry they have nick-named the steel ingots in which the metal finally leaves the Bessemer Department on flatcars, calling them "hot tamales."

I make all due allowance for the diabolical hypnotism exercised over the men in a steel mill, from highest to lowest, by the overwhelming majesty of the instruments with which they work. And for that very reason I believe in the intervention of the public authorities, and in the supervision that is exercised over industrial establishments in many of the countries of Europe by public officials who have not been hypno-tized by daily intercourse with Bessemer converters.

And at the same time I wish to give all due credit to the present management of the Illinois Steel Company. It has shaken itself almost awake from the hypnotism of the Bessemer converters. It has devoted itself, so far as its lights extend, to the reformation of its plant. It has established a Safety Department. This department is partly selfish, partly philanthropic. It has photographers who take a picture of every accident, just as soon as it has happened, for the purpose of furnish-ing evidence in the courts if the relatives of the deceased should sue for damages. But it also suggests changes to be made in the construc-tion of the plant for the purpose of preventing future accidents. The motive in this case is, I fully believe, disinterested. The present laws of Illinois on the subject of industrial accidents furnish no other ade-quate motive. And, on the basis of the recommendations of its Safety Department, the Illinois Steel Company made three thousand changes last year in the construction of its plant. This fact is an eloquent commentary not only on the present awakenment of the company but also on the previous condition of the plant.

The operating men who manage the Illinois Steel Company are human beings. They do not wish to commit either murder or suicide. But Steel is War. And it is also Dividends. All the operating men in South Chicago, from William A. Field down to the lowest "Huniak" who now sculls the ladles that Mr. Field used to scull, are bound, hand and foot, by the desire to produce more steel this month than was ever before produced in South Chicago. The figures that indicate production and profits are the only figures handled and scrutinized by the members of the board of directors of the United States Steel Corporation. Steel is War. And it is a war in which the commanding officers as well as the privates are exposed to the immediate fire of the enemy.

The greatest steel man that America ever produced, Bill Jones, was killed by a blast furnace. At the time of his death he was drawing a salary equal to that of the President of the United States. He went from this world to the world beyond in company with a dollar-a-day Hungarian laborer. Bill Jones was the man who put the United States ahead of Great Britain in the rapid and economical production of iron and steel. And if Bill Jones was killed by a blast furnace, why not Steve Bragosimshamski?

That is the spirit of the War of Steel.

It is not surprising, therefore, that on the sixth of February, this year, the Building Department of the City of Chicago, being a department of peace, was forced to intervene in the aftermath of an accident in the pig-casting department of the Illinois Steel Company. Ten or twelve men had been injured. A thirty-ton ladle had tipped all the way over and had wrecked the roof and sides of the building, besides subjecting the ten or twelve men above mentioned to considerable bodily discomfort.

During the previous year the company had made those three thousand changes in its plant. But it hadn't been able to make that pig-casting department safe. Building Commissioner Bartzen suggested that the thirty-ton ladles of hot iron should be anchored to the columns of the building in order to prevent them from tipping over. The company apparently had not thought of that. According to the public records of the Building Department in the City Hall in Chicago, the Illinois Steel Company accepted almost every suggestion made to it by the Building Department during the regime of Building Commissioner Bartzen. But it did not divine those suggestions on its own account before they were made.

I do not blame the Illinois Steel Company for failing to divine those suggestions. A company whose nose is close up against a thirty-ton ladle of molten iron has an almost sufficient excuse. But it is for that very reason, as I have previously indicated, that I here make an argument for public supervision.

This argument is based only in part on considerations of humanity. For practical purposes it rests on solid motives of self-interest. There is not a single accident that happens to a laborer in the plant of the Illinois Steel Company or in any other industrial plant without tending, directly or indirectly, to loosen the strings of the public purse.

What happens to Steve Bragosimshamski's widow? What happens to his orphans, twelve years, ten years, eight years, six years, four years, two years, six months old? They do not evaporate. They do not comfortably disappear.

In eight cases out of ten, as I am prepared to prove by competent authority, the death of a Steve Bragosimshamski throws no legal money-liability on the company. What do the widow and the orphans do?

Ask the South Chicago Charitable Association. Ask the South Chicago Women's Benevolent Association. Ask the Catholic Aid Association. Ask the authorities at Glenwood, at Feehanville, at the St. Charles Home for Boys. Ask the superintendent of the Hudleston Home for Boys at Ewing. Ask the probation officers of the Juvenile Court. Ask the County Agent who distributes coal in wintertime. Ask the police officers of the Fifteenth Precinct station just off Commercial Avenue. Ask the officials of the County Poorhouse at Dunning. Ask the women who keep the houses of ill fame which line the street that runs along beside the high white fence of the company's plant south of Eighty-ninth Street.

For these things society pays. For poverty, demoralization, vice and crime, the price is laid down by society either through the generosity of private individuals or through the expensive and cumbrous action of public officials.

Nothing is gained without its price. If it is cheap to kill Steve Bragosimshamski, it is expensive to support his wife and family. And since society, in the long run, supports that wife and that family, it is inevitable that society shall seek to understand and to prevent the industrial accidents which encumber it with such burdens.

There are two remedies, therefore, that will certainly be applied to situations of the kind that we have been studying.

The first is complete publicity, including a report to the public authorities on every accident, fatal or nonfatal. And the second is the granting of power to the public authorities to supervise all machinery in all industrial establishments and to suggest and enforce such changes, within specified limits, as shall seem necessary.

A law embodying the first of these remedies was passed through the Illinois state legislature this year in the teeth of violent opposition. If it is enforced, it will do a world of good. A full public report on every industrial accident happening in the State of Illinois will inform the people as to the character and proportions of one of the greatest modern sources of pauperism, vice and crime; it will stimulate the public demand for the public regulation of all dangerous machinery; it will excite the manufacturers to greater carefulness; and, above all, it will remove that veil of secrecy and mystery behind which the great manufacturing corporations now operate and through which the public eye discerns all the faults of these corporations with indistinctness, suspicion, exaggeration and hatred. When there is complete publicity with regard to all accidents, the manufacturing corporations will be more popular than they are today. One of the strongest fostering causes of class antagonism will have been eliminated.

I can give an apposite illustration of what I mean.

It is commonly believed in Chicago (and I have heard it given as a plain fact by scores of citizens) that the Illinois Steel Company conceals a large number of the deaths that happen in its plant and that it buries its victims secretly in mounds of slag. It is also reported that in the Illinois Steel Company hospital the patients are barbarously treated, and that while still in the delirium of pain they are forced to sign legal documents releasing the company from all legal money-liability for the accidents in which they were injured.

These stories are currently reported and implicitly credited. And they are absolutely untrue. The company does not, and cannot if it would, conceal any death in its plant. Its hospital is excellently appointed and superbly managed, and the chief surgeon, Dr. Burry, is a man of the highest professional standing and of the most sensitive self-respect. And there is no proof of any kind that Mr. Haynie, the lawyer in charge of the company's damage suits, has ever countenanced any extorting of releases from delirious or infirm patients.

But I had to disprove these stories by my own efforts. I should never have been obliged to go to that trouble, and the company would never have been suspected of any such abominable practices, if there had always been complete publicity for all industrial accidents in all the manufactories of Illinois.

The second remedy I have suggested (namely, public supervision of dangerous machinery) was defeated in the last legislature by the Illinois Manufacturers' Association after a long fight in which the representatives of the Illinois Steel Company bore a conspicuous part. It was a selfish, short-sighted, inhuman fight. The manufacturers claimed to be in favor of the spirit of the bill but alleged that it was unreasonable. Nevertheless they did not exert themselves to suggest amendments that would have removed its unreasonable features. They simply fought it. And they defeated it. In doing so they prepared a day of judgment for themselves. By their actions, if not by their words, they have taken the position that the public is not concerned with what happens in their plants. I have shown that the public is vitally concerned. And when such facts as I have presented in this article, without exaggeration and without malice, are completely understood, some even more severe bill than that which the Illinois Manufacturers' Association defeated at the last session of the legislature will be enacted into law and will place all dangerous machinery in all manufacturing establishments under the inspection and supervision of public experts.

The only persons who would ultimately suffer by the enactment of such a law would possibly be the undertakers. My last recollection of South Chicago will be the undertakers. They made a kind of raid last year on the Illinois Steel Company plant in order to get the trade that comes with the inquests that are held on the corpses from the Illinois Steel Company hospital.

Every corpse goes to the nearest undertaker unless the relatives intervene. In consequence of this custom it is extremely desirable to have a location near the company's big gate. Hence the raid.

First Mr. Finerty, from 345 Ninety-second Street, moved down to 168. That move gave him precedence. But it did not last long. Mrs. Murphy abandoned her original location, moved along the street and settled down between Mr. Finerty and the mills. So far, so good. Mrs. Murphy was ahead of the game. But then came Mr. Adams, all the way from the outside of South Chicago, and swooped down on the corner of Mackinaw and Eighty-ninth. He is the final winner. He is closer to the plant today than either Mr. Finerty or Mrs. Murphy.

This comic interlude in the grim tragedy of South Chicago remains firmly fixed in the memory of the spectator, like the antics of the gravedigger in *Hamlet*. More essential incidents, more important facts, may fade away and disappear. But when you leave the cave of smoke on the north bank of the Calumet River; when you gaze at all that abomination of desolation in the foreign quarter of South Chicago, where no steel magnate, even though blessing a multitude of distant prairie towns with libraries, has ever left a single discernible trace of benevolence for the people who actually make the steel that pays for the libraries; when you send your mind back over the wonderful, gigantic machinery, the superhuman processes, hidden in the cave of smoke behind you; why, even then, even while all these things are pressing upon your attention, they suddenly slip away from you, and as you take your seat in the train the last image that is presented to you is the race of those undertakers on toward the great gate of the plant. You see them coming closer and closer. You see them settling down and waiting. And then you see the dead bodies coming out from the plant and being carried into the back rooms and being lawfully viewed and having true presentment made as to how and in what manner and by whom or what they came to be what they are now.

Is the public concerned? If it says it is, then it is.

Everybody's Magazine
November 1907

CHILD LABOR

CHILD LABOR had existed in the United States from its early days. But not until the latter decades of the nineteenth century, with the development of the factory system, did child labor become a serious menace.

More and more children became caught in the spreading factory octopus. It is estimated by some sources that by 1900 at least 1.7 million children were employed, of whom about 40 per cent were in factories, mines, tenement workshops and textile mills.

It was in these industrial concerns that the conditions were the worst and the exploitation the most ruthless.

The muckrakers were not the first to decry or expose these conditions. Other writers, including John Spargo, Robert Hunter and Mrs. Van Vorst, had done so in the past. Together with the muckrakers, they helped to create a changed attitude toward child labor, and their studies gave impetus to child labor legislation.

Edwin Markham, who attained world fame with his poem "The Man with the Hoe," and has been called the "poet of the muckrakers," created a sensation with a series of articles titled "The Hoe-Man in the Making."

With irony and brilliance he told of the yearly sacrifice of children in the glass factories, at the loom, in the mines, in box factories and sweatshops, cigar and tobacco shops and candy factories.

Cosmopolitan in announcing the series in its August 1906 issue said that "Edwin Markham, author of 'The Man with the Hoe,' has written a wonderfully strong series of articles against child-labor and kindred evils, under the title 'The Hoe-Man in the Making.' This series, which shows how the Man with the Hoe, the brother to the ox, has sprung into being, will run for several months in the Cosmopolitan. It is written in the beautiful poetic prose of our acknowledged foremost man of letters."

Two months later, Cosmopolitan told its readers that Markham "struck twelve in his first installment . . . [nobody else] has presented so startling and convincing a document."

The magazine urged its readers to join the Child Labor Federation as "all these movements tend to sway legislation in favor of the child-workers."

In November, Cosmopolitan pointed out "the widespread indignation aroused by Edwin Markham's portrayal of child-labor conditions and the responses that keep pouring in to the new Child Labor Federation, show the detestation with which the exploitation of children is viewed."

Also contributing to the literature of exposure on child labor was William Hard in "De Kid Wot Works at Night."

Mr. Hard recalls that his article "had a considerable influence in promoting adequate child-labor legislation in my then state of Illinois. Such legislation had been denounced by many employers as 'Socialism.' My article . . . did a lot to explode that foolish charge in the Illinois State Legislature." [141]

By 1907, two-thirds of the states had either initiated or passed or improved protective legislation for children. Congress enacted a law in 1916 excluding from interstate transportation products of factories which employed children under fourteen years of age. The law became effective September 1, 1917. But on June 3, 1918, by a five-to-four vote, the Supreme Court of the United States declared the law unconstitutional. In 1919 Congress imposed a 10 per cent tax on net profits of factories employing children. Here again the Supreme Court in May 1922 held the law unconstitutional.*

Muckraking as a movement was already dead when the Sixty-eighth Congress in 1924 submitted to the states a proposal for an amendment which would give it the "power to limit, regulate and prohibit the labor of persons under 18 years of age."

The proposed amendment was not adopted because of lack of ratification by the necessary three-quarters of the states, but child-labor regulation through Federal legislation was finally adopted through the Fair Labor Standards Act of 1938 and its 1949 amendments.

* Hammer *v.* Dagenhart and Bailey *v.* Drexel Furniture Co.

EDWIN MARKHAM

The Hoe-Man in the Making

O NCE, so the story goes, an old Indian chieftain was shown the
ways and wonders of New York. He saw the cathedrals, the sky-
scrapers, the bleak tenements, the blaring mansions, the crowded circus,
the airy span of the Brooklyn Bridge. "What is the most surprising thing
you have seen?" asked several comfortable Christian gentlemen of this
benighted pagan whose worship was a "bowing down to sticks and
stones." The savage shifted his red blanket and answered in three slow
words, "Little children working."

It has remained, then, for civilization to give the world an abominable custom which shocks the social ethics of even an unregenerate
savage. For the Indian father does not ask his children to work, but
leaves them free till the age of maturity, when they are ushered with
solemn rites into the obligations of their elders. Some of us are won-
dering why our savage friends do not send their medicine men as missionaries, to shed upon our Christian darkness the light of barbarism.
Child labor is a new thing in human affairs. Ancient history records
no such infamy. "Children," says the Talmud, "must not be taken from
the schools even to rebuild the temple." In Greece and Rome the children of both slave and master fared alike in a common nursery. The
trainers worked to build up strong and beautiful bodies, careless of the
accident of lineage or fortune. But how different is our "Christian
civilization"! Seventeen hundred thousand children at work! Does the
enumeration bring any significance to our minds when we say that an
army of one million seven hundred thousand children are at work in our
"land of the free"? This was the figure in 1900; now there are hundreds
of thousands more. And many of them working their long ten or fourteen hours by day or by night, with only a miserable dime for a wage!
Can the heart take in the enormity?

Picture the procession of them all—enough to people a modern Babylon—all held from the green fields, barred from school, shut out of home, dragged from play and sleep and rest, and set tramping in grim, forced march to the mills and mines and shops and offices in this our America—the land whose name we have been told is Opportunity! We of the "upper crust" give our children books and beauty by day, and fold them into white beds at night; and we feel all this caretaking to be only the natural order of things. Do we ever think of the over two million children who—in free America—are pushed out as little burden bearers to share the toils and strains and dangers of the world of battling men?

Let us glance into the weaving rooms of the cotton mills and behold in the hot, damp, decaying atmosphere the little wan figures flying in hideous cotillion among looms and wheels—children choked and blinded by clouds of lint forever molting from the webs, children deafened by the jar and uproar of an eternal Niagara of machines, children silenced utterly in the desert desolation in the heart of the never-ceasing clamor, children that seem like specter-shapes, doomed to silence and done with life, beckoning to one another across some thunder-shaken Inferno.

Is it not shameful, is it not astounding that this craft that was known to the toilers of Memphis and Shushan, of Sardis and Tadmor, should now, after all the advance of the ages, be loaded in any degree upon the frail, half-formed bodies of little children? To what purpose then is our "age of invention"? Why these machines at all, if they do not help to lift care from the soul and burden from the back? To what purpose is our "age of enlightenment," if, just to cover our nakedness, we establish among us a barbarism that overshadows the barbarism of the savage cycle? Is this the wisdom of the wise? Is this the Christianity we boast of and parade in benighted Madagascar and unsaved Malabar? Is this what our orators mean when they jubilate over "civilization" and "the progress of the species"?

After all these ages, more children are crowded into this limbo of the loom than into any other cavern of our industrial abyss. In the southern cotton mills, where the doors shut out the odor of the magnolia and shut in the reeking damps and clouds of lint, and where the mocking bird outside keeps obbligato to the whirring wheels within, we find a gaunt goblin army of children keeping their forced march on the factory floors—an army that outwatches the sun by day and the stars by night. Eighty thousand children, mostly girls, are at work in the textile mills of the United States. The South, the center of the cotton industry, happens to have the eminence of being the leader in this social infamy. At the beginning of 1903 there were in the South twenty thousand children at the spindles. *The Tradesman,* of Chattanooga, estimates that with the springing up of new mills there must now be fifty thousand children at the southern looms. This is 30 per cent of all the cotton workers of the South—a spectral army of pygmy people sucked in from the hills to dance beside the crazing wheels.

Let us again reckon up this Devil's toll. In the North (where, God knows, conditions are bad enough), for every one thousand workers over sixteen years of age there are eighty-three workers under sixteen (that young old-age of the working-child); while in the South, for every one thousand workers in the mills over sixteen years of age there are three hundred and fifty-three under sixteen. Some of these are eight and nine years old, and some are only five and six. For a day or a night at a stretch these little children do some one monotonous thing—abusing their eyes in watching the rushing threads; dwarfing their muscles in an eternity of petty movements; befouling their lungs by breathing flecks of flying cotton; bestowing ceaseless, anxious attention for hours, where science says that "a twenty-minute strain is long enough for a growing mind." And these are not the children of recent immigrants, hardened by the effete conditions of foreign servitude. Nor are they Negro children who have shifted their shackles from field to mill. They are white children of old and pure colonial stock. Think of it! Here is a people that has outlived the bondage of England, that has seen the rise and fall of slavery—a people that must now fling their children into the clutches of capital, into the maw of the blind machine; must see their latest-born drag on in a face of servility that reminds us of the Saxon churl under the frown of the Norman lord. For Mammon is merciless.

Fifty thousand children, mostly girls, are in the textile mills of the South. Six times as many children are working now as were working twenty years ago. Unless the conscience of the nation can be awakened, it will not be long before one hundred thousand children will be hobbling in hopeless lock-step to these Bastilles of labor. It will not be long till these little spinners shall be "far on the way to be spiders and needles."

Think of the deadly drudgery in these cotton mills. Children rise at half-past four, commanded by the ogre scream of the factory whistle; they hurry, ill fed, unkempt, unwashed, half dressed, to the walls which shut out the day and which confine them amid the din and dust and merciless maze of the machines. Here, penned in little narrow lanes, they look and leap and reach and tie among acres and acres of looms.

Always the snow of lint in their faces, always the thunder of the machines in their ears. A scant half hour at noon breaks the twelve-hour vigil, for it is nightfall when the long hours end and the children may return to the barracks they call "home," often too tired to wait for the cheerless meal which the mother, also working in the factory, must cook, after her factory day is over. Frequently at noon and at night they fall asleep with the food unswallowed in the mouth. Frequently they snatch only a bite and curl up undressed on the bed, to gather strength for the same dull round tomorrow, and tomorrow, and tomorrow.

When I was in the South I was everywhere charmed by the bright courtesy of the cultured classes, but I was everywhere depressed by the stark penury of the working people. This penury stands grimly out in the gray monotonous shells that they call "homes"—dingy shacks, or bleak, barnlike structures. And for these dirty, desolate homes the workers must pay rent to the mill owner. But the rent is graded according to the number of children sent to work in the mill. The more the children, the less the rent. Mammon is wise: he knows how to keep a cruel grip upon the tots at the fireside.

And why do these children know no rest, no play, no learning, nothing but the grim grind of existence? Is it because we are all naked and shivering? Is it because there is sudden destitution in the land? Is it because pestilence walks at noonday? Is it because war's red hand is pillaging our storehouses and burning our cities? No, forsooth! Never before were the storehouses so crammed to bursting with bolts and bales of every warp and woof. No, forsooth! The children, while yet in the gristle, are ground down that a few more useless millions may be heaped up. We boast that we are leading the commercialism of the world, and we grind in our mills the bones of the little ones to make good our boast.

Rev. Edgar Murphy of Montgomery, Alabama, has photographed many groups of these pathetic little toilers, all under twelve. Jane Addams saw in a night-factory a little girl of five, her teeth blacked with snuff, like all the little girls about her—a little girl who was busily and clumsily tying threads in coarse muslin. The average child lives only four years after it enters the mills. Pneumonia stalks in the damp, lint-filled rooms, and leads hundreds of the little ones out to rest. Hundreds more are maimed by the machinery, two or three for each of their elders. One old mill hand carries sixty-four scars, the cruel record of the shuttles.

The labor commissioner of North Carolina reports that there are two hundred and sixty-one cotton mills in that state, in which nearly forty thousand people are employed, including nearly eight thousand children. The average daily wage of the men is fifty-seven cents, of the women thirty-nine cents, of the children twenty-two cents. The commissioner goes on to say: "I have talked with a little boy of seven years who worked for forty nights in Alabama, and with another child who, at six years of age, had been on the night shift eleven months. Little boys turned out at two o'clock in the morning, afraid to go home, would beg a clerk in the mill for permission to lie down on the office floor. In one city mill in the South, a doctor said he had amputated the fingers of more than one hundred children, mangled in the mill machinery, and that a horrible form of dropsy occurs frequently among the overworked children." . . .

But not alone upon the South lies the blame of these human hells. Many of the mills of the South are owned by New England capitalists, the machinery having been removed from the North to the South, so as to be near the cotton fields, near the water power, and shame to record, near the cheap labor of these baby fingers, for the brief time before they shall be folded waxenly and forever. It was the New England shipper, greedy for gold at any cost, who carried the blacks to the South, planting the tree of slavery in our soil. And now it is the northern money-grubber who is grafting upon our civilization this new and more terrible white slavery. "South Carolina weaves cotton that Massachusetts may wear silk!"

This new slavery of the mills is worse than the old slavery of the cotton fields. For the Negro of the old days was well fed and sure of shelter; he did his work under the open sky, singing as he toiled, and finding time to weave out of his mystic brain a wild balladry and a poetic folklore. But the slavery of the white women and children sucks life dry of all vigor and all joy. These white workers are stunted, slow and sad; their lives are emptied of passion and poetry. In the long revolution of the wheel of Change, in the irony of the grim Destinies who laugh behind the veil, it is now the stiff-necked whites—they who of old would not work beside the Negro—who in this generation must bear all the burden of the mill. The young Negro, not cunning enough to speed the spindle, is spared. It is now the white child who is in bondage, while the little [Negro] is out in the cotton fields under the open heavens.

These little white children often begin work in the mill with no fragment of education. And often after a year of this brain-blasting labor they lose the power to learn even the simple art of reading. There is sometimes a night school for the little workers, but they often topple over with sleep at the desks, after the long grind of the day. Indeed they must not spend too many wakeful hours in the night school, shortening their sleep-time; for the ogre of the mill must have all their strength at full head in the morning. The overseer cannot afford to be sending his mounted "poker-up" to their homes to rout them out of bed day after day, nor can he be continually watching lest they fall asleep on the mill floor while working or eating. Nor can he afford to keep a clerk busy docking the wages of these little sleep-starved workers for the constant mistakes and accidents of the fatigued and fumbling fingers. For these little drudges are fined for their lacks and lapses; and they are sometimes in debt to the concern at the week's end.

But worse than all is the breakdown of the soul in these God-forgetting mills. Here boys and girls are pushed into the company of coarse men who are glib with oaths and reeking jests. Torrents of foul profanity from angry overseers wash over the souls of the children, till they, too, grow hardened in crusts of coarseness. Piled on all these are the fearful risks that the young girls run from the attentions of men "higher up," especially if the girls happen to be cursed with a little beauty.

What avail our exports, our tariffs, our dividends, if they rise out of these treasons against God? All gains are losses, all riches are poverties, so long as the soul is left to rot down. What the friends of mercy are pleading, is the old, old plea of the Friend of Children—the plea of him who cried out, "Be not afraid of them which kill the body, but are not able to kill the soul: but rather fear him which is able to destroy both body and soul in hell."

The poor remnant of these young toilers, they who do not crumble down in an early death, or drift to the gutter or the brothel, are left, alas! to become fathers and mothers. Fathers and mothers, forsooth! What sort of fatherhood and motherhood can we hope for from these children robbed of childhood, from these children with the marrow sucked out of their bones and the beauty run out of their faces? Tragical is it beyond words to think that any of these poor human effigies should ever escape to engender their kind and to send on a still more pitiable progeny. What child worthy of the name can spring from the loins of these withered effigies of men? What babe worthy of the name can be mothered in the side of this wasted and weakened woman who has given her virgin vitality to the Moloch of the mill? And what wonder that, if expelled from the factory as no longer competent to be a cog or a pulley in the vast machine, they have no ambition but to sit idly in the sun? What wonder that the commonwealth, having fostered these dull degenerates, should be forced to care for them in her almshouses, her jails, her asylums? What wonder that only the cheapest and coarsest pleasures can stir their numb spirits? The things of the soul which they have missed, they will never know that they have missed. They sit idly in the sun, a sorrowful type of the savage created by civilization, and sad protest against civilization—the starved, the stunted, the stunned, who speak no protest! . . .

What boots a social order that makes thousands of degenerates as the by-product of its exquisite linens and delicate muslins? Must we take our civilization on such terms as this? Must thousands fall and perish that a few may soar and shine? Let us rather go back to the clout of the savage, for "the body is more than raiment." The savage, the grim son of the forest, has at least a light step, a sound body, a brood of lusty children and a treasure of poetic legend and song. But our savage of civilization, what of him? Look at his wasted body, his empty face, his beauty-robbed existence. Men are such cravens before custom that they often think a thing right because it has been long in existence. But child labor has about it no halo of antiquity. It is a thing of yesterday—a sudden toadstool in the infernal garden. It shot up with the coming of steam and loom at the end of the eighteenth century. England began to fight the villainy in 1802, yet today the black shadow of it lies wide upon America.

The factory, we are told, must make a certain profit, or the owners (absentee proprietors generally, living in larded luxury) will complain. Therefore the president is goaded on by the directors. He in turn whips up the overseer; the overseer takes it out on the workers. So the long end of the lash cuts red the backs of the little children. Need we wonder, then, that cotton-factory stock gives back portly profits—25, 35, yes, even 50 per cent? It pays, my masters, to grind little children into dividends! And the silks and muslins do not show the stain of blood, although they are splashed with scarlet on God's side. . . .

"Rob us of child labor and we will take our mills from your state." This is the frequent threat of the mill owners in the chambers and lobbies of legislation. And, alas! we are in a civilization where such a threat avails. Still, in spite of the apathy of the church, in spite of the assault of the capital, the friends of mercy have in all but four states forced some sort of a protective law: no child under twelve years of age shall work for longer than eight hours, nor any without a common-school education. This reads fairly well; but a law on the statute book is not always a law on the factory-floor. The inspectors are often vigilant and quick with conscience. Some mills desire to keep the law. But others are crooked: they have their forged and perjured certificates, their double payrolls—one for the inspector, another for the countinghouse. They have, also, the device of bringing children in as "mothers' helps," giving the mothers a few more pennies for the baby fingers.

Hard masters of mills, shiftless or hapless parents, even misguided children themselves, all conspire to hold the little slaves to the wheel. Yes, even the children are taught to lie about their age, and their tongues are ever ready with the glib rehearsal. Some mills keep a lookout for the inspector, and at the danger signal the children scurry like rats to hide in attics, to crouch in cellars, behind bales of cotton, under heaps of old machinery. But God's battle has begun. Still there must be a wider unification of the bands of justice and mercy, a fusing and forcing of public opinion. Let the women of America arise, unite, and resolve in a great passion of righteousness to save the children of the nation. Nothing can stand against the fire of an awakened and banded womanhood.

Cosmopolitan
September 1906

WILLIAM HARD

C&X

"De Kid Wot Works at Night"

WHEN THE SHADES of night look as if they were about to fall; when the atmosphere of Chicago begins to change from the dull gray of unaided local nature to the brilliant white of artificial illumination; when the Loop District, the central crater of the volcano, is filling up rapidly with large numbers of straps [streetcars] which have been brought downtown from outlying carbarns for the convenience of those who have had enough and who now wish to withdraw; when the sound of the time clock being gladly and brutally punched is heard through every door and window—

When all these things are happening, and, besides—

When all the fat men in the city get to the streetcars first, and all the lean and energetic and profane men have to climb over them to the inner seats; when the salesladies in the department stores throw the night-covers over bargain ormolu clocks just as you pant up to the counter; when the man who has just bought a suburban house stops at the wholesale meat market and carries home a left-over steak in order to have the laugh on the high-priced suburban butcher; when you are sorry your office is on the fifth floor because there are so many people on the eleventh floor and the elevator goes by you without stopping, while you scowl through the glass partition—

When all these things are happening, and, besides—

When the clocks in the towers of the railway stations are turned three minutes ahead so that you will be sure to be on time and so that you will also be sure to drop into your seat with fractured lungs; when the policeman blows his whistle to make the streetcar stop, and the motorman sounds his gong to make the pedestrian stop, and both the motorman and the pedestrian look timorously but longingly at the area of death just in front of the fender; when the streets are full and the straps are full, and the shoes of the motor-cars of the elevated trains are throwing yellow sparks on the shoulders of innocent bystanders; when the reporters, coming back to their offices from their afternoon assignments, are turning about in their doorways to watch the concentrated agony of an American home-going and are thanking God that they go home at the more convenient hour of 1 A.M.—

When all these things are happening, and when, in short, it is between five and six o'clock in the afternoon, the night newsboy and the night messenger boy turn another page in the book of experience and begin to devote themselves once more to the thronging, picturesque, incoherent characters of the night life of a big American city.

Then it is, at just about five o'clock, that the night messenger boy opens the door of his office by pushing against it with his back, turns around and walks sidewise across the floor, throws himself down obliquely on his long, smooth bench, slides a foot or two on the polished surface, comes to a stop against the body of the next boy, and begins to wait for the telegrams, letters and parcels that will keep him engaged till one o'clock the next morning and that may lead his footsteps either to the heavily curtained drawing rooms of disorderly houses in the Red Light district or to the wet planks of the wharves on the Calumet River twelve miles away, where he will curl up under the stars and sleep till the delayed boat arrives from Duluth.

Then it is that the night messenger boy's friend and ally, the night newsboy, gets downtown from school, after having said good-by to his usually mythical "widowed mother," and after having assumed the usually imaginary burden of the support of a "bereaved family." Then it is, at about five o'clock, that he approaches his favorite corner, grins at the man who owns the corner news stand, receives "ten *Choinals*, ten *Murrikins*, ten *Snoozes*, and five *Posts*"; goes away twenty feet, turns around, watches the corner-man to see if he has marked the papers down in his notebook, hopes that he hasn't marked them down, thinks that perhaps he has forgotten just how many there were, wonders if he couldn't persuade him that he didn't give him any "*Murrikins*," calculates the amount of his profit if he should be able to sell the "*Murrikins*" without having to pay the corner-man for them, turns to the street, dodges a frenzied automobile, worms his way into a hand-packed streetcar (which is the only receptacle never convicted by the city government of containing short measure), disappears at the car door, comes to the surface in the middle of the aisle, and hands a *News* to a regular customer.

From the time when the arc lamps sputter out bravely against the evening darkness to the time when they chatter and flicker themselves into extinction before the cold, reproving rays of the early morning sun, what does the street-boy do? What does he see? What films in the moving picture of a big American city are unrolled before his eyes? These are questions that are important to every American city, to every mission superintendent, to every desk sergeant, to every penitentiary warden, to every father, to every mother.

Night, in these modern times, is like the United States Constitution. It is an admirable institution, but it doesn't know what is happening beneath it. Night comes down on Chicago and spreads its wings as largely and as comfortably now as when the *Tribune* building was a sand dune. You stand on Madison Street and look upward, through the glare of the arc lamps, and you see old Mother Night still brooding above you, calmly, imperturbably, quite unconscious of the fact that her mischievous children have lined her feathers with electricity, kerosene, acetylene, coal gas, water gas, and every other species of unlawful, unnatural illuminating substance. She still spreads her wings, simply, grandly, with the cosmic unconcern of a hen that doesn't know she is hatching out ducks instead of chickens; and in the morning she rises from her nest and flutters away westward, feeling quite sure that she has fulfilled her duty in an ancient, regular and irreproachable manner.

She would be quite maternally surprised if she could know what her newsboys and messenger boys are doing while she (good, proper mother!) is nodding her head beautifully among the stars.

I do not mean by this remark to disparage the newsboy. He occupies in Chicago a legal position superior to that of the president of a railway company. The president of a railway company is only an employee. He receives a weekly, a monthly, or at least a yearly salary. The newsboy does not receive a salary. He is not an employee. He is a merchant. He buys his papers and then resells them. He occupies the same legal position as Marshall Field & Co. Therefore he does not fall within the scope of the child-labor law. Therefore no rascally paternalistic factory inspector may vex him in his pursuit of an independent commercial career.

At about five o'clock he strikes his bargain with the corner-man. The corner-man owns the corner. It is a strange and interesting system, lying totally without the pale of recognized law. Theoretically, Dick Kelly, having read the Fourteenth Amendment to the Constitution of the United States, and having become conscious of his rights, might try to set up a news stand at the southwest corner of Wabash and Madison. Practically, the Constitution does not follow the flag as far as that corner. Mr. Kelly's news stand would last a wonderfully short time. The only person who can have a news stand at the corner of Wabash and Madison is Mr. Heffner.

Mr. Heffner is the recognized owner, holder, occupant, possessor, etc., of some eighty square feet of sidewalk space at that point, and his sovereignty extends halfway down the block to the next corner southward, and halfway down the other block to the next corner westward. When Mr. Heffner has been in business long enough he will deed, convey and transfer his rights to some other man for anywhere between $5 and $1,500.

These rights consist exclusively of the fact that the newspapers recognize the corner-man as their only agent at that particular spot. When the corner-man wishes to transfer his corner to somebody else, he must see that the newspapers are satisfied with his choice of a successor.

The newsboy deals, generally speaking, with the corner-man. The corner-man pays the *Daily News* sixty cents for every hundred copies. He then hands out these hundred copies in "bunches" of, say, ten or fifteen or twenty to the newsboys who come to him for supplies. Each newsboy receives, as a commission, a certain number of cents for every hundred copies that he can manage to sell. This commission varies from five to twenty cents. The profit of the corner-man varies therefore with the commission that he pays the newsboy. The public pays one hundred cents for one hundred copies of the *News*. The *News* itself gets sixty cents; the newsboy gets from five to twenty cents; the corner-man gets what is left, namely, from thirty-five down to twenty cents in net profit.

On the basis of this net profit, plus the gross profit on his own sales made directly by himself to his customers, there is more than one corner-man in Chicago who owns suburban property and who could live on the income from his real-estate investments.

From five o'clock, therefore, on to about half past six, the newsboy flips streetcars and yells "turrible murdur" on commission. But pretty soon the corner-man wants to go home. He then sells outright all the papers left on the stand. The newsboy makes him an offer. It is like a fire sale.

"Forty cents fer de whole lot," says the newsboy.

"Fifty cents," says the corner-man.

"Forty. Dat's all."

"Fifty. I'll sell 'em to the nigger kid."

"Forty. Youse seen me lick dat kid meself yestiddy. He ain't no good."

"Oh, you ain't so much yerself. Sammy Ryan, that works fer the man on the next corner, I seen him more than halfway down to this corner ten times today. W'y didn't you hand it to 'im? Because you can't. That's w'y. Fifty cents fer the lot!"

"Nit. Say, dat nigger kid got six *Snoozes* from yer today and youse forgot to put 'em down. Forty!"

"You're a liar! That nigger kid is the only one of all twelve of you kids that don't hand it to me like that. He's honest, he is! An' I bet he kin lick any Dago in the town."

At this point the "nigger kid," through no fault of his own, gets pushed off the sidewalk into a pool of dirty water by an extremely angry "Dago."

The "Dago" then returns to the corner-man and says simply but majestically:

"Youse saw me. Forty cents fer de lot!"

"All right. Take 'em, you little pirate," says the corner-man, and thereupon puts on his coat and goes home.

The Italian newsboy is now in full possession of the stand. If he sells the papers for a total of more than forty cents, he wins. If he can't sell them for that, he loses. He has embarked upon a speculation.

This element of speculation is one of the reasons why the Italian boy is distancing all other boys in the business of selling newspapers. He is almost as good a bargainer as the Jewish boy, while at the same time, he is almost as good a fighter as the Irish boy. His power of bargaining and fighting simultaneously renders him almost irresistible, especially when it is combined with his marvelous power of persistence. The Italian boy will stay at his stand till the last paper is sold.

A few years ago a Chicago publisher, making a Sunday morning tour in his automobile, happened to notice that the Irish corners were deserted very early in the day. The Irish boy was a skillful salesman, but as soon as he had made as much money as he needed for temporary purposes he closed up his stand and went to a picnic. The Italian boy, on the other hand, never had money enough until all his papers had been exchanged for an equal number of nickels. The Irish boy was interested in getting money to spend. The Italian boy was interested in getting money.

Therefore, although the Italian is a comparatively late arrival, he already leads the newspaper-selling business. A short time ago Hull House, in connection with other settlements, made a comprehensive investigation of the subject. Out of 1,000 newsboys investigated, cross-examined, tracked to their lairs and tabulated, there were 211 who came from south of the Alps.

Next to the Italians came the "Americans," whatever that may mean. There were 208.

Next to the "Americans" came the Germans, 180 of them. Next to the Germans, occupying fourth place in the list, came the Irish, numbering only 113. Just as the Irishman has lost his place among the "day laborers" and has moved upward into the ranks of the foremen, so he has lost his place among the newspaper vendors of America and has moved upward into the superior financial stratum in which the boys of the family are more likely to be kept at home.

Below the Irish in the Hull House census there follow, with decreasing numbers, the Negroes, the Scandinavians, the Jews, the Poles, the English, the Bohemians, the Dutch, the French, the Canadians, the Greeks, the Scotch, and the Arabians, in the order named. Finally, at the bottom of the list, encompassed with enemies, bobbing irrelevantly in the vortex of the international whirlpool, there are descried the heads of one Austrian, one Dane, one Lithuanian, one Roumanian and one Syrian.

The best specimen of the finished type of newsboy, within my knowledge, is an Italian boy named "Jelly." His father's surname is Cella, but his own name has been "Jelly" ever since he can remember.

"Jelly" was born on the great, sprawly West Side. His father worked during the summer, digging excavations for sewers and gas mains. His mother worked during the winter, making buttonholes in coats, vests, and pants. Neither parent worked during the whole year.

This domestic situation was overlooked by the Hull House investigators. In their report on newsboys they found that the number of paper-selling orphans had been grossly overestimated by popular imagination. Out of 1,000 newsboys in their final tabulation, there were 803 who had both parents living. There were 74 who had only a father living. There were 97 who had only a mother living. There were only 26, out of the whole 1,000, who had neither a father nor a mother to care for them.

But "Jelly" occupied a peculiar position. He had both parents living and yet, from the standpoint of economics, he was a half-orphan, since neither parent worked all the year.

At the age of ten, therefore, "Jelly" began selling papers. His uncle had a news stand on a big important corner not far from "Jelly's" house on the West Side. At the age of ten "Jelly" was selling papers from five to eight in the morning and from five to eight in the evening.

He was therefore inclined to go to sleep at his desk when he was receiving his lesson in mental arithmetic in the public school where he was an unwilling attendant. Nevertheless, he showed an extraordinary aptitude for mental arithmetic a few hours later when he was handing out change to customers on his uncle's corner.

"Jelly" was a pretty good truant in those days. There was no money to be made by going to school and it looked like a waste of time. His acquaintance among truant officers came to be broad and thorough. He was dragged back to school an indefinite number of times. Yet, with the curious limitations of a newsboy's superficially profound knowledge of human nature, he has confided to me the fact that every truant officer gets $1 for every boy that he returns to the principal of his school.

Besides being a pretty good truant, "Jelly" became also a pretty good fighter.

His very first fight won him the undying gratitude of his uncle.

It happened that at that time the struggle between the circulation departments of the evening newspapers was particularly keen. "Jelly's" uncle allowed himself, unwisely, to be drawn into it. The local circulation experts of the *News* and the *American* noticed that on the news stand kept by "Jelly's" uncle the *Journal* was displayed with excessive prominence and the *News* and the *American* were concealed down below. It was currently reported in the neighborhood that "Jelly's" uncle was receiving $10 a week from the *Journal* for behaving in the manner aforesaid.

In about twenty-four hours the corner owned by "Jelly's" uncle bore a tumultuous aspect. The *News* and the *American* had established a rival stand on the other side of the street. This stand was in charge of a man named Gazzolo. Incidentally it happened that a man named Gazzolo had beaten and killed a man named Cella in the vicinity of Naples some five years before.

Gazzolo's news stand had confronted Cella's, frowning at it from across the street, for about a week, when it began to be guarded by some six or seven broad-chested persons in sweaters. Meanwhile Cella's news stand had also acquired a few sweaters inhabited by capable young men of a combative disposition.

On the afternoon of the eighth day the sweatered agents of the *News* and the *American* advanced across the street and engaged the willing agents of the *Journal* in a face-to-face and then hand-to-hand combat.

At least three murders have happened in Chicago since that time in similar encounters. "Nigger" Clark, an agent of the *News*, was killed on the South Side, and the Higgins brothers were killed on the Ashland

Block corner in the downtown district itself, within view of the world-wide commerce transacted in the heart of Chicago. And a Chicago publisher has told me that these three open murders, recognized by everybody as circulation-department murders, must be supplemented by at least six or seven other clandestine murders before the full story of the homicidal rivalry between the agents of Chicago afternoon newspapers is told.

It was amateur murder before the *American* arrived. Then circulation agents began to be enlisted from the ranks of the pupils in the boxing schools, and since that time the circulation situation has become increasingly pugnacious, until today it has reached the State Attorney's office and has come back to the street in the form of indictments and prosecutions.

Typical of this warfare was the fray that followed when the sweatered agents of the *News* and the *American* came across the street and fell rudely upon the news stand of "Jelly's" uncle.

"Jelly's" uncle had his shoulder-blade broken, but "Jelly" himself, being young and agile, escaped from his pursuers and was instantly and miraculously filled with a beautiful idea.

The agents of the *News* and the *American*, coming across the street to attack "Jelly's" uncle, had left Gazzolo's corner unprotected. "Jelly" traversed the cedar blocks of the street and reached Gazzolo in an ecstatic moment when he was surveying the assault on Cella's shoulder-blade with absorbing glee. Just about one-tenth of a second later Mr. Gazzolo was pierced in the region of the abdomen by the largest blade of a small and blunt pocket-knife in the unhesitating right hand of Mr. Cella's nephew, "Jelly."

It was a slight wound, but in consideration of his thoughtfulness in promptly perceiving Mr. Gazzolo's unprotected situation and in immediately running across the street in order to take advantage of it, "Jelly" was transferred by his uncle to a position of independent responsibility. He was put in charge of a news stand just outside an elevated railway station on the South Side.

Nevertheless, even after this honorable promotion, "Jelly's" father continued to take all his money away from him when he came home at night. And the elder Cella did not desist from this practice till his son had been advanced to the supereminent honor of selling papers in the downtown district.

This final transfer happened to "Jelly" when he was fifteen. He still retained his stand on the South Side, selling papers there from five to ten in the morning, but he also came downtown and sold papers at a stand within the Loop from five to nine at night. His uncle had prospered and had been able to invest $1,000 in a downtown corner, which was on the point of being abandoned by a fellow Italian who desired to return to the hills just south of Naples.

Thereafter, till he was sixteen years old, "Jelly" led a full and earnest life. He rose at four; he reached his South Side stand by five; he sold papers there till ten; he reached the downtown district by eleven; he inspected the five-cent theaters and the penny arcades and the alley restaurants till five in the afternoon; he sold papers for his uncle on commission till half past six; he bought his uncle's left-over papers at half past six and sold them on his own account till nine; and then, before going home at ten in order to get his five hours of sleep, he spent a happy sixty minutes reinspecting the five-cent theaters and the penny arcades and dodging Mr. Julius F. Wengierski.

Mr. Wengierski is a probation officer of the Juvenile Court. At that time he was making nightly tours through the downtown district talking to the children on the streets and trying to induce them to go home. He made a special study of some fifty cases, looking into the home circumstances of each child and gathering notes on the reasons why the child was at work. He was assisted by the agents of a reputable and conscientious charitable society.

In only two instances, out of the whole fifty, was the boy's family in need of the actual necessaries of life. In one instance the boy's father was the owner of his house and lot and was earning $5 a day. He also had several hundred dollars in the bank. In only a few instances did the family, as a family, make any considerable gain, for the purposes of household expenses, from the child's labor.

Some fathers, it is true (notably the one who owned his house and lot), used the child selfishly and cruelly as a worker who required no wages and whose total earnings could be appropriated as soon as he came home. It was the same system as that to which "Jelly" had been subjected from ten to fifteen. But these cases were exceptional.

One of the boys was working in order to get the money for the installment payments on a violin, and another was working in order to pay for lessons on a violin of which he was already the complete and enthusiastic owner.

One little girl was selling late editions in the saloons on Van Buren Street in order to have white shoes for her first communion. Another little girl needed shoes of the same color for Easter. Still a third was working in order that after a while she might have clothes just as good as those of the girl who lived next door.

In at least ten of Mr. Wengierski's cases, the reason for earning money on the street at night was the penny arcade and the five-cent theater. The passion for these amusements among children is intense. They will, some of them, work until they have a nickel, expend it on a moving-picture performance, and then start in and work again until they have another nickel to be spent for the same purpose at another "theatorium."

The earnings of these children, according to the Hull House investigation, which is the only authoritative investigation on record, vary from ten cents a day when the children are five years old up to ninety cents a day when they are sixteen. This is the average, but of course there are many children who make less and many who, because of superior skill, make more. Among these latter is "Jelly."

"Jelly's" high average, which used to reach almost $2 a day, was due partly to his own personal power and partly to the fact that on Saturday night he employed the services of his little sister.

Saturday night was "Jelly's" big time. On other nights he went home by ten o'clock. He had to get up by four and it was necessary for even him to take some sleep. But on Saturday night he gave himself up with almost complete abandon to the opportunities of the street.

On that night he used to close up his stand by eight o'clock and then go down to the river and sell his few remaining papers to the passengers on the lake boats. "Last chanst ter git yer *Murrikin!*" "Only one *Choinal* left! De only *Choinal* on de dock!" "Buy a *Post,* mister! Youse won't be able ter sleep ter-night on de boat! De only paper fer only two cents!" "Here's yer *Noose!* Only one cent! No more *Nooses* till youse comes back! Last chanst! Dey will cost yer ten cents apiece on de boat!" "Git yer *Murrikin.* No papers sold on de boat!" "Git yer *Post.* Dey charges yer five cents w'en youse gits 'em on de boat!"

Slightly contradictory those statements of his used to be, but they attained their object. They sold the papers. And as soon as the boats had swung away from their moorings, "Jelly" would come back to the region of the five-cent theaters and the penny arcades and resume his nocturnal inquiries into the state of cheap art.

At half past ten he went to an elevated railway station to meet his little sister. She was ten years old. She had dressed herself for the part. From her ragged and scanty wardrobe she had chosen her most ragged and her scantiest clothes.

Accompanied by his sister, "Jelly" then went to a flower shop and bought a bundle of carnations at closing prices. With these carnations he took his sister to the entrance of the Grand Opera House. There she sold the whole bundle to the people coming out from the performance. Her appearance was picturesque and pitiful. Her net profit from the sale of her flowers was usually about thirty-five cents.

As soon as the flowers were sold and the people had gone away, "Jelly" took his sister back to the elevated station. There he counted the money she had made and put it in his pocket. He then handed her out a nickel for carfare and, in addition, a supplementary nickel for herself. "Jelly" was being rapidly Americanized. If he had remained exactly like his father, he would have surrendered only the nickel for carfare.

It was time now to go to the office of the *American* and get the early morning Sunday editions. "Jelly" began selling these editions at about twelve o'clock. He sold them to stragglers in the downtown streets till two. It was then exactly twenty-two hours since he had left his bed. He began to feel a little bit sleepy. He therefore went down to the river and slept on a dock, next to an old berry crate, till four. At four he rose and took the elevated train to the South Side. There he reached his own news stand and opened it up at about five o'clock. This was his Saturday, Saturday-night, and Sunday-morning routine for a long time. On other nights "Jelly" slept five hours. On Saturday nights he found that two hours was quite enough. And his ability to get along without sleep is characteristic of newsboys and messenger boys rather than exceptional among them.

The reason why "Jelly" used to dodge Mr. Wengierski is now explainable. To begin with, his opinion of all probation officers is unfavorable. He classes them with truant officers. They are not "on the level." They discriminate between different classes of boys. "Jelly" was once accosted by a probation officer at about ten o'clock at night on Clark Street. He gave this probation officer a good tip about a lot of boys who were staying out nights attending services in the old First Methodist Church. These boys had been seen by "Jelly" going home as late as half past ten. The probation officer took no action in their case while at the same time he advised "Jelly" to stop selling papers at an early hour.

Incidents like this had convinced "Jelly" that probation officers were certainly not on the level and were possibly "on the make." But in Mr. Wengierski's case he had an additional reason. Mr. Wengierski was looking for boys of fourteen and under, and, while "Jelly" was entitled by age to escape Mr. Wengierski's notice, he was not so entitled by size. He was sixteen, but he looked not more than thirteen. The street had given him a certain superficial knowledge, but it had dwarfed his body just as surely as it had dwarfed his mind.

Mr. J. J. Sloan, when he was superintendent of the John Worthy School (which is the local municipal juvenile reformatory), reported that the newsboys committed to his care were, on the average, one-third below the stature and one-third below the strength of average ordinary boys of the same age. In the face of testimony of this kind, which could be duplicated from every city in the United States, it seems absurd to talk about the educative influence of the street. That it has a certain educative influence is undeniable, but it is equally undeniable that the boys who are exposed to this influence should be prevented, by proper legislation, from exposing themselves to it for too many hours a day and should especially be prevented from exposing themselves to it for even a single hour after seven o'clock in the evening.

"Jelly" has now become a messenger boy and has been given a new name by his new associates. He will some day go back to the newspaper business because there is more money in it, and "Jelly" is fundamentally commercial. But there seems to be, after all, a certain struggling, unruly bubble of romanticism in his nature and it had to rise to the surface and explode.

"Jelly" first thought of the messenger service when he was attending a five-cent theater. "Jelly" went in. The fleeting pictures on the screen at the farther end of the room were telling a story that filled him with swelling interest. A messenger boy is run over by an automobile. He is taken to the hospital. He regains consciousness in his bed. He remembers his message. He calls for a portable telephone. He phones the message to the young man to whom it was addressed. The young man comes at once to the hospital. The young woman who had sent the message also comes. She wants to find out what has happened to the message. The young man and the young woman meet at the bedside of the messenger boy. They fall into each other's arms and the messenger boy sinks back on his pillow and dies. And it is a mighty good story even if the rough points are not rubbed off.

"Jelly" determined at once to be a messenger boy, without delay.

Messenger boys differ from newsboys in several particulars.

In the first place, when they work at night, they earn a definite wage instead of being out for themselves as independent commercial adventurers. The night messenger boy, from five in the afternoon to one in the morning, earns $1. After that hour he earns overtime at a definite rate. What he picks up incidentally in the way of tips is "velvet." There are messenger boys in Chicago who, at the age of sixteen, are earning at least $60 a month.

In the second place, the night messenger boy, being an employee instead of an independent "merchant," must be at least sixteen years old, under the child-labor statutes of Illinois.

In the third place, the night messenger boy has a point of view that is much more objective and much more artistic than that of the night newsboy. The night messenger boy is not working for himself. He is not worrying about his income. Consequently, he can take a much more disinterested interest in what happens to him.

It was a messenger boy who gave me the last word on the necessary qualifications of a political leader.

He was telling me why it was that messenger boys always act, not as individuals, but in mass. For instance, when one messenger boy is reading a novel, all the others are also reading novels. They will sit in the office, quiet as mice, with a long row of yellow-backs in their hands. Each boy has bought one book, a book of the general character of "Tin-toothed Tom of Tennessee," in exchange for a nickel. Then, by a system of universal transfers, each boy reads every other boy's book before the fad expires. An expenditure of one nickel has provided him with the perusal of some thirty or thirty-five volumes.

But when the novel-reading fad has reached its climax, it ceases suddenly, totally. After that no one would read a novel if he were paid for it. Everybody plays craps. And after everybody has played craps, everybody stops playing craps at the same moment and goes simultaneously, in a body, to the nickel theaters and the penny arcades.

These waves of popular fancy are governed largely by the boy who happens at the time to be "leader."

"And what must a boy do to be leader?"

The answer was instantaneous and comprehensive:

"He must be brave and he must know how ter shoot de gab."

And it might puzzle James Bryce himself to construct a better definition of popular leadership in a pure democracy.

The messenger service is a democracy of the purest kind, courageous, pugnacious, unterrified, irreverent. When the boys went on strike a year or two ago there was an injunction issued against them. The servitors of the court were afraid that they would not be able to find the boys in order to get service on them. But there was no such trouble. The boys made no effort to avoid a knowledge of the court's wishes. They gathered in large numbers and listened with vast satisfaction to the words that the court had used. And then the man who had read the injunction was almost mobbed because he didn't have a copy of it to give to each one of his auditors. The few boys who managed to get written specimens of the court's order became celebrities.

A certain number of boys work out from two offices in the very center of the Red Light district. Some of these boys stop working at one. Others work through till morning. There is no business in that district in the morning hours except the business of disorderly houses and all-night saloons. And even during the earlier hours of the night there is very little business of any other kind. The only effective reason for keeping an all-night office in that district is to share in the profits of vice.

There was once a woman who owned a big disorderly house in the district and who got her one son into the Red Light messenger service under an assumed name in order that in the course of his nightly duty he might be more or less under her protecting eye. Outside of this case there has never been much evidence of maternal care in the life of the boys who spend their working hours carrying messages and parcels almost exclusively among disreputable characters.

All night long these boys may be seen, slouching out of their offices, shambling along the street with the peculiar foot-dragging shuffle of their kind, passing the rows of open-faced saloons, turning down into the rows of droop-eyed, close-curtained houses, climbing the steps of a brothel, disappearing into the interior, coming out again after a while, and lounging languidly back to headquarters.

From carrying messages for the women of the town they go on to carrying cocaine and other drugs for them. They learn where the illicit vendors of forbidden drugs have their salesrooms. They learn where the friends of the women drink their favorite drinks over their favorite bars. They make appointments between those who have fallen and those who are being tempted to fall. They become part of the mechanism of vice. And then they become part of vice itself. It is a process of inevitable absorption.

The disease of vice penetrates the whole body of the street service among boys. When Mr. J. J. Sloan, who has already been quoted, was managing the John Worthy School, he said that one-third of the street boys sent to him were suffering from the loathsome distempers of which the Red Light district is the propagating center.

Who can look at a boy, sixteen or seventeen years old, employed for no other purpose than that of delivering messages to prostitutes, and not feel that the shame of the fact adduced by Mr. Sloan throws its shadows over other persons besides the boys themselves?

Many night messenger boys, whose "trick" lasts only from five in the afternoon to one in the morning, volunteer to work after that time in order to earn some overtime money. When they do this they are likely, at the age of sixteen, to approximate the income of some of the adult telegraph operators. They do it, of course, at the cost of their health.

Even when these boys stop working, they find it difficult to make up their minds to go home. They are likely to go instead to the restaurant that happens to be in favor with the boy who happens to be leader.

Just at present there is a restaurant in the southern part of the downtown district where at two o'clock in the morning there is a gathering of a large part of the wisdom of the street.

After going down into the basement where the food is served and after doing their best to make the cashier accept street-railway tickets instead of money for the sandwiches and coffee that they have consumed, the boys come back to the surface and sprawl on the sidewalk and spend a few quiet evening hours under the glare of the corner arc lamp.

"Fade me?" It is the first formal question in the game of craps. It is like "May I play, partner?" in bridge. "Fade me?"

"Wot are yuh playin'?"

"A nickel."

The challenged boy draws a street-railway ticket out of his pocket, a ticket given to him by the company and saved by himself through the simple expedient of ignoring the conductor or else of walking to his destination. Most messenger boys have a few surviving tickets on their persons.

Two hours and a half pass playing craps. The honesty of the engineering construction of the dice is several times impugned. And, apparently, not without reason. The boy who is winning at any given time is the boy who is playing with his own dice.

At about half past four a very old man, about thirty-six years of age, stumbles by. He turns and comes back. He is carrying a satchel. He steadies himself and begins to tell the boys that in that satchel he has a machine that will make him a millionaire. His eyes stagger almost as much as his legs. He is thin. His skin is drawn tightly over his face. His clothes hang loosely on his frame. After explaining the value, though not the character, of the machine in his satchel, he explains further that he is not only a future millionaire, but that he has already been a millionaire, having owned at one time a factory 500 feet long and more than that broad.

The boys rise up from their sprawling attitudes on the sidewalk under the glare of the arc lamp. In turn, solemnly, they kick the stranger's satchel. It is battered in, on both ends. It is then cracked open in the middle. It is revealed as being empty. The boys change from solemnity to gaiety and kick the satchel all together instead of in succession. The man staggers out into the street. A policeman turns the corner.

"Time to go swimmin'," yells the leader. He has seen the policeman and has demonstrated his right to be leader.

The light of dawn is chilling and freezing the warm nocturnal radiance of the arc lamp. The policeman's face is gray and sick. To the man who has worked all night it seems unreasonable, impossible, like a nightmare, that within another hour or two thousands of people should be resuming their frantic, insane, energetic labor in the office-buildings about him. The perpetually renewed strenuosity of the world seems like the mocking laugh of a demon who is laughing in order to hear himself. It seems to have no other excuse or explanation.

But these messenger boys, living their whole life all at once, emphatic and condensed, are yelling: "Come on! Swimmin'!"

They rush in a body down the street and turn the corner toward the lake.

The policeman looks down the street, eastward, after them. A gleam of sunlight strikes the metal on his helmet. The night is over.

Everybody's Magazine
January 1908

PART TEN

Vice

THE COUNTRY had been reading about the alliance between business and politicians and the corruption of both. This was the theme of Lincoln Steffens. Now the public began to read the muckrakers' stories about the connection between liquor, gambling, crime, political corruption and prostitution.

The nation was shocked with the sensational charges in *McClure's Magazine* about the highly organized, efficient, and wide extent of traffic in women and its association with political corruption.

S. S. McClure had given George Kibbe Turner the assignment of exposing vice. Turner had been associated with the Springfield *Republican*. He joined the staff of *McClure's* soon after Ray Stannard Baker, Lincoln Steffens, Ida M. Tarbell, Finley Peter Dunne and others left the magazine to publish and edit their own *American Magazine*.

S. S. McClure had had an idea for a story on Chicago. He had been clipping news stories from Chicago newspapers for some time as a basis for this. However, before he published his article, he sent Turner to Chicago to study the situation. What resulted was Turner's "City of Chicago," which appeared in April 1907. The article pointed to the "business of dissipation" that came from the liquor trade, prostitution and gambling.

"The effect of this single article was indescribable. Coming as it did four years after Steffens began his investigations into municipal crime, it found a national audience ready and able to appreciate it and apply its lessons at home. Prostitution had hitherto been mentioned in generalities; it was significant that the public now seized upon it rather than upon municipal corruption as a whole. Prostitution was the subject the people wanted elaborated." [142]

The article acted like a clarion call to Chicago reformers and a vice commission * was named by the Mayor in 1910 which resulted in its report "The Social Evil in Chicago."

* 1910 Vice Commission appointed by Chicago's Mayor Fred A. Busse, headed by The Very Rev. Walter T. Sumner, Dean, Episcopal Cathedral SS. Peter and Paul. Members included Dr. W. L. Baum, Chicago Medical Society; David Blaustein, Superintendent, Chicago Hebrew Institute; Rev. James F. Callaghan, Pastor, Saint Malachy's Roman Catholic Church; Dr. Anna Dwyer, President, Mary Thompson Hospital; Dr. W. A. Evans, Health Commissioner; Rev. Albert Evers, Pastor, Saint Boniface's Roman Catholic Church; Dr. Frank W. Gunsaulus, President, Armour

A month later, McClure's article, "Chicago As Seen by Herself; Epidemic of Crime," appeared.

U.S. Congressman Barratt O'Hara,* who at the time of the Chicago Vice Commission was lieutenant-governor of Illinois and who later was to be chairman of the Vice Commission of the Illinois State Senate, which investigated vice and low wages, writes: "I am not in a position to say that the Turner article in *McClure's Magazine* in April 1907 was responsible for the creation of the vice commission . . . but I have no doubt it was a large contributing factor. . . . This committee did a really good work. . . . But because of some of the personnel of the commission the large emphasis in the placing of blame was put on dance halls, manner of conduct of houses of prostitution and similar phases. The fact that at that time it had been established that no girl could live on less than $8.00 a week, and that at least 50% of the girls in such respectable establishments as Marshall Fields and Sears Roebuck were getting considerably less than that amount in wages was not given what I thought the proper emphasis. . . .

"While I cannot say that in any direct sense did the writings of the McClure 'muckrakers' influence the creation or the investigation of the Senate Vice Committee, it is undoubtedly true that these writings had a large indirect influence. That is, the 'muckrakers' had prepared the climate for the public reception of the exposures, and inasmuch as the wide public indignation over the fact brought out by the Senate Vice Committee that women workers were being paid less than they could live on, resulted in the enactment of the first State Minimum Wage laws.

"I think that in this area you must give the 'muckrakers' plenty of credit." [143]

Turner followed his Chicago article two years later with an exposé of the social evil in New York City. "Tammany's Control of New York by Professional Politicians" charged that prostitution had been practically legalized in that city. Five months later, Turner wrote "Daughters of the Poor," which was a tale of immigrant girls caught in the white slave trade of New York.

In announcing "Daughters of the Poor," *McClure's Magazine,* using an advertisement in *Collier's,* called it "the most startling and important article

---

Institute; W. W. Hallam, Corresponding Secretary, Chicago Society of Social Hygiene; Dr. Abram W. Harris, President, Northwestern University; Dr. William Healy, President, Psychopathic Institute; Dr. James M. Hyde, Professor, Rush Medical College; Mrs. Ellen M. Henrotin, Federation of Women's Clubs; Rev. Abram Hirschberg, Rabbi, North Chicago Hebrew Congregation; Rev. E. A. Kelly, Pastor, Saint Anne's Roman Catholic Church; Rev. John G. Kircher, Pastor, German Evangelical Church; Louis O. Kohtz, Agent, Aetna Fire Insurance Company; P. J. O'Keeffe, lawyer; Judge Harry Olson, Chief Justice, Municipal Courts; Judge Merritt W. Pinckney, Judge, Juvenile Court; Alexander Robertson, Vice-President, Continental National Bank; Julius Rosenwald, President, Sears, Roebuck & Company; Dr. Louis E. Schmidt, Professor, Northwestern Medical College; Bishop C. T. Shaffer, African Methodist Episcopal Church; Edwin W. Sims, United States District Attorney; Edward M. Skinner, Association of Commerce; Professor Graham Taylor, President, Chicago Commons; Professor William I. Thomas, University of Chicago; Professor Herbert L. Willett, University of Chicago; and John L. Whitman, Superintendent, House of Correction.

* Second district, Illinois.

published in years—a plain story . . . of how the White Slave Trade in American girls developed in New York under Tammany Hall and has spread to every large city of the United States." [144]

Two months after "Daughters of the Poor" appeared, a grand jury was impaneled in New York to investigate white slave trade in that city. It was headed by John D. Rockefeller, Jr.

The *New York Times* of January 4, 1910 announced:

ROCKEFELLER HEADS
VICE GRAND JURY

Son of the Standard Oil Man
Demurs Because of Youth and
Business, but Is Overruled.

TO TAKE UP WHITE SLAVERY

Judge O'Sullivan, in Strong Charges,
Says Organized Traffic Should Be
Thoroughly Investigated

"This investigation was precipitated by Turner's articles, as was another . . . in Chicago." [145]

A year after the publication of "Daughters of the Poor," *McClure's* referred to the article "as one of the most notable things that the magazine ever published . . . largely instrumental, together with reports to the national Government of the Immigration Commission, in causing legislation dealing with the 'white slave' traffic to be passed in many States. So influential, indeed, was this article that in the public mind it has gained a large share of the credit which is due to the two years' investigation of the national Government. . . ." [146]

The impetus to investigation, as a result of these three Turner articles, also led to such vice commission reports as that in Minneapolis, 1911; Portland, 1913; and Hartford, 1913.

A strong case can also be made out that these writings had their effect in helping to pass the Mann Act. Designed to deal with the traffic of women through the Federal power over interstate commerce, the Mann Act was first introduced in December 1909 by Representative James R. Mann of Chicago, and passed by Congress on June 25, 1910.

GEORGE KIBBE TURNER

The City of Chicago

A STUDY OF THE GREAT
IMMORALITIES

D URING THE PAST year three great American cities, Chicago, San
Francisco and Pittsburgh, have been swept by "waves of crime,"
so-called—sudden and unexplained outbursts of criminal violence.
Women have been beaten down, men murdered, even streetcars robbed
by highwaymen on the thoroughfares, with all the nonchalance of the
wild and vacant frontier. This thing is not new; in some cities it is
constantly recurring—so constantly that it is questionable whether these
"waves of crime" are not ordinary conditions, emphasized by chance
and the special attention of the daily press. Why do these conditions
exist? What forces are there, hidden in American cities, which are
dragging them, according to the record of their own press, into a
state of semibarbarism?

Chicago, in the mind of the country, stands pre-eminently notorious
for violent crime. It is the second city on the continent; it is, all things
considered, perhaps the most typically American of our cities; it is
intimately known by millions; and its press is especially active and
alert in the discussion of local affairs. The reputation of Chicago
for crime has consequently fastened itself upon the imagination of the
United States as that of no other city has done. It is the current conventional belief that the criminal is loose upon its streets, that the
thug and holdup man go patrolling them by night.

Take Chicago, then, not because it is worse than or different from
other cities of America, but, on the contrary, because it is so typical,

and because it is so well known. Why have the primary basic guarantees of civilization broken down in Chicago? Why has the city, year after year, such a flood of violent and adventurous crime? The answer can be simple and straightforward: because of the tremendous and elaborate organization—financial and political—for creating and attracting and protecting the criminal in Chicago.

The criminal is a savage, nothing more nor less. Civilization builds up painfully our definite, orderly rules of life—work, marriage, the constant restraint of the gross and violent impulses of appetite. The criminal simply discards these laws and slides back again along the way we came up—into license, idleness, thieving and violence. He merely lapses back into savagery. To understand the matter of crime in great cities, the first step is to measure the positive forces working continually to produce savagery there. These forces are today, as they always have been, greater than can easily be imagined.

The City—from scarlet Babylon to smoky Chicago—has always been the great market place of dissipation. In the jungle you would call this thing savagery. In the city there is a new side to it. The dweller of the city—true to the instincts of city life—has made it a financial transaction. He has found it a great source of gain, of easy money. There has grown up, therefore, a double motive in promoting it—the demand for the thing itself and the stimulus of the great profit in providing it. You may call the sale of dissipation in the city savagery by retail. Ethically considered, this thing is hideous beyond belief; socially considered, it is suicidal. But to be understood and followed through intelligently, it must first be considered neither ethically nor socially. Its methods and motives are the methods and motives of pure business and must be considered as such. There is no other way. That is what I must recognize in describing conditions in Chicago. I must talk cold business, as the saying goes. No emotion, no squeamishness, not even sympathy; simply a statement of fact.

The sale of dissipation is not only a great business; it is among the few greatest businesses in Chicago. The leading branch of it—as you would naturally expect of the savage European stock from which we sprang—is the sale of alcoholic liquor. In the year 1906 the receipts in the retail liquor trade in Chicago were over $100,000,000; they were probably about $115,000,000. There was one retail interest greater than this. The sellers of food—grocers and meat men—had gross receipts of, perhaps, double these figures.

At the same time, the liquor interests are vastly more extended in Chicago than any other. There are 7,300 licensed liquor sellers in

Chicago, and in addition about a thousand places where liquor is sold illegally. The only business which approaches this in number of establishments, according to the Chicago directory, is the grocery trade, which has about 5,200. The city spends at least half as much for what it drinks as for what it eats—not counting the cost of the cooking and serving of food.

The great central power in the liquor business in America is the brewery. In the past thirty-five years, the per capita consumption of spirituous liquor in the United States has increased not at all. The per capita consumption of malt liquor has trebled. This increase has come partly because of the demand for a milder drink, but largely also because of another fact: because the breweries own or control the great majority of the saloons of American cities. They have a distinct policy: if there are not as many saloons as there can be, supply them. This is what has been done in Chicago. Fully 90 per cent of the Chicago saloons are under some obligation to the brewery; with at least 80 per cent, this obligation is a serious one.

The business of the brewery is to sell beer. There are excellent men in the brewing trade, but that fact has never interfered with the carrying out of the development of the industry to its utmost limit. It could not be allowed to do so. The brewery, under present conditions in Chicago, must sell beer at all cost, or promptly die. This is because the brewing business has been overcapitalized and overbuilt there for at least ten years. There has been furious competition—"beer wars"—which have left financial scars that are not yet and probably never will be entirely obliterated. And at the present time a full third of the capital invested in the forty companies and fifty plants is not earning dividends. Under these circumstances, the breweries of Chicago can have but one aim—to fill Chicago with beer to the point of saturation.

Each brewer disposes of his product by contracting with special saloonkeepers to sell his beer and no other. The more saloons he has, the better. Up to a year ago, there was absolutely no legal hindrance to the multiplication of saloons. The brewers employ special agents to watch continually every nook and cranny in Chicago where it may be possible to pour in a little more beer. If a rival brewery's saloonkeeper is doing well, his best bartender is ravished from him and set up in business alongside. If a new colony of foreigners appears, some compatriot is set at once to selling them liquor. Italians, Greeks, Lithuanians, Poles—all the . . . tribes which have been drawn into Chicago —have their trade exploited to the utmost. Up to last year, no man with $200 who was not subject to arrest on sight need go without a saloon in Chicago; nor, for that matter, need he now. The machinery is constantly waiting for him. With that $200 as a margin, the brewery sorts him out a set from its stock of saloon fixtures, pays his rent, pays his license, and supplies him with beer. He pays for everything in an extra price on each barrel of beer. The other supplies of his saloon— liquor and cigars—are bought out of his $200 cash capital.

Under this system of forcing, Chicago has four times as many saloons at it should have, from any standpoint whatever, except, of course, the brewers' and the wholesalers'. A new license law, passed last year, now limits the number to one in every 500 people; but it will be years before that law will have any appreciable effect. There is now one retail liquor dealer to every 285 people, disregarding, of course, the one thousand unlicensed dealers. In the laboring wards the licensed saloons run as many as one to every 150. Take the stockyards. Around that long and dismal stockade, at every hole from which a human being can emerge, a shop or group of shops sits waiting. At the main entrance they lie massed in batteries. At the rear—on Ashland Avenue—"Whisky Row"! To the north, the vileness of Bubbly Creek; to the east, the bare, gaunt, high-shouldered buildings of the yard; to the west and south, scattering, shabby dwellings. Just forty-eight saloons —and two that have recently died—housed in opposing rows of stagger- ing wooden buildings, down a distance across which a strong man could throw a stone; located nowhere in particular in space, except due east of that ugly little hole in the stockade from which the men run out to drink in their brief half-hour's nooning.

The Chicago market is thoroughly saturated with beer, and in- cidentally with other liquor. Reckoning it out by population, every man, woman, and child in Chicago drank, in 1906, two and one-quarter barrels of beer—that is, seventy gallons—three and one-half times the average consumption in the United States. Each also drank about four gallons of spirituous liquor—two and two-thirds times the average. The main object of the brewing business is well fulfilled; the consumers of Chicago expended not less than $55,000,000 for beer in 1906.

Now, if the competition is red-handed among the breweries, it is simply ravenous among the saloonkeepers. There is a popular fallacy that there is great profit in the retail saloon business. The saloonkeepers themselves believe this when they go into it. The hope of easy money and easy life is the motive which brings men into this trade. Now, this is in reality the kind of business it is: in the lean years between 1897 and 1901, one-third of the license holders in Chicago gave up their licenses every year and were replaced by other licensees. In other words, one-third of the saloons of Chicago failed every year. In the Seventeenth Ward—a territory of working folk—a special study of the liquor business was made a year ago. In one block and a half, it was shown, eighteen saloons had been started and had died in the course of eighteen months. Of the saloonkeepers of Chicago, less than 10 per cent have resources enough to entitle them to any rating by a commercial agency. The pressure of the brewery to sell beer almost crushes the retailer out of existence.

All this means one thing—a premium on the irregular and criminal saloonkeeper. The patronage of a saloon is a very fickle and elusive thing. A place is popular, or it is nothing. Consequently, the need of drawing and holding a good trade is imperative. There are two general business methods of attracting it: by giving unusually large measures and big bonuses of free lunch; or by carrying illegitimate and illegal side lines. The first, generally speaking, does not leave large margins of profit; the second does. A year ago the license fee was raised in Chicago from $500 to $1,000. It was hoped that this would wipe out the criminal saloon. It did, of course, nothing of the sort. The poor miserable little dives in the working man's ward, each snatching a starvation living from the lips of the dwellers of the dozen smoke-befouled frame tenements about it, staggered down—a few hundred of them—and died. The man with the side line of prostitution and gambling naturally survived and had the benefit of the others' failure.

So much for the great legalized branch of the sale of dissipation in Chicago. The net results of that free and undisciplined struggle have been two: the thorough saturation of Chicago—especially of the tenement districts—with alcoholic liquor; and a high and successful premium on the criminal saloon.

The effect of the latter can be told when the sale of other forms of dissipation is considered. The effect of the former is felt immediately and directly. A great part of the crime in Chicago is committed by men under the influence of drink. This is true in any city. But conditions in Chicago are peculiarly favorable to this class of crime. A population of hundreds of thousands of rough and unrestrained male laborers, plied, with all possible energy and ingenuity, with alcoholic liquor, can be counted on, with the certainty of a chemical experiment, for one reaction—violent and fatal crime. There would be crime of this kind from such a population under any circumstances. But the facilities of Chicago double and treble it. The European peasant, suddenly freed from the restraints of poverty and

of rigid police authority, and the . . . Negro from the countryside of
the South—especially the latter—furnish an alarming volume of savage
crime, first confined to their own races, and later—as they appreciate
the lack of adequate protection—extended to society at large. None
of these folk, perhaps, have progressed far along the way of civilization;
but under the exploitation of Chicago they slip back into a form of city
savagery compared to which their previous history shows a peaceful
and well-ordered existence. Their children are as quickly and surely
rotted as themselves by the influence of the saloon upon the neighborhood of their homes.

And now a short sketch of the second great business of dissipation—
prostitution. The gross revenues from this business in Chicago, in
1906, were $20,000,000—and probably more. There are at least ten
thousand professional prostitutes. Average annual receipts of $2,000
each are brought in by these women. They do not themselves, however,
have the benefit of this revenue. Much of it is never received by them.
They are, in fact, exploited by large business interests.

There are four large interests which are concerned in the exploitation
of prostitution. The first of these is the criminal hotels, the second
is the houses of ill fame, the third the cheap dance halls and saloons,
and the fourth the men . . . who deal in women for the trade. There
are large indirect interests—such as, for instance, the leasing or sub-
letting of tenements to the business, an operation which yields enormous percentages of profit—but these are the four principal direct
interests in the trade.

The hotels constitute probably the largest of these. There are 292
of these houses known and recorded in Chicago—with a capacity of
10,000 rooms. Twenty-one of them contain each 100 rooms or over;
the largest has 250. The gross receipts of these enterprises cannot
be less than $4,000,000 a year; they are probably $5,000,000. The total
amount expended there cannot be less than $8,000,000; it is probably
$10,000,000. These places have been extremely profitable, because their
expenses are low, and their patronage is large. At present they are
not so good an investment as formerly, because the city authorities—
urged to action by a desperate woman's throwing herself out of an
upper story window—have passed a hotel license ordinance, which is
intended to do away with this business. The largest of the hotels, some
of which have for some time pooled their legal and political interests
in the hands of a manager, are now fighting this ordinance as unconstitutional.

Under ordinary conditions—that is, when there is no particular agitation against them—there are at least 350 good-sized houses of prostitution in Chicago. There are in all more than 4,000 women in these. The annual gross receipts are not less than $8,000,000; they are more likely over $10,000,000. These houses are disposed throughout the city according to the demand, which is affected to some extent by public opinion.

The profits of these houses are, of course, very large and quick. Much of the money made here is dissipated, yet there are at least half a dozen persons now interested in this business who are credited with fortunes running into the hundreds of thousands. Their profits are not only from their shares in the women's wages, but from excessive prices for liquor. They also secure large returns from furnishing clothing and other necessities of life to their employees, at prices ranging from 100 to 200 per cent higher than the usual retail price. By this system the wages of the women are largely secured by the proprietors of the establishments. The plan is not different in principle from the familiar "company store" system of the manufacturing and mining district. It is a first rule of the business, as generally conducted, to keep the employees continuously in debt, so that they are unable to leave the establishments unless the proprietors desire it.

The business of the small places, the flats, cannot be estimated, but it is very large and is growing constantly, especially since the official attacks which have frightened away customers from the criminal hotels. There are certainly not less than two thousand women in these flats, and annual expenditures are certainly not less than $4,000,000. In some sections of the city there are scores of these small places. One building of over seventy apartments is said to contain nothing else.

These places and the hotels cater to the demand for ruining young girls—especially the low-paid employees of department stores and factories, which furnish the majority of the English-speaking women in the profession in Chicago. The dance halls and irregular saloons also take a part of the profit from this source. The direct business of supplying women to the trade, while not so large as these others, is also profitable. Some of the more enterprising of the keepers of the regular houses of ill fame have private arrangements with men, who ruin young girls for their use. Most of the young women who come into the business in this way do so before reaching the age of nineteen.

The largest regular business in furnishing women, however, is done by a company of men . . . [who] have a sort of loosely organized association extending through the large cities of the country, their chief centers being New York, Boston, Chicago and New Orleans. In Chicago they now furnish the great majority of the prostitutes in the cheaper district of the West Side Levee, their women having driven out the English-speaking women in the last ten years. From the best returns available, there are some ten or a dozen women offered for sale at the houses of prostitution in the Eighteenth Ward every week. The price paid is about $50 a head. In some exceptional cases $75 has been given. This money, paid over to the agent, is charged up to the debt of the woman to the house. She pays, that is, for her own sale. In addition, she gives over a large share of her earnings to the man who places her.

There is a minor business, financially speaking, which is closely connected with prostitution: this is the selling of cocaine. The average life of a woman in the business of prostitution ranges from five to ten years. She is, of course, continually drinking alcoholic stimulants. Later, however, these do not satisfy the women, and toward the end of their career they acquire some drug habit. Formerly they depended largely on morphine. During the past ten years, however, cocaine has come into general use. This drug is very attractive to persons who are unfortunate or despondent. It produces an extravagant feeling of buoyancy and well-being. Although taken by many persons throughout the country, especially by Negroes, it is now recognized generally to be the special drug of the prostitute. The chief markets for it in Chicago follow very closely the markets of prostitution. In its effect this is much quicker than any other drug habit, through its action upon the brain cells. After a time the taker is subject to various acute hallucinations—the most characteristic of which is the belief that worms are crawling just underneath the skin. The cocaine taker in this condition often slashes his skin with a knife in the attempt to get them out. Death is likely to come within two or three years from the unrestricted use of the drug, although some individuals survive for a long time. It is largely a question of temperament.

The profit on the retail sale of cocaine is very large, running as high as 300 or 400 per cent, as the drug is usually heavily adulterated with acetanilid. There have always been, consequently, a number of drugstores and some saloons at which it could be obtained by its users. Various estimates of the number of the takers of this drug in Chicago have been made, many of them extravagant. The number of confirmed users in the city probably does not exceed 7,000. It is more likely about 5,000. A great proportion of these are prostitutes. At the same time, the drug is exceedingly convenient to take, the crushed crystal or flake—

according to the common custom—being merely snuffed up from the back of the hand; and on this account its use spreads easily. Boys, especially messengers and newsboys, are apt to experiment with it, and many young men in the early twenties acquire the habit. Deprived of their drug, these men often resort to petty crime and sometimes to violent crime to secure means to get it. The drug fiends are usually ghastly in appearance; a grim sight is afforded by the procession of haggard women who appear in the gray light of the early morning to secure the drug from the big dealers on the West Side Levee.

The chastity of woman is at the foundation of Anglo-Saxon society. Our laws are based upon it, and the finest and most binding of our social relations. Nothing could be more menacing to a civilization than the sale of this as a commodity. To the average individual woman concerned, it means the expectation of death under ten years; to practically all the longer survivors a villainous and hideous afterlife. There is a great profit in this business, however. Chicago has it organized— from the supplying of young girls to the drugging of the older and less salable women out of existence—with all the nicety of modern industry. As in the stockyards, not one shred of flesh is wasted.

The third large business of dissipation in Chicago is gambling. In an average year—1906, for example—its gross receipts cannot be less than $15,000,000. Policy shops, the race track, and open poolrooms and gambling houses have been quite generally closed out in Chicago during the past few years. The largest gambling interest is now the making of "handbooks" on the horse races. The gross receipts from this must be above $12,000,000 a year. During the latter part of 1906, when the business was running with comparative freedom, there were at least five hundred agents of "handbook" systems in Chicago. These systems are in the hands of a few favored gamblers or groups of gamblers, who have their arrangements so nicely made that they can divide the territory of the city between them; and no newcomer can enter the field without their consent. If he does, he is raided by the police. Besides these "handbook men" there is a floating poolroom—the steamer *City of Traverse*, owned by a large number of professional gamblers—which is supposed to leave South Chicago and run out of the city limits into Lake Michigan, although, as a matter of fact, it does not always do so.

In addition to the receipts from this betting on the horse races, there was in 1906 at least $2,000,000 net revenue from general gambling in Chicago. General open gambling is not in evidence, but there are large games, in a few specially favored places, and many smaller ones, open to those who have inside information, throughout the city. Altogether, the gambling interests in 1906 took at least $7,000,000 in gross profits out of the Chicago public, doubtless the amount was considerably larger.

The dealers in dissipation in Chicago, then, have a total revenue of at least $135,000,000 a year—that is, receipts at least two-thirds as large as those of the retail grocers and meat men. There are more than 40,000 persons directly employed by them. This is one of the few greatest businesses of the city, but beyond that it bears a relation to society and government which nothing else can bear. Every cent of that great sum of money is taken in, and every action of that great company of proprietors and employees takes place either under the strict regulation of law, or in direct defiance of it.

The business can be divided into two general classes. In the first, the dealers—including the brewers, the wholesale liquor dealers, and the great majority of the saloonkeepers—have no direct interest in breaking the law, although they all may profit indirectly, and some of them do profit to a great extent, because of the breaking of the law by others. But the first interest of this class is to resist the constant attacks of its enemies looking toward the further restriction of its trade. It must, therefore, be continually in politics. Its political alliances are naturally with the other interests of dissipation. The members of the second class—the dealers in prostitution and gambling, and the criminal saloonkeepers—must violate the law to exist. They consequently have made careful business arrangements to break the law. To do this, they also must go into politics.

The gross receipts of this illegal class of business are some $45,000,000 a year. About four-fifths of this—$35,000,000—is concentrated in the chief markets of dissipation near the center of the city—for the sale of dissipation, in any city, merely follows the natural laws of trade and locates where the demand is, near the large centers of population. In two downtown wards of Chicago—the First and the Eighteenth— are situated five-sixths of the criminal saloons and of the dealers in prostitution, and at least two-thirds of the gambling interests. The owners of these enterprises turn over the organization of their political business to the natural agent—the ward boss.

The business of the political boss has not always been clearly understood. The boss is simply a middleman. He buys votes and sells privileges. He pays for his votes either in cash or in privileges; he sells his privileges either for cash or its equivalent, or for votes. The difference between his income and outgo of money is, of course, his personal profit. The direction of the political business of concerns with a gross annual income of $35,000,000 and the peculiar necessities of the sellers of vice naturally offers unusual financial opportunities to the ward boss. . . . [See BEHIND POLITICAL DOORS—The Ward.]

Until the present time the local criminal courts in Chicago have been in charge of the police magistrate, one of the relics of the old town government, of which Chicago has been full. Sixty justices of the peace were nominated by the circuit-court judges in Cook County; were appointed by the governor and confirmed by the senate of the state. It was this transaction, undoubtedly, which excited in the mind of George E. Cole, the abrupt and active Chicago reformer, the pessimism which led him to exclaim: "I wouldn't trust the judges to appoint a committee to lead my dog to the pound!" From these sixty justices of the peace, the mayor chose and assigned to the different districts in the city sixteen police magistrates. The First and Eighteenth Wards secured exactly the police magistrates they desired. The relation between these officials and the leaders of the wards were so close and informal, that the leaders, in many instances, did not trouble to arrange in person for the justice to be meted out to their various unfortunate constituents. It was a common occurrence, in at least one court, for a ward leader's assistants to telephone before the morning session the disposition he desired to have made of the various cases, which had been called to his attention.

The arrangement with the police force is an easy matter. The administration can be relied upon in one way or another to respect the wishes of the ward in regard to this service. And the police department furnishes a large supply of exactly the officials desired by the interests of these wards.

Under this system of protection from the law, there has been established in Chicago a condition unique in this country. The center of Chicago, all things considered, is the cheapest market of dissipation in Caucasian civilization. The prices in European cities, no doubt, are absolutely lower, but relative to the ease of obtaining means to spend, either by begging or stealing or casual labor, they are not to be compared with the great, rough, bountiful American city. A full quart of beer is sold in the saloon for five cents; prostitution is as low as ten cents. As for the expense of living, a lodging for the night costs five and ten cents, and meals, if you buy them, can be had as low as a nickel. With ten cents—five cents for a bed and five cents for a glass of beer, and access to the free lunch—a man may cover the space of twenty-four hours and pay his way. A "town bum" in Chicago said recently: "I have not had my legs under a table for six years."

Chicago is the great inland center of the country; trains by hundreds drop in there every day. Around it is the best territory in the world for tramping and for casual labor; about it, in an unholy ring, stand penitentiaries by the dozen. And when the service and the tramping and the casual labor are done, the criminals and the half-criminals and the quarter-criminals come drifting back into Chicago. They come there by choice, of course: for one chief reason. There they can enjoy, with the least disturbance, at the lowest cost, cheap dissipation—the kind of life they wish to live. Nights, the ten-cent lodging-house. Days, and the long evenings, the "barrel house"—that curious dive so strangely like the thieves' den of the Middle Ages. "Town bums" are there, jerky, pompous cocaine fiends, "gay-cats" and "hoboes," blown in from the four corners of the earth; and in the evening, those great husky, hideous beggars who hitch and crawl about the Chicago streets by day; and now and then the real tramp-burglar—the "yeggman," with his bag of "soup" across the soft muscles of his belly—nitroglycerine enough to blow the whole unlikely company back to limbo.

In the center of Chicago are now two small cities of savages—self-regulating and self-protecting. In one of these there are 35,000 people; in the other, 30,000. It is a region of adults—one child in every eight or nine people, while there is one in three in the general population of the city. The inhabitants neither labor regularly nor marry. Half of the men are beggars, criminals, or floating laborers; a quarter are engaged in the sale of dissipation; and a third of the women are prostitutes. A great share of the men spend most of their waking hours thoroughly drugged with cheap alcohol. Society here has lapsed back into a condition more primitive than the jungle.

It would be difficult to estimate the cash payment which must be made every year by the interest of dissipation, for the privilege of breaking the law. So many people receive the money, so many give it out. There is such a variation from time to time. However, there cannot be less than $500,000 a year paid out now. There is probably much more. Prostitution pays at least $250,000; the remainder is largely paid by gambling. . . .

The purchase of the police in Chicago is made simply by the fact that the upper half of the force—that is, the half that furnishes the officials—came into the service when the police force was freely and frankly for sale to the interests of dissipation. Of course, not all of the officials of the Chicago police force are for sale. It is clear, however, that the dealer in dissipation could not receive adequate protection unless there were a thorough organization in the police department, to see that this was given. Otherwise, there must be, at any time, some individual officer or official, who would blunder in and attempt to enforce the law. There is, as a matter of fact, just such an organization. It is not a formal thing; naturally, it does not elect officers or pass bylaws; but, in a large sense, it is just as efficient. It is spoken of as the System.

The System comes about very simply. The influence of the ward bosses in the districts of dissipation secures from the administration the police officials they desire. These officials see that the men under them carry out the business agreements which they themselves make with the leaders of the ward. If a new policeman does not enter into relations with the System or acquiesce in its working, he is "jobbed." That is, by various technical charges against him by his superior officer, he is kept under continual suspicion and finally either shipped off to some outlying district of the city or even discharged from the department on trumped-up charges. The Chicago department is now under civil service and has been for ten years, but this effective and simple method makes it possible to beat the civil service rules and to organize the force so that the required protection can be guaranteed to the interests of dissipation.

Inside the department there is either an astonishing fear of this System or a loyalty to it that is simply amazing. Occasionally, however, a revolt discloses its methods of operation. An interesting example of this came in the case of the discharge of Lieutenant Roger Mulcahy, last year. Mulcahy did two things which two police officers could not stomach. A labor leader met in a saloon a Negro, took offense at something he said, and wantonly shot him in the leg; the man's leg was afterwards amputated. About the same time a well-known Negro was arrested and shown to have had a wholesale career in a vile crime which was terrifying the whole vicinity. Both men [the offenders] had strong political influence. Mulcahy, the police lieutenant, because of this influence, brought them up on minor charges before the court and arranged the machinery for their discharge. The two policemen went into rebellion. "There are some things I won't stand for," said one, with a great oath. They themselves took the matter to the Grand Jury, and both of the criminals were severely punished. In the meanwhile, Mulcahy had started out after the two rebels in the usual fashion of the System. In the two months before the Grand Jury acted, Mulcahy had one man up five times on minor charges before the police trial board. In May he recommended the discharge of the other man from the department for drunkenness. He was going through, in fact, the usual forms of "jobbing." This time, however, the process had disastrous results. The men were retained with honor, and developments at their trial brought about the discharge of the lieutenant himself.

There must be, at a conservative estimate, $200,000 a year paid over to the police, for protection to the business of dissipation. Just where that money goes into the department is, of course, almost impossible to tell. It is a matter of fact, for instance, that the gambling squad—eight or ten men under the personal command of the chief of police—sit and watch the operations of "handbook" makers and even bet themselves. It is also a fact that when personal information has been given to the chief of police concerning a betting place, that place has been perfunctorily raided and has been in operation again a half hour after this was done. But it would be impossible to demonstrate from this evidence that the present chief of police was paid to protect gambling in Chicago. It is true that criminal saloons and houses of prostitution have an understanding with the police that they may violate the law until someone protests, and that then they will be notified by the police and kept in touch with the situation until it is advisable for them to resume the practices which are objected to. But who gets the pay for this and what the pay is, has not yet been determined with legal exactitude. It is worth while, perhaps, as showing the possibilities in the case, to recall that one ex-chief of police said, in a burst of confidence, that he had put away $187,000 during his few years of office.

The result of all this is not difficult to imagine. The City Council of Chicago, in the paroxysm of excitement over the reign of crime of a year ago, voted for 1,000 new policemen, most of whom have now been added to the force. It was asserted then that there were not men enough to protect that great and wide-lying city. This was certainly true, but it was an understatement of the case. The exact condition was stated by Captain Alexander R. Piper, an expert who, with Roundsman William F. Maher of New York, made a special investigation of the Chicago police in 1904. He said in summing up: "It is not necessary for me to tell you that you have practically no protection on your streets. You all know it, and you know how seldom you see an officer at night. Your patrolmen pull the box on the hour or half-hour and then lounge in their holes or some saloon." These conditions exist today.

The reason for all this is clear. The business of dissipation, working through ward politics, has bought the protection of the Chicago police force. This fact necessarily deprives the police force of its usefulness to the public. The officials who are actually receiving pay for granting protection are in a combination to break the law. This combination extends below them to a certain extent into the department; and it encourages, of course, every patrolman who is at all dishonest to break or help to break the laws. Various members of the force have, in the past, formed alliances with criminals; men who have been convicted from time to time of crimes ranging from shoplifting to burglary. Indeed, it is a fact that criminals, attracted by the possible chances of profits, are continually trying to get into the department. In a recent call for 450 men, 35 applicants were found to have criminal records. Of course, there can be no discipline under these conditions. There is, as Roundsman Maher said, practically no patrolling. There is continual loafing on the beat, with petty grafting down at the bottom of the department. The condition of the department is summed up in the statement that in two years, 1904 and 1905, over half the force was before the police trial board for one cause or another.

The addition of the police force completes the great organization for the exploitation of savagery in the City of Chicago. The dealer in dissipation, the ward boss and the police official are its chief members. I have tried to show clearly the simple and inevitable process by which this organization was built up. A business interest absolutely against the law must make positive arrangements to break the law in order to exist. It buys the right to do this out of its huge income—first, politically, through its business agent, the ward boss; and, second, by the purchase of the authorities which society employs to protect itself— particularly the police. In doing this it consolidates every influence hostile to well-organized society, from the robber and prostitute to the corrupt police official, in a great body whose continual influence is to impair or break down civilization.

The one clue to the workings of this organization is the money of dissipation which finances it. Every dollar of this, it might be said, is subtracted from the sum total of the assets of the civilization of Chicago. The making of savages is not likely to be interfered with greatly so long as it merely costs some hundreds or thousands of individual lives a year. Society does not busy itself sufficiently with the affairs of its members for this. But, unfortunately, the savages, once created and located in a city, begin to reach out and prey upon the civilized and orderly population about them. They must find their own living according to their own methods. There is continual tribute levied; and, now and then, when the season is ripe, or some other particular conditions exist, there break out those "waves of crime" which terrify and anger the population which is preyed upon.

The great specialty of Chicago crime is, of course, the holdup; that is, the robbery on the open street. This is either the work of the savages who congregate in the First and Eighteenth Wards, or of the young foreigners who are taught by the example of these men and stimulated by their early education in dissipation and their personal knowledge of the opportunities offered by the absence of proper police regulation. They are looking for easy money, and they know of no simpler method to secure it than this. Nothing more absolutely fish-blooded and in-human has been produced by modern civilization than the type of the "carbarn bandits," who shot down human beings with exactly the same dispassionate accuracy that they employed against the rocking images in the State Street shooting galleries of Ward One, where they created, night after night, their astonishing skill with firearms. The most disturbing thing about all these holdups is, naturally, the cold certainty of their producing just so many murders and just so many violent assaults year after year.

It is this one particular thing—the murderous street robbery—which more than all others has given Chicago its reputation for crime. This is not the only point, however, at which the savages overrun the city. Burglaries are much too frequent—not high-class jobs, but mostly the cheap and violent work which must be expected from the irruption of the low-class criminal from the territory of cheap dissipation. Morning after morning the vigorous beggars move out over the boundaries of savagery and limp and crawl and wriggle down the Chicago streets. When the weather is right to gather them in, and they feel the courage of numbers and the sharp necessities of the season—as they have during the past winter—the beggar and the "hobo" easily become the holdup man.

The murders of Chicago are generally personal matters between the savages. The great exception, of course, is when the savage, in his at-tacks on members outside his class, finds it necessary or advisable to kill his prey. There is a strong belief that murder in America is in-creasing because of our failure to enforce the death penalty. This, no doubt, has its influence. But the murders in Chicago are principally murders of dissipation and passion, committed by individuals who never calculated in their life the chances of the death penalty, and certainly never could consider it, in their mental condition at the time the murder was committed. The only authority which could possibly touch their imagination would be the visible symbol of an honest and efficient police force—which they do not have. Of 187 homicides in Chicago from December 1, 1904 to December 1, 1905, 175 were by shooting or blows; and only three by poison. Of the 176 in the year closing last December 1, 167 were by shooting or other violent means, and only eight by poisoning. These murders were hasty, savage acts of a crude population, and not in the least the calculating crimes of a calmer and more intellectual civilization. But the loss of life among the savages themselves is alarming. The death rate from murder in Chicago is six or eight times greater than in the cities of Great Britain, and twenty or twenty-five times greater than in the cities of Germany. In Europe it is only approached and surpassed in the black murder belt of Lower Italy.

There are two chief exploiters of the cities of America—the public service corporation and the business of dissipation. Attention has been directed during the past few years almost entirely to the former. It has become the orthodox belief that the public service corporation was the original corrupter of American cities. This is not true, especially in large cities. Long before the public service corporation existed, the corrupt ward politics of cities was organized by the business of dissipation. When the corporation arrived for the first time in that murky region, it found the herd already there—feeding, feeding, feeding on the rich filth of the sale of savagery. The corporation merely dumped its contribution in and left it in the general pile. The leaders of the herd may find their provender in the largess of the corporation, but the herd itself, the organization of the ward, has always been and will continue to be nourished by the vastly greater interests of dissipation. As a matter of fact, it does not receive mere gifts from these interests as it does from the corporation. The members of the political organization take the profits themselves. They are not in ward politics; they are ward politics. And this business divides millions of dollars, while the corporation divides hundreds of thousands, in American city politics.

The City of Chicago is just completing a splendid victory over corrupt public service corporations. It is now turning its attention to this second great business interest which is debauching it. This will be far more difficult to fight than the other one. The difference can be stated by mere statistics. The gross receipts of the surface street railways, which the City of Chicago has at last brought into reasonable subjection, are $16,000,000 a year—that is, only four-fifths of the receipts for prostitution. If you add to that sum the receipts of the elevated roads, you have $23,000,000 as the entire receipts of the traction interests in Chicago. This amount is less than two-thirds of the annual receipts for prostitution and gambling in the City of Chicago. But this is only a partial statement. The profits and the political necessities of the business of dissipation are incomparably greater than those of the public service corporation. . . .

There are two main causes for the excessive crime in Chicago. The first is the saturation of the poorest classes with alcoholic liquor, by the agents of a business under a terrible economic pressure to produce revenue. The time is coming in America and Europe when the important and delicate function of the distribution of intoxicants to city populations will be taken from these purely selfish interests which now hold it; when the reasonable safeguarding of the public, and not the necessities of private enterprises operated on the streets of a wolfish competition, will be the main compelling motive in the conduct of this trade.

The second great cause of crime is the purchase of the right to break the law by the dealers in illegal dissipation—that is, by the sellers of savagery. This is the chief reason for waves of crime in great cities. It is more immediately alarming than the unregulated sale of liquor: not only because every act committed under it impairs or breaks down our civilization; but because, indirectly, the purchase of authority—particularly the police—rots society at its foundations and atrophies the power of dealing with crime of all descriptions.

It is the custom to call the tribute of illegal establishments to the police of great cities blackmail. This term is neither comprehensive nor accurate. The operation is merely one phase in the working out of the business of a great financial and political organization. Inroads have been made and will be made upon the influence of this organization by attacks on particular powers—as has been done in Chicago. Such attacks will probably not achieve final results.

The fact is that under present conditions the financial interests of dissipation have more direct representation in the administration of the people. In Chicago the dealer in vice reaches directly through the ward organization, who hands over bodily the function of enforcing the law—concerning which he himself is and must be to a large extent ignorant—to a political appointee at the head of the police department. With the simplification of the processes of city government; with the abolishing of the ward and the ward boss and the ward delegate in the nominating conventions; with the substitution of nominations and elections by the people—not the mayor, nor of the present machinery for the representative of special interests in city government, but of men to act as department heads, nominated directly, elected directly, and held directly responsible to the people—the organization for the sale of dissipation in cities will lose its present control in city administration, and the people will gain it. At that time the will of the people—whatever it may be—will express itself in city government. There will be an end to the present grotesque and alarming spectacle of a civilization which is stultifying itself; of a society which enacts and desires to administer laws, but is unable to do so because of the control of its machinery by the huge financial interests which owe their very existence to the sale of savagery.

McClure's Magazine
April 1907

GEORGE KIBBE TURNER

The Daughters of the Poor

T HERE ARE NOW three principal centers of the so-called white slave
trade—that is, the recruiting and sale of young girls of the poorer
classes by procurers. The first is the group of cities in Austrian and
Russian Poland, headed by Lemberg; the second is Paris; and the third
the City of New York. In the past ten years New York has become the
leader of the world in this class of enterprise. The men engaged in it
there have taken or shipped girls, largely obtained from the tenement
districts of New York, to every continent on the globe; they are now
doing business with Central and South America, Africa and Asia. They
are driving all competitors before them in North America. And they
have established, directly or indirectly, recruiting systems in every large
city of the United States.

The story of the introduction of this European business into New
York, under the protection of the Tammany Hall political organization,
its extension from there through the United States, and its shipments
of women to the four corners of the earth, is a strange one; it would
seem incredible if it were not thoroughly substantiated by the records
of recent municipal exposures in half a dozen great American cities,
by two independent investigations by the United States government
during the past year, and by the common knowledge of the people of
the East Side tenement district of New York, whose daughters and
friends' daughters have been chiefly exploited by it.

The ancient and more familiar white slave trade was the outright
sale of women from eastern Europe into the Orient through the big
general depot of Constantinople. The chief recruiting ground for this
was the miserable ghetto of Europe in the old kingdom of Poland, now
held by Austria and Russia, where the Jews were herded out of the rest
of Christendom by the persecutions of the Middle Ages. This section

408

is known from Alexandria to Shanghai for its shipment of women like
"Anne of Austria" in Kipling's "Ballad of Fisher's Boarding-House" in
India:

> From Tarnau in Galicia
> To Jaun Bazar she came,
> To eat the bread of infamy
> And take the wage of shame.

The recruiting ground for the supplies of women for this trade, East
or West, is always the section inhabited by the very poor. Out of this
racial slum of Europe has come for unnumbered years the Jewish kaftan,
leading the miserable Jewish girl from European civilization into Asia.
The Jewish church fought the kaftan with all its power. In life he was
ostracized; in death, dragged to an unholy grave. But to this day he
comes out of Galicia and Russian Poland, with his white face and his
long beard—the badge of his ancient faith—and wanders across the
face of this earth. Occasionally members of the fraternity come into
New York: men of seventy, sometimes, with gray beards, following their
trade through life to the very end. Within the year there was in New
York an individual of this profession, known as "Little Bethlehem,"
from the scene of his former business—the Holy Land.

In the last part of the last century a new field opened for this European industry. Great masses of young male laborers went westward out
of Europe to do the work of establishing civilization in a new hemi-
sphere. There were two or three men to one woman in this great shift-
ing of population, which is still taking place. And the social relations
of the whole world were affected by it. One great market for the procurer's supplies, from the time of the Middle Ages, had been the camps
of armies. In the last fifty years two continents have been filled, in city
and country, with a new and similar market—the camps of male
laborers.

The Jewish kaftan, for some reason, did not try his trade with North
America. He exploited South America instead; and in Argentine Republic he found a market that rivaled the East. He could transfer
women there, for a lump sum, into what are known to the New York
trade as "slave houses"; or, in accordance with the more Occidental
development of the business common to most Western countries, one
youth could marry or pretend to marry one girl, travel abroad with her,
and live with her as her manager.

So largely have these people emigrated to Argentina that there is a
considerable colony of them in the suburbs of Buenos Aires. Excluded
from the society of other persons of their own race and religion, they

have secured burial places of their own—somewhat similar to that which has been established in New York—and have even set up their own synagogue, in which they hold ghastly caricatures of religious services. The colony is strong on ceremonial forms, and Jewish holidays are strictly dedicated by the women to devotion. These people still remain in Buenos Aires. But recently—as part of an agitation extending across the civilized world—the Argentine Republic has made their business of importation difficult by new and stringent laws.

It remained for Paris, the second center of the business in Europe, to develop the white slave trade with North America. The Parisian type of trader is so old an institution that his common name, *maquereau* ("mackerel"), appears in the French dictionary. His trade became to all intents and purposes a recognized calling, with a distinguishing costume of its own, consisting of black velvet trousers, a blouse, and a peculiar silk cap known as the *bijou*. These *maquereaux* start in the business—and most of them remain in it—as the manager of one girl of the poorer classes, whom they place to the best possible advantage. From one, the more successful advance to the business management of a number of girls. In all this theirs is exactly similar to the American type of trade which has developed in New York. The *maquereaux* reached the height of their prosperity in Paris during the fashionable and amusement-loving reign of Louis Napoleon in the '60s. With the simpler and more democratic feeling at the beginning of the present French Republic, public sentiment turned more against the traffic. Its operators were frequently transported to the penal colonies in New Caledonia and French Guiana. They gradually discarded their costume and slunk out of sight. And in the '70s they began to emigrate in large numbers, and now may be found across the entire globe. The chief points of export were London and New York. But so much more profit and freedom from law were obtained in the capital of the new continent that it very soon received more attention from the exporters of women than any other place in the world.

Up to this time prostitution had existed in the United States—as most people assume that it exists today—without having attracted the business management of men to securing and exploiting its supplies. So far as it had management, it was entirely a woman's business. Its supplies came, as they must always come, from poor and unfortunate families. From 1850 to the present time, the poorest and most unprotected class has been the newest European emigrants. The most exposed and unprotected girls are those in domestic service. For over half a century this class of population has been called upon to furnish the great bulk of the supplies of girls in our large cities, and this class of employment far more than any other.

In 1857 the police of New York, under the direction of Dr. W. W. Sanger, the resident physician of the institutions on Blackwell's Island, gathered statistics on carefully prepared blanks from two thousand of the six thousand prostitutes then supposed to be in New York. Of these over three-fifths were born abroad, and at least three-quarters were of foreign birth or parentage; one-half had been servants before entering the profession. The new immigration of the time was Irish and German; it furnished the greatest number of women, simply because of their exposed position in the city slums. More than one-third of the two thousand women were born in Ireland—noted throughout Europe for the chastity of its women.

The French *maquereau* was immediately successful in a country where the business had developed in so haphazard a way. The women he brought to this country he dressed well; he kept them abstemious from liquors, and implanted in their minds the ambition of acquiring a competence and returning to live in France. They tended from the first to replace the disheveled and desperate creatures produced by the American slums.

But, though extremely successful in America at first, and still prosperous in the majority of our greater cities, the French *maquereau* was not the type finally adapted to conduct the business in the self-governing American municipalities. He intended to return to France after securing a competency, frequented his own exclusive boardinghouses and clubs, and did not even learn the language. He failed to identify himself with any political organization. He consequently had no direct political influence, and obtained his right to break the law simply by payments of money. In this way he occupied very much the same position as the Chinese gambler in the community of lawbreakers. Both are always able to do business in a large city, but they are much more liable to extortion and blackmail than persons who are directly identified with the political machine. It was necessary for the procuring and selling of girls to become an integral part of slum politics—as the tenement-house saloon and gambling houses had been preceding it—before it could be established on its present firm footing.

About twenty-five years ago the third great flush of immigrations, consisting of Austrian, Russian and Hungarian Jews, began to come into New York. Among these immigrants were a large number of criminals, who soon found that they could develop an extremely profitable business in the sale of women in New York. The Police Department and the police courts, before which all the criminal cases of the city were first brought, were absolutely in the hands of Tammany Hall, which, in its turn, was controlled by slum politicians. A great body of minor workers among this class of politicians obtained their living in tenement-house saloons or gambling houses, and their control of the police and police courts allowed them to disregard all provisions of the law against their business. The new exploiter of the tenement-house population among the Jews saw that this plan was good, and organized a local Tammany Hall association to apply it to the business of procuring and selling girls.

The organization which they formed was known in the Lexow investigation as the Essex Market Court gang, but named itself the Max Hochstim Association. Among various officers of this organization was Mr. Martin Engel, the Tammany Hall leader of the Eighth Assembly District in the late '90s; and with him a group of Tammany Hall politicians in control of this district and the Third Assembly District along the Bowery, just to the east.

This Jewish district, as it was when Mr. Martin Engel was leader, opened the eyes of the minor politician of the slums to the tremendous financial field that a new line of enterprise, the business of procuring and the traffic in women, offered him. The red light district, operated very largely by active members of the local Tammany organization, gave to individual men interested in its development in many cases twenty and thirty thousand dollars a year. Very few of the leading workers in the tenement saloons or gambling enterprises had been able up to that time to make half of that from the population around them.

The supplies of girls for use in the enterprises of the political procurers did not at first come entirely from the families of their constituents. The early Jewish immigration contained a great preponderance of men, and comparatively few young girls. The men in the business made trips into the industrial towns of New England and Pennsylvania, where they obtained supplies from the large number of poorly paid young mill girls, one especially ingenious New Yorker being credited with gaining their acquaintance in the garb of a priest. But, gradually, as the population grew and the number of men engaged in the business increased, the girls were taken more and more from the tenement districts of the East Side.

When this misfortune began to develop among the Jewish people of the East Side, it was a matter of astonishment, as well as horror. The Jewish race has for centuries prided itself upon the purity of its women. Families whose daughters were taken away in the beginning of the

New York traffic often formally cast them off as dead; among the very orthodox, there were cases where the family went through the ancient ceremonial for the dead—slashing the lapels of their clothing and sitting out the seven days of mourning in their houses. But individual families of new immigrants, often not speaking English, naturally had little chance against a closely organized machine. The Essex Market gang, as was shown in the Lexow testimony, not only could protect their own business in women, but had the facilities to prove entirely innocent women guilty.

The business grew so rapidly under these favoring auspices that the East Side was soon not only producing its own supplies, but was exporting them. The first person to undertake this export trade with foreign countries, according to the verbal history of the East Side, was a man who later became a leading spirit in the Tammany organization of the district; he took one or two girls in 1889 or 1890 to compete with the Russian and Galician kaftan in the Buenos Aires market. This venture was not very successful, and the dealer soon returned to New York. Since that time a few hundred New York girls have been taken to Buenos Aires, but, generally speaking, it has not proved a successful market for the New York trade.

South Africa, on the contrary, proved an excellent field, as mining districts always are. In the middle of the '90s—during the lean years of Mayor Strong's administration—stories of the fabulous wealth to be made in the South African gold and diamond fields came to the attention of the New York dealers, and they took women there by the hundred. They proved successful in competition with the dealers from the European centers in Paris and Poland, and established colonies of New Yorkers through the southern end of the continent. Large sums of money were made there, and a few considerable fortunes were acquired, which their owners brought home and put into various businesses in New York—including gambling houses and "Raines law" hotels.* The English government in recent years has been more stringent against the trade, and under a new law gave imprisonment and lashing to men engaged in it. One man, now occupied in a Raines law hotel enterprise in New York, was among those imprisoned, having recently served a sentence of one year. The campaign against the business made South Africa a much less attractive field than formerly; but there are still small New York colonies in various cities there.

* So called after John Raines, New York legislator, who introduced the law which was passed in 1896. The law gave special preference to hotels in selling liquor on Sunday; hence saloons set up enough rooms on their premises to pass as hotels. It was these establishments which became centers of prostitution.

Once acquainted with the advantages of the foreign trade, the New York dealer immediately entered into competition with the French and Polish traders across the world. There are no boundaries to this business; its travelers go constantly to and fro upon the earth, peering into the new places, especially into spots where men congregate on the golden frontiers; and the news comes back from them to Paris and Lemberg and New York. After South Africa, the New York dealers went by hundreds into the East—to Shanghai and to Australia; they followed the Russian army through the Russo-Japanese war; they went into Alaska with the gold rush, and into Nevada; and they have camped in scores and hundreds on the banks of the new Panama Canal. However, the foreign trade was not large compared with the trade with the cities of the United States, which was to develop later. The demand was naturally not so great.

In the meantime, the business grew and strengthened and developed its own institutions in its headquarters at New York. The best known of these is the Jewish society that goes under the name of the New York Independent Benevolent Association. This organization was started in 1896 by a party of dealers who were returning from attendance at the funeral of Sam Engel, a brother of Martin Engel, the Tammany leader of the red light assembly district. In the usual post-funeral discussion of the frailty of human life, the fact was brought out that the sentiment of the Jews of the East Side against men of their profession barred them generally from societies giving death benefits, and even caused discrimination against them in the purchase of burial places in the cemetery. A society was quickly incorporated under the laws of New York, and a burial plot secured and inclosed in Washington Cemetery in Brooklyn. This plot contains now about forty dead, including some ten young children. Of the adults, about a third have died violent or unnatural deaths.

The Independent Benevolent Association guarded its membership carefully, but grew to contain nearly two hundred persons. As most of its people were prosperous, it was able, as a body, to exert a continual influence through political friends to prevent punishment of individual members. Matters of mutual trade interest were discussed at its gatherings, and later, when the more enterprising men in it found larger opportunities in the other cities of the country, its members would naturally inform one another of conditions of business in different sections. In New York, as various members grew to undertake larger business enterprises, the usual difference of trade interest between the retailer and the wholesaler grew up; and the leading operators formed a strictly trade association among themselves—the association whose meeting place was discovered and broken into during business sessions by the District Attorney's force in his campaign of 1907.

In the freedom of the Van Wyck administration of the late '90s, the latest type of slum politician that New York has developed demonstrated further his peculiar value to politics, and the great rewards of politics for him. Like the saloonkeeper before him, he had large periods of the day to devote to planning and developing political schemes; there were a great many dependents and young men connected with the business; and there grew up in the various political and social centers of the East Side so-called "hangout joints," saloons and coffee-houses, where these men came together to discuss political and business matters. It soon became evident that these gangs were exceedingly valuable as political instruments in "repeating" or casting a great number of fraudulent votes.

Yet, in spite of this growth of an entirely new element of political strength, Tammany Hall was defeated in the election of 1901, largely because of a revulsion of popular feeling against some phases of the white slave trade. This feeling was especially directed against the so-called cadets—a name now used across the world to designate the masses of young men engaged in this trade in and out of New York, exactly as the name of *maquereau* is used to designate the Paris operator. As the women secured for the business are at first scarcely more than children, the work of inducing them to adopt it was naturally undertaken most successfully by youths not much older than themselves. In this way the specialization of the business in New York produced the New York cadet—the most important figure in the business in America today. The Committee of Fifteen—which made a thorough and world-wide investigation bearing upon the conditions of life in New York developed by the disclosures of 1901 and 1902—defined this new American product as follows:

"The cadet is a young man, averaging from eighteen to twenty-five years of age, who, after having served a short apprenticeship as a 'watch-boy' or 'lighthouse,' secures a staff of girls and lives upon their earnings. The victim of the cadet is usually a young girl of foreign birth, who knows little or nothing of the conditions of American life."

A general feeling of resentment because the Tammany organization of the East Side had developed this new institution, and others connected with it, among the unprotected immigrants of that district, caused the destruction of the red light district by an anti-Tammany administration, and a great lessening of the freedom of the business in

New York City. In a way, however, this temporary period of reform was a means of greatly extending the business in the United States and eventually in New York. The larger operators in this business established themselves throughout the various larger cities of the country; and the cadets still secured their supplies in the old recruiting grounds of the East Side, where they were in no particular danger. An elaborate campaign against them a little later resulted in the arrest and imprisonment of seven of these men as vagrants. They were released long before the expiration of their terms, by the influence of political friends.

The new type of political industry developed in New York proved very successful in other cities of the country—so much so that it has now established itself to some extent in at least three-quarters of the large cities of the United States. The first places to be developed were naturally the nearest. One of the earliest was Newark, New Jersey, within ten miles of New York.

A group of members of the Independent Benevolent Association came into that city in the early 1900s, and soon after the New York red light district had been broken up they obtained control of practically the entire business of Newark. They secured as supplies the ignorant immigrant girls taken from the East Side of New York, and they brought with them from New York, or educated in Newark, their own staff of cadets—who not only worked vigorously as "repeaters" in local elections, but returned to form some of the most vigorous voters in the lower Tammany Hall districts of New York. But in 1907 the attempt of one member of the Benevolent Association to defraud another out of his business by the aid of local political forces led to a disruption in the body of men who were so well established in Newark. An exposé followed this disagreement, which broke up, for the time at least, the local business, with its importations of New York women, and temporarily stopped the return supply of illegal voters to New York. The testimony of the time showed that these men had worked industriously in the interests of the Tammany leaders in the downtown tenement districts of New York, from which the supply of Newark girls was largely obtained. In Newark the chief of police killed himself subsequent to the exposure.

Another group of Jewish operators transferred themselves from New York to Philadelphia. They secured their supplies of women—largely young immigrant girls—from New York, and retained their New York cadets. The members joined the Mutual Republican Club of the Thirteenth Ward of Philadelphia, whose president was the sheriff of the county; and their cadets were extremely valuable to the political machine as "repeaters," and as managers of the growing Jewish vote in Philadelphia. These "repeaters" are incredibly efficient, some having the record of working in three states—at Philadelphia, Newark, and New York—on the same election day.

The public exposé in Philadelphia did not, of course, come through any political source in Philadelphia—there is but one political party there. It was started by the case of Pauline Goldstein, one of the Russian-Jewish immigrant girls, who was obtained in New York, and later thrown out, scantily clothed, upon the streets of Philadelphia, when sick. The matter was taken up by the Law and Order Society. Some hundred places were found being operated by the New York Jewish group, with several hundred foreign immigrant girls. The investigation showed that there was a close community of interest among this body of men, and that a small group had charge of the relations with the politicians and police. Some sixty men were given jail sentences. "Jake" Edelman, one of the leaders, was the man arrested in the case of the Goldstein girl. He "jumped his bail"; went to join the New York colony in South Africa; returned, to be arrested on the Bowery in New York; and at his trial he was represented by New York counsel, accompanied by a large group of New York friends. The prosecution of these men in Philadelphia was very largely responsible for the eighteen months of reform administration in that city in 1905 and 1906. But since then the New York operator is returning to Philadelphia, and the cadet is firmly established in the local life.

In Chicago the New York operators secured an even stronger hold. Several hundred New York dealers came into the West Side section after the Low administration and established there an excellent reproduction of the red light district. At its height it contained between 750 and 1,000 Jewish girls from New York—largely new immigrants, who could scarcely speak the language. Local crusades have sent a great number of the New York men farther west; but the cadet is now one of the prominent features of the local slum life, and a considerable number of New York Jews still remain in positions of business and political leadership there.

A detailed statement of the spread of activities of the New York dealer and cadet through the United States since the exodus from New York after 1901 would serve as a catalogue of the municipal scandals of the past half dozen years, and would include the majority of the large cities of the country. The New York Jewish cadets were found to be present in hundreds in San Francisco at the great exposé there, and took a prominent part in the rottenness that preceded it; they were strong in Los Angeles before the disclosing of conditions in their line of business changed the administration there a year ago; and two of the most notorious dealers of New York's East Side were prominent figures in the political underworld uncovered by Folk in St. Louis. Today they are strong in all the greater cities; they swarm at the gateway of the Alaskan frontier at Seattle; they infest the streets and restaurants of Boston; they flock for the winter to New Orleans; they fatten on the wages of the government laborers in Panama; and they abound in the South and Southwest and in mining regions of the West.

The growth of this new factor in American city politics was due, not alone to the advantages it offered, but to a general necessity on the part of the slum politician to concentrate his attention upon prostitution as a means of getting a living. This condition was brought about by the astonishing success of the campaign against gambling, beginning some ten years ago, both in New York and in most of the large cities of the country. Policy is almost obliterated, poolrooms are rapidly declining, and little by little gambling at race tracks is dwindling throughout the country. To anyone remembering the condition of public sentiment and the frank and open operation of gambling in American cities fifteen years ago, this change is little less than startling.

One principal reason for the change was the awaking of the personal interest of the richer and more influential classes against gambling. Practically all of the gambling enterprises fed upon the earnings of the poor—a sure tax levied upon the people by the slum politician, who stooped in his policy games to pick up the last and meanest penny of the child. But too many small embezzlements from their employers were made by clerks and bookkeepers to pay the race track and poolroom gambler. The imagination and interest of the employing class became enlisted, and gambling enterprises were pursued with a vigorous attention which drove them out. The net result of all this to the slum politician was succinctly expressed by an observant old-time policeman upon the Bowery of New York about a year ago:

"Where's a district politician goin' to get a bit of money nowadays? The poolrooms are all shut down; policy's gone. There ain't no place at all but the women."

Because of this narrowing tendency in the field of slum politics, the politicians of Tammany Hall below Fourteenth Street found themselves in an exceedingly delicate position after the exposure that defeated them in the red light campaign. The decline of gambling was already evident, and its thousands of political employees—a mainstay in illegal voting—had been discharged; and new election machinery made difficult the wholesale voting of broken tramps and town loafers. Not only was some participation in the sale of women necessary, but the use of the gangs of young procurers and thieves, who had their beginning in the red light days, became almost indispensable if the politicians were to secure the vote upon which their power rested, both in their party and out.

This situation was met with adroitness. The district below Fourteenth Street had now come under control of the slum politicians in the United States, known the country over. Martin Engel, the old Tammany Hall leader of the red light district, was solemnly deposed; a husky young politician was made leader of the district, seriously put on a pair of kid gloves, called in the reporters, and pounded with great pomp and ceremony the persons of a few unfriended cadets. After this drama, it was announced with stern and glassy front that cadets were forever banished from the district—and one of the most useful Tammany myths ever sent gliding down the columns of the local newspapers was launched on its long way. The district retained the chief disorderly-house keepers and captains of cadets upon its list of election captains—where it keeps them yet; and the bands of cadets and thieves worked in its service as they had never worked before. But in the Third District—about the Bowery—they began to have their real headquarters.

It is, of course, the belief—fostered by the great ignorance and indifference of the more influential classes as to the conditions of the alien poor in a city like New York—that the cadet died out largely with the red light. On the contrary, he has largely multiplied—as every close observer of the conditions of the East Side knows. The whole country has been opened up for the supplies of New York procurers since the red light days; the development of the lonely woman of the street and tenement has increased the field for these young cadets greatly; and not only the lower but now the upper East Side of New York City is full of them. The woman they live upon, and her daily necessity of political protection, brings them into public life, and makes them the most accessible of political workers. They have a hostage to fortune always on the street.

It is interesting to see how the picking up of girls for the trade in and outside of New York is carried on by these youths on the East Side of New York, which has now grown, under this development, to be the chief recruiting ground for the so-called white slave trade in the

United States, and probably in the world. It can be exploited, of course, because in it lies the newest body of immigrants and the greatest supply of unprotected young girls in the city. These now happen to be Jews—as, a quarter and a half century ago, they happened to be German and Irish.

The odds in life are from birth strongly against the young Jewish-American girl. The chief ambition of the new Jewish family in America is to educate its sons. To do this the girls must go to work at the earliest possible date, and from the population of 350,000 Jews east of the Bowery tens of thousands of young girls go out into the shops. There is no more striking sight in the city than the mass of women that flood east through the narrow streets in a winter's twilight, returning to their homes in the East Side tenements. The exploitation of young women as money-earning machines has reached a development on the East Side of New York probably not equaled anywhere in the world.

It is not an entirely healthy development. Thousands of women have sacrificed themselves uselessly to give the boys of the family an education. And in the population of young males raised in this atmosphere of the sacrifice of the woman to the man, there have sprung up all sorts of specialization in the petty swindling of women of their wages. One class of men, for instance, go about dressed like the hero in a cook's romance, swindling unattractive and elderly working women out of their earnings by promising marriage, and borrowing money to start a shop. The acute horror among the Jews of the state of being an old maid makes swindling of Jewish women under promise of marriage especially easy.

But the largest and most profitable field for exploitation of the girls of the East Side is in procuring them for the white slave traffic. This line of swindling is in itself specialized. Formerly its chief recruiting grounds were the public amusement parks of the tenement districts; now for several years they have been the dance halls, and the work has been specialized very largely according to the character of the halls.

The amusement of the poor girl of New York—especially the very poor girl—is dancing. On Saturdays and Sundays the whole East Side dances after nightfall, and every night in the week there are tens of thousands of dancers within the limits of the city of New York. The reason for all this is simple: dancing is the one real amusement within the working girl's means. For five cents the moving picture show, the only competitor, gives half an hour's diversion and sends its audience to the street again; for five cents the cheaper "dancing academies" of the East Side give a whole evening's pleasure. For the domestic servant and the poorer shop girl of the East Side there is practically no option, if she is to have any enjoyment of her youth; and not being able to dance is a generally acknowledged source of mortification.

There are three main classes of dance halls, roughly speaking, which are the main recruiting places. In two of them are secured the more ignorant, recent immigrants, who appear in the houses kept by the larger operators of the Independent Benevolent Association. The halls of the first class are known by the East Side boys by the name of "Castle Gardens." To these places, plastered across their front with the weird Oriental hieroglyphics of Yiddish posters, the new Jewish immigrant girl—having found a job—is led by her sister domestics or shopmates to take her first steps in the intricacies of American life. She cannot yet talk the language, but rigid social custom demands that she be able to dance. She arrives, pays her nickel piece and sits—a big, dazed, awkward child—upon one of the wooden benches, along the wall. A strident two-piece orchestra blasts big, soul-satisfying pieces of noise out of the surrounding atmosphere, and finally a delightful young Jewish-American man, with plastered hair, a pasty face, and most finished and ingratiating manners, desires to teach her to dance. Her education in American life has begun.

The common expression for this process among the young dance hall specialists of the East Side is "to kop out a new one." Night after night the cheap orchestra sounds from the bare hall, the new herds of girls arrive, and the gangs of loafing boys look them over. The master of the "dancing academy" does not teach dancing to these five-cent customers; he cannot, at the price; he simply lets his customers loose upon the floor to teach themselves. Some of the boys are "spielers"— youths with a talent for dancing—who are admitted free to teach the girls, and are given the proceeds of an occasional dance. The others pay a ten-cent fee. The whole thing, catering to a class exceedingly poor, is on a most inexpensive scale. Even the five-cent drink of beer is too costly to be handled at a profit. The height of luxurious indulgence is the treat at the one- and two-cent soda stands on the sidewalk below the dance hall. Contrary to the common belief, intoxicating liquor plays but a small part in securing girls from this particular type of place. These lonely and poverty-stricken girls, ignorant and dazed by the strange conditions of an unknown country, are very easily secured by promise of marriage, or even partnership.

A class very similar to this, but of different nationality and religion, is furnished by a second kind of dance hall on the East Side. Just north of Houston Street are the long streets of signs where the Polish and

Slovak servant girls sit in stiff rows in the dingy employment agencies, waiting to be picked up as domestic servants. The odds against these unfortunate, bland-faced farm girls are greater than those against the Galician Jews. They arrive here more like tagged baggage than human beings, are crowded in barracks of boardinghouses, eight and ten in a room at night, and in the morning the runner for the employment agency takes them, with all their belongings in a cheap valise, to sit and wait again for mistresses. Every hand seems to be against such simple and easily exploited creatures, even in some of the "homes" for them.

Just below this section of the Poles and Slavs lies the great body of the Jews, and in the borderland several Hebrews with good political connections have established saloons with dance halls behind them. For the past five or six years the Jewish cadets have found these particularly profitable resorts. These girls are so easily secured that in many cases the men who obtain control of them do not even speak their language.

For a third of a century, at least, the young slum politician in Tammany has danced and picnicked his way into political power. The chief figures in New York slum politics followed this method. And thus arose the "grand civic ball" of the Bowery district—of which, perhaps, since its completion, the present Tammany Hall Building in Fourteenth Street has been the center. But the recent political gangs that have formed the chief strength of the slum districts of Tammany Hall have had a much closer connection with dance halls than any political bodies before them, because their membership is so largely composed of cadets. Practically all the big gangs that have figured in slum politics in recent years started about cheap dance halls. Paul Kelly's began in the halls about the lower Bowery; Eastman's grew strong about new Irving Hall in the Russian-Jewish district below Delancey Street; and Kid Twist's about a dance hall for the Galician Jews in the far East Side.

These gangs of political cadets naturally gravitate toward Tammany Hall for their larger affairs, when they are strong enough to do so. In this way Tammany Hall itself, among the many "tough" dance halls in the city, has come to be the leading headquarters for disreputable dances. It is this class of dances that plays a most prominent part in finally procuring the American-bred girl for the cadet.

The American-bred Jewish girl does not attend the "Castle Garden" dancing academies for "greenhorns." Generally she is able to take dancing lessons, and her dancing is done at weddings or balls. A large number of these balls are given by the rising young political desperadoes, who form for the East Side girls local heroes, exactly as the football captains do for the girls in a college town. The cadets, who make up these men's followers, become acquainted with the girls upon the street at noon hour or at closing time, when the young toughs hang about the curbings, watching the procession of shop girls on the walks. Nothing is more natural than the invitation to the ball; and nothing is more degrading than the association, at these balls, with the cadets and their "flashy girls."

There is liquor at these dances, which plays its part in their influence; but the tale of drugging is almost invariably a hackneyed lie—the common currency of women of the lower world, swallowed with chronic avidity by the sympathetic charitable worker. The course of a girl frequenting these East Side balls is one of increasing sophistication and degradation. At its end she is taken over by the cadet by the offer of a purely commercial partnership. Only one practical objection to the life remains to her—the fear of arrest and imprisonment.

"That's all right; you won't get sent away," says the cadet. "I can take care of that."

His indispensable service in the partnership is the political protection without which the business could not exist. How well he performs his work in New York was demonstrated by the recent testimony, before the Page commission of the legislature, of the immunity of women of this kind from serious punishment by the local courts.

These three classes of girls form the principal sources of the supply that is secured in New York. The ignorant "greenhorns" are taken over more by the larger operators into the houses. The American-bred girl is the alert and enterprising creature who is going through the cities of the United States with her manager, establishing herself in the streets and cafés. The cadet in the past was almost always Jewish; now the young Italians have taken up the business in great numbers. There are a number of "dancing academies" in the Jewish section near the Bowery, where the Italian cadet secures immigrant girls. He attends and conducts balls of his own, which are attended by both Christian and Jewish girls, and he has developed an important field for Slavic and Polish girls in the saloon dance halls of the employment agency district just north of the "Little Italy" in Harlem.

There is a smaller special business in the lower part of New York, which brings in and sends out of the city a number of girls, and which corresponds more closely in its methods to the old white slave trade of the Orient. For a number of years a small group of Italians, who have been very active in the cause of the Tammany Hall organization of the Third Assembly District, has procured Italian girls for the Italian trade in America. The girls in the Italian population of New York are guarded as carefully by their mothers as any class of girls in America, and for this reason are not picked up in any considerable number in the ordinary way by the New York cadet. It has been necessary to secure them from Italy. The plan that is, perhaps, most frequently worked, is to get them through various "wise" members of the great mass of young Italian laborers who return to Italy every year for the winter. These youths induce young peasant girls to accompany them back to America under promise of marriage. When they arrive here, they are satisfied to give up the girls to the dealers in New York upon payment of their passage money and a small bonus.

In the survey of the conditions of the procuring business in the United States during the recent government investigations, no more melancholy feature was discovered than that of the little Italian peasant girls, taken from various dens, where they lay, shivering and afraid, under the lighted candles and crucifixes in their bedrooms. Fear is more efficacious with this class than any other, because of the notorious tendency of the low-class Italian to violence and murder. These girls are closely confined, see only their managers and Italian laborers, do not talk English, and naturally do not know how to escape. At last, of course, they become desperate and hardened by the business. The American trade in them centers in the Bowery Assembly District in New York. From there they are sent in small numbers to various cities where the Italian laborer is found in considerable numbers, including Philadelphia, Pittsburgh, Chicago and Boston.

This is a rough outline of the system of procuring and sending girls out of New York City under the safeguard of political protection. Detectives of the Federal government, who have made within the past year a special investigation of this business in all of the large cities in this country, estimate that about one-half of all the women now in the business throughout the United States started their career in this country in New York. This estimate includes, of course, the women imported into this city, as well as those taken from the population. This estimate may be large, but there can be little doubt, since recent developments, of New York's growth to leadership as the chief center of the white slave trade in the world.

The Galician and Russian kaftan of Lemberg and Warsaw has had one chief market almost destroyed by the recent drastic laws in Argentine Republic, which leave his present field of operation much narrowed. The same loss of trade by legal attack has come now upon the

French trader in his greatest single market, the United States. During the past year two independent Federal investigations—one by the regular government immigration service and one by a special commission appointed by Congress—have been conducted. Their attention has centered chiefly on the activities of the French trade. This branch of the white slave trade in America has been thoroughly frightened by the government's activity, and the number of *maquereaux* in this country has greatly decreased for this reason.

The movement that is driving the French importer out of America has proved ineffectual against the operator from New York who secures immigrant girls after they have landed. In the campaign of the Federal authorities of Chicago, Joseph Keller and Louis Ullman, the former a member of the New York Independent Benevolent Association, were each sentenced to one and a half years of imprisonment for harboring two Jewish immigrant girls they had brought to Chicago from the East Side of New York. They appealed to the United States Supreme Court, and this held that while directly importing girls could be punished by Federal law, the provision punishing men for merely harboring girls taken after they arrive here was not constitutional; and that the exploiting of such girls must be punished by the state law, if at all.

Thus, while the business out of Poland and Paris has been severely curtailed in the past few years, there has so far been no practical setback for the trader from New York. He has today several thousands of girls, secured from the population of New York, established in various sections of the earth. And month after month the ranks of these women must be filled or extended out of the East Side population. This is a matter of desperate seriousness to the population that is being drawn upon for this supply, and a staring advertisement of New York's disgrace across the world; but for the United States at large it is less serious than another phase of the development of the business out of New York—the extension of its political cadet system throughout the cities of the United States.

During the past six or seven years the police of most large American cities outside of New York have noticed a strange development which they have never been able to explain entirely to themselves. The business enterprises for marketing girls have passed almost entirely from the hands of women into those of men. In every case these men have the most intimate connections with the political machines of the slums, and everywhere there has developed a system of local cadets.

The date of this new development of the white slave trade outside of New York corresponds almost uniformly with the time when the traders and cadets from the New York red light district introduced New York methods into the other cities of the country in 1901 and 1902. Hundreds of New York dealers and cadets are still at work in these other cities. But much more important are the local youths, whom these missionaries of the devil brought by the sight of their sleek prosperity into their trade. Everywhere the boy of the slums has learned that a girl is an asset which, once acquired by him, will give him more money than he can ever earn, and a life of absolute ease. In Chicago, for example, prosecutions in 1908 conducted by Assistant State's Attorney Clifford G. Roe caused to be fined or sent to prison 150 of these cadets, nearly all local boys, who had procured local working girls from the dance halls and cheap pleasure resorts in and around Chicago.

There is little doubt that from now on the larger part of the procuring and marketing of women for the United States will be carried on by the system of political procurers developed in New York. The operation of this system has a double influence upon our large cities. On the one side, it has great political importance, for the reason that more and more, with the growing concentration of the slum politician upon this field, the procurer and marketer of women tends to hold the balance of power in city elections. This is true not alone in New York; analyzers of recent political contests in Philadelphia and Chicago have been convinced that the registration and casting of fraudulent votes from disorderly places in those cities may easily determine the result in a close city election, for false votes by the thousand are cast from these resorts.

Certainly this is not an overscrupulous class to hold the balance of political power in a community. But it is the other influence of the development that counts most—its highly efficient system for procuring its supplies. The average life of women in this trade is not over five years, and supplies must be constantly replenished. There is something appalling in the fact that year after year the demands of American cities reach up through thousands to the tens of thousands for new young girls. The supply has come in the past and must come in the future from the girls morally broken by the cruel social pressure of poverty and lack of training. The odds have been enough against these girls in the past. Now everywhere through the great cities of the country the sharp eyes of the wise cadet are watching, hunting her out at her amusements and places of work. And back of him the most adroit minds of the politicians of the slums are standing to protect and extend with him their mutual interests.

The trade of procuring and selling girls in America—taken from the

weak hands of women and placed in control of acute and greedy men—
has organized and specialized after its kind exactly as all other business has done. The cadet does his procuring, not as an agent for any
larger interest, but knowing that a woman can always be sold profitably
either on the streets or in houses in American cities. The larger operators conduct their houses and get their supplies from the cadet—take
him, in fact, into a sort of partnership, by which every week he collects the girl's wages as her agent. The ward politician keeps the disorderly saloon—a most natural political development, because it serves
both as a "hangout" for the gangs of cadets and thieves, and a market
for women. And, back of this, the politician higher up takes his share
in other ways. No business pays such toll to the slum politicians as this
does. The First Ward ball of "Hinky-Dink" Kenna and "Bathhouse
John" Coughlin, the kings of slum politics in Chicago; the Larry Mul-
ligan ball in New York; the dances of the Kelly and East Side and
Five Points New York gangs, all draw their chief revenue, directly or
indirectly, from the source. From low to high, the whole strong organization gorges and fattens on the gross feeding from this particular
thing.

It is the poor and ignorant girl who is captured—the same class that
has always furnished the "white slaves" of the world. Interesting figures
made by the police concerning the newcomers into the South Side
Levee district of Chicago tell the same story as the statistics of New
York in 1857. All but 12 or 15 per cent are of foreign birth or parentage. About one-third were of the domestic servant class before they
entered the life of prostitution.

Meanwhile, New York, the first in the development of this European
trade in America, remains its center, and its procuring interests are
the strongest and most carefully organized of all. The young cadet has
his beginning, as well as the woman he secures. These boys learn in the
primary schools of the farther East Side, from the semipolitical gangs
in the dance halls; step by step, as they grow in the profession, they
graduate into the Third Assembly District, the chief "hangout" place
of the procurer in the world. In all the East Side districts of Tammany
Hall these youths have representatives who look out for their interests;
but here two-thirds of the active workers are or have been interested in
markets of prostitution.

Around the district's eastern edge in lower Second Avenue hang the
mass of the Jewish cadets, who are members of the strong East Side
political gangs. Many of them are determined thieves as well. Farther
along is a mixture of the more leisurely class, who devote all their

attention to their work as managers of women. Among them are scores —and through the nearby East Side hundreds—of youths who have women at work throughout this country, especially in the West and Southwest, or abroad, but who prefer to remain, themselves, in the companionship and comfort of the national headquarters of their trade. Correspondence on the condition of the white slave trade comes here from all over the world. On the lower Bowery and in Chatham Square are the Italian cadets.

There are scores of "hangouts" for cadets in the Third District, and in all the notorious saloons the waiters are managers of women, and receive their jobs on the recommendation of politicians. Special lawyers defend the cadets when they are caught, and all have their direct access to the political machine, largely through the political owners of their special "hangouts." Altogether, it is a colony of procurers not equaled throughout the world in its powers of defense and offense.

This class of political criminal has a distinct tendency toward greater and greater license. The type of youth first known as cadets was a slinking, cowardly person, who was physically formidable only to the more timid foreign immigrants. Now, and especially since the young Italian has taken up this profession in New York, the gangs of these men have constantly grown uglier and bolder. A curious similarity is shown between these gangs as they have developed in New York, and the Apaches, the bands of city savages in Paris, whose violent crimes were responsible for the recent reintroduction of capital punishment in France. A statement by M. Bay, head of the Research Brigade in that city, concerning the outbreak of crime there in 1902, shows how identical the gangs of New York are with those that have formed in the capital of France, about the same business that is their mainstay there.

"Paris," he said, "is empty; the women upon whom the great mass of these hooligans prey are unable to obtain money. Result—the scoundrels, none of whom are capable of doing an hour's honest work, fall back on the knife, the revolver, or the burglar's jimmy. All of these articles can be purchased cheaply. Another reason for the street fights which take place with revolvers is jealousy. A woman leaves her 'protector' and takes up with sworn enemies, and a regular vendetta is started between them. They gather their friends and in pitched battles try to kill each other."

The highway assaults, murders and street fights that New York has suffered from in the last five years have come from an exactly similar class of organization. For two years past the operations of these gangs have been curtailed by the activity against them of the Police Department, under the administration of General Bingham. Gradually his campaign led to the higher and more important enterprises which they made headquarters for themselves and their women. It extended first through the centers about the Bowery, Second Avenue and Chatham Square, and finally to the associated summer headquarters at Coney Island. Then, suddenly, General Bingham was removed by Mayor McClellan.

The various interests dependent upon the procuring and sale of women considered this event their first victory. But now all eyes of these people are concentrated on the main issue of this fall. Will or will not Tammany be elected? The whole future of their career in New York hangs upon the issue of this event. And they are preparing to work for the Democratic party with every means in their power.

The exploitation of a popular government by the slum politician is a curious thing, always. I sat some time ago with a veteran politician, for many years one of the leading election district captains of the Tammany Bowery organization, conversing sociably in the parlor of his profitable Raines law hotel.

"The people love Tammany Hall," said my host. "We use 'em right. When a widow's in trouble, we see she has her hod of coal; when the orphans want a pair of shoes, we give it to them."

It was truly and earnestly said. As he spoke, the other half of the political financing was shown. The procession of the daughters of the East Side filed by the open door upstairs with their strange men. It was the slum leader's common transaction. Having wholesaled the bodies of the daughters at good profit, he rebates the widow's hod of coal.

The so-called "human quality" is the threadbare defense of slum politics. But all its charitable transactions have been amply financed. From the earliest time it has been the same old system of rebates to the poor. First, the rebate of the tenement saloon at the death of the drunken laborer; then, the rebate from the raking up of the last miserable pennies of the clerk and laborer and scrubwoman, by the poolrooms and policy; and now, smiling its same old hearty smile, it extends to the widow and orphan its rebates from the bodies of the daughters of the poor.

It is a source of perennial wonder how much longer the poorer classes will be cajoled and threatened and swindled into taking them. . . .

McClure's Magazine
November 1909

EPILOGUE

THE MUCKRAKERS believed in fair play and in democracy; they believed that if man knew of the wrongs, he would rise to his stature and do something about them. They muckraked because they loved the world. Though they were angry at the injustices, there was no bitterness, no hatred.

They were writers and reporters interested in human nature. Sometimes they worked together; mostly they worked alone. Though they were not organized as a group, they had a common cause: to expose. Generally they offered no cures.

Some of their paths crossed again after the era of the muckraker was over; others found themselves in different arenas. Some turned conservative; a few—like Sinclair, Steffens and Russell—veered to the left. With the mass-circulation magazines no longer interested in publishing muckraking articles, these writers whose words had blazoned across the American scene to awaken an apathetic public now began to look toward other areas of activity.

Upton Sinclair, in reminiscing, calls his muckraking colleagues simply "men of courage." He explains: "The times required a great deal of it, for the things they were after were certainly serious defects in our political, social and economic life." [147]

Ida M. Tarbell, on the other hand, wrote that she often heard the comment that it required courage on the part of *McClure's* to undertake her series on Standard Oil. "But courage implies a suspicion of danger. Nobody thought of such a thing in our office. . . . We were neither apologists nor critics, only journalists intent on discovering what had gone into the making of this most perfect of all monopolies. What had we to be afraid of?" [148]

431

Sinclair recalls some of his fellow writers of the muckraking era: "Ida Tarbell was largely a conventional-minded lady, sweet and gracious. David Graham Phillips never classified himself, but he expressed an old-fashioned American radicalism not identified with any economic theory. He associated with Socialists.

"Lincoln Steffens was very enthusiastic in the early days about Communists, but later he became disillusioned and disappointed with them.

"Ray Stannard Baker was very mild, sweet, kind, a New England conscience, cultured. He muckraked conscientiously; he was shocked by the wrong. I tried to make a fighting radical out of him, but Baker was too gentle; he had no economics, or very little.

"Finley Peter Dunne made fun with Mr. Dooley and he laughed freely; he had a wonderful sense of humor," recalls Sinclair.[149]

William Hard, who during the muckraking era wrote about child labor, politics and industrial accidents, is today proud of his muckraking, and asserts that "in my opinion, the best of us muckrakers was Lincoln Steffens. He dealt principally, of course, with politics and government. He was a charming character as well as a great magazine writer."[150]

In the 1912 election, Sullivan and Irwin campaigned for Roosevelt; Baker was on the Wilson team; Russell and Sinclair found in Socialist Eugene Victor Debs their ideal candidate.

As World War I came closer to involving the United States, more muckrakers supported President Wilson. Steffens, Tarbell and Adams joined the Wilson banner. When the United States declared war, Sinclair and Russell broke with the Socialist party's antiwar stand. Adams, Baker, Connolly, Irwin and Russell were among the muckrakers who joined the "blue-ribbon list" of 150,000 "Four Minute Men" who delivered the government's message in motion picture theaters throughout the country during the war.

Upton Sinclair wrote that he gave his support to the war and has "no apology to make for that course. . . . But my support of the war did not mean that I had given myself into the hands of war-profiteers."[151]

In their later writings, many of the muckrakers turned to biography as well as to autobiography. They wrote novels, short stories, articles, plays, but few—if any—kept to the muckraking theme.

Ida M. Tarbell (1857-1944) wrote friendly biographies of Judge Gary of U.S. Steel and Owen D. Young of the General Electric Company, and sympathetic articles in defense of big business. She was a member of President Wilson's Industrial Conference and a member of President Harding's Unemployment Conference. She lectured on the Chautauqua circuit and pleaded for sex equality.

Samuel Hopkins Adams (1871-1958) wrote novels, including *Flaming Youth*, a title which was used to characterize the hedonistic, flamboyant years after World War I. He wrote biographies of President Harding, Alexander Woollcott and Daniel Webster, plus mystery novels and movies. Several of his novels were made into successful movies, such as *It Happened One Night* and *The Gorgeous Hussy*.

Thomas Lawson (1857-1925) completely forgot muckraking and turned his interest to horticulture and the pink rose, thoroughbred horses and art collections. In the early twenties, there was talk that he would go back on Wall Street to attempt to amass another fortune, but if he did, it was done quietly with no fanfare, and no one heard about it. His fortune dwindled and four months after his death, executors of his estate announced that he died "without a five-cent piece."

Charles Edward Russell and Upton Sinclair took part in a number of Socialist political campaigns. Russell (1860-1941) in 1913 ran for mayor of New York, and the following year for United States senator, on the Socialist ticket. He was a member of the Wilson Industrial Commission, and was appointed by the President to a diplomatic mission under Elihu Root. During the New Deal NRA days, he was on the Clarence Darrow Review Board. In his later years, Russell was a friend of the Irish republic, and was keenly interested in the plight of the Jews. At the time of his death, he was vice-president of the American Association Opposed to Capital Punishment. He too turned to biography—that of Julie Marlowe and Theodore Thomas.

"I'm the only one of the muckrakers who kept at muckraking," said Upton Sinclair (1878-   ) on his eightieth birthday. "But I'm also a working Socialist." The octogenarian participated in many a Socialist campaign, and he wrote historic pamphlets about industrial events in America and on the international scene. He decried newspapers in *The Brass Check*; he wrote about the Spanish civil war in *No Pasaran*; about Ford-America in *The Flivver King*. His Lanny Budd series of novels were best sellers and book club selections. He also rained havoc on California politics when he captured the Democratic party nomination of the state in the thirties with his End Poverty in California (EPIC) campaign; but he was defeated in the election.

William English Walling (1877-1936), a wealthy Socialist, lectured and wrote in his later years. In 1924 he was a Progressive Democratic candidate for Congress from the fourth district in New York; he was a founder and director of the National Association for the Advancement of Colored People; and in 1930 he went to Cuba to study conditions there for the International Labor News service.

William Hard (1878-   ), after his muckraking days, went to Washington as a correspondent, first for *The New Republic*, then *The Nation*. He also worked for the Cosmopolitan News service, owned by David Lawrence, until he became a roving editor for *Reader's Digest* in 1936. In 1928 Hard published a biography of Herbert Hoover. Irreconcilably against the League of Nations, today Mr. Hard is an ardent advocate of the United Nations.

An assassin's bullet cut David Graham Phillips' (1867-1911) life short. In 1915 his novel *Susan Lenox* was posthumously serialized in Hearst's *International* magazine, and its appearance stirred the country as much as his "Treason of the Senate" had. Libelous and obscene, said the critics when the series was published in book form two years later. Pressured by the Society for the Suppression of Vice, the first edition was withdrawn and subsequent editions had about 100 pages deleted.

George Kibbe Turner (1869-1952) wrote short stories and did Hollywood scenarios. Among his motion pictures were *Held in Trust*, *Those Who Dared*, and *Street of Forgotten Men*.

Mark Sullivan (1874-1952), who was known as the "official journalist of the Progressive movement," became conservative as the years passed, and his conservatism was accelerated during the F.D.R. administration. After leaving the editorship of *Collier's*, he joined the New York *Evening Post* as a political columnist, and then the New York *Herald Tribune* as a commentator. He was a correspondent to the Paris peace conference in 1919. He was opposed to the League of Nations, but in 1946 came out in favor of Churchill's Fulton, Missouri, speech in which the phrase "iron curtain" was first used. His six volumes of *Our Times* are a lively history covering the first quarter of this century.

Will Irwin (1873-1948) wrote a biography of President Herbert Hoover, as well as novels and plays. In addition to his muckraking articles in *Collier's*, he also wrote about baseball. He collaborated on two plays, each having a successful run. *The Thirteenth Chair* was written with Bayard Veiller and was a hit in 1916; in 1930 he wrote *The Lute Song* with Sidney Howard, which was produced on Broadway in 1946.

Ray Stannard Baker's (1870-1946) life ranged from a "crusading editor's chair to the Thoreauesque calm of a New England retreat." He went to Paris with President Wilson in 1919 as director of the press bureau of the American commission to negotiate peace. He reviewed labor troubles in the twenties. In 1927 he wrote the first of an eight-volume biography of Wilson, the last two volumes of which won him a Pulitzer prize in 1940. Under the name of David Grayson, he presented his philosophy in *Adventures in Contentment* and *Adventures in Understanding*: "It's to make better men, nobler men—and after that still nobler men. . . . Not to blink sorrow or evil or ugliness, but never to fear them."

Lecturer, lawyer and writer, C. P. Connolly (1863-1933) in his later years wrote for national magazines, but there was no muckraking to his theme. During the debate on the Eighteenth Amendment, he spoke and wrote in favor of the enactment of prohibition.

John L. Mathews (1874-1916), newspaperman and magazine editor, wrote extensively on conservation. He was a student of waterways. In addition to his articles for *Hampton's*, he wrote a series on economics for *Harper's* Magazine.

Edwin Markham (1852-1940) insisted that "I am neither an economist nor a politician. In my writings I have only attempted to depict life as it appears to me. If they disclose there is something wrong," said the poet of the muckrakers, who became famous almost overnight with his poem "The Man with the Hoe," "that is as much as can be expected of them. I am no back-seat driver. I leave guidance of our political state to the men who have learned to direct it." After his rise to fame, Markham was always ready to lend his name to any cause he considered worthy. In 1930 he voiced an appeal for the starving Jews in eastern Europe and to rebuild Palestine in a poem, "Bread and Home."

Lincoln Steffens (1866-1936) covered revolutions and wars after his muckraking days; he lectured in this country on the meaning of the Mexican and Russian revolutions. Returning from a visit to Russia after the revolution, he told associates, "I have looked at the millennium, and it works." He attended the Versailles Peace conference; he became secretary of the Committee for Russian Relief, and also renewed his drive for the amnesty of American political and labor prisoners. He saw Mussolini as a new kind of political boss. It took Steffens five years to write his *Autobiography*, a classic in which he tells the lessons of his experiences, as well as the nature and technique of corruption.

Whether their paths turned to the left or to the right, they all agreed with Charles Edward Russell when he wrote, "There is no such thing in this world as a wasted protest against any existing evil."[152]

NOTES

1. C. C. Regier, *The Era of the Muckrakers* (Chapel Hill: University of North Carolina Press, 1932), p. 13.
2. June 27, 1895.
3. Henry F. Pringle, *Theodore Roosevelt* (New York: Harcourt, Brace & Co., 1931, pp. 163-164.
4. Eric F. Goldman, *Rendezvous with Destiny* (New York: Alfred A. Knopf, 1952), p. 176.
5. Louis Filler, *Crusaders for American Liberalism* (New York: Harcourt, Brace & Co., 1939), p. 53.
6. Vernon Parrington, *Main Currents in American Thought* (New York: Harcourt, Brace & Co., 1930), III, 406.
7. Walter Lippmann, *Drift and Mastery* (Mitchell Kennerley, 1914), pp. 4-5.
8. John Chamberlain, *Farewell to Reform* (New York: Liveright, Inc., 1932), p. 140.
9. *American Magazine*, "The Man with the Muckrake," May 1906.
10. June 1906.
11. C. C. Regier, *The Era of the Muckrakers*, p. 201.
12. In a letter to the editors.
13. Harold Laski, *The American Democracy* (New York: The Viking Press, 1948), p. 621.
14. John Chamberlain, *Farewell to Reform*, pp. 127-128.
15. In conversation with the editors.
16. In conversation with the editors.
17. February 1914.
18. John Chamberlain, *Farewell to Reform*, pp. 141-142.
19. Will Irwin, *The Making of a Reporter* (New York: G. P. Putnam's Sons, 1942), p. 170.
20. In conversation with the editors.
21. Ellery Sedgwick, *The Happy Profession* (Boston: Little Brown & Company, 1946), pp. 142-143.
22. Ray Stannard Baker, *An American Chronicle* (New York: Charles Scribner's Sons, 1945), p. 169.
23. Louis Filler, *Crusaders for American Liberalism*, pp. 357-358.
24. S. S. McClure, *My Autobiography* (New York: Frederick A. Stokes Co., 1913), pp. 244-245.
25. *Ibid.*, p. 245.
26. Chicago *Sunday Record-Herald*, April 15, 1906.
27. Ray Stannard Baker, *An American Chronicle*, p. 203.
28. Lincoln Steffens, *The Autobiography of Lincoln Steffens* (New York: Harcourt, Brace & Co., 1931), p. 581.
29. Elting E. Morison, *The Letters of Theodore Roosevelt* (Cambridge: Harvard University Press, 1954), VIII, 959.
30. Charles Edward Russell, *Bare Hands and Stone Walls* (New York: Charles Scribner's Sons, 1933), pp. 142-143.
31. Isaac F. Marcosson, *David Graham Phillips and His Times* (New York: Dodd, Mead & Co., Inc., 1932), p. 89.
32. February 1906.

33. November 17, 1906.
34. Elting E. Morison, *The Letters of Theodore Roosevelt*, V, 269.
35. Louis Filler, *Crusaders for American Liberalism*, pp. 256-257.
36. *Collier's*, March 2, 1907.
37. Mark Sullivan, *The Education of an American* (New York: Doubleday, Doran & Co., Inc., 1938), p. 248.
38. George French, "The Damnation of the Magazines," *Twentieth Century*, June 1912.
39. *Collier's*, April 2, 1910.
40. *Twentieth Century*, June 1912.
41. Mark Sullivan, *The Education of an American*, p. 244.
42. September 6, 1906.
43. In a letter to the editors from Jack Ryan, Director of Publications and News Service, Montana State University.
44. C. B. Glasscock, *The War of the Copper Kings* (Indianapolis: The Bobbs-Merrill Company, 1935), p. 176.
45. November 9, 1933.
46. Lincoln Steffens, *The Autobiography of Lincoln Steffens*, p. 364.
47. *Ibid.*, p. 368.
48. *Ibid.*
49. *Ibid.*, p. 373.
50. Lloyd Morris, *Postscript to Yesterday* (New York: Random House, 1947), p. 289.
51. Lincoln Steffens, *The Shame of the Cities* (New York: Peter Smith, 1948), pp. 3-4.
52. *McClure's*, June 1904.
53. Louis Filler, *Randolph Bourne* (American Council on Public Affairs, 1943), p. vi.
54. Arthur M. Schlesinger, *Political and Social History of the United States, 1829-1925* (New York: The Macmillan Company, 1925), p. 442.
55. Herman Kogan and Lloyd Wendt, *Chicago: A Pictorial History* (New York: E. P. Dutton & Co., Inc., 1958), p. 168.
56. Will Irwin, *The Making of a Reporter*, p. 156.
57. December 8, 1908.
58. December 12, 1908.
59. Chicago *Record-Herald*, December 14, 1908.
60. December 14, 1908.
61. Pp. 156-157.

62. *New York Times*, September 16, 1909.
63. Norman Hapgood, *Changing Years* (New York: Farrar & Rinehart, Inc., 1930), p. 182.
64. Henry F. Pringle, *The Life and Times of William Howard Taft* (New York: Farrar & Rinehart, Inc., 1939), p. 470.
65. A. T. Mason, *Bureaucracy Convicts Itself* (New York: The Viking Press, 1941), p. 212.
66. May 25, 1940.
67. Edward Bok, *The Americanization of Edward Bok* (New York: Charles Scribner's Sons, 1922), p. 340.
68. Mark Sullivan, *The Education of an American*, pp. 188-189.
69. *Ibid.*, p. 191.
70. October 7, 1905.
71. September 30, 1905.
72. Will Irwin, *The Making of a Reporter*, p. 155.
73. *Collier's*, June 23, 1906.
74. *Cosmopolitan*, "What Life Means to Me," October 1906.
75. In conversation with the editors.
76. *Cosmopolitan, ibid.*, October 1906.
77. Mark Sullivan, *Our Times: The United States, 1900-1925* (New York: Charles Scribner's Sons, 1927), II, 479.
78. Louis Filler, *Crusaders for American Liberalism*, p. 279.
79. Ray Stannard Baker, *An American Chronicle*, p. 192.
80. March 1907.
81. *Collier's*, September 19, 1908.
82. Arthur S. Link, *American Epoch* (New York: Alfred A. Knopf, Inc., 1955), p. 76.
83. Mary White Ovington, *How the National Association for the Advancement of Colored People Began*, 1914 (pamphlet).
84. S. S. McClure, *My Autobiography*, p. 237.
85. *Ibid.*, p. 238.
86. *Ibid.*
87. Ida M. Tarbell, *All in the Day's Work* (New York: The Macmillan Company, 1939), p. 203.
88. *Ibid.*
89. *Ibid.*, p. 215.
90. *Ibid.*, p. 225.
91. *Ibid.*, p. 227.
92. *Ibid.*, p. 240.
93. *Ibid.*, p. 241.

94. Elbert Hubbard, *The Standard Oil Co.* (East Aurora, N. Y.: Roycroft Shop, 1910), pp. 13-14.
95. January 5, 1905.
96. January 5, 1905.
97. Allan Nevins, *John D. Rockefeller* (New York: Charles Scribner's Sons, 1940), II, 520-521.
98. *Ibid.*, p. 522.
99. *New York Times*, February 9, 1925.
100. *Everybody's*, July 1904.
101. *Ibid.*
102. December 29, 1904.
103. January 19, 1905.
104. C. C. Regier, *The Era of the Muckrakers*, p. 130.
105. *Ibid.*
106. Allan Nevins, *John D. Rockefeller*, II, 526-527.
107. Arthur S. Link, *American Epoch*, p. 76.
108. Louis Filler, *Crusaders for American Liberalism*, p. 188.
109. February 25, 1925.
110. Thomas Lawson, *Frenzied Finance* (The Ridgway-Thayer Co., 1905), pp. 415-416.
111. *Era*, November 1904.
112. *Ibid.*, April 1905.
113. P. 781; published by American Conservation Co., 1936.
114. Mark Sullivan, *Our Times: The United States, 1900-1925*, III, 67.
115. October 7, 1905.
116. Arthur M. Schlesinger, *Political and Social History of the United States, 1829-1925*, p. 442.
117. Allan Nevins, *John D. Rockefeller*, p. 527.
118. Arthur M. Schlesinger, *Political and Social History of the United States, 1829-1925*, II, 440.
119. Louis Filler, *Crusaders for American Liberalism*, p. 212.
120. *Collier's*, August 11, 1906.
121. Louis Filler, *Crusaders for American Liberalism*, p. 211.
122. August 11, 1906.
123. October 1905.
124. Ray Stannard Baker, *An American Chronicle*, p. 194.
125. Arthur S. Link, *American Epoch*, p. 76.
126. *The Independent*, February 18, 1909.
127. Charles Edward Russell, *Bare Hands and Stone Walls*, pp. 146-147.
128. *Everybody's*, February 1909.
129. P. 30; published by The Macmillan Company, 1902.
130. Charles Edward Russell, *Bare Hands and Stone Walls*, p. 147.
131. June 1908.
132. July 17, 1908.
133. July 15, 1908.
134. As reprinted in the Atlanta *Constitution*, July 21, 1908.
135. As reprinted in the Atlanta *Constitution*, July 21, 1908.
136. Atlanta *Constitution*, July 24, 1908.
137. September 20, 1908.
138. *Everybody's*, September 1908.
139. *Ibid.*, June 1912.
140. "The Newark Factory Fire," April 1911.
141. In a letter to the editors.
142. Louis Filler, *Crusaders for American Liberalism*, p. 288.
143. In a letter to the editors, February 23, 1960.
144. *Collier's*, October 23, 1909.
145. Louis Filler, *Crusaders for American Liberalism*, p. 290.
146. October 1910.
147. In conversation with the editors.
148. Ida M. Tarbell, *All in the Day's Work*, p. 206.
149. In conversation with the editors.
150. In a letter to the editors.
151. Upton Sinclair, *The Brass Check* (Girard, Kansas: Haldeman-Julius Publications), p. 378.
152. Charles Edward Russell, *Bare Hands and Stone Walls*, p. 422.

BIBLIOGRAPHY

Other Muckraking Articles

Adams, Samuel Hopkins, "Fraud Medicines Own Up," *Collier's*, January 20, 1912.

Adams, Samuel Hopkins, "The Law, the Label, and the Liars," *Collier's*, April 13, 1912.

Adams, Samuel Hopkins, "Fraud Above the Law," *Collier's*, May 11, 1912.

Baker, Ray Stannard, "Capital and Labor Hunt Together," *McClure's*, September 1903.

Baker, Ray Stannard, "Trust's New Tool—The Labor Boss," *McClure's*, November 1903.

Baker, Ray Stannard, "Organized Capital Challenges Organized Labor," *McClure's*, July 1904.

Baker, Ray Stannard, "The Railroad Rate," *McClure's*, November 1905.

Baker, Ray Stannard, "Railroad Rebates," *McClure's*, December 1905.

Baker, Ray Stannard, "Railroads and Popular Unrest," *Collier's*, August 11, 1906.

Baker, Ray Stannard, "The Negro's Struggle for Survival in the North," *American*, March 1908.

Baker, Ray Stannard, "The Tragedy of the Mulatto," *American*, April 1908.

Baker, Ray Stannard, "The Black Man's Silent Power," *American*, July 1908.

Baker, Ray Stannard, "The Case Against Trinity," *American*, May 1909.

Baker, Ray Stannard, "The Godlessness of New York," *American*, June 1909.

Bingham, Theodore A., "The Organized Criminals of New York," *McClure's*, November 1909.

Brandeis, Louis D., "The Greatest Insurance Wrong," *Independent*, December 20, 1906.

Connolly, C. P., "Raiding the People's Land," *Collier's*, January 8, 1910.

Connolly, C. P., "Ballinger—Shyster," *Collier's*, April 2, 1910.

Connolly, C. P., "Who Is Behind Ballinger?", *Collier's*, April 9, 1910.

Connolly, C. P., "Big Business and the Bench," *Everybody's*, February-July 1912.

Crosby, Ernest Howard, "Militarism at Home," *Arena*, January 1904.

Crosby, Ernest Howard, "Wall Street and Graft," *Cosmopolitan*, February 1907.

Dorr, Rheta Childe, "The Prodigal Daughter," *Hampton's*, April 1910.

Flynt, Josiah, "In the World of Graft," *McClure's*, February-April 1901.

Flynt, Josiah, "Pool Room Vampire and Its Money-Mad Victims," *Cosmopolitan*, February 1907.

Flynt, Josiah, "Pool Room Spider and the Gambling Fly," *Cosmopolitan*, March 1907.

Flynt, Josiah, "The Men Behind the Pool Rooms," *Cosmopolitan*, April 1907.

Flynt, Josiah, "Telegraph and Telephone Companies as Allies of the Criminal Pool Rooms," *Cosmopolitan*, May 1907.

French, George, "Masters of the Magazines," *Twentieth Century*, April 1912.

French, George, "The Damnation of the Magazines," *Twentieth Century*, June 1912.

Galvin, G. W., "Inhuman Treatment of Prisoners in Massachusetts," *Arena*, December 1904.

Glavis, L. R., "The Whitewashing of Ballinger," *Collier's*, November 13, 1909.

Hampton, Benjamin B., "The Vast Riches of Alaska," *Hampton's*, April 1910.

Hard, William, "Labor in the Chicago Stockyards," *Outlook*, June 16, 1906.

Hard, William, "Law of the Killed and Wounded," *Everybody's*, September 1908.

Hendrick, Burton J., "The Story of Life Insurance," *McClure's*, May-November 1906.

Irwin, Will, "Tainted News Methods of the Liquor Interests," *Collier's*, March 13, 1909.

Irwin, Will, "The American Newspaper," *Collier's*, January 21-July 29, 1911.

Kennan, George, "The Fight for Reform in San Francisco," *McClure's*, September 1907, November 1907.

Keys, C. M., "The Money Kings," *World's Work*, October-December 1907, February 1908.

Lewis, Alfred Henry, "A Trust in Agricultural Implements," *Cosmopolitan*, April 1905.

Lewis, Alfred Henry, "The Lesson of Platt," *Cosmopolitan*, April 1906.

Lewis, Alfred Henry, "Owners of America," *Cosmopolitan*, 1908-1909.

Lewis, Alfred Henry, "The Betrayal of a Nation," *Pearson's*, 1909.

Lewis, Alfred Henry, "What Is Joe Cannon?", *Cosmopolitan*, April 1910.

Lewis, Alfred Henry, "The Apaches of New York," *Pearson's*, 1911-1912.

Lewis, Alfred Henry, "The Viper on the Hearth," *Cosmopolitan*, March 1911.

Lewis, Alfred Henry, "The Trail of the Viper," *Cosmopolitan*, April 1911.

Lewis, Alfred Henry, "The Viper's Trail of Gold," *Cosmopolitan*, May 1911.

Lindsey, Benjamin B., "The Beast and the Jungle," *Everybody's*, October 1909-May 1910.

London, Jack, "My Life in the Underworld," *Cosmopolitan*, May-October 1907.

Mathews, John L., "Water Power and the Pork Barrel," *Hampton's*, October 1908.

Mathews, John L., "Water Power and the Price of Bread," *Hampton's*, July 1909.

Mathews, John L., "The Trust That Will Control All Other Trusts," *Hampton's*, August 1909.

McClure, S. S., "The Tammanyizing of a Civilization," *McClure's*, November 1909.

Moody, John, "The Conservation of Monopoly," *Arena*, October 1905.

Moody, John, and Turner, George Kibbe, "The Master of Capital in America," *McClure's*, November-December 1910 — January-March 1911.

Norcross, Charles P., "The Beet-Sugar Round-Up," *Cosmopolitan*, November 1909.

Norcross, Charles P., "The Rebate Conspiracy," *Cosmopolitan*, December 1909.

Norris, Frank, "A Deal in Wheat," *Everybody's*, August 1902.

Oskison, J. M., "Competing with the Sharks," *Collier's*, February 5, 1910.

Oskison, J. M., "Round-up of the Financial Swindlers," *Collier's*, December 31, 1910.

Perkins, George C., "The United States Senate and the People," *Independent*, April 12, 1906.

Phillips, David Graham, "David B. Hill," *Everybody's*, November 1902.

Phillips, David Graham, "The Delusion of the Race Track," *Cosmopolitan*, January 1905.

"Q. P.," "Changes in the 'Big Three' Companies," *World's Work,* November 1905.

"Q. P.," "The Life Insurance Machine," *World's Work,* November 1905.

"Q. P.," "Irresponsible Insurance Millions," *World's Work,* January 1906.

"Q. P.," "The Life Insurance Remedy," *World's Work,* February 1906.

"Q. P.," "Life Insurance Corruption," *World's Work,* March 1906.

Reuterdahl, Henry, "Needs of Our Navy," *McClure's,* January 1908.

Russell, Charles Edward, "The Growth of Caste in America," *Cosmopolitan,* March 1907.

Russell, Charles Edward, "Where Did You Get It, Gentlemen?", *Everybody's,* August 1907-March 1908.

Russell, Charles Edward, "At the Throat of the Republic," *Cosmopolitan,* December 1907, January, March 1908.

Russell, Charles Edward, "Beating Men to Make Them Good," *Hampton's,* September, October, November 1909.

Russell, Charles Edward, "What Are You Going to Do About It?", *Cosmopolitan,* July 1910-January 1911.

Russell, Charles Edward, "The Keeping of the Kept Press," *Pearson's,* January 1914.

Sinclair, Upton, "Is Chicago Meat Clean?", *Collier's,* April 22, 1905.

Sinclair, Upton, "Stockyard Secrets," *Collier's,* March 24, 1906.

Sinclair, Upton, "The Condemned Meat Industry," *Everybody's,* May 1906.

Steffens, Lincoln, "The Shamelessness of St. Louis," *McClure's,* March 1903.

Steffens, Lincoln, "Pittsburgh, A City Ashamed," *McClure's,* May 1903.

Steffens, Lincoln, "Philadelphia: Corrupt and Contented," *McClure's,* July 1903.

Steffens, Lincoln, "Enemies of the Republic," *McClure's,* March 1904.

Steffens, Lincoln, "Illinois," *McClure's,* August 1904.

Steffens, Lincoln, "Wisconsin," *McClure's,* October 1904.

Steffens, Lincoln, "Rhode Island: A State for Sale," *McClure's,* February 1905.

Steffens, Lincoln, "New Jersey: A Traitor State," *McClure's,* April-May 1905.

Steffens, Lincoln, "Ohio: A Tale of Two Cities," *McClure's,* July 1905.

Steffens, Lincoln, "Breaking into San Francisco," *American,* December 1907.

Steffens, Lincoln, "It: An Exposition of the Sovereign Political Power of Organized Business," *Everybody's,* September 1910-March 1911.

Teague, Merrill A., "Bucket-Shop Sharks," *Everybody's,* June-September 1906.

Turner, George Kibbe, "Our Navy on Land," *McClure's,* February 1909.

Van Vorst, Bessie and Marie, "The Woman That Toils," *Everybody's,* September-December 1902—January 1903.

Welliver, Judson C., "The National Water Power Trust," *McClure's,* May 1909.

Welliver, Judson C., "The Mormon Church and the Sugar Trust," *Hampton's,* January 1910.

Welliver, Judson C., "The Secret of the Sugar Trust's Power," *Hampton's,* May 1910.

White, William Allen, "Folk," *McClure's,* December 1905.

Periodicals

Alger, George W., "The Literature of Exposure," *Atlantic,* August 1905.

Archer, William, "The American Cheap Magazines," *Fortnightly Review,* May 1910.

Brooks, G., "Still the Muckraker," *Independent,* May 3, 1906.

Cassidy, Edward E., "Muckraking in the Gilded Age," *American Literature,* June 1941.

Cline, H. F., "Benjamin Orange Flower and *The Arena,* 1889–1909," *Journalism Quarterly,* June 1940.

Cline, H. F., "Purpose and Content," *Journalism Quarterly,* September 1940.

Destler, Chester McA., "Wealth Against Commonwealth, 1894-1944," *American Historical Review*, October 1944.

Dickason, David H., "Benjamin Orange Flower, Patron of the Realists," *American Literature*, May 1942.

Donohoe, Dennis, "The Truth About Frenzied Finance," *Public Opinion*, January-February 1905.

Fairfield, Roy P., "Benjamin Orange Flower, Father of the Muckrakers," *American Literature*, Vol. 22, No. 3.

Francis, C. M., "Fighting Magazines," *Bookman*, July 1910.

French, George, "Masters of the Magazines," *Twentieth Century*, April 1912.

French, George, "Damnation of the Magazine," *Twentieth Century*, June 1912.

French, George, "Everybody's Business," *Twentieth Century*, July 1912.

Givens, W. R., "Wall Street's Estimate of Lawson," *Independent*, May 18, 1905.

Kemp, W., "Value of the Exposé," *Bookman*, October 1905.

Kittle, William, "The Interests and the Magazines," *Twentieth Century*, May 1910.

Lawson, Thomas W., "Fools and Their Money," *Everybody's*, May 1906.

Lawson, Thomas W., "The Muckraker," *Everybody's*, August 1906.

Lawson, Thomas W., "Why I Gave Up the Fight," *Everybody's*, February 1908.

Lowndes, Arthur, D.D., "Trinity Church in the City of New York," *Independent*, May 13, 1909.

Merwin, Samuel, "The Magazine Crusades," *Success*, June 1906.

Peters, John P., D.D., "The Tale of Trinity," *Independent*, February 18, 1909.

Ross, Edward A., "The Suppression of Important News," *Atlantic*, March 1910.

Russell, Charles Edward, "Trinity's Tenements—The Public's Business," *Everybody's*, February 1909.

Russell, Charles Edward, "The Magazines Soft-Pedal," *Pearson's*, February 1914.

Sedgwick, Ellery, "The Man with the Muckrake," *American*, May 1906.

Sinclair, Upton, "My Cause," *Independent*, May 14, 1903.

Sinclair, Upton, "What Life Means to Me," *Cosmopolitan*, October 1906.

Sinclair, Upton, "Muckrake Man," *Independent*, September 3, 1908.

Smith, F. H., "Muckrake as a Circulation Boomer," *Critic*, June 1906.

Smith, Goldwin, "Profits of Unrest," *Forum*, August 1890.

Tugwell, R. G., "Sources of New Deal Reformism," *Ethics*, July 1954.

Turner, William Jewett, "The Progress of the Social Conscience," *Atlantic*, September 1915.

Von Lestrich, John, "Lawson and the Life Insurance Companies," *Overland*, March 1905.

"After Exposure, What?" *Nature*, March 22, 1906.

"Campaign Against the Wholesale Poisoners of a Nation's Food," *Arena*, July 1906.

"Deterioration of the Popular Magazine in America," *Current Opinion*, July 1916.

"Exposure of Wrong Doing," *Current Literature*, May 1906.

"Lawson's Crusade: Strength and Weakness," *Arena*, September 1905.

"Literature of Exposure," *Independent*, March 22, 1906.

"A Little Talk About an Important Group of Magazines," *Hampton's*, August 1911.

"Magazines in the Grip of Privileged Wealth," *Arena*, January 1909.

"Muckrake versus the Muck," *Arena*, June 1906.

"Muck-Shielding the Hope of the Thieves and Corruptionists," *Arena*, July 1906.

"Nation that Clears Out its Muck," *Hampton's*, June 1910.

"New Policy for Trinity Church," *Outlook*, May 1, 1909.

"The Privileged Interests that Prey on the People and their Upholders," *Arena*, September 1906.

"Secret of Lawson's Career," *Current Literature*, March 1908.

"Strangling the Magazines," *Nation*, May 2, 1912.

"Value of Literature of Exposure," *Current Literature*, January 1906.

"Vicious Philosophy Which Is the Hope of the Grafters and Corruptionists," *Arena*, October 1905.

"Why *Hampton's* Has Succeeded," *Hampton's*, April 1910.

"Why So Mild with the Muckrakers," *Hampton's*, February 1911.

"Will It Go Out of Style?", *Independent*, March 22, 1906.

"Word to the Muckrakers," *Independent*, February 9, 1911.

Books

Aaron, Daniel, *Men of Good Hope: A Story of American Progressives* (New York: Oxford University Press, 1951).

Addams, Jane, *A New Conscience and an Ancient Evil* (New York: The Macmillan Company, 1912).

Baker, Ray Stannard, *American Chronicle* (New York: C. Scribner's Sons, 1945).

Beard, Charles A. and Mary R., *A Basic History of the United States* (New York: The Blakiston New Home Library, 1944).

———, *The Rise of American Civilization* (New York: The Macmillan Company, 1927).

Bishop, Joseph Bucklin, *Theodore Roosevelt and His Time, Shown in His Own Letters*, Vol. 2 (New York: Charles Scribner's Sons, 1920).

Bliss, William Dwight Porter, *The New Encyclopedia of Social Reform* (New York and London: Funk & Wagnalls Company, 1908).

Bok, Edward, *The Americanization of Edward Bok* (New York: Charles Scribner's Sons, 1922).

Bowers, Claude G., *Beveridge and the Progressive Era* (Boston: Houghton Mifflin Company, 1932).

Bridge, James Howard, *Millionaires and Grub Street; Comrades and Contacts in the Last Half Century* (New York: Brentano's, 1931).

Brooks, John Graham, *As Others See Us—A Study of Progress in the United States* (New York: The Macmillan Company, 1910).

Brooks, Van Wyck, *The Confident Years, 1885-1915* (New York: E. P. Dutton & Co., Inc., 1952).

Butt, Archibald Willingham, *Taft and Roosevelt—the Intimate Letters of Archie Butt, Military Aide* (Garden City, New York: Doubleday, Doran & Company, Inc., 1930).

Cargill, Oscar, *Intellectual America: Ideas on the March* (New York: The Macmillan Company, 1941).

———, *The Social Revolt: American Literature from 1888 to 1914* (New York: The Macmillan Company, 1933).

Chamberlain, John, *Farewell to Reform* (New York: Liveright, Inc., 1932).

Commager, Henry Steele, *The American Mind: An Interpretation of American Thought and Character since the 1880's* (New Haven: Yale University Press, 1950).

Coulter, E. Merton, *A Short History of Georgia* (Chapel Hill: The University of North Carolina Press, 1933).

Croly, Herbert, *Progressive Democracy* (New York: The Macmillan Company, 1915).

———, *The Promise of American Life* (New York: The Macmillan Company, 1909).

Curti, Merle Eugene, *The Growth of American Thought* (New York and London: Harper & Brothers, 1943).

Davis, Oscar King, *Released for Publication: Some Inside Political History of Theodore Roosevelt and His Times, 1898–1918* (Boston and New York: Houghton Mifflin Company, 1925).

Dell, Floyd, *Upton Sinclair: A Study in Social Protest* (New York: G. H. Doran Co., 1927).

Dix, Dr. Morgan, *A History of the Parish of Trinity Church in the City of New York* (New York: G. P. Putnam's Sons, 1901).

Duffy, Herbert Smith, *William Howard Taft* (New York: Minton, Balch & Co., 1930).

Fales, William E. S., *The Life of Lawson* (New York: "Dixie" Book Shop).

Faulkner, Harold Underwood, *American Political and Social History* (New York: F. S. Crofts & Co., Inc., 1937).

———, *The Decline of Laissez Faire, 1897-1917* (New York: Rinehart & Co., Inc., 1951).

———, *The Quest for Social Justice, 1898-1914* (New York: The Macmillan Company, 1931).

Fetter, Frank Albert, *The Masquerade of Monopoly* (New York: Harcourt, Brace and Company, 1931).

Filler, Louis, *Crusaders for American Liberalism* (New York: Harcourt, Brace and Company, 1939).

———, *Randolph Bourne* (Washington, D.C.: American Council on Public Affairs, 1943).

Flynn, John T., *God's Gold: The Story of Rockefeller and His Times* (New York: Harcourt, Brace and Company, 1932).

Gabriel, Ralph Henry, *The Course of American Democratic Thought: An Intellectual History since 1815* (New York: The Ronald Press Co., 1940).

Garland, Hamlin, *A Son of the Middle Border* (New York: The Macmillan Company, 1928).

Glasscock, C. B., *The War of the Copper Kings* (Indianapolis, New York: The Bobbs-Merrill Company, 1935).

Goldman, Eric F., *Rendezvous with Destiny, a History of Modern American Reform* (New York: Alfred A. Knopf, 1952).

———, *Two-Way Street: The Emergence of the Public Relations Counsel* (Cambridge, Mass.: Bellman Publishing Co., Inc., 1948).

Grimes, Alan Pendleton, *American Political Thought* (New York: Henry Holt & Co., 1955).

Hapgood, Norman, *Changing Years* (New York: Farrar & Rinehart, Inc., 1930).

Haworth, Paul Leland, *America in Ferment* (Indianapolis: The Bobbs-Merrill Company, 1915).

Hendrick, Burton J., *The Age of Big Business: A Chronicle of the Captains of Industry* (New Haven: Yale University Press, 1919).

Hicks, John D., *The Populist Revolt: A History of the Farmers' Alliance and the People's Party* (Minneapolis: The University of Minnesota Press, 1931).

Hofstadter, Richard, *The Age of Reform: From Bryan to F.D.R.* (New York: Alfred A. Knopf, 1955).

———, *The American Political Tradition and the Men Who Made It* (New York: Alfred A. Knopf, 1948).

———, *Social Darwinism in American Thought, 1860-1915* (Philadelphia: University of Pennsylvania Press; London: H. Milford, Oxford University Press, 1944).

Holbrook, Stewart H., *The Golden Age of Quackery* (New York: The Macmillan Company, 1959).

———, *Lost Men of American History* (New York: The Macmillan Company, 1946).

Howard, Joseph Kinsey, *Montana; High, Wide and Handsome* (New Haven: Yale University Press, 1943).

Howe, Frederic C., *The Confessions of a Reformer* (New York: Charles Scribner's Sons, 1926).

Howland, Harold, *Theodore Roosevelt and His Times: A Chronicle of the Progressive Movement* (New Haven: Yale University Press, 1921).

Hubbard, Elbert, *The Standard Oil Co.* (East Aurora, N. Y.: The Roycrofters, 1910).

Hunter, Robert, *Poverty* (New York: The Macmillan Company; London: Macmillan & Co. Ltd., 1907).

Ickes, Harold L., *The Autobiography of a Curmudgeon* (New York: Reynal & Hitchcock, Inc., 1943).

Irwin, Will, *The Making of a Reporter* (New York: G. P. Putnam's Sons, 1942).

Johnson, Walter, *William Allen White's America* (New York: Henry Holt and Company, 1947).

Johnson, Willis Fletcher, *Theodore Roosevelt: Addresses and Papers* (New York: The Sun Dial Classics Co., 1908).

Josephson, Matthew, *The President Makers: Politics and Leadership in an Age of Enlightenment, 1896–1919* (New York: Harcourt, Brace & Co., 1940).

———, *The Robber Barons: The Great American Capitalists, 1861–1901* (New York: Harcourt, Brace & Co., 1934).

Kazin, Alfred, *On Native Grounds: An Interpretation of Modern American Prose Literature* (New York: Reynal & Hitchcock, 1942).

Kogan, Herman and Wendt, Lloyd, *Chicago: A Pictorial History* (New York: E. P. Dutton & Company, Inc., 1958).

Laski, Harold J., *The American Democracy* (New York: The Viking Press, 1948).

Lawson, Thomas, *Frenzied Finance: The Crime of Amalgamated* (New York: The Ridgway-Thayer Co., 1905).

Lewis, Edward R., *A History of American Political Thought from the Civil War to the World War* (New York: The Macmillan Company, 1937).

Lewis, Lloyd and Smith, Henry Justin, *Chicago: The History of Its Reputation* (New York: Harcourt, Brace & Co., 1929).

Lief, Alfred, *Brandeis: The Personal History of an American Ideal* (New York; Harrisburg, Pa.: Stackpole Sons, 1936).

Lindsey, Ben B. and O'Higgins, Harvey J., *The Beast* (New York: Doubleday, Page & Co., 1911).

Link, Arthur S., *American Epoch: A History of the United States Since the 1890's* (New York: Alfred A. Knopf, 1955).

Lippmann, Walter, *Drift and Mastery: An Attempt to Diagnose the Current Unrest* (New York: Mitchell Kennerley, 1914).

Marcosson, Isaac F., *David Graham Phillips and His Times* (New York: Dodd, Mead & Co., 1932).

Markham, Edwin, with Lindsey, Benjamin B. and Creel, George, *Children in Bondage* (New York: Hearst's International Library Co., 1914).

Mason, Alpheus Thomas, *Brandeis: A Free Man's Life* (New York: The Viking Press, 1946).

———, *Brandeis: Lawyer and Judge in the Modern State* (Princeton: Princeton University Press, 1933).

———, *Bureaucracy Convicts Itself: The Ballinger-Pinchot Controversy of 1910* (New York: The Viking Press, 1941).

McClure, S. S., *My Autobiography* (New York: Frederick A. Stokes Co., 1913).

McHale, Francis, *President and Chief Justice; The Life and Public Services of William Howard Taft* (Philadelphia: Dorrance & Co., 1931).

Morison, Elting E., *The Letters of Theodore Roosevelt* (Cambridge: Harvard University Press, 1954).

Morison, Samuel Eliot and Commager, Henry Steele, *The Growth of the American Republic*, Vol. 2, 1865–1950 (New York, London: Oxford University Press, 1956).

Morris, Lloyd R., *Postscript to Yesterday* (New York: Random House, 1947).

Mott, Frank Luther, *A History of American Magazines, 1885-1905* (Cambridge: Harvard University Press, 1957).

Mowry, George Edwin, *The Era of Theodore Roosevelt, 1900-1912* (New York: Harper & Brothers, 1958).

———, *Theodore Roosevelt and the Progressive Movement* (Madison: University of Wisconsin Press, 1946).

Nevins, Allan, *American Press Opinion, Washington to Coolidge: A Documentary Record of Editorial Leadership and Criticism, 1785–1927* (Boston, New York: D. C. Heath & Co., 1928).

———, *John D. Rockefeller* (New York: Charles Scribner's Sons, 1940).

Nye, Russel B., *Midwestern Progressive Politics: A Historical Study of Its Origins and Development, 1870–1950* (East Lansing: Michigan State College Press, 1951).

O'Donnell, Terence, *History of Life Insurance in Its Formative Years* (Chicago: American Conservation Co., 1936).

Parkes, Henry Bamford, *Recent America* (New York: Thomas Y. Crowell Co., 1941).

Parrington, Vernon Louis, *Main Currents in American Thought*, Vol. 3 (New York: Harcourt, Brace & Co., 1930).

Pattee, Fred Lewis, *The New American Literature, 1890–1930* (New York: The Century Co., 1930).

Paxson, Frederic L., *Recent History of the United States* (Boston, New York: Houghton Mifflin Co., 1921).

Pringle, Henry F., *The Life and Times of William Howard Taft* (New York, Toronto: Farrar & Rinehart, Inc., 1939).

——, *Theodore Roosevelt* (New York: Harcourt, Brace & Co., 1931).

Regier, C. C., *The Era of the Muckrakers* (Chapel Hill: University of North Carolina Press, 1932).

Rich, Everett, *William Allen White, the Man from Emporia* (New York, Toronto: Farrar & Rinehart, Inc., 1941).

Riis, Jacob A., *The Battle with the Slum* (New York: The Macmillan Company; London: Macmillan & Co., Ltd., 1902).

——, *Theodore Roosevelt: the Citizen* (The Outlook Co., 1903).

Roosevelt, Theodore, *Works of Theodore Roosevelt* (New York: Charles Scribner's Sons, 1926).

Ross, Edward Alsworth, *Changing America: Studies in Contemporary Society* (New York: The Century Co., 1912).

——, *Sin and Society: An Analysis of Latter-day Iniquity* (Boston: Houghton Mifflin Co., 1907).

Russell, Charles Edward, *Bare Hands and Stone Walls: Some Recollections of a Side-line Reformer* (New York: Charles Scribner's Sons, 1933).

——, *Lawless Wealth: the Origin of Some Great American Fortunes* (B. W. Dodge & Co., 1908).

——, *Why I Am a Socialist* (New York: Hodder & Stoughton, George H. Doran and Company, 1910).

Schlesinger, Arthur Meier, *Political and Social History of the United States, 1829-1925* (New York: The Macmillan Company, 1925).

——, *The Rise of the City, 1878-1898* (New York: The Macmillan Company, 1933).

Sedgwick, Ellery, *The Happy Profession* (Boston: Little Brown and Company, 1946).

Sinclair, Upton, *The Brass Check* (Pasadena, Calif.: Published by author, 1919).

——, *The Jungle* (New York: Doubleday, Page & Co., 1906).

Spiller, Robert E.; Thorp, Willard; Johnson, Thomas H.; and Canby, Henry Seidel, *Literary History of the United States* (New York: The Macmillan Co., 1948).

Steffens, Lincoln, *The Autobiography of Lincoln Steffens* (New York: Harcourt, Brace & Co., 1931).

——, *The Struggle for Self-Government* (New York: McClure, Phillips & Co., 1906).

Sullivan, Mark, *The Education of an American* (New York: Doubleday, Doran & Co., Inc., 1938).

——, *Our Times: The United States, 1900-1925, Vol. 1, The Turn of the Century, 1900-1904* (New York: Charles Scribner's Sons, 1926).

——, *Our Times: The United States, 1900-1925, Vol. 2, America Finding Herself* (New York: Charles Scribner's Sons, 1927).

——, *Our Times: The United States, 1900-1925, Vol. 3, Pre-War America* (New York: Charles Scribner's Sons, 1930).

——, *Our Times: The United States, 1900-1925, Vol. 4, The War Begins, 1909-1914* (New York: Charles Scribner's Sons, 1932).

Tarbell, Ida M., *All in the Day's Work* (New York: The Macmillan Company, 1939).

Tassin, Algernon, *The Magazine in America* (New York: Dodd, Mead and Company, 1916).

Thayer, John Adams, *Astir: A Publisher's Life Story* (Small, Maynard & Co., 1910).

Trent, W. P. and other editors, *Cambridge History of American Literature, Vol. 3, Chapter xix*, by Cairns, W. B., "*Later Magazines*" (New York: G. P. Putnam's Sons, 1921).

Underwood, John Curtis, *Literature and Insurgency* (Mitchell Kennerley, 1914).

Van Vorst, Mrs. John and Marie, *The Woman Who Toils* (New York: Doubleday, Page & Co., 1903).

Villard, Oswald Garrison, *Fighting Years: Memoirs of a Liberal Editor* (New York: Harcourt, Brace & Co., 1939).

Walker, Albert H., *The Administration of William H. Taft* (1912).

Ware, Louise, *Jacob A. Riis: Police Reporter, Reformer, Useful Citizen*

(New York: D. Appleton-Century Co., Inc., 1938).

Waterman, Willoughby Cyrus, *Prostitution and Its Repression in New York City, 1900-1931* (New York: Columbia University Press; London: P. S. King & Son, Ltd., 1932).

White, Morton G., *Social Thought in America, The Revolt Against Formation* (New York: The Viking Press, 1949).

White, William Allen, *The Autobiography of William Allen White* (New York: The Macmillan Company, 1946).

——, *The Old Order Changeth* (New York: The Macmillan Company, 1911).

Whitlock, Brand, *Forty Years of It* (New York, London: D. Appleton & Co., 1914).

Wiley, Dr. Harvey Washington, *An Autobiography* (Indianapolis: The Bobbs-Merrill Company, 1930).

Wish, Harvey, *Contemporary America, the National Scene Since 1900* (New York: Harper & Brothers, 1955).

——, *Society and Thought in Modern America, Vol. 2: A Social and Intellectual History of the American People from 1865* (New York: Longmans, Green & Co., 1952).

The Social Evil in Chicago, a Study of Existing Conditions with Recommendations by The Vice Commission of Chicago (Chicago: Gunthorpe-Warren Printing Co., 1911).

A Report Prepared Under the Direction of The Committee of Fifteen, The Social Evil with Special Reference to Conditions Existing in the City of New York (New York: G. P. Putnam's Sons, 1902).

ABOUT THE EDITORS

Both the Weinbergs are experienced writers as well as editors. Arthur Weinberg went from college to a career as a professional journalist in Chicago. He has since won national acclaim as the man who created the enormously successful study of Clarence Darrow, Attorney for the Damned. *In* The Muckrakers, *however, he has turned his astute eye to another aspect of the American past, this time collaborating with his wife, Lila, who for ten years has served as an editor in many fields, including work on books and magazines.*

Mr. Weinberg has occasionally taken time away from his writing to give a course at the University of Chicago, and his name frequently appears on book reviews in that city.

The Weinbergs live in Chicago with their three daughters.